MADHOUSE

AT THE

END

OF THE

EARTH

MADHOUSE

AT THE

END

OF THE

EARTH

THE *BELGICA'S* JOURNEY INTO THE DARK ANTARCTIC NIGHT

JULIAN SANCTON

ALLEN

1

WH Allen, an imprint of Ebury Publishing,
20 Vauxhall Bridge Road,
London SW1V 2SA

WH Allen is part of the Penguin Random House group of companies
whose addresses can be found at global.penguinrandomhouse.com

First published in the United States by Crown in 2021
This edition published in the United Kingdom by WH Allen in 2021

www.penguin.co.uk

A CIP catalogue record for this book is available from the British Library

Hardback ISBN 9780753553442
Trade Paperback ISBN 9780753553459

Book design by Simon M. Sullivan

Printed and bound in Great Britain by Clays Ltd, Elcograf S.p.A.

The authorised representative in the EEA is Penguin Random House Ireland,
Morrison Chambers, 32 Nassau Street, Dublin D02 YH68.

Penguin Random House is committed to a sustainable future for
our business, our readers and our planet. This book is made from
Forest Stewardship Council® certified paper.

For Jess, Maya, and Leila (and Suki)

CONTENTS

MADHOUSE

AT THE

END

OF THE

EARTH

PROLOGUE

THE LIGHT OF A COLD GRAY DAWN FILTERED THROUGH THE GRATING that covered the narrow windows of the Leavenworth penitentiary hospital. Exhausted after his sixteen-hour shift, the old doctor tidied his station and signaled to the guard that he was ready to be escorted to his cell. When he passed his duties off to the regular prison physician, he became just another prisoner, inmate #23118.

The doctor collapsed on his bed. It had been a long night. The country was then in the grip of an opiate epidemic of unprecedented scale, and after dark the top floor of the hospital became, in the doctor's words, a "narcotic mad house," as addicts in the agony of withdrawal howled for a fix. The doctor's cell was a well-lit room within the three-story brick building. It had a single bed, a chair, and running water. On the walls were elaborate needlework pictures he had made. His were more comfortable accommodations than those afforded to some of his contemporaries in the prison, including the Chicago gangster Big Tim Murphy (who had become a friend and protector) and, later, Carl Panzram, the prolific and unrepentant serial killer (who would not). But then, inmate #23118's offenses were of a different nature. The sixty-year-old had been convicted of fraud in connection with what amounted to a pyramid scheme involving stock in an oil company. He was on year three of a fourteen-year sentence, a punishment far harsher than that usually doled out for similar crimes, but one in proportion with his notoriety.

In his half-remembered youth, long before his fall from grace, the doctor had been a celebrated polar explorer. His claim to have conquered the North Pole in 1908 had made him a national hero until it was suspected that he had falsified that feat, among several others.

"He will count for ever among the greatest impostors of the world," *The New York Times* would assert. "That and not the discovery of the north pole shall be his claim to immortality."

In the afternoon, a guard informed him that he had a visitor. Since entering prison, the previous year, the doctor had refused to see friends and family. The man waiting for him today was perhaps the only person alive for whom he was willing to make an exception. Rarely a day passed when the prisoner didn't think of his former comrade, a strapping, fifty-three-year-old Norwegian with whom he had served on a harrowing expedition to Antarctica nearly three decades earlier. Once the doctor's apprentice in polar matters, the Norwegian had gone on to become one of the greatest explorers the world had ever known—the legitimate conqueror of the *South* Pole. His headline-grabbing exploits, and the apparent ease with which he accomplished them, had conferred upon him an almost mythic aura. An international lecture tour had taken him through the United States, and he had made it a point to pay his respects to his former mentor.

News spread that the illustrious explorer was meeting with Leavenworth's best-known inmate, and within minutes reporters swarmed to the prison. With this public gesture of support for the discredited doctor, the Norwegian was risking his own reputation. But the visit was not merely an act of pity for an old friend in need. Years of single-minded competition for the planet's most coveted geographic prizes had taken their toll. The fire within him had burned him up. He had grown bitter and paranoid, with few friends who understood him as well as the doctor from whom he had learned so much in simpler times, when all that mattered was survival. Above all, the Norwegian felt honor-bound to visit the man he credited with saving his life.

The two men's fates had diverged dramatically since they'd last seen each other, and it showed on their faces. Imprisonment had drained the doctor of color and vitality. His slate-hued eyes had lost some of their electric quality, his once luxuriant hair had thinned, and his large nose had, if possible, grown even larger. But there was a flash of his younger self when he smiled, revealing several gold teeth.

The Norwegian visitor towered over the doctor. His face "was brown, deeply burned from polar snows, lined with deep wrinkles and a pleasing fresh vigor," the doctor later recalled. The explorer "was at the apex of glory [while] I was in the ditch of penal condemnation. . . . The effect to me was at first appalling, but soon old cordiality burned all barriers. We were as brothers."

They grasped each other's hands and didn't let go. To confound the eavesdroppers, they began to speak in what the doctor described as the "mixed lingo of the Belgica." The *Belgica* was the ship on which they'd met, in the prime of their lives, on their first journey to Antarctica. The various languages spoken by the scientists, officers, and crew blended into one Babel-like amalgam of French, Dutch, Norwegian, German, Polish, English, Romanian, and Latin. The voyage taught both men how the cold and the dark can ravage the human soul. It was on this expedition that the doctor had come to worship the sun. Then, too, he had been a prisoner, held captive not by bars and locks but by an infinite expanse of ice. Then, too, he had heard shrieks in the night.

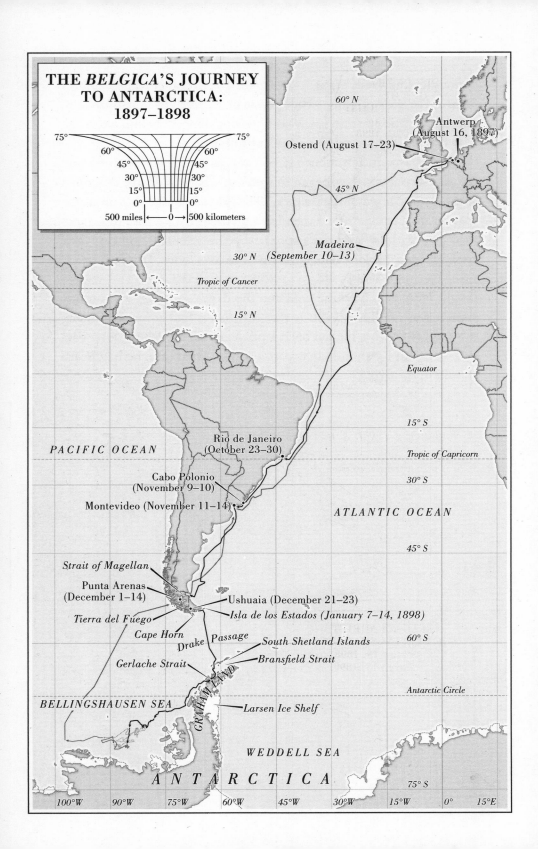

THE *BELGICA*'S JOURNEY TO ANTARCTICA: 1897–1898

75°
60°
45°
30°
15°
0°

75°
60°
45°
30°
15°
0°

500 miles ←|→ 500 kilometers
0

60° N

Antwerp
(August 16, 1897)

Ostend (August 17–23)

45° N

Madeira
(September 10–13)

30° N

Tropic of Cancer

15° N

Equator

15° S

Rio de Janeiro
(October 23–30)

Tropic of Capricorn

PACIFIC OCEAN

30° S

Cabo Polonio
(November 9–10)

Montevideo (November 11–14)

ATLANTIC OCEAN

45° S

Strait of Magellan

Punta Arenas
(December 1–14)

Ushuaia (December 21–23)

Tierra del Fuego

Isla de los Estados (January 7–14, 1898)

Cape Horn

Drake Passage

South Shetland Islands

60° S

Gerlache Strait

Bransfield Strait

BELLINGSHAUSEN SEA

GRAHAM LAND

Larsen Ice Shelf

Antarctic Circle

WEDDELL SEA

ANTARCTICA

75° S

100°W   90°W   75°W   60°W   45°W   30°W   15°W   0°   15°E

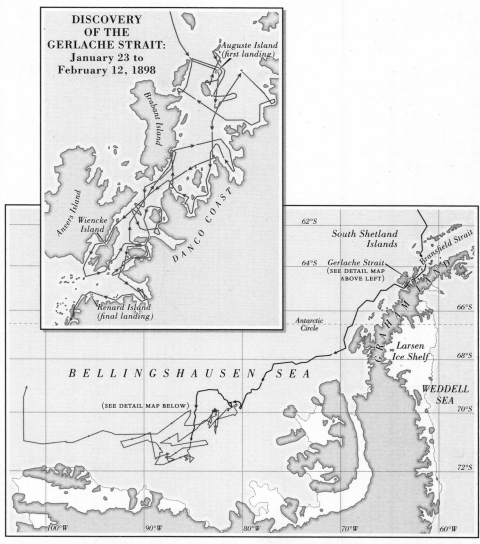

DISCOVERY OF THE GERLACHE STRAIT: January 23 to February 12, 1898

Auguste Island (first landing)

Brabant Island

Anvers Island

Wiencke Island

D A N C O C O A S T

Renard Island (final landing)

62°S

64°S

South Shetland Islands

Gerlache Strait (SEE DETAIL MAP ABOVE LEFT)

Bransfield Strait

66°S

G R A H A M   L A N D

Antarctic Circle

Larsen Ice Shelf

68°S

WEDDELL SEA

B E L L I N G S H A U S E N   S E A

(SEE DETAIL MAP BELOW)

70°S

72°S

100°W   90°W   80°W   70°W   60°W

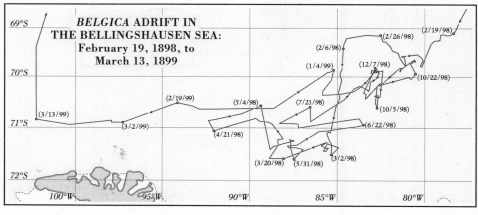

69°S

BELGICA **ADRIFT IN THE BELLINGSHAUSEN SEA:** February 19, 1898, to March 13, 1899

(2/19/98)

(2/26/98)

(2/6/98)

(1/4/99)

(12/7/98)

(10/22/98)

70°S

(2/19/99)

(5/4/98)

(7/21/98)

(10/5/98)

(3/13/99)

(3/2/99)

(4/21/98)

(6/22/98)

71°S

(3/20/98)   (5/31/98)   (3/2/98)

72°S

100°W   95°W   90°W   85°W   80°W

PART I

Sometimes science is the excuse for exploration.
I think it is rarely the reason.

—GEORGE LEIGH MALLORY

CHAPTER 1

Why Not Belgium?

THE RIVER SCHELDT WOUND LANGUIDLY FROM NORTHERN FRANCE through Belgium, taking a sharp westward turn at the port of Antwerp, where it became deep and wide enough to accommodate oceangoing ships. On this cloudless summer morning, more than twenty thousand people flocked along the city's riverfront to salute the departure of the *Belgica* and exult in its glory. Freshly painted steel gray, the 113-foot-long, three-masted steam whaler, fitted with a coal-powered engine, was headed to Antarctica to chart its unknown coasts and collect data on its flora, fauna, and geology. But what drew the crowds today was not the promise of scientific discovery so much as national pride: Belgium, little Belgium, a country that had declared its independence from Holland sixty-seven years earlier and was thus younger than many of its citizens, was staking a claim to the next frontier of human exploration.

At ten o'clock, the vessel weighed anchor and sailed at a regal pace in the direction of the North Sea, so freighted with coal, provisions, and equipment that her deck floated just a foot and a half above the water. Escorted by a flotilla of yachts that carried government officials, well-wishers, and press, the *Belgica* paraded before the city. She glided past the flag-bedecked townhouses lining the waterfront, past the flamboyant Gothic cathedral that dominated the skyline, past Het Steen, the fortress that had loomed over the river since the Middle Ages. From a pontoon, a military band played "La Brabançonne," Belgium's national anthem, a theme as grand as the country was small. Cannons fired in tribute, from both banks of the river. Vessels from around the world blew their foghorns and hoisted Belgium's black, yellow, and red flag. Cheers rippled across the crowd as the *Belgica* sailed by. The entire town seemed to vibrate.

Gazing back at this roiling sea of banners and hats and handkerchiefs from the bridge of the ship was the expedition's commandant, thirty-one-year-old Adrien de Gerlache de Gomery. His face betrayed little emotion, but behind his heavy-lidded eyes he burned with excitement. Every detail of his appearance had been meticulously attended to in preparation for this moment, down to the twist of his mustache, the crop of his beard, and the knot of his cravat. De Gerlache's dark, double-breasted greatcoat was too warm for this August morning, and not nearly warm enough for the frigid ends of the earth, but it lent him a dashing air befitting a man in the process of making history. Now and again, basking in the acclamation, he pulled off his *Belgica*-emblazoned cap by its patent-leather brim and waved it at the jubilant multitude. He had long hungered for these cheers. The starting point felt to him like the finish line. "My state of mind," he wrote, "was that of a man who has just reached his goal."

In a way, he had. That the ship was leaving at all was a personal triumph. Despite the heartfelt patriotism on display this morning, the Belgian Antarctic Expedition was less a national endeavor than the manifestation of Adrien de Gerlache's steadfast will. He had spent more than three years planning, staffing, and raising funds for the journey. His determination alone had won over skeptics, loosened purse strings, and rallied a nation behind him. Now, though he remained ten thousand miles from his destination, he was already enjoying a taste of glory. But on this euphoric day, with his countrymen hip-hip-hooraying him, it was easy for de Gerlache to forget that this glory was on credit. To earn it, he would have to survive one of the most hostile environments on earth, a continent so inimical to human life that no man had yet spent more than a few hours on its shores.

Belgium's border with Holland stretched across the Scheldt a dozen miles northwest of Antwerp. Before crossing it, the *Belgica* docked at Liefkenshoek quay to attend to one last order of business. Even as the merriment continued on deck and aboard the yachts that swarmed around the vessel, the crew shuttled between the quay and the *Belgica*'s hold in order to load a half ton of tonite, an explosive believed to be more powerful than dynamite. The tonite sticks, which took up several large crates in the ship's hold, were de Gerlache's insurance policy. He didn't know what to expect from the Antarctic ice, only that a continent that had succeeded in staving off humanity until the nineteenth century demanded respect. He could imagine several ways the ship could be destroyed: she could slam into an iceberg or an uncharted reef. But perhaps the most dreaded possibility was that the *Belgica* would be caught in the ice and either crushed by the pressure or kept captive indefinitely, leaving her men to starve to death. Several notorious expeditions to the northern polar regions had met such fates. De Gerlache presumed that a half ton of tonite would more than suffice to break the grip of the sea ice. It was the first time he underestimated the power of Antarctica, but it would not be the last.

As the crew packed tonite into the hold, a gaggle of dignitaries left one of the accompanying yachts and boarded the *Belgica* to wish de Gerlache and his men good luck. A sailor to his core, the commandant was far more comfortable at sea than in a crowd, and over the last three years he had grown weary of glad-handing. He had spent more time scrounging for funds than he expected to spend in Antarctica. As he exchanged pleasantries with government ministers, wealthy patrons, and the wise old men of the Royal Belgian Geographical Society, which had sponsored the expedition, he felt the weight of his obligations to them. If it can be said that he didn't fear the frozen continent enough, then he feared the judgment of these men too much.

If he failed in his mission, he would shoulder the disappointment of an entire country. Far worse, in his mind, was the dishonor it would bring to his illustrious family. The de Gerlaches were one of Belgium's oldest aristocratic dynasties, able to trace their origins to the fourteenth century. A relative, Baron Etienne-Constantin de Gerlache, had been among the founders of the Belgian nation, a principal author of its constitution, and its first prime minister (though his tenure lasted just eleven days). Both Adrien's grandfather and father had been decorated military officers. The public expected greatness from a de Gerlache. In the press and in Brussels high society, Adrien's family had made a show of support for his Antarctic project, wagering their good name on his success. This only added to the pressure the commandant felt.

Adrien's parents, sister, and brother—a promising army lieutenant—had also come aboard the *Belgica*, and remained there after the dignitaries returned to their yacht. The only patron allowed to stay was the socialite Léonie Osterrieth, the expedition's most dedicated and passionate backer. The plump, fifty-four-year-old widow of a prominent Antwerp trader, she treated de Gerlache like her own son. He, in turn, called her "Maman O." and considered her his most trusted confidante. (For her generous contributions to the expedition, the men would nickname her "Mère Antarctique," which means "Mother Antarctica," but is also a homophone of "Mer Antarctique," or "Antarctic Sea.") When it came time for goodbyes, Adrien's patrician father, Auguste, embraced every member of the expedition, from the lowliest deckhand to the scientists, and with a tremor in his voice called them all his "dear children." The commandant's mother, Emma, sobbed inconsolably, as if she'd had a premonition that she would never see her eldest boy again. The *Belgica*'s twenty-eight-year-old captain, the short and scrappy Georges Lecointe, vowed that he and the rest of the men would devote themselves entirely to her son. He was not the type of man to break a promise. Lecointe then led the crew in three rousing cheers of "Long live Madame de Gerlache!" While the last cry was still echoing down the Scheldt, the captain shouted out orders to the crew.

"Now, everyone back to his post!"

The de Gerlache family left the ship and boarded a yacht named the *Brabo,* which turned back in the direction of Antwerp. Waving his cap from the deck of the *Belgica,* the commandant managed to hold back tears, but in the words of one observer, "A violent emotion seized his face."

"*Vive la Belgique!*" he yelled across the water as the *Brabo* pulled away. He scurried up the rigging with the agility of an acrobat. It took him fewer than fifteen seconds to climb to the crow's nest—a repurposed barrel—where he continued to wave his cap until the vessel carrying nearly everyone he loved disappeared beyond the river bend.

. . .

De Gerlache had never lived anywhere other than Belgium, yet in many ways he felt more at home in the cabins of ships, wherever they happened to bring him. He was born in Hasselt, Belgium, on August 2, 1866. Unlike his brother, father, grandfather, and a long line of de Gerlache men going back centuries, he had no interest in a military career. A pacifist at heart, he dreamed of a life at sea, an unusual fascination for a boy growing up in Belgium, which, after its secession from Holland in the 1830 revolution, was left with a virtually nonexistent navy, a bare-bones merchant marine, and only forty miles of coastline.

As a child, de Gerlache wasn't the type to play at war with other boys. Instead, he spent countless hours alone building intricate miniature ships. His masterpiece was a magnificent sailing vessel with functional rigging, which he constructed over the course of a winter with the help of his doting mother. When he was finished, he lowered the ship into a stream near his family home and beamed with pride as the wind filled her finely hemmed sails, then looked on helplessly as the current took hold of her and sent her careening over a dam. The *Cambrier*, as he'd christened her, was the first ship under his command, and his first shipwreck.

The heartbreaking incident did little to dampen his maritime ambition. At first his family indulged his passion, deeming it a boyhood phase, but as the years passed, his fixation on the sea only grew as he gorged on stories of nautical derring-do. He matriculated at the Free University of Brussels at the age of sixteen and excelled in his studies. During summers he enlisted as an apprentice sailor on transatlantic ocean liners traveling from Antwerp to New York or Philadelphia, among other destinations.

Colonel Auguste de Gerlache disapproved of Adrien's chosen vocation, which he felt was unworthy of his son's social class and education. It pained him to imagine Adrien scrubbing decks, sleeping on coils of rope, eating rock-hard sea biscuits, and suffering the usual indignities of greenhorn sailors. He urged Adrien to find a more respectable career, but it quickly became obvious that the boy was miserable on land. "As soon as he came home he became nostalgic,"

Adrien's sister, Louise, recalled. "Out of duty and obedience he pursued his engineering studies in good conscience; soon his health deteriorated seriously, he became terribly melancholy, his eyes took on that look particular to sailors and voyagers, that veiled and unfathomable gaze which, even when it points straight into your eyes, seems to contemplate infinite expanses much farther away."

Auguste eventually dropped his resistance. He allowed his son to follow a navigation course and enroll in the Belgian Navy, skeletal as it was. De Gerlache worked hard to prove himself worthy of his father's faith. His instructors discovered that he had a natural affinity for boats and a gift for reading winds and currents. De Gerlache traded his baggy sailor suits and oversized sou'westers for the trim uniforms of an officer in training. In short order, he became one of Belgium's top naval prospects. This was not saying much, since the Belgian Navy oversaw little more than a ferry service in the North Sea. To gain the experience necessary to become a ship captain, de Gerlache had no option but to serve on foreign vessels. These journeys gave him a sense of the sea's awesome, destructive power. On one such voyage, bound for San Francisco via Cape Horn, the British ship on which de Gerlache was serving, the *Craigie Burn,* was pummeled so viciously by the winds and rocks off Tierra del Fuego that she had to be abandoned. It was his second shipwreck.

After several years working on Dutch ocean liners, he was made full lieutenant and assigned to the Ostend–Dover ferry line. It was on this route, in 1890, that de Gerlache first met the Belgian king, who was heading to London. Tall and imperious, with a hatchet nose and a gray slab of a beard, Leopold II had taken an interest in de Gerlache's career, both because of his family name and because word of his talent had gotten around. The monarch sought the twenty-three-year-old lieutenant on the bridge. Did he enjoy serving the Belgian state? the king asked. De Gerlache responded with the candor of youth. "Very much, Sire," he said, "only, as navigation goes, it's rather monotonous, but it's all we have in this country and we don't have a choice."

Leopold, for whom the lack of a serious Belgian maritime presence was a source of national shame, was stunned by de Gerlache's frankness.

"Yes," said the king. "For the moment."

Soon after, de Gerlache was given the opportunity to help chart the river system in the Congo Free State, a million-square-mile swath of central Africa that Leopold had claimed not as a Belgian colony but as his personal property, to exploit for his own enrichment. The assignment would have placed de Gerlache in the same murky waters as Kurtz and Marlow in Joseph Conrad's *Heart of Darkness,* and greatly benefited his career by ingratiating him to Leopold.

At the risk of vexing the king once again, the lieutenant declined. He had interest neither in freshwater navigation nor in the Congo, having already set his course for colder horizons.

While vast areas of the world were still uncharted by Western explorers—primarily in Africa, South America, and Central Asia— one continent remained virtually unknown to all humankind: Antarctica. The southernmost region of the earth, an area larger than North America, lay blank on world maps, save for a few sketchy coastlines where a handful of explorers, whalers, and sealers had ventured since land was first spotted, in 1820. It was yet to be determined whether what lay beyond that outline was open water, an ocean of ice, or a vast, solid continent. Antarctica was the last great geographical mystery.

Only three expeditions had ever sailed south of the 70th parallel. Such journeys were dangerous and expensive, and it had been almost half a century since the last. There was a growing consensus among the world's geographical societies that a new era of Antarctic exploration was overdue. De Gerlache, who had long thrilled to narratives of polar adventure, was determined to take part in it. In 1891, hearing that the Swedish explorer Baron Adolf Erik Nordenskiöld was planning an Antarctic expedition, de Gerlache applied for a position and offered to help raise financing for it in Belgium. His letter went unanswered. While others might have been discouraged by the rejection, the twenty-five-year-old lieutenant saw it as an opportunity. When Nordenskiöld's endeavor failed to materialize and nobody else stepped up to take his place, the seed of an idea that had long been germinating in de Gerlache's mind blossomed into a plan. Brushing aside his relative lack of experience, he resolved to mount an expedition himself, one that would bring glory both to him and to Belgium.

The questions *Why me?* and *Why Belgium?* do not seem to have occurred to him. Instead he asked himself, *Why* not *me? Why* not *Belgium?*

One obvious answer was the cost involved. To raise the money required for the multiyear voyage he had in mind, de Gerlache would have to convince his compatriots of its value, and of his. This would require a campaign of persuasion as delicately assembled as the model ships he had once built.

De Gerlache understood that his prospective financiers might hesitate to take a chance on what could be dismissed as the boyish fantasy of an untested commander. He decided to appeal to their patriotism. He'd sensed the nationalistic winds blowing across Europe and, astute navigator that he was, maneuvered to harness them. He would argue that the young nation could hardly dream of better publicity than an expedition that would fly the Belgian flag to the ends of the earth and draw global press coverage.

Second, the young lieutenant believed that his best chance of drumming up support for his plan was to frame it as a scientific expedition. The nineteenth century was a time of exploratory frenzy, as European nations scrambled to colonize territories that could extend their global influence and provide the resources to feed their insatiable domestic industries. Yet the justifications for exploration had evolved over the course of the century. Explorers were now as likely to be natural scientists, like Charles Darwin or Alexander von Humboldt, as sailors, soldiers, merchants, or missionaries. Data—on plants, animals, geology, populations—became as coveted a prize as gold or spices or cheap labor had been in earlier ages. Having conquered much of the known world, the West now endeavored to understand it. There developed among the geographical societies of Europe and America a culture of sporting competition in which the ultimate trophy was scientific advancement and national bragging rights. If valuable natural resources were discovered along the way, all the better.*

---

* By the same token, science was often invoked as a pretext for colonization and profit-driven exploration. Indeed, Leopold II had at first framed his brutal exploitation of the Congo as a scientific mission.

Science might have been a means to an end for de Gerlache, but he took it seriously enough to seek the counsel of several esteemed Belgian scholars. Though they surely recognized his last name, they'd never heard of him. They nonetheless expressed enthusiasm for his Antarctic plan. With their support, he put together a long proposal that he submitted, in late 1894, to the Royal Belgian Geographical Society in Brussels, which had a say in all exploration under the Belgian flag and advised on government funding. Composed in tidy handwriting, it looked and read like the work of a dutiful schoolboy. Aware that the society might balk at his youth, he strove for a grand tone, employing the first-person plural, the royal "we": "Having always felt an irresistible attraction towards all that relates to the knowledge of polar regions, we asked ourselves whether it would not be possible to organize a Belgian expedition for the exploration of the Antarctic Sea."

The society invited him to present his plan at the stately, neoclassical Academy Palace in central Brussels. On January 9, 1895, the twenty-eight-year-old de Gerlache stood before the graybeards of Belgium's scientific establishment and described his project in detail. He argued that, while the world had long seen a steady flow of expeditions to the Arctic—no fewer than four were vying for the North Pole that very year—"the Austral Sea remains unexplored, scientifically at least." De Gerlache laid out a broad program of scientific observations he planned to carry out. He intended, among other things, to collect zoological, botanical, oceanographical, and meteorological data; to measure terrestrial magnetism; and to study the poorly understood phenomenon of the southern lights. He would chart the coastline from the tip of the Antarctic Peninsula all the way down to Victoria Land, on the other side of the globe, where the intrepid British navigator James Clark Ross had, more than fifty years earlier, established the standing farthest-south record of latitude 78°09′ south.

The expedition he proposed would last almost two years. It would leave in September 1896, reach Antarctica in early December, and pursue a southern course until the middle of the following year. De Gerlache expected to wait out the grueling winter (which coincides with the Northern Hemisphere's summer) in Australia and return to

Antarctica when the sea ice broke up in the spring. No human had ever witnessed a winter below the antarctic circle, when the sea ice solidifies and the sun disappears for weeks. De Gerlache didn't plan to either, though he held out hope that with the right ship, he might push farther into the pack ice than anyone had before.

When he finished speaking, the lecture hall resounded with applause. Energized by de Gerlache's boldness and youthful vigor, the scientists in attendance expressed their unequivocal support for a Belgian Antarctic expedition.

To go down in history—and prove to his father that his dreams of nautical glory were not misplaced—de Gerlache would need to come home with a record, a "first" of some kind. Polar exploration had long been predicated on heroic exploits: who could reach the highest latitudes, withstand the lowest temperatures, cover the longest distances. Such achievements electrified the public and satisfied a deep human urge to make inroads into the unknown.

He settled on such a goal in consultation with his scientific advisers. They were particularly interested in his proposed study of magnetism. "Its consideration alone," the astronomer Charles Lagrange argued, "would be sufficient to give this expedition its raison d'être." Lagrange suggested that the discovery of the South Magnetic Pole, which had eluded Ross in 1841, would "make history."

The South Magnetic Pole was then thought to lie around the 75th parallel.* Determining its exact location would be of some utility, since it would allow navigators to adjust their compass readings with more accuracy. Crucially, it would also be a major coup. De Gerlache amended his itinerary: he now planned to leave a four-man landing party to establish a winter camp in Victoria Land, immediately south of New Zealand, and make a dash to the magnetic pole at the earliest sign of spring.

---

* The South Magnetic Pole is the spot in the Southern Hemisphere where the lines of the earth's magnetic field shoot vertically into the sky. It's not to be confused with the geographic South Pole, at latitude 90° south, the point where all meridians converge and from which every direction is north. The southern and northern magnetic poles are in continual motion, depending as they do on the eternally churning layer of molten iron around the earth's solid core.

The geographical society's validation could not have been better timed. Just over six months later, in July 1895, the Sixth International Geographical Congress—a gathering of the world's geographical societies—met in London and determined that the exploration of the Antarctic was an urgent priority. In its official report, the congress set a deadline: "This work should be undertaken before the close of the century." The Antarctic race was on, pitting one plucky, little-known young Belgian naval officer against the major seafaring nations of Germany, Britain, and Sweden, which soon announced plans to send expeditions to the continent.

De Gerlache would have to move fast. Yet there was a significant hitch: while the society offered him its blessing, it wouldn't provide funding. De Gerlache estimated that the expedition would cost about 300,000 francs ($1.8 million in current U.S. dollars). His scientific advisers thought the sum far too low—and indeed it represented a fraction of the budgets proposed for other Antarctic expeditions being considered around the world—but de Gerlache felt it had the advantage of being achievable.

De Gerlache set out to find a wealthy benefactor. He first approached Belgium's most prominent citizen, King Leopold himself. After all, he thought, the monarch might be enticed by the prospect of having a newly discovered land named after him. De Gerlache sent a prospectus on the expedition to the royal palace but received no response. The lieutenant presumed Leopold still harbored a grudge over de Gerlache's refusal to take part in the Congo project.

Undeterred, de Gerlache made appeals across Belgium's upper class, making use of his family's extensive social connections. From his parents' elegant townhouse in a leafy Brussels neighborhood, he embarked on an exhausting letter-writing campaign. In reply, he received a flood of heartfelt encouragements, but no money.

Just as he was about to abandon hope, he secured a commitment of 25,000 francs from the fifty-seven-year-old soda ash tycoon Ernest Solvay, said to be Belgium's richest man, who devoted much of his fortune to the advancement of science. De Gerlache's audacity appealed to him, perhaps reminding him of his own up-from-his-bootstraps ascent. Solvay's credit suddenly made the Belgian Antarctic

Expedition seem like less of a pipe dream. Other donors soon followed his lead. Emboldened, de Gerlache began shopping for a ship, which would represent his largest single expense.

He had toyed with the idea of having a ship specially built, but soon realized that would have cost more than his entire budget. De Gerlache thought it wise, instead, to purchase or even lease a craft that had already proven herself in polar conditions. There were none of those to be found in Belgian shipyards, so he looked northward, to Scotland and Norway, for vessels specially braced to withstand the suffocating pressures of the ice. In March of 1895, on the invitation of a ship broker, he left for a three-month whaling and seal-hunting voyage off the coast of Greenland, aboard a handsome, steam-powered Norwegian three-master called the *Castor*. She had prowled the perimeter of Antarctica just two years earlier, and she was for sale. The purpose of the journey was twofold: it would allow de Gerlache to get a feel for the ship, and it would give him a chance to learn the ropes of polar navigation. For all his years at sea, he knew nothing of the ice.

It was a bountiful hunting season in the Arctic, and de Gerlache witnessed, with some uneasiness, the flensing of bottlenose whales and the brutal clubbing of thousands of seal pups, whose fur was of the most desirable softness. A number of other sealers were patrolling the waters, and though he was courting the *Castor*, he stole glances at the competition. Off Jan Mayen, a fleck of volcanic land in the Arctic Ocean halfway between Norway and Greenland, his eye landed on an eleven-year-old bark called the *Patria*. Her figure was less graceful than the *Castor*'s. At 100 feet and 244 tons, she was the runt of the Norwegian whaling fleet, yet he admired how nimbly she negotiated the ice, how tough she could be, ramming past icebergs, sliding up on top of the pack ice, and crushing it under her weight. He had fallen for her, but when he discreetly inquired about her price, he was told she wasn't for sale. Not that it mattered: despite commitments from Solvay and others, he still had just a fraction of the money he needed to buy a vessel.

De Gerlache returned to Belgium shipless in August 1895. It seemed like his grand project was destined to fail. A year after de Gerlache first proposed it, the Belgian Antarctic Expedition still consisted of little more than Adrien de Gerlache, his ink, and his paper. He could think of no other potential patrons to turn to. And yet to abandon his endeavor now that he'd announced his bold intentions across Belgian society, to have to turn down Ernest Solvay's offer, would represent an intolerable humiliation.

Having come up empty in his appeals to the king and the government, de Gerlache turned directly to the people. Starting in January 1896, the Royal Belgian Geographical Society helped him mount a national subscription campaign to fund the expedition. Donations large and small poured in: a schoolteacher gave one franc, a mailman three, a senator one thousand. The society, as well as local supporters and patrons such as Léonie Osterrieth, organized events across the country, including concerts, lectures, a cycling competition, and hot-air balloon rides.

In all, 2,500 Belgian citizens contributed. The effort would bring in a total of 115,000 francs by May 1896. Now that de Gerlache's plans were starting to materialize, the government finally opened its coffers: in June, both chambers of the legislature voted to approve a supplemental 100,000-franc credit. The expedition had suddenly gained a new dimension, one that filled de Gerlache with excitement but also anxiety. These contributions did more than subsidize his Antarctic dream. The journey that had lived only in his mind for many years now lived, too, in the minds of his countrymen, hungry to share in the glory. He had made it real, but in doing so he had generated a national emotional investment that he had no choice but to pay back. This weight would be with him always going forward, creeping into his thoughts, shading his glowing ambition with the fear of failure and shame.

From then on, de Gerlache realized, the expedition had ceased to be entirely his. Meeting the conflicting expectations of the geographical society (which insisted on the utmost scientific rigor), his financial backers (who expected their money to be spent wisely), the glory-hungry public (who demanded death-defying heroics), and his own family (who counted on him not to sully their name) would prove to be an impossible juggling act.

· · ·

De Gerlache could at last afford a ship. Via an intermediary—Johan Bryde, the Norwegian-born director of the Belgian consulate in Sandefjord—he made an offer on the *Patria,* the ship that had rebuffed his advances the previous year. A savvy negotiator, Bryde was able to secure her for 70,000 francs. In the summer of 1896, de Gerlache traveled to Sandefjord, Norway, to claim his prize. He felt the deck beneath his feet and ran his hand along the gunwales. At last he had a vessel he could call his own, the first since the model ships of his youth. On July 5, he rechristened her the *Belgica.*

It was around the time that de Gerlache had initially hoped to leave for Antarctica, but he was not nearly ready. He was forced to postpone departure for a full year, since he wanted at all costs to avoid arriving in Antarctica during the terrifying austral winter.

De Gerlache stayed in Sandefjord for several months to oversee the modifications required to prepare the *Belgica* for her journey. In that time, he would learn to speak fluent Norwegian. The ship's hull was sheathed in the sturdiest wood available, a tropical variety called greenheart, to defend against the wrenching assaults of the ice. Working with a shipbuilder named Lars Christensen (who happened to be Bryde's father-in-law), de Gerlache added layers of felt and wood to insulate the interior and guard against shipworms. Christensen replaced the engine and added a new steel propeller that could be retracted in case the ice closed in on the ship. He expanded the poop deck, and built a wardroom for the officers and a darkroom in which to develop photographic plates. Finally, he constructed two on-deck laboratories that de Gerlache equipped with cutting-edge scientific instruments, ordered from across Europe. When Christensen was done, the *Belgica* had lost her greasy patina and pervasive blubbery odor and taken on the gleaming appearance of a pleasure yacht.

Now that he'd acquired his vessel, de Gerlache had to find scientists and sailors to inhabit her. In this, de Gerlache immediately ran into a problem that would continue to bedevil him long after he left port, but one that loomed perhaps far larger in his mind than in reality. Dreading dishonor more than death, he had formed an almost pathological fear of the jingoistic Belgian press, which he suspected would savage him were the ship manned by a crew and scientific staff that weren't entirely, proudly Belgian. But this was a virtually impossible demand. De Gerlache never had much hope of finding enough competent sailors in Belgium to man his expedition, given the country's paltry maritime tradition. The journey he was proposing, moreover, was both dangerous and unprofitable: Belgian thrill seekers were far more likely to chase their fortunes in the Congo. And while the country had no shortage of good scientists, the best had already come and gone. Shortly after the expedition was first announced, de Gerlache received eager commitments from several eminent Belgian scholars, but as the preparations dragged on, they dropped out one by one. They had grown frustrated with the delays and wary of what they feared was a poorly financed and disorganized affair.

The only man who had not abandoned de Gerlache was Emile Danco, one of his oldest friends, who had accompanied him on the whaling journey the previous year. The two had been drawn to each other as the reserved, cloistered children of military fathers. While de Gerlache went on to pursue a naval career, Danco enlisted in the Belgian Army and rose to the rank of artillery lieutenant. Though he looked the part of an Antarctic adventurer, with his sturdy build and square-jawed good looks, he was neither a scientist nor a sailor. But what he lacked in qualifications he made up for in enthusiasm. His mother had died when he was young; after the death of his wealthy but domineering father, he was left with a sizeable inheritance and a desperate desire to see the world beyond Belgium. De Gerlache would not find a more committed collaborator. Danco not only went without pay but also offered to contribute several thousand francs to the expedition. As soon as the assignment was made official—which required a special military dispensation signed by Leopold II—Danco began addressing his childhood friend as *"mon commandant,"* also switching from the informal pronoun *tu* to the more deferential *vous*.

But two men alone could not fill a roster. Faced with the choice of recruiting a number of foreigners, resorting to unqualified Belgians, or further delaying, if not canceling, the voyage, de Gerlache decided to risk compromising the patriotic nature of the project. Relying wholly on an ill-prepared Belgian crew meant dooming the expedition. Nor could he embark on a scientific mission without scientists. The Belgian Antarctic Expedition thus became international by default—and for the better.

De Gerlache's second hire was Henryk Arctowski, a brilliant but destitute Polish chemist and geologist affiliated with the University of Liège, in Belgium, a man whose unsmiling mien, crisp suits, voluminous beard, and extensive publication record made him seem far older than his twenty-three years. It was several months before Arctowski confessed that he didn't, strictly speaking, have a diploma. "I must tell you that I have no academic title," he wrote to de Gerlache. "I have pursued a totally independent course of study, and I'm still far from the goal that I have set for myself." De Gerlache had too few alternatives to be picky. Arctowski kept the job. The *Belgica* would be his diploma.

It took de Gerlache longer to find his zoologist. Emile Racovitza,* age twenty-seven, was born into a wealthy Romanian family and studied at the Sorbonne, in Paris, where his exceptional work on pelagic life, particularly sea worms, had greatly impressed his professors. Though Arctowski had recommended him, the two could hardly have been more different. Their personalities reflected their chosen fields of study: while the geologist was dry, rigid, and flinty, the zoologist was warm and spirited. Perhaps just as enticing for de Gerlache was Racovitza's offer to serve without pay.

Then came the crew. The Belgian crew members de Gerlache was able to wrangle over the course of a year were far from the cream of the crop. They included a navy mechanic, Joseph Duvivier, whose superior officer wrote a letter of recommendation that read much more like a warning: "In summation, *it is possible* that Mr. Duvivier might figure out how to work a very simple engine, like the *Belgica*'s, but I cannot guarantee it." De Gerlache hired him.

Another Belgian applicant was Louis Michotte, a twenty-eight-year-old ne'er-do-well who had just returned from a five-year stint in Africa with the French Foreign Legion, during which a local man had bitten off one of his thumbs. "As a youth I committed a few youthful

* This is how he signed his name when writing in French. The Romanian spelling is Emil Racoviță.

peccadilloes," he wrote to de Gerlache, "and my father still holds them against me, but if I could accompany you in any capacity, then, Sir, I hope to be pardoned, and you, Sir, you would have a good deed to add to your glory." Michotte cited his skill at fencing among his qualifications for Antarctic exploration. De Gerlache hired him, too.

For the bulk of his crew, however, de Gerlache would need dependable men who could navigate through ice and extreme weather. Norway—with its flourishing shipping industry and extensive coastline; with its Viking traditions and briny myths—was a natural place to look. It was difficult to find a Norwegian who knew nothing of boats. While in Sandefjord with the *Belgica*, de Gerlache hired a number of eager Norsemen, veterans of Arctic campaigns as well as teenage novices.

In late July 1896, de Gerlache received a letter that caught his attention:

To Lieutenant A. de Gerlache,
As I have just been informed that you don't intend to launch your Antarctic expedition until next year, I would like to ask if there is still an open position among the personnel of your expedition. If so, I would be grateful for a spot as a sailor.
    I'm 24 years old and I served in 1894 on the "Magdalena" with Captain Stöcksen in the glacial sea and this year aboard the "Jason," Captain Evensen.
    I have passed my middle school exams, the baccalaureate, and my navigation school exam. I have the best certificate as regards my health. Finally, I might add that I am used to skiing and that I have undertaken difficult ski trips in the high mountains.
    I would be grateful if you would kindly respond soon. . . .
    Roald Amundsen

De Gerlache was intrigued enough to meet with Amundsen in person. He found a man who seemed to have been torn from the pages of the adventure novels he'd read as a child. More than six feet tall and a muscular two hundred pounds, the hawk-faced Amundsen looked like a modern-day Viking. De Gerlache was particularly impressed by Amundsen's avowed skills as a cross-country skier. Skiing had only recently begun to spread beyond its birthplace in the Scandinavian hinterlands, and if de Gerlache was going to make a dash to the South Magnetic Pole, he would need a practiced skier alongside him. Just as enticing: Amundsen, like Danco and Racovitza, did not expect payment. He was interested solely in the experience.

It was Bryde who had passed Amundsen's application to de Gerlache. In the corner, the diplomat had scrawled an enthusiastic note to the commandant: "Take him, my friend!" De Gerlache had stumbled upon a gem. Never the best judge of men, even he could tell that this Norwegian would be wasted as a rank-and-file crew member. Though Amundsen had applied for a spot as a mere sailor, de Gerlache named him first mate,* a position that would, under maritime custom, place him in line to inherit command of the *Belgica*. The possibility that a Norwegian might take the helm of the ship was far from ideal. Danco suggested it might encourage the Norwegian crew to split their allegiance, possibly even to mutiny.

It was only a matter of time before the press found out that only half the men on the Belgian Antarctic Expedition were Belgian. The team the commandant had assembled would be among the first truly international scientific expeditions in history, but this was not the kind of first de Gerlache was hoping to achieve. Among the workarounds he briefly explored was to have some of the men take on Belgian citizenship; he abandoned this idea after Arctowski told him that he planned one day to return to Poland, and that under czarist Russian rule, any subject who took foreign citizenship without permission was sentenced to hard labor.

He found a more convenient solution in June 1897, just two months before the *Belgica*'s departure, when he secured one of the few major Belgian naval talents aside from himself. The twenty-eight-year-old Georges Lecointe, a former classmate of Danco's at the Royal Mili-

---

*Historians disagree on whether to call Amundsen first or second mate. His official title was reported alternatively as first or second lieutenant, but French and Belgian maritime ranks don't conform exactly to the Anglo-American hierarchy. Since Amundsen performed the typical duties of a first mate and there was neither a lieutenant nor a mate above him, this book will refer to him as first mate, as Amundsen did himself.

tary School, was a lieutenant in the Belgian Navy then serving with the French forces. Known as an expert in celestial navigation, Lecointe would become the captain of the *Belgica*, second to Commandant de Gerlache, moving Amundsen down a peg in the hierarchy.* Described by one Belgian journalist as short, "all nerves, with the vivacity of the squirrel," Lecointe had a pugnacious leadership style that contrasted with de Gerlache's natural placidity.

In late June, the *Belgica* made her way from Sandefjord to Vlissingen, Holland, where Lecointe was set to come aboard. On the twenty-eighth, before the captain's arrival, the ship ran aground on a sandbar off the port town of Den Helder. Lecointe wondered what he'd gotten himself into: if the crew couldn't negotiate well-charted European waters, how could they handle the unknown perils of the Antarctic? "Nothing seemed more extraordinary to me," he wrote, "than this ship that would embark on its campaign, the crew of which, still incomplete, already included several undisciplined and even dangerous sailors." But if he doubted de Gerlache, he would never question him; he would become, in fact, his greatest defender.

Through clever cajoling of the government—and by offering tours of the *Belgica* to paying visitors at the port of Antwerp—de Gerlache finally raised his 300,000-franc budget. Yet the muster roll continued to change until the last day. De Gerlache hired Jan Van Mirlo, a young, impulsive Antwerp native, who applied in order to dodge military service and lied about having any sailing experience. (The only job he'd ever held had been to deliver bread on a tricycle for his father, a baker.) Around the same time, the commandant brought on a hulking, irascible French cook named Albert Lemonnier, who had a fondness for drink and a tendency to insult everyone within earshot.

In a preview of the disciplinary problems to come, several Belgian sailors left the ship without permission for extended periods. A sub-officer named Coene outright deserted. After the chief mechanic, Henri Somers, went on a two-day bender through Antwerp, an

---

*The terminology of rank is confusing here as well. De Gerlache was the leader of both the expedition and the ship: he was for all intents and purposes the captain of the *Belgica*. Yet Lecointe was accorded the title of captain because of an equivalency between his rank in the French Navy—"ship's lieutenant"—and that of "captain-commandant" in the Belgian Army.

alarmed Lecointe reported him to de Gerlache: Somers, he wrote, "gravely compromised, in public, the good reputation of the crew, by getting scandalously inebriated (while in uniform)." Lecointe recommended that de Gerlache fire Somers immediately. With his dismissal, the *Belgica*'s engine was left in the incapable hands of Duvivier.

Stymied by a mixture of self-sabotage and bad luck, De Gerlache struggled most of all in acquiring a surgeon. The first candidate, Dr. Arthur Taquin, had been handpicked early on by the secretary-general of the Royal Belgian Geographical Society, but the commandant feared that Taquin would act as a Trojan horse for the society and wrest control of the expedition away from him. Since de Gerlache shrank from confrontation, his father did the dirty work for him. Colonel Auguste de Gerlache used his considerable influence to have Taquin ousted, citing past malpractice and threatening legal action.*

Several other physicians were considered before de Gerlache settled on a young Belgian doctor named Jules Pouplier, fresh out of medical school. But on August 15, the day before the ship was to set sail, Pouplier's older brother wrote de Gerlache a note saying that Pouplier was needed at home to care for their ailing sister and was thus unable to travel.

De Gerlache realized the foolishness of departing for the most treacherous waters on earth with a less-than-ideal crew and no doctor. But if he didn't leave now, he might never leave at all. Amid the hurrahs and music and fluttering Belgian flags on August 16, de Gerlache convinced himself that it would all somehow work out.

Once the yacht carrying his family was out of sight, de Gerlache descended from the *Belgica*'s crow's nest. The commandant felt blissfully free. "I was done with the thankless duties that had consumed

---

*De Gerlache père alleged that Taquin had neglected his duty as physician aboard a ship sailing from Congo to Belgium. The doctor was said to have remained in his cabin throughout the journey, during which four people died. To make his case, Adrien's father interviewed dozens of passengers, six of whom confirmed on paper that Taquin could have done more. Taquin, in his own defense, claimed that he'd been ill with food poisoning.

me for three years, done with solicitations, with compromises, with the endless hunt for indispensable resources. . . . This departure meant deliverance, escape . . . infinite hopes."

The *Belgica* anchored for the night off the Dutch port town of Vlissingen, at the mouth of the Scheldt. As the setting sun illuminated his starboard-facing cabin—decorated with polar scenes and a photograph of his father that loomed above his bunk—he sat down at his desk and let his thoughts fill the silence. By selling his polar dream as a patriotic undertaking, he had subjected himself to pressures as intimidating to him as those he expected to face in the ice. While a successful expedition would buff Belgium's global cachet, de Gerlache knew that he alone would shoulder the blame if anything went wrong.

The very next day, something did. Just as the *Belgica* entered the open sea and the crew fired her steam engine, the condenser overheated and broke down, on Duvivier's watch. De Gerlache was forced to dock in Ostend, along the coast of the North Sea, for repairs—an abject humiliation after such a momentous send-off.

De Gerlache surely hoped his layover in Ostend would go unnoticed, but he picked the worst spot to drop anchor—right next to King Leopold's yacht, the *Clémentine,* on which the king's presence was soon expected. The inevitable encounter ended in the most embarrassing possible fashion when Leopold emerged to address the *Belgica*'s crew and pretended not to recognize the ship.

Leopold asked if he could come aboard. The short visit was an awkward moment for de Gerlache, who still harbored a grudge against his sovereign for not contributing to his Antarctic endeavor. "The King asked us rather banal questions and wished us good luck," he confided to Léonie Osterrieth. "He was polite, but no more. In his opinion, I succeeded because I didn't find support in high places. In other words, he did us a favor by not taking an interest in us!!!"

Perhaps seeing a bad omen in the engine malfunction, three men quit the expedition in Ostend. Two seasoned Norwegian crew members—the carpenter and the boatswain—complained that their Belgian shipmates refused to take orders from them, and a mechanic called out sick and never returned. Desperate, de Gerlache rehired Henri Somers, the engineer who had been cashiered for public drunkenness. The commandant understood the bad precedent his mercy set, but the incident with the condenser had made him nervous about keeping Duvivier as the sole mechanic.

It was "almost in hiding" that de Gerlache returned to Antwerp to find new recruits. There he replaced the two departed Norwegians with two far less experienced Norwegians, Engelbret Knudsen and Ludvig Hjalmar Johansen. But the insubordination of the Belgian sailors was threatening to cause serious trouble. The commandant was especially wary of a clique consisting of Frans Dom, Maurice Warzée, and Jan Van Damme, three skilled but unruly Belgian sailors with chips on their shoulders about working with foreigners. As tempted as he might have been to kick them off the ship, he feared the consequences. Firing them would not only shrink the crew at the start of the voyage, but it would also increase the proportion of non-Belgians. This gave the clique leverage over de Gerlache, hobbling his authority from the get-go. His sensitivity to the accusation that he was biased against his own countrymen allowed them to act with impunity.

While in Ostend, he took on an extra scientist, a young student named Antoni Dobrowolski. An acquaintance and compatriot of Arctowski's, Dobrowolski was an outspoken Polish separatist who had been sentenced to three years in a czarist prison. He had recently escaped, and had since been living in poverty in Belgium, reduced to sating his hunger "with air or the like." His offer to serve on the *Belgica* without pay and to perform grunt duties suited de Gerlache just fine.

However grateful he might have been for the position—and the regular meals—Dobrowolski privately harbored grave doubts about the expedition, its crew, and its leader. "Somehow I trust neither the *Belgica*—a tiny little thing with flaws in its construction—nor its captain [de Gerlache]—who does a good job of posing, but doesn't seem like such a wizard," the new recruit wrote in his diary. "We'll see, at any rate. Discontent with [him] was visible among the deckhands right from the start."

This left only the matter of the physician. Just days before the *Belgica* would have to leave Ostend, de Gerlache took a train to Ghent in a last-ditch attempt to hire a Belgian doctor. The commandant was unsuccessful.

He had received several offers from abroad but had not previously considered them, knowing he'd be lambasted in the press for hiring yet another foreigner. But now he faced a choice between a foreign doctor and no doctor at all. He turned his attention to a telegram he had received and dismissed a few weeks earlier, sent from Brooklyn, New York.

COULD I JOIN YOUR EXPEDITION AT MONTVIDEO [sic]
WILL SUBSCRIBE BRING ARCTIC EQUIPMENT ALSO
SOME ESKIMO DOGS ANSWER MY EXPENSE. + DR
COOK

CHAPTER 2

"Gold and Diamonds"

ON THE HUMID EVENING OF AUGUST 19, A UNIFORMED WESTERN Union messenger raced through the streets of Brooklyn by bicycle, weaving between the screeching electric streetcars that regularly mowed down pedestrians and had inspired the local baseball team's new nickname, the Brooklyn Trolley Dodgers. He rushed to 687 Bushwick Avenue, a townhouse on an upscale block, to deliver a telegram.

At that address, Dr. Frederick Albert Cook was seeing the last of his patients for the day and readying himself for dinner. After struggling for years to build a clientele, the thirty-two-year-old physician was finally enjoying success. He was known throughout the neighborhood for making house calls in his sporty cabriolet, pulled by a resplendent white horse. Cook had made a name for himself as the surgeon on a famous Arctic expedition, bona fides that brought prestige to his practice and, for his patients, a frisson of adventure to routine checkups.

Cook had a remarkable ability to connect with his patients, to gain their trust, even their love, and perhaps this skill allowed him to cover for the fact that these days he was not fully present. His mind was thousands of miles away, drifting over the icescapes of Antarctica, a destination he'd never stopped fantasizing about. His reveries bled into his medical notebooks, where in between pages of shorthand notes—about Mr. Luran's persistent cough or Mrs. Greene's obesity and frequent flatulence—were clippings of articles about the as-yet-unattained South Pole, iceberg formation, or the midnight sun of the polar summer. Cook was drawn to the poles as if by magnetism. His wanderlust, his insatiable thirst for adventure and glory, kept him from being satisfied with the comfortable, sedentary life of a family doctor.

He heard a knock out front. When Cook opened his door, the Western Union boy thrust in his hand a ticket to the world of his secret dreams.

It was his restless nature that allowed Frederick Cook to escape the crippling poverty of his youth. His early life was one story among the many that collectively formed the mythology of American opportunity. Cook was born in rural New York, across the Delaware River from Pennsylvania, two months after the end of the Civil War. His father, a German immigrant named Theodor A. Koch, had served as a surgeon during the war. It was then that the family name was anglicized to Cook. Frederick spoke German at home with his parents. After his father died of pneumonia in 1870, his mother, Magdalena, was able to support her five children for a while by collecting unpaid debts from Theodor's former patients. But that income soon ran out. Cook grew up, in his words, "underfed and overschooled." The table was often bare. The occasional woodchuck was a delicacy.

Forced to look for work, Magdalena moved the family down the river and eventually to Brooklyn, where she landed a job as a seamstress for a sweatshop. They rented a shack on South First Street in Williamsburg, a damp, industrial neighborhood along the East River, saturated with the sickly-sweet stench emanating from the nearby sugar refinery. Soon after they arrived, Cook's younger brother, August, died of scarlet fever.

Cook began earning his keep at age twelve in a succession of jobs. A broad-featured boy, with a nose well on its way to prominence, he toiled in the magmatic glow of fires at a glass factory and worked as a streetlamp lighter. He and his brother William later manned a fruit and vegetable stall at the Fulton Market in Manhattan. Despite the punishing hours—from two a.m. to noon—Cook managed to keep up with his schoolwork.

Emulating a father he hardly remembered, Cook decided to go to medical school. That he couldn't afford it didn't dissuade him. A childhood spent tearing through the woods barefoot among the feral boys of Sullivan County had toughened Cook and taught him how to survive on little; an adolescence spent in Brooklyn had taught him how to hustle. Even as a young man, he had a talent for problem solving and invention, which he would draw on for the rest of his life. With his meager savings, he bought a small, secondhand printing press, which he used to make posters, flyers, ads, and greeting cards for local merchants. As soon as his business began to thrive, he sold it to launch a new one. He purchased a milk route that he operated with his older brothers. The Cook Bros Milk & Cream Company expanded rapidly, delivering as far as Rockaway Beach. Cook devised ingenious ways to best the competition. When the Great Blizzard of 1888 blanketed the East Coast under several feet of snow and paralyzed New York traffic, he and his brothers affixed sledge runners to a boat, which, once hitched to a horse, allowed them to deliver much-needed coal throughout the city—and reap a handsome profit.

In 1887, Cook enrolled in the College of Physicians and Surgeons at Columbia University. When Columbia moved its campus to uptown Manhattan, he transferred to New York University's medical school, then on Twenty-sixth Street. The shorter commute allowed him to deliver milk in Brooklyn at night and study during the day—and sleep very little.

He somehow found the time to court a young stenographer named Libby Forbes, whom he met at a temperance festival at a Methodist church in Williamsburg. The two married in the spring of 1889, and Libby became pregnant in the fall. Cook saw his future clearly: Within nine months, he would graduate from medical school and become a father. He'd sell his milk business and open a practice. The feverish pace of life would slow down, and the Cook family would ease into the routine of what was not yet called the upper middle class. Or at least that's what he told himself. Nothing about Cook's life so far suggested he would find happiness in settling down. But he never got a chance to find out.

Just as he arrived within reach of this comfortable life, it was ripped away from him. Libby gave birth to a baby girl in the summer of 1890, but there were complications and the infant died within hours. Libby followed her a week later, succumbing to peritonitis. Among the last things Cook would have told her was that he had passed his exams.

Heartbroken, Cook moved across the river and opened a medical office in Manhattan. At just twenty-five, he had already known the struggle and the grief of a much older man, but it didn't show on his boyish face. He grew a beard, as men often do when going through dark times, but also as young doctors then did in an effort to be taken seriously. Despite his hopes of finding solace in work—and despite his impressive whiskers—few patients sought his services.

For the first time in more than a decade, Cook had nothing to do. Sitting idly in his office only reinforced the loneliness and desolation of city life. The country boy had never taken to New York—"It was slushy and dirty when snow came, stuffy, hot, and sweaty in summer," he wrote—and since his wife's death it had grown even more intolerable to him. He whiled away the empty hours reading about distant corners of the earth, places far hotter and far colder than New York. Cook was particularly taken by the narratives of adventurers like Elisha Kent Kane, the swashbuckling American physician who in the 1850s survived a succession of brutal winters aboard a ship encased in the Arctic ice, and Henry Morton Stanley, the self-promoting Welsh American explorer who charted much of central Africa at the behest of Belgium's King Leopold II.

Stanley's voyages, as well as several famous polar expeditions, were chronicled at length in *The New York Herald,* which Cook read assiduously. A desire to travel far away began to grow in him. "With time to think and plan there developed a longing to get out over the world into the unknown to blaze the trail for a life of useful adventure," he wrote.

In the early spring of 1891, Cook saw a short newspaper article, datelined Philadelphia, that would redirect his life poleward. A naval engineer named Robert E. Peary was planning an expedition far above the arctic circle to determine the northern limits of Greenland and was in search of volunteers. The notice sparked him to action. He sent an application and a few weeks later found himself meeting with Peary in Philadelphia. Cook had not traveled outside the state of

New York, and his brief experience as a doctor contained little that would apply to the brutal, almost combat-like conditions of a polar expedition. But he knew people, knew what they wanted to hear, and when Frederick Cook desired something badly enough, he could usually talk his way into it. Peary sensed the doctor's passion, his fearlessness. By the time Cook headed back to Brooklyn, he had secured a position as the expedition's surgeon and ethnologist.

The Peary party consisted of the engineer, Cook, four other men, and Peary's wife, Josephine, one of the few women to take part in early polar exploration. Sailing aboard an aging, steam-powered barkentine called the *Kite,* they arrived at northwestern Greenland's Melville Bay, around latitude 76° north, in early July. Cook was introduced to the ruthlessness of the Arctic before he even left the ship. On July 11, as the *Kite* was battering past the floes that formed around the coast, he heard a bloodcurdling scream coming from the deck. The ship's rudder had caught on a chunk of ice, whipping the iron tiller into Peary's right leg and crushing it against the deckhouse. Cook set Peary's shattered bones and fashioned a splint and cast for him, as well as a pair of crutches. The doctor's companions on the journey would frequently remark on his uncanny resourcefulness. "Dr. Cook," recalled the young Norwegian adventurer Eivind Astrup, the sole non-American on the expedition, "has a lucky gift of being able to make good and useful things out of strange materials."

The party built a lodge atop a rocky bluff on McCormick Bay. For the six months it took Peary's leg to heal, Cook was left in charge of establishing contact with nearby Inuit families, whose knowledge of the region the explorers depended on and with whom they hoped to trade for fresh meat, sled dogs, furs, boots, and other necessities. Never a quick study with foreign languages, Cook nonetheless learned enough of the local tongue to make himself understood, aided by hand signals and his natural charisma.

As the expedition's designated ethnologist, Cook posed Inuit men and women unclothed for Peary's camera and took detailed measurements of their bodies, objectifying practices then typical of the nascent field of anthropolology. But his curiosity and empathy probed deeper.

The Inuit came to consider Cook as something like an *angakok,* or shaman. "Now and then," Cook recalled, "I was able to perform some bit of surgery or administer some drug, very much to the delight of the Eskimos who finally came to endow me with supernatural powers." As such, they allowed him to observe their rituals more closely. He ate caribou meat with them and listened to their stories. He saw how they grew despondent during the monthslong winter night, and how their passions were reignited when the sun returned. Cook grew fascinated with animistic Inuit beliefs, or what he understood of them: with the notion that light had divine powers, that the souls of people resided in their shadows, and that the seasonal disappearance of the sun caused a kind of a vanishing of the spirit. In time, he would come to consider these concepts as something more than folklore.*

One night in February 1892, Cook underwent the kind of ordeal that forever changes the way a man thinks of mortality. After climbing to a high plateau from which they hoped to welcome the long-absent sun, Cook, Astrup, and Peary (whose leg had mended) took shelter from a violent blizzard in a poorly constructed igloo. They slipped into their reindeer-skin sleeping bags and fell asleep in relative comfort. By early morning, the roof—built flat atop beams made of skis rather than domed in the Inuit fashion—had collapsed in the gale, and the three men awoke to find themselves entombed in snow.

Cook and Peary struggled free. In a panic, they began scratching at the mound of snow that covered Astrup from head to toe. They kept a breathing hole open for the Norwegian as they dug him out with their hands at first, and then with a shovel. The three men crouched behind the ruins of the igloo's wall to keep from toppling over in the deafening wind. They were still in their undergarments, their shoes and furs inaccessible under several feet of snow. All they could do was wait out the storm, with no shelter but their dampen-

---

*Cook's characterizations of Inuit beliefs are necessarily incomplete and inexact. He was not trained in anthropology—which wasn't yet firmly established as an academic discipline—and he understood little of the language. Yet they are valuable in that they represent what he took away from his experience among the Inuit.

ing sleeping bags. They remained braced against the wind for a full day, each minute an agony of whipping precipitation from which there was no escape.

Peary, Cook, and Astrup dipped in and out of sleep as the snow turned to hail, then to icy rain. Every so often, shouting to be heard, Peary reminded them to wriggle around to keep from freezing in place. After a while, moonlight pierced through the dark clouds and the snow stopped falling, though the wind continued to sweep it across the plateau. The temperature plummeted. Cook felt his extremities go numb and began to shiver uncontrollably. His sleeping bag was encased in ice. He couldn't move, which only exacerbated the cold. Peary dug a grave-shaped hole and, after chiseling Cook free, rolled him into it and curled himself along the edge of the hole to protect the doctor from the wind. Cook did not record what he felt in that moment, lying paralyzed beneath Peary, whether he was stricken with fear or rendered numb and silent by the shock. But it's hard not to imagine that he wondered if this first adventure would be his last. When the storm died down and the feeling returned to his arms and legs, he realized that he had survived his baptism by the polar elements. The ordeal impressed upon him the immense power of the ice and snow—how easy it was to meet one's fate near the poles.

The Peary expedition was Cook's education as an explorer. He endured a bitter Arctic winter. He learned much from his companions, including how to ski and shoot, and he taught himself how to scale cliffs of ice and snow by carving out footholds with an ax. Even more valuable, perhaps, was Cook's time among the Inuit, from which he acquired not only practical skills he would come to depend on—such as dog running, proper igloo building, and hide tanning—but also a profound humility before the forces of nature.

"In our short acquaintance with polar aborigines, we learned to discount civilized intelligence in exchange for the more useful perspective of the primitive," Cook wrote. "If one must live in the Arctic, the sooner he reverts to habits of the wilderness folk, the better."

Crediting Cook for "the almost complete exemption of the party from even the mildest indispositions," Peary invited Cook to accompany him as surgeon and second-in-command on his next Arctic journey. Cook initially accepted the offer, but after Peary refused to let the doctor publish his observations of the Inuit in a scientific journal, citing the convention that the publication of any findings collected on an expedition was the prerogative of its leader, Cook resigned. He refused to remain in the shadow of another explorer. The two parted ways, amicably for the time being.

Back in Brooklyn, heading up a new practice, Cook found that having one's name in the papers did wonders for business. Yet even as he saw patients at his Rutledge Street office, his imagination strayed to extreme latitudes. Greenland had transformed him. He longed for lungfuls of Arctic air, for the vast white vistas that made America's largest city seem small. Perhaps most intoxicating was the sensation of having cheated death. He had no choice: he would return to the ice.

Cook planned to mount a polar expedition of his own. In part because he didn't want to compete with Peary in the North, and in part because he had sensed the same opportunity as de Gerlache would in the South, Cook set his sights on the little-explored Antarctic.

He believed that adopting Inuit modes of travel and dress would increase his chances of success in Antarctica. Before formally announcing his plans, he would need to return to Inuit territory to acquire sled dogs and fur garments, and to complete his study of "Arctic Highlanders," as many then called the Inuit. To that end, as well as to help fund his Antarctic journey, Cook organized a cruise to Greenland for a few paying customers. It was largely subsidized by a wealthy Yale arts professor whose pole-obsessed son had heard Cook speak about his Arctic adventures at the university and was desperate to visit the northern wastelands.

In the summer of 1893, Cook chartered and refitted a seventy-eight-foot schooner called the *Zeta* and led his well-to-do clients on a cruise to Labrador and western Greenland. He returned to Brooklyn in early October with a dozen or so Greenland dogs, several trunks full of animal skins, and two Inuit teenagers, Kahlahkatak and Mikok, whom he called Clara and Willie. He had seen the beautiful sixteen-year-old Kahlahkatak perform an entrancing traditional dance in the trading outpost of Rigolet, Labrador, and envisioned the sensation she would provoke in the United States. Cook convinced the girl's father to let him take her and her brother, Mikok, back to New York, promising to return them the following spring. They would get to see the big city, and Cook would be able to show them off on the lecture circuit as living props.

The Inuit children stayed in a tent in the backyard of Cook's mother's new house on Fifty-fifth Street in Manhattan. Cook would draw crowds whenever he walked through Midtown with his Inuit wards at his side and his pack of panting huskies leading the way. He entered the dogs in the Westchester Kennel Club show, where they won three prizes. But they didn't take well to the New York summers. Several died of the heat, and the doctor sent the survivors to his brother's farm in Sullivan County, where he hoped to breed them. Kahlahkatak and Mikok didn't relish the summer either, and both found ice cream revolting. In the winter, they complained of the cold. Cook helped them build an igloo.

Counting on lectures to help finance his Antarctic project, Cook hired the flamboyant promoter Major J. B. Pond, who had managed tours for Peary, Stanley, P. T. Barnum, Mark Twain, and a young Winston Churchill. (Churchill later dismissed Pond as a "vulgar Yankee impresario.") The doctor proved to be a natural showman, with a keen sense of what could fire the public imagination. "Dr. Cook had a knack for holding the attention of his audiences," recalled the owner of a Manhattan dime museum where Cook did a four-week run and where Harry Houdini regularly performed around that time. Framed as an anthropological lecture, Cook's traveling Arctic presentation—which he delivered up to nine times a day—was a less outwardly sensationalist but equally exploitative version of Buffalo Bill's Wild West shows or Barnum's bearded lady sideshows. He dressed up in his polar furs and recounted his Arctic adventures, with liberal embellishments. With Kahlahkatak and Mikok beside him onstage, he described the harrowing, monthslong winter night and the exotic practices of the Northern Greenland Inuit. (That these practices had little connection to Kahlahkatak and Mikok, who came from a relatively Westernized trading outpost well below the arctic circle, was of little importance to Pond or Cook.)

Toward the end of his lecture, he unfolded a grand vision for his proposed Antarctic journey. The expedition he had in mind was not dissimilar to de Gerlache's plan, nor was his approach to pitching it. In 1894, he sent a proposal to the American Geographical Society, in which he made the case that while the Arctic had been thoroughly explored, "the south-polar regions have been neglected, and very little is known of the antarctics." Like the Belgian lieutenant (of whom he had yet to hear), Cook intended to travel by steam whaler, "especially fitted for work in ice-bound seas," and to conduct scientific observations throughout the journey.

Where the two plans differed was in Cook's ambition from the outset to be the first to winter on the continent and to travel by dog-sled as far south as possible, perhaps even to the geographic pole, the following summer. There was another fundamental difference between Cook's and de Gerlache's plans: because Cook had already experienced some of the cruelties of a polar winter, he understood the necessity of preparing his men for the soul-withering ravages of prolonged darkness. "As the sun disappears," he wrote in his proposal, "explorations in the field must cease, and a systematic routine of mental and physical exercise begin."

The doctor estimated the expedition would cost $50,000, slightly less than de Gerlache's anticipated budget. "This money I expect to raise by private subscriptions and through the aid of scientific societies," he wrote. "Much of it has already been promised, and some of it I expect to derive from a course of lectures."

In reality, he had secured virtually no money from private donors. Yet confident of his eventual success, the doctor nonetheless ordered stationery marked "Official Bureau of the American Antarctic Expedition. Dr. Frederick A. Cook, Commanding." While his lectures hadn't earned him enough to purchase a ship, let alone to staff or equip one, they had generated enough publicity and interest for him to organize a second tourist excursion to Greenland, which he hoped might get him close to the $50,000 he needed for his Antarctic adventure.

Cook advertised an expedition to hunt polar bears, learn about the Inuit, and study the natural history of Greenland. The asking price was $500 per person. In short order, Cook sold fifty-two tickets, most of them to students and professors from elite universities. The trip would allow him to bring Kahlahkatak and Mikok back home, along with several Inuit from Labrador who had been left stranded in the United States after being exhibited at the 1893 World's Columbian Exposition in Chicago.

To accommodate this large group, Cook chartered a 220-foot iron steamer called the *Miranda,* disregarding her reputation as a cursed ship notorious for her numerous collisions with rocks and other vessels. Cook's expedition only confirmed her snakebitten status. On July 17, 1894, off the coast of Newfoundland, passengers at breakfast heard a cutlery-jangling crash that some mistook for an explosion, followed by the screech of grinding metal. The *Miranda* had barreled into an enormous iceberg. The impact stove in her starboard side and sent huge chunks of ice crashing down onto the angled deck. Three weeks later, after crossing the Labrador Sea to Greenland, the *Miranda* smashed into a reef, causing another panic on board. "I reckon we been sounding with the keel," one sailor told Cook.

The damage was far worse than after the first collision: the *Miranda* was taking on water and could not be relied upon to carry the passengers any farther. Demonstrating the coolness that had earned him Peary's admiration, Cook led a small party in an open whaleboat for a hundred miles along the wind-scoured Greenland coast in hopes of finding a ship that might offer the *Miranda* castaways passage back to a major port. One of Cook's Inuit guides spotted the fishing schooner *Rigel,* out of Gloucester, Massachusetts. Her captain agreed to cut his fishing campaign short in order to help his fellow Americans—in exchange for $4,000 and a share of whatever could be salvaged from the *Miranda.* Cook had no choice but to accept. It became increasingly clear that this expedition would end up costing him more than it brought in and would set him even further back from his goal of reaching the South Pole. Cook and his group carried on to Halifax, where they boarded the *Portia,* which happened to be the *Miranda*'s sister ship and proved just as star-crossed. On the morning of September 10 off Cuttyhunk Light, Massachusetts, the *Portia* sailed broadside into a schooner called the *Dora M. French,* splitting her cleanly in two. Three of the schooner's men, caught in the tangled rigging, were sucked into the ocean along with her.

Speaking to reporters at his Brooklyn home upon his return, Cook played down the failures of the journey. Ever the self-promoter, he even tried to spin it as a success: "a delightful trip, replete with adventures, abounding in situations, not free from danger, and taken all in all, I have not heard one member of the party that had a complaint to make." Cook was lying through his teeth, having endured a steady barrage of complaints ever since the collision with the iceberg off Nova Scotia. Few blamed the doctor personally, but the *Miranda* disaster nevertheless clung to Cook like a bad smell, marring his reputation and compromising his ability to raise funds for his Antarctic expedition.

He redoubled his efforts to publicize his polar plan and adjusted his sales pitch to overcome the swell of misgivings. Out of desperation, he cut his asking price in half: Cook now estimated that the expedition would cost a mere $25,000, rather than the $50,000 he'd cited originally. Reflecting the influence of his impresario, the histrionic J. B. Pond, Cook ramped up the drama of his proposal to Barnumesque levels. He hinted at the possibility of a southern gold rush to rival the Californian bonanza of the late 1840s. "We cannot say Antarctica has not gold and diamonds as well as Africa," the doctor said, as paraphrased by a *New York Times* reporter. Cook suggested that the expedition might even discover a new civilization. His basis for this was a mysterious entry in the diary of the Norwegian captain Carl Anton Larsen, who on a whaling expedition to the tip of the Antarctic Peninsula in 1893 claimed to have discovered some "balls made of sand and cement resting upon pillars composed of the same constituents. We collected some fifty of them, and they had the appearance of having been made by man's hand." That the samples Larsen claimed to have taken with him had subsequently been destroyed in a fire struck skeptics as all too convenient but allowed Cook to give Larsen the benefit of the doubt.

"This is the first evidence of human existence in the Antarctic," Cook pronounced in his lilting tenor, which rose at the end of sentences. "To my mind human habitation on the antarctic shores is not impossible, nor do I deem it by any means improbable to find there an isolated tribe of men, feeding and dressing from the liberal sea farms."

Though Cook never failed to entertain and intrigue his audiences, financiers were loath to open their checkbooks—or at least to be the first to do so. Months went by, and the only offers Cook received were from cranks and crackpots, such as the Brazilian inventor who claimed to have constructed a bird-shaped vehicle that could glide over the ice at 120 miles per hour.

The more time that passed without anyone investing in Cook's plan, the less viable it seemed. His Antarctic dream was slowly withering, taking a piece of his soul along with it. In early 1897, Cook made a desperate attempt to find a patron who would cover the entire cost of his expedition. As with his other endeavors, in this, too, Cook was outsized: why bother with merely rich men, he thought, when you could go straight to the richest? He decided to pursue Andrew Carnegie, the sixty-one-year-old Pittsburgh steel magnate and already a figure of international renown. Somehow, Cook secured a meeting.

Carnegie received Cook at the Union League Club in Manhattan, a grandiose colonnaded palace on the corner of Fifth Avenue and Thirty-ninth street, the embodiment of Gilded Age excess. As Carnegie sat back and listened to the explorer's pitch, dappled in the multicolored light coming through the intricate stained-glass windows designed by Louis C. Tiffany, the scowl that seemed frozen on his bearded face gradually thawed. Given Carnegie's reputation as a cutthroat businessman, it surprised Cook to see him show genuine enthusiasm for his project. Perhaps the once penniless Scottish immigrant recognized that he and Cook were cut from the same threadbare cloth, both children of Europe who found that America imposed no limit on their ambitions. The two spoke amiably of polar exploration for an hour, after which Carnegie got up, shook Cook's hand, and said, "Doctor, I would like to get interested in your ice business. What color have you to exchange for gold? See me next Monday or write me."

Carnegie was challenging Cook to show how the expedition might be profitable, evidently not convinced by Cook's allusion to a potential Antarctic gold rush. At their second meeting, in the corner of a lavish club room redolent of cigar smoke, pleasantries were put aside. Cook knew that he could not rely on charm and tall tales this time, and so he had prepared a detailed explanation of his proposed scientific program and its concrete benefits. He "talked utility fast and strong," as he later recalled. Cook's pitch appeared to be having an effect. But just as the doctor reached his crescendo, a fellow club member approached Carnegie and "rudely interrupted what seemed like a compact." By the time Cook recovered Carnegie's attention, the moment had passed.

Carnegie rose and walked Cook to the stairs.

"Doctor, there is so much to be done in this world nearer by," he said. "Three miles above is all the ice we will ever need. Find a way to fetch it down." Cook was devastated. He now realized that when Carnegie had expressed interest in his "ice business," he had literally meant the business of ice—the possibility of harvesting Antarctica's glaciers for the mundane purposes of refrigeration and chilling cocktails.

Carnegie's refusal sealed the fate of Cook's American Antarctic Expedition. Finally defeated, Cook resigned himself to a respectable, if unexciting, life as a Brooklyn physician. Barring a windfall that would allow him to see Antarctica with his own eyes, he could one day look back fondly on his polar adventures as the escapades of youth. The mother of his late wife was now running his household and lived there with her two remaining daughters, both schoolteachers; Cook began courting the younger of the pair, Anna Forbes, and soon they were engaged to be married.

Even as he saw patients, he continued to read every book and clip every article he could find about Antarctica. Interest in the frozen continent had swelled ever since the Sixth International Geographical Congress of 1895 called for its urgent exploration. It pained Cook to learn about so many aspirants suddenly bidding for what he still, deep down, considered his prize. He took spiteful comfort in seeing all of them fall short.

All of them, that is, but one. While perusing the New York *Sun* on August 6, 1897, Cook's eye snagged on a small item about the imminent departure of an Antarctic expedition from—of all places—Belgium.

The news filled the doctor with an intoxicating mix of envy and excitement. Lieutenant Adrien de Gerlache, whoever he was, had succeeded where Cook had failed. Yet the very fact that a major scientific mission was leaving for Antarctica gave Cook a vicarious thrill.

The article made no mention of the difficulty de Gerlache had encountered in finding a surgeon, nor, indeed, that he was seeking additional men. In Cook's mind, ever alive to opportunity, this made no difference: the announcement might as well have been an invitation. He had expected to lead an expedition by this point in his life, not merely participate in one, especially not under an unknown and inexperienced commander, and *especially* not one that would redound to the glory of a country other than the United States. And yet such chances to bolster his bona fides as a polar explorer were too rare to pass up and might vanish entirely once he settled into married life.

On August 6, Cook cabled de Gerlache, expressing his desire to join the expedition. He offered to pay his way and bring his remaining Greenland dogs.

De Gerlache's response came a few days later: to his regret, he had to decline Cook's generous offer since all the berths on the *Belgica* had been spoken for.

Cook could still feel the sting of de Gerlache's rejection on the evening of August 19, when he heard a knock on his front door. The out-of-breath Western Union boy handed the doctor a telegram from Ostend:

POUVEZ REJOINDRE MONTEVIDEO, MAIS
N'HIVERNEREZ PAS—CDT DE GERLACHE

This looked like good news—why else would de Gerlache write him again?—but not speaking a word of French, let alone telegrammatic French, Cook couldn't be sure. Around midnight, cable in hand, he crossed the Brooklyn Bridge and headed to the still-bustling Manhattan offices of the *Sun* to consult with his friend Cyrus Adams, the paper's geographic editor. Cook showed Adams the telegram, and through his walrus mustache, the editor translated the message: "Can join in Montevideo, but will not winter."

Elated, Cook replied by cable at two a.m.: "YES AM READY TO COMMAND."* Just before the *Belgica*'s final departure, Cook received updated instructions to meet the ship in Rio de Janeiro.

As he prepared for his journey, Cook spoke with a reporter for the New York *World* about the expedition. "For years," the doctor told him, "I have been in correspondence with Lieut. Adrien de Gerlache." This was an outright lie—the first contact between the two men had taken place just a month earlier. Cook wanted to make his appointment to the *Belgica* seem less like the act of desperation that it was, both for him and for de Gerlache. And after so many years of trying to sell himself, bending the truth had become second nature.

Cook announced that he would take the Rio-bound steamship *Hevelius* on Saturday, September 4. By eight o'clock that morning, a large crowd had formed at Manhattan's Fulton Street Pier to bid the doctor farewell. Among the group were Cook's mother and sister, as well as curious New Yorkers there to catch a glimpse of the man who would become the first American to cross both polar circles. Men and women craned their necks to spot him, but by the time the ship was scheduled to leave, Cook had still not arrived. Reporters begged the steamship's captain to delay departure. As Cook was the vessel's most illustrious passenger, the captain obliged. But after a few minutes, he decided he could wait no longer. The ship pulled away.

While the *Hevelius* was still in sight, cruising past the Statue of Liberty, news arrived that Cook had examined the shipping timetables and realized that he could leave later in the month and still meet the *Belgica* in time. But in truth Cook had gotten cold feet. His fiancée, Anna, had fallen ill, and while New York University doctors could find nothing wrong with her, Cook suspected tuberculosis. He had already buried a wife and could not bear to leave Anna alone. He stayed by her bedside, and after a few weeks her condition appeared to improve. Seeing how despondent Cook was at the thought of the *Belgica*'s sailing to Antarctica without him, Anna assured him she felt better and urged him to go.

---

* Even for a telegram, this clipped phrasing is odd, since Cook knew de Gerlache was the expedition's commander. Perhaps he meant "Yes, I am ready and at your command," but this cable remains something of a mystery.

At the Fulton Street Pier, on the cool and drizzly afternoon of September 20, Cook walked up the gangway and disappeared into the bowels of the steamship *Coleridge*, followed by a seemingly endless procession of luggage that included two sledges, a pair of skis, a medicine chest, and fifteen trunks containing snowshoes, books, Greenland furs, materials for tent making, assorted Arctic equipment, and a ten-by-fifteen-foot silk American flag. But no dogs.

The *Coleridge* pushed off from the pier and began to lumber her way out of New York harbor. As he watched Manhattan shrink, Cook found the concerns of city life receding from his mind as well. The circumstances of his departure for the icy continent were not as he'd imagined. But although he knew almost nothing about de Gerlache, his plans, or his men, he had no regrets. "The antarctic has always been the dream of my life," he later wrote, "and to be on the way to it was then my ideal of happiness."

CHAPTER 3

Tribute to Neptune

THE *BELGICA* LEFT OSTEND AT SUNSET ON AUGUST 23, 1897. "THIS TIME we're off," the commandant wrote to Léonie Osterrieth. "I preferred to depart 'without drums or trumpets.'" He was finally on his way, with thirteen Belgians, ten foreigners, and two cats named Nansen and Sverdrup.

Well before the *Belgica* confronted the unknown dangers of Antarctica, she endured the all-too-notorious storms of the Bay of Biscay, off the coast of France. Strong winds propelled her southward. As the ship seesawed up and down precipitous waves, the view through the rectangular window of de Gerlache's cabin swung between the storm clouds and the frothing ocean. To calm the thrashing sea, he called for bags of oil to be thrown overboard and dragged through the water, a common practice in the late nineteenth century. A couple of quarts were enough to spread a layer of oil over a vast area; just one molecule thick, the slick film prevented the wind from gaining traction. Instead of whipping up whitecaps, the gales would in theory glide smoothly over the surface of the water. But while the oil worked to soothe the waters immediately around the ship, it did nothing to slow the giant waves rolling in from far away.

Seasickness took hold, sparing almost nobody. One of the young Norwegian sailors, Carl August Wiencke, painted a graphic scene in his diary: "The captain [Lecointe] stands on the bridge, steering and vomiting. The scientists lie on the hatch and vomit. The engineers sit in the engine room and vomit and the deckhands vomit down from the top deck."

Wiencke was among the few who were immune from the ship-wide nausea. While his comrades were folded over the gunwales, he zealously obeyed every order, bounding across the rocking deck and swinging from the rigging with little regard for his safety. With his beardless cheeks and rounded features, Wiencke still looked like a boy, especially in his striped sailor's outfit and *Belgica* cap. He had enlisted on the *Belgica* for a shot at adventure and turned twenty the day before the expedition's departure. Wiencke was smart and curious, a hard worker beloved by all. While he never showed anything but total devotion to the expedition, his diary entries reveal deep misgivings about its leaders.

"Captain Lecoint [*sic*] showed an exceedingly bad side of himself today," he wrote on August 31, while the *Belgica* was still being tossed about like a bath toy in the Bay of Biscay.

> "Sverdrup," did its business on the deck. As the captain was suffering from seasicknesses, he found it hard to steady himself and headed straight towards it. He became so angry that he grabbed the cat by the neck and threw it overboard. The wretched animal swam and screeched for as long as it was in sight. Such behavior doesn't serve to endear him with the other men.

Wiencke made similarly unvarnished observations about de Gerlache. He scoffed at the commandant's insistence that the men of the *Belgica* were all equals and that officers and scientists were not to receive special treatment. "Gerlache's comments about equality are entirely satirical," he wrote. "One cannot speak to an officer unless spoken to and on the whole there is the greatest distance between the superiors and the crew."

The combination of inexperience and defiance among some of the crew members caused trouble from the outset. In early September, it nearly led to catastrophe. Heading straight into southwesterly winds, the *Belgica* could advance only by steam power. The air in the middle deck was stifling in the best conditions, but at the beginning of the journey, when gas-emitting coal was stacked to the ceiling, the tanks brimmed with water, and the insatiable furnace roared, the atmosphere was unbearably thick. Steam hissed out of joints and valves and condensed along the walls. Water dripped from the low ceilings, and sweat formed rivulets on the men's blackened faces. After heaving coal for almost two hours, Jan Van Mirlo dropped his shovel, fell to the ground, and wept.

His fellow sailors helped him to his feet and took him upstairs to get some fresh air. Nobody noticed when he grabbed a revolver off the wall. Once on deck, he jumped onto the railing and brandished the gun.

Amundsen didn't know whether Van Mirlo meant to use the gun on himself or on his shipmates—or to jump overboard. Not waiting to find out, he barreled toward the Belgian, threw him down, and yanked the revolver out of his hand. The two grappled on the deck: Amundsen was the largest and strongest man on the ship, but Van Mirlo had worked himself into such a frenzy that it took five more sailors to subdue him.

After he'd calmed down, Van Mirlo was examined by the Romanian zoologist, Emile Racovitza, who until Cook's arrival would be the closest thing to a doctor on board. Van Mirlo's bout of insanity, Racovitza determined, was due to mental strain brought on by overwork.

Remarkably, Van Mirlo was put back to work a few days later, as if nothing had happened. But the disturbing episode only deepened de Gerlache's doubts about his men. In his hurry to get the mission afloat, he had been forced to make compromises and take on a number of inexperienced or otherwise underqualified sailors. He hoped the southern journey would be sufficient preparation for the mental and physical challenges of the Antarctic, but order was already starting to break down.

Although de Gerlache was concerned about the reliability and emotional stability of his men, there was little he felt he could do about it. Aloof and sensitive, with an intellectual disposition, he was not the type of exhortative leader who could inspire his men to prove their devotion to the mission. Nor was he a natural disciplinarian or a hothead like Lecointe—one couldn't imagine *him* throwing a cat overboard for defiling the deck. And de Gerlache had few means of imposing discipline even if he'd been so inclined. Since the *Belgica* had no official naval commission—she technically flew under the burgee of the yacht club of Antwerp—he could not threaten a court-martial or keep offenders in shackles. Unlike the officers, most of the crew members hadn't signed a binding contract. The commandant's only recourse was to kick insubordinate sailors off his ship, and stops on the way to Antarctica were few and very far between. And yet de Gerlache blanched even at that option, fixated as he was on how the press back home might react were he to fire a Belgian sailor.

And so problems festered. It was not easy to keep control of a fractious, multilingual, multicultural crew. Ethnic rifts ran throughout the ship, dividing officers and crew: Norwegians versus Belgians, Dutch-speaking Belgians from Flanders versus French-speaking Belgians from Wallonia. Meanwhile, no one could get along with the belligerent French cook, Lemonnier. The task of maintaining order frequently fell to Lecointe and Amundsen, who, despite being younger than de Gerlache, were better able to keep the crew in line. Their leadership styles were as different as their builds. Lecointe was short, feisty, and quick to anger; Amundsen was physically imposing and more laconic. But they complemented each other effectively, with Lecointe keeping a close eye on the rowdy Warzée–Dom–Van Damme clique, and Amundsen acting as the liaison with the more cooperative Norwegians.

After a three-day layover at the Portuguese island of Madeira, the *Belgica* weighed anchor on September 13, and now the trade winds pushed her steadily along. To save on coal, the furnace was allowed to cool and the sails were unfurled in all their majesty. As the ship approached the tropics, the heat became hard to bear. Sailcloth was wrapped around all the brassware on the bridge to prevent the men from scalding themselves. The extra layers of insulation designed to keep out the Antarctic cold also prevented hot air from escaping; temperatures belowdecks reached 130 degrees.* It became impossible to sleep in the cabins, so hammocks were strung on the deck amidships.

To slice through tropical waters, propelled by wind alone, was a blissful sensation. "There is a pleasant, mild breeze and the music of waves against the ship's side," Wiencke wrote in his diary one night,

---

* All temperatures are in Fahrenheit unless otherwise noted.

presumably while swaying gently in his hammock. "Now and again there is the slap of a sail that makes us look up and notice the sail and the rigging against the moonlight, and you cannot hope to see a more beautiful sight than that."

Competing with the spectacle of a moonlit night in the trade winds was the glow given off by the sea itself, as the ship and the dolphins that escorted it cut trails of bluish-white light through swarms of bioluminescent life. Explosions of light marked the collision of dolphins with large jellyfish. Once in a while, flying fish would soar over the gunwales and flop onto the deck, to the delight of Nansen, the ship's remaining cat.

Some evenings after supper, the crew gathered on the foredeck to make merry. The sixteen-year-old Norwegian deckhand Johan Koren, a gifted draftsman, captured one such scene in his sketchbook: Using a hatch cover as a dance floor, two sailors jigged to music from a small crank organ, accompanied by an accordion and a cornet. The rest of the crew spread out around them, smoking pipes and singing. Bawdy Belgian shanties alternated with melancholy Norwegian tunes.

Wafting back to the stern, where the officers and scientists congregated, these wistful melodies made Amundsen think of home. One can picture him looking out over the bulwark toward the horizon as the music played on, his thin but ludicrously wide mustache, shaped like a seagull in flight, flapping slightly in the breeze. Amundsen had fantasized about polar exploration for so long that this journey felt to him like destiny.

Roald Amundsen had, like Cook, been compelled to follow in the footsteps of a father he'd hardly known. A shipowner and captain, and something of a war profiteer, Jens Amundsen was away for most of Roald's life and died at sea when the boy was fourteen. The younger Amundsen got to know his father largely through the many stories told about him—some exaggerated, some certainly true. According to one, he survived a brutal ax attack and ultimately defeated a mutiny while transporting three hundred Chinese laborers to Havana. A ruthless disciplinarian, he'd forced the Chinese mutineers to hang their own leader. Jens took on a mythical aura in his son's mind, one Roald strove to live up to. He would forever be chasing a legend.

Like de Gerlache, Amundsen had grown up enthralled by polar narratives. A year after his father's death, Amundsen discovered another guiding figure in the early-nineteenth-century British explorer Sir John Franklin. A bald and doughy naval officer whose voyages in the Canadian Arctic were marked by tragedy and bad judgment, Franklin was an unlikely role model. He came to be known as "the Man Who Ate His Boots" after much of his party died of disease, murder, and starvation while surveying the Coppermine River by foot from 1819 to 1822. In the mid-1840s, Franklin commanded the HMS *Terror* and HMS *Erebus* in an attempt to sail through the Northwest Passage, but both vessels were crushed by the ice, and approximately 130 of their men perished. Rumors of cannibalism hovered over both of Franklin's above-mentioned expeditions. But this hardship was the very thing that captured Amundsen's imagination. "Strangely enough the thing in Sir John's narrative that appealed to me most strongly was the sufferings he and his men endured," Amundsen wrote. "A strange ambition burned within me to endure those same sufferings."

But the most influential figure in Amundsen's life was the Norwegian scientist and polar explorer Fridtjof Nansen. Eleven years Amundsen's senior, Nansen had made international headlines after he successfully crossed the Greenland ice cap on skis in 1888. Tall and blond, with a powerful brow and piercing blue eyes, he looked like the Norsemen of legend. He was hailed as a national hero before Norway, under Swedish rule since Napoleon's day, was officially a nation once more. The sixteen-year-old Amundsen was among the thousands who thronged along the Kristiania Fjord* to welcome Nansen home on May 30, 1889—"a red-letter day in many a Scandinavian boy's life," Amundsen recalled. "Certainly it was in mine."

Nansen topped that triumph four years later when he allowed his ship, the *Fram,* to be encased in the ice for three years and spiraled along ocean currents closer to the North Pole than any man had ever

*Now known as the Oslo Fjord.

been. He and a shipmate made a final poleward dash on skis and by dogsled to 86°13'6" north, about 227 miles from the pole, establishing a new farthest-north record. After a grueling journey back south, Nansen and his companion were unable to find the *Fram*, which had, as they'd expected, drifted away in the pack ice. They built a stone hut in which they waited out the winter, surviving on bear and walrus meat, before resuming their southern course in the spring. Improbably, they were rescued by a passing British expedition.

Inspired by Franklin and Nansen, Amundsen resolved from a young age to become a polar explorer, an unwavering ambition that bordered on obsession. He had less interest than de Gerlache and Cook in the scientific aspects of exploration; he cared mainly for the glory it could bring. Amundsen subjected himself to an intense physical and mental training program at the expense of everything else in his life, including schoolwork and romantic entanglements. He slept with his bedroom window open throughout the winter to inure his body to the cold and went on frequent excursions in the mountains outside Kristiania.

To improve his cross-country skiing and test the limits of his endurance, Amundsen attempted in January 1896 to cross the fearsome Hardangervidda, a hundred-mile plateau west of Kristiania, with his brother Leon. In the dark winter months, the vast, snow-swept Hardangervidda was a dead ringer for the treacherous polar wastelands Amundsen yearned to explore. Eleven days into the journey, the brothers lost their way in a whiteout blizzard. As temperatures dipped below −10 degrees, they stopped for the night in the lee of a small outcropping. Since they'd counted on finding shelter in an unoccupied shepherd's hut, they hadn't brought a tent. Amundsen had to improvise. He dug a narrow, oblong cavity in the snow, slid into it headfirst, and pulled his sleeping bag up to his chin.

As Amundsen slept, snow continued to fall and eventually blocked the opening of his cave. Temperatures dropped further and the snow, moistened by the heat of Amundsen's body, turned to hard ice. His shelter had become a sarcophagus. "In the middle of the night I woke up," he remembered. "My muscles felt cramped and I made the instinctive move to change my position. I could not move an inch. I was practically frozen inside a solid block of ice! I struggled desperately

to free myself, but without the slightest effect. I shouted to my companion. Of course he could not hear."

Amundsen's panicked cries died in the snow. The air grew scarce,
and he stopped screaming to conserve what was left of it. He panted
in his icy coffin, scratching uselessly at the ice, until Leon—who in
the night had had the presence of mind to wake up and shake the
snow off himself—saw the bristles of Amundsen's reindeer-skin
sleeping bag poking through the snow and dug him out. Amundsen
had literally been a hair's breadth from death. His experience on the
Handangervidda was a humbling lesson on the importance of proper
preparation. It was also the first time he made the local paper.

The next step in Amundsen's self-imposed curriculum was to gain
experience at sea so he could one day lead his own expedition. He
joined the crews of the sealers *Magdalena* and *Jason* during summer
campaigns in the Arctic. It was upon the *Jason*'s return to the Norwegian port of Sandefjord in July 1896 that Amundsen first caught sight
of the *Belgica,* which was still being outfitted for her Antarctic journey. When he heard that de Gerlache was looking for men to staff his
expedition, Amundsen applied, seeing a chance to further his polar
education.

Since Amundsen had never held a position of authority, de Gerlache's decision to hire him as the ship's first mate was a gamble. But
to Amundsen, the appointment was a natural stage in his inexorable
march to polar glory. Ever methodical, Amundsen signed on to another merchant ship to hone his navigational skills in the year between his hiring and the launch of the expedition. He then studied
French in Cognac and Flemish in Antwerp so he could give orders to
the *Belgica*'s multilingual crew.

He was back in Sandefjord on June 18, 1897, when he joined the
Belgica. The timing was fortuitous: the next day, Fridtjof Nansen visited the ship ahead of her departure for Antwerp. A wave of excitement washed across the deck as Nansen strode up the gangway, his
white sailor's cap cocked at a jaunty angle. At well over six feet, he
had the stature of a demigod, looming over Amundsen and even
more steeply over the rest of the starstruck crew. After posing for
photographs, Nansen left de Gerlache with a picture of himself, in-

scribed "To Adrien de Gerlache with best wishes for prosperity, from Fridtjof Nansen."

To Amundsen, Nansen's blessing of the expedition felt like an induction into the small club of polar explorers. Amundsen already imagined himself as Nansen's successor. He almost certainly had a hand in naming the *Belgica*'s cat after his hero, never mind that she was female.

Amundsen's route to Antarctica had been methodical, charted out to the finest detail. The one thing he hadn't prepared for was the heat of the tropics, which became unbearable as the *Belgica* entered the doldrums around the equator. Amundsen was one of thirteen men aboard who had never crossed into the Southern Hemisphere. An elaborate ceremony was planned to initiate the equatorial virgins on the day they sailed over the line, October 6.

The equator-crossing ceremony is a longtime custom in navies and merchant marines around the world. It varies in its particulars, but the basic script remains the same, involving an interrogation by Neptune, the Roman god of the sea, and some form of ritual humiliation. That Amundsen ranked above the men performing the hazing did not exempt him. Tradition was tradition. De Gerlache, who had endured similar treatment years earlier on an American ship taking the long way to San Francisco, looked on with amusement.

Amundsen was the first to be baptized. At ten in the morning, dressed in tatters, he was led to a seat amidships by two of Neptune's "henchmen" and watched his tormentors stream onto the deck. In his diary that night, he described the procession: "Neptune"—played by the truculent Belgian sailor Maurice Warzée—"arrives with his retinue: his wife, a priest, a barber and finally people from various nations."

Neptune's costume consisted of a long beard, a wide-brimmed wizard's hat, and a trident made of a serving fork tied to the end of a long staff. Surrounding him was a motley assemblage of racial stereotypes—one man in blackface and a turban, another dressed as a Chinese sailor with a painted-on beard and a long piece of rope for a braid—clutching guns and looking like storybook pirates.

Lemonnier, the nasty French cook, played the barber, in his cook's whites. Relishing the role, he towered menacingly over the seated Amundsen, wielding what looked like an enormous straight razor made of wood. Neptune stood next to him, holding a shaving brush lathered in a foul black paste made of flour, water, lard, and soot.

"What is your name?" shouted Neptune, waving the brush in Amundsen's face.

Unacquainted with the ritual, Amundsen foolishly attempted to respond. As soon as he opened his mouth, Neptune shoved a brushful of the vile mixture into it. Gagged by gunk, Amundsen couldn't protest when Neptune began to sloppily lather the first mate's face. "If you are unfortunate enough to have a beard," Amundsen wrote in his diary, not without amusement, "then you may be certain that it will take you at least a week to get it clean."

With his prizeworthy mustache caked in filth, Amundsen subjected himself to Lemonnier's "razor," then received the sacred anointment: three buckets of seawater to the face. His torture complete, he washed up, lit a cigar, and sat back to "enjoy the suffering of others." The new graduates were handed mock diplomas that featured caricatures of the neophytes. Amundsen cherished this certificate as much as any official recognition he received in his life.

The ceremony and ensuing festivities achieved the true purpose of such initiation rituals: to bond men together in brotherhood. Differences of hierarchy and nationality fell away. The *Belgica* was a family, at least for the evening. Music and dancing lasted through the night. "At ten o'clock," Amundsen wrote, "we crossed the equator to the sound of popping champagne corks."

It was raining torrentially on the afternoon of October 22 when the *Belgica* sailed past Sugarloaf Mountain, off her port bow. The downpour veiled most of Guanabara Bay and the sprawling city of Rio de Janeiro. It also marred the grand entrance de Gerlache had hoped to make as the first Belgian ship to arrive there in years. But evidently the *Belgica* had been spotted: a small steamboat approached. The members of the expedition presumed the boat would be carrying the physician with whom de Gerlache had set a rendezvous in Rio, a man nobody on board had ever seen but whose reputation preceded him.

The officers and crew of the *Belgica* rushed to the railing to greet the famous Dr. Cook. They picked out passengers who looked the most like their idea of an American doctor.

"He's the short, fat, eager-looking one!"

"No way, he's the tall, skinny one!"

"Couldn't it be that man with the wild grey beard?"

He was none of them. The steamboat carried a Belgian delegation and a packet of letters from home, but no Cook. As the men would soon learn, the doctor had arrived two weeks earlier and was living in luxury forty miles away in the tony mountain town of Petrópolis, a guest of a Belgian minister, Count van den Steen de Jehay.

Only the next morning, as the sun shone on the bay, the horseshoe of pristine white sand, and the lush green mountains beyond, did the men understand why Rio de Janeiro was known as one of the most beautiful ports in the world. The serenity of the panorama gave way to chaos once the officers stepped ashore and got lost in Rio's tortuous, overflowing streets. The city had a mad, improvisational quality. Wealthy elites of Portuguese origin, dressed in the latest European fashions, rubbed shoulders with poor native Amazonians and descendants of African slaves. It was a time of political turmoil, of uprisings and assassinations. Crime was rampant and the police corrupt. Strolling by the docks at night, one of the *Belgica*'s sailors was held up by policemen, bludgeoned with the flat of a sword, and robbed clean.

An epidemic of yellow fever had taken hold of Rio, one of the reasons Cook had decided to stay in the mountains with Van Steen de Jehay. Early one morning shortly after the *Belgica*'s arrival, Cook and the count took a train from Petrópolis, winding slowly down the verdant mountainside, across valleys, and along Rio's steep cogwheel railway until they arrived at Guanabara Bay. They embarked on a steam-powered tugboat and made their way across the water to the *Belgica*. Approaching what would be his home for the foreseeable future, Cook was disheartened by how ungainly the ship seemed next to the elegant schooners, sleek yachts, and majestic frigates that populated the bay. He compared her to "a little bull-dog amid a group of large greyhounds—small, awkward, and ungraceful."

As he climbed the sea ladder to the *Belgica* that sweltering morning, Cook could see vapor rising from the ship's rain-soaked deck.

First in line to greet him on the gangway was the *Belgica*'s squirrelly captain, Georges Lecointe, who uttered momentous words of welcome. As they were in French, they were entirely lost on Cook, who, despite his unbounded curiosity in so many fields, spoke no language but English, a smattering of the Greenland Inuit tongue, and fragmentary German half-remembered from his childhood. Cook next shook hands with Commandant de Gerlache, whose time on American ocean liners made him one of the few men aboard who could speak passable English. At his side were Danco and Amundsen. The welcoming committee was rounded out by the scientists Racovitza and Arctowski, with whom Cook soon found that he could converse in a semblance of German.

To the doctor's new shipmates, Cook must have appeared less like a sober physician than a character from an operetta. They would have been struck by his peninsula of a nose. His fine clothes, too warm for the weather, together with his thick beard and the gold teeth in his big American smile, brought to mind an Alaskan prospector who had struck it rich. "Cook looks like a real Yankee," wrote Wiencke, "and goes around in a fur coat."

Considering that all lives aboard would soon be in Cook's hands, the language barrier didn't bode well. But there was something magnetic about him, something—in the men's minds, at least—quintessentially American, an irrepressible sunniness that transcended language. Cook's role in Robert Peary's Greenland expedition of 1891–92 had made him famous among polar enthusiasts worldwide. The Norwegians, Amundsen in particular, would have read about him in their compatriot Eivind Astrup's popular memoir of that journey. Amundsen admired Astrup, so he admired Cook by association. He had been looking forward to their meeting ever since the *Belgica*'s departure from Antwerp. A diligent student of polar travel, Amundsen set about to learn everything he could from the doctor.

Even amid the tumult of turn-of-the-century Brazilian politics, the *Belgica*'s presence in Guanabara Bay was national news. Fêted throughout the town, journalists tailing them wherever they went, the expeditioners spent evenings in revelry and daylight hours nursing hangovers. (Cook lingered in bed especially late. Ever since his insomniac adolescence in New York, studying by day and running a business by night, he never missed an occasion to sleep in.) These soirées were bacchanalian affairs, with toast upon toast to the Antarctic explorers, in multiple tongues.

The most stirring tribute, the one that would resonate in the hearts of the *Belgica*'s men as they sailed toward the ice, took place during a solemn reception at the Brazilian Historic and Geographic Institute. The organization's official orator, Dr. Alfredo Nascimento, offered a long, grandiloquent toast to the explorers' courage. At the climax of his speech, he couched their quest in literary terms:

> Voyagers! In his fantastic dreams, the imaginative Jules Verne placed the famous Hatteras on the North Pole; and in the submarine *Nautilus,* he brought Captain Nemo to the 90th latitude south, to plant his black and gold flag on the Antarctic pole. Well! Gentlemen, the progress of science has already realized the fantastic *Nautilus,* and today submarines are no longer chimerical visions of the imagination. Now complete the realization of the prophecy: go rip out from the South Pole this black flag from a nation that doesn't exist and put in its place the banner of [your] people. . . . Erase from this spot the name of Captain Nemo—which means nobody—and engrave in its place that of Adrien de Gerlache!

The Belgian Antarctic Expedition was sold as a scientific mission, but at its core it was a romantic endeavor. De Gerlache conceived the journey because the blank space at the bottom of the map drew him in like a vacuum. Up until then, that void, which the *Belgica*'s scientists hoped to fill with cold, hard facts, had been filled with fiction. The men's conceptions of the unknown Antarctic were necessarily formed by literature, just as Jules Verne's fantasies had been inspired by science.

Throughout the nineteenth century, the barren poles became fertile ground for the imaginations of popular novelists, especially Verne. As boys, de Gerlache and his men would have thrilled to Verne's books. In 1870, Verne published *Twenty Thousand Leagues Under the Sea,* which pictured the South Pole as a rock protruding from an endless sea of ice beneath which the *Nautilus* could navigate freely. By 1897, when the *Belgica* set sail, knowledge of the Antarctic had barely advanced; no one could categorically debunk Verne's fanciful descriptions. The southernmost continent, if indeed it *was* a continent and not an ocean of ice, remained as mysterious as the other distant frontiers of Verne's oeuvre: the center of the earth, the abysmal depths of the ocean, the surface of the moon.

Like de Gerlache—perhaps in part *because* of de Gerlache—Verne sensed Antarctica in the zeitgeist. Starting in January of 1897, the aging French author revisited the South Pole in a serialized novel titled *Le sphinx des glaces*. Published in English as *The Sphinx of the Ice Fields* (and more recently as *An Antarctic Mystery*), the story describes a mountain of ice shaped like the winged riddler of Thebes, so magnetically charged that it draws ships hurtling toward it at impossible speeds and dashes them to splinters against its side. De Gerlache, who treasured the book, referred to the deep Antarctic as a "sphinx."

Verne wrote *An Antarctic Mystery* as a sequel and homage to Edgar Allan Poe's only completed novel, *The Narrative of Arthur Gordon Pym of Nantucket,* published in 1838. Among the most macabre entries in the canon of nautical fiction, this work is haunting even by Poe's standards, largely due to its mystical final image. After surviving a succession of grisly episodes across the South Seas, the novel's protagonist and his companion drift in a small open boat through the uncharted waters at the bottom of the globe, albatrosses circling above them. As they approach the South Pole, the sea turns milky, and a white ash rains down on their boat. They begin to drift "with a hideous velocity," pulled along by an unseen force. Before them, through the dissipating mist, emerges a form of breathtaking magnitude: "I can liken it to nothing but a limitless cataract," reports Pym, "rolling silently into the sea from some immense and far-distant rampart in the heaven. . . . It emitted no sound." In the novel's final paragraph, Pym arrives at the foot of this vertical ocean—the end of the earth:

And now we rushed into the embraces of the cataract, where a chasm threw itself open to receive us. But there arose in our pathway a shrouded human figure, very far larger in its proportions than any dweller among men. And the hue of the skin of the figure was of the perfect whiteness of the snow.

The book ends there, with the demise of its narrator.

A luxuriously bound edition of Poe's collected stories, translated by the renowned French poet Charles Baudelaire, lay hidden away in the *Belgica*, waiting to be unwrapped. De Gerlache's sister, Louise, had selected books for her brother to give to each of the scientists and officers on the *Belgica* at Christmas. She chose Poe's stories for the American Dr. Cook, whose initials were sewn on its specially embroidered cover.* Among the works contained in the volume was "MS. Found in a Bottle," which, like *Pym*, involves a boat drifting ineluctably southward to Antarctica. In this case, the world ends not with an infinitely high waterfall but with a bottomless maelstrom.

The concept of the North and South poles as sources of an irresistible, malevolent force that draws men in and drives them to madness was a theme that had run throughout nineteenth-century literature ever since Samuel Taylor Coleridge's *The Rime of the Ancient Mariner* (1798), about a ship that becomes cursed after a sailor takes a potshot at an albatross and finds itself helplessly ensnared in the Antarctic ice. By the time the *Belgica* departed, the literary link between polar obsession and insanity had been firmly established. The forbidding, unexplored poles served as perfect settings for whatever lay beyond human comprehension.

However metaphorical, these stories inevitably seeped into the minds of the *Belgica*'s men. Their own diaries and accounts of the expedition, even those of the scientists, are littered with novelistic flourishes that owe a debt to—and even directly reference—the likes of Poe and Verne. The journals would grow only more gothic in tone as the events they described began to fit the archetype of the polar horror story.

* Of course, he wouldn't have understood a word of the French translation.

CHAPTER 4

Showdown

A DELEGATION OF BRAZILIAN DIGNITARIES WAS MILLING ABOUT ON the *Belgica* in the early afternoon, amiably shaking hands, patting the gunwales, and gripping the lines, when Josef Duvivier began to make a scene. Though the bay was placid, the Belgian machinist stumbled across the deck as if on a storm-tossed sea. Reeking of alcohol, he repeatedly insulted a Brazilian vice admiral, undoing much of the goodwill the *Belgica* crew had built during their stay.

Amundsen reported the incident to Lecointe, who called Duvivier into the officers' quarters. The unhumbled mechanic shouted back at his captain, stormed out past the Brazilian visitors, and lurched toward the forecastle. He screamed at Amundsen, calling him, in so many words, a fucking Norwegian. In his drunken fury, Duvivier reached for the two revolvers that hung from the gun rack (and had for some reason not been locked away after Van Mirlo's episode the previous month). As the crew wrestled with Duvivier, the Brazilians must have wondered how on earth this bunch would survive Antarctica if they could barely make it out of Rio alive. When de Gerlache, who was in Petrópolis at the time, was told of the incident, he agreed to forget what happened.

The discipline problem aboard the ship would soon prove more consequential than de Gerlache had imagined. His confident handling a week later of the notorious pampero winds—chilling southwesterly squalls bringing cold air from across the South American pampas—and the onboard mayhem that followed after the ship dropped anchor at Montevideo on November 11 showed how much more adept he was at bringing ships to heel than in imposing order among his men. The proximity of land meant the proximity of li-

quor, which only exacerbated the men's misbehavior. Alcohol in-
flamed long-smoldering grudges. The initial spark was a newspaper
article about the expedition that claimed the Norwegians, because
of their familiarity with the cold and their even-keeled demeanor,
were better suited to the Antarctic than were the hot-blooded Belgians. The angrier the Belgian sailors got about the article, the more
they proved its point. "The quick, mercurial Belgians were livid over
the relative calm and indifference of the sons of the North," the im-
partial Dobrowolski recalled. "And after the article, the acute deterioration of the relations between the nationalities on the ship was
brewing."

The Belgian ringleader for the night, Frans Dom, was spoiling for
a fight. "These foreigners, God verrrdamelt,* want to be better than we
Belgians, we Belgians," growled the burly Flemish sailor, thumping
his barrel of a chest. Since the Belgians and the Norwegians were
about evenly matched, Dom redirected his liquor-soaked rage at the
Frenchman Lemonnier, who was sleeping, or attempting to, in one
of the bunks along the V-shaped forecastle. Months of heaping abuse
on his shipmates had left the cook with few allies, even if the only offense he had committed that night had been to prepare a disappoint-
ing meal of peas and water. The reckoning had been a long time
coming.

Dom jumped to Lemonnier's bed and threw his fists up.

"Get out of here, God verrrdamelt," he shouted at the cook.

Lemonnier leapt out of his bunk and stood tall, his enormous head
nearly touching the ceiling.

With all his might, Dom lifted the twenty-five-gallon pan that contained the crew's drinking water and emptied it onto Lemonnier,
flooding the forecastle. After waiting a beat to register the shock, the
two gripped each other by the throat and fell to the ground with a
splash. Another Belgian, Jan Van Damme, tumbled into the scrum.
"Having an older grudge against the cook, [Van Damme] smashed
his face with his fist so hard that he spilled his blood," Dobrowolski
recalled. The Polish scientist tried to break up the mêlée but was

---

*This is how Dobrowolski, who didn't speak Dutch, transcribed Dom's "goddamit,"
emphasizing the guttural "r." The correct spelling would be godverdomme.

pushed away. Two other men attempted to pull the combatants apart but ended up pummeling Lemonnier instead.

The bloodied cook staggered out the door and across the deck toward the officers' quarters. Back in the flooded forecastle, the mood had improved since the ousting of the common enemy. The Belgians, realizing they would have to account for their actions in the morning, resolved to tell de Gerlache that either the cook or they would have to go. The Norwegians, who had their own grievances against Lemonnier and no desire to further antagonize the Warzée–Dom–Van Damme clique, agreed to back them up.

"The water was soon mopped up, overturned tables were picked up and bottles that had been stowed in the forepeak, for safety's sake, were steadily opened," Wiencke wrote. The festivities continued until three in the morning, with the Belgians and the Norwegians— and the Polish scientist—singing arm in arm, alternating choruses of their respective national anthems.

The next morning, having seen Lemonnier's face and heard the boisterous carousing at the other end of the ship, Lecointe opened an investigation. He entered the forecastle at dawn and found it immaculate, crew members standing at attention in crisp uniforms. Lecointe called them one by one to his quarters to determine what had happened. The crew had conspired to frame Lemonnier, and all reported the same lies and half-truths in their interviews with the captain: The cook had started the fight, they agreed. What's more, he had grossly insulted de Gerlache and the other officers. Finally, the crew insisted, Lemonnier planned to sabotage the expedition because he blamed de Gerlache for having prevented him from becoming the personal chef for King Leopold II.

Faced with a united front, Lecointe had little choice but to send Lemonnier packing. He passed on the news to de Gerlache, who feared that the crew was only growing more disorderly as they approached the Antarctic. The commandant hired a Swede to replace Lemonnier, but the new hire immediately fell ill and had to be disembarked. Van Damme, who had just beaten the daylights out of the cook, became the cook.

De Gerlache was happy to let Lecointe discipline the crew. He had risen through the ranks because he loved the ocean, because he was unusually good at reading winds and currents, not because he relished power. He often yearned for simpler times, when he was a lowly sailor taking orders rather than giving them.

One day, he strolled through a lively Montevideo marketplace with a Belgian expat, negotiating with vendors for fresh fruit, vegetables, fish, and meat in order to give the crew a break from the insipid canned food. As he breathed in the market smells and the balmy spring air, he thought back to the last time he had been there. It was a similarly warm day ten years earlier, when he was serving as a sailor on the *Craigie Burn*, a British sailing vessel bound for San Francisco. The ship had been fatally battered in the thrashing storms off Tierra del Fuego and had returned to Montevideo to be sold off for parts. One of just a handful of crew members who had not deserted or been fired, de Gerlache had accompanied the captain to the same Montevideo market to buy victuals, wearing nothing but a loose flannel shirt and sailcloth pants. He'd savored the feeling of firm ground beneath his bare feet as he ambled back to the ship with a live, flailing turkey in each hand.

The pleasant memory set off a bout of melancholy. "I've [since] become a captain and an expedition leader. But am I happier for it?" de Gerlache wrote. "It was a tough life in those days, bent in passive obedience; but I was twenty years old, I was carefree, confident about the future. The future I dreamed of then already is the present of today. But what reality has ever equaled the sweet splendor of dreams! I now answer to nobody but myself, and yet I must obey still, obey the obligations and responsibilities of all sorts that weigh down on me. . . . It was simpler then."

Chief among the worries burdening the commandant at that moment was the knowledge that he would soon face the same treacherous waters off Cape Horn, to say nothing of the unforgiving Antarctic, with a crew he could not trust. Getting rid of Lemonnier had improved morale, he acknowledged, yet there were still loose cannons in the forecastle—particularly Duvivier, Van Mirlo, Dom, Warzée, and Van Damme—who threatened every day to dishonor the expedition, or worse.

. . .

The first albatross was spotted off the coast of Argentina on November 17. Two days later, the men saw their first penguin, likely of a small, warm-water variety known as the Magellanic penguin. (The species, with its splotchy bands of black and white across its breast, was named after the Portuguese explorer Ferdinand Magellan, who saw the birds swimming in those same waters in 1520, during his voyage around the globe.) The days grew cooler as the *Belgica* approached the tip of South America. They grew longer, too, the sun dipping below the horizon just long enough to allow a glimpse of the Southern Cross in the indigo sky.

On November 27, the *Belgica* faced her first real test. Freezing hurricane-force winds walloped her from the northeast, then whipped around to the southwest, blocking her progress and pounding her into submission. The sea became a mountain range in motion, and the men struggled to stay on their feet. Enormous waves crashed over the gunwales, flooding the galley and the laboratories before spilling back out through the scuppers, the openings in the bulwark at the level of the deck. Wind screeched through the spars, strong enough to blow a man overboard and loud enough to cover the sound of his screams.

The elements inflicted the kind of punishment de Gerlache had both feared and daydreamed about when bound to his desk begging Belgium's wealthy to back his expedition. The responsibilities of leadership had begun to wear him down, and the rising indiscipline gave him reason to fear that he was not up to the task. Now, at last, was a chance to prove himself.

The oil bags that he dropped into the ocean did little to calm it. Unable to proceed farther down the coast, de Gerlache decided to tack toward the Falkland Islands, a day's sail away to the southeast. At his orders, deckhands rushed to the blocks, pulling frantically at the lines to unfurl the fore-topmast staysail and the topgallant sail. For several hours the seamen sailed hard into the wind, until, just as abruptly as it had formed, the storm abandoned the fight. "The clouds part and the first constellation that reveals itself is the Southern Cross," wrote de Gerlache. "Without being superstitious, might I not see in this a good omen?"

With his deft evasion, de Gerlache had earned the admiration of all on board. The crew had acquitted itself well in the crisis, but most impressive was the performance of the ship: she had snapped to every command, her sails held strong, and she had taken almost no water. She had shown herself to be remarkably seaworthy, vindicating de Gerlache's decision to choose her over more handsome vessels. Cook, who had been so unimpressed by the *Belgica* when he first saw her in Guanabara Bay, had a change of heart. "As she takes us farther and farther away from our homes, we become daily more dependent upon her," he wrote. "She already has a place in our affections as definitely as a pet horse."

For the men of the *Belgica*, the storms off Argentina marked the true beginning of the expedition. Like the Flood of the Old Testament, they washed away enmities. Belgians and Norwegians were getting along, especially since the departure of Lemonnier, and Cook was forming close bonds with his shipmates despite his linguistic shortcomings. "Strange thing!" wrote Captain Lecointe. "The doctor and I understood each other only with signs, and yet we became fast friends. Moreover, a point of contact brought us even closer together: Cook, too, suffered from seasickness!"

The ship rounded Cape Virgenes and sailed on into the Strait of Magellan, which winds through Tierra del Fuego, connecting the Atlantic and the Pacific. On the afternoon of December 1, she arrived at the Chilean port of Punta Arenas. Her arrival would hardly have been noticed in the crowded harbor. Before the completion of the Panama Canal, most ships sailing from one ocean to the other cut through the Strait of Magellan to avoid ending up in the nautical graveyard off Cape Horn. Almost all stopped in Punta Arenas.

The city had a haunted past, beginning life as a penal colony before evolving into a rough-and-tumble settlement that was destroyed twice in thirty years following a pair of grisly revolts. From the ghost town that remained, however, two decades' time had borne a lively little city of six thousand, teeming with gauchos and gold diggers, Fuegians and bounty hunters. There reigned an atmosphere of lawless freedom not unlike that of the boomtowns of the American West. Punta Arenas had become, as the men discovered, one of the most permissive places in the world. Seemingly every other address was a bar or a brothel. They even served alcohol in church, and not just at Communion. Houses were made from empty wine bottles mortared together. "Alcohol is at the base of all the crimes and most of the pleasures of Punta Arenas," Cook observed.

Under the effects of liquor, the onboard peace that had followed the great storm was quickly broken. Captain Lecointe, in his log, relates a crescendo of defiance and drunken recklessness:

Saturday December 4.—[Somers] and [Warzée] are severely inebriated; they cause a scandal on board, insulting and provoking each other. I intervene and they quiet down; then, two minutes later, the quarrel begins with renewed vigor.

Sunday 5.—[Somers] has forgotten himself to the point of striking a novice. At midnight, [Tollefsen] returns to the ship, drunk. [Michotte] and D . . . remained in port.

Monday 6.—The commandant sends orders for [Warzée], who was on land with a dinghy, to transport to the ship two cases of clothing *for the crew*. [Warzée] refuses, answering that he is not a longshoreman.

The bad actors among the crew—led by Van Damme, Dom, and Warzée—were testing the commandant, and he was failing the test. Even some of the more dutiful sailors had fallen under their influence. Instances of insubordination continued throughout the week, growing more frequent and more brazen the longer they went unpunished. Night after night, men left the ship as they pleased, and drank and fought and whored their way through Punta Arenas. De Gerlache's inability to impose discipline from the start had allowed resentments to fester. The power dynamic aboard the *Belgica* was no longer dictated by the chain of command, but by a more primal struggle for dominance.

On the evening of December 9, Jan Van Damme showed up at de Gerlache's door and demanded an advance on his wages so he could go ashore. It was less a request than a shakedown. When the commandant refused, meekly pointing out that Van Damme had not received permission to leave the ship and had already spent more than he was owed for the entire expedition, the sailor threatened to quit.

He stared at de Gerlache with the confidence of a man who knows he has the upper hand. The difference in both men's experiences of the sea could be read on their faces: De Gerlache had the smooth skin of a life spent largely behind desks and in officers' quarters; Van Damme, though only twenty-seven, looked a decade older than the commandant, his rugged, sun-worn features bespeaking years of toil on unsheltered decks. Reluctant to lose one of his few good Belgian mariners (who now also served as cook), de Gerlache backed down, granted him shore leave, and gave him the money he'd asked for.

De Gerlache had hoped to appease Van Damme. Instead, he'd only emboldened him. Van Damme roped five crew members—four Belgians and one impressionable Norwegian, Ludvig Hjalmar Johansen—into joining him on an all-night bender in town. At daybreak, the officers sent a dinghy to retrieve them. Van Damme told the boatswain that he didn't feel like coming back just yet; others, including Dom and Johansen, followed his lead. A lifelong student of maritime history, de Gerlache knew this was how mutinies began: when a charismatic crew member commanded more loyalty than a ship's leaders.

De Gerlache, Lecointe, and Amundsen spent the rest of the day attempting to corral the stragglers, who had dispersed back into the drinking holes of Punta Arenas. Dom came back aboard in his own time and went straight to his bunk to sleep. Van Damme returned soon after and began packing his bags, intent on leaving the ship one way or another. Lecointe burst into the forecastle and asked him if he was sick. Dom said no, he was just wretchedly hungover and wanted to be left alone. Both Van Damme and Dom were openly insolent to the officers, having made a drunken pact the night before to instigate a final confrontation with the *Belgica*'s command.

The showdown came when Van Damme took clothes that belonged to the expedition, including his *Belgica* uniform, and stuffed them in his bag. De Gerlache, who could apparently tolerate a drunk but not a thief, at last put his foot down and demanded he hand over the clothes. Van Damme refused and insulted the commandant to his face, in vulgar terms, in view of the entire crew.

There was no turning back. For de Gerlache to let this open insubordination go unanswered would be to lose control of the ship for good. But he also knew that there were multiple disgruntled sailors and a number of available guns on board. The commandant did not know exactly how many men would side with Van Damme and Dom in the event of a conflict, but he recognized that he had few chips to gamble with. If the situation spiraled into violence, there was no guarantee that he, Lecointe, and Amundsen would not be wounded or killed in the struggle. Having failed to make himself respected before, he could hardly do so now. He had no choice but to call for help.

De Gerlache had Lecointe fly a red flag from the mainmast to alert the Chilean Navy and the Punta Arenas port authority and signal that their assistance was required immediately. Unlike him, they had the power to sequester troublesome sailors. The hours ticked by, the tension on deck growing with each passing minute, yet the Chileans still did not arrive. Soon the sun began to set. Fearing the authorities wouldn't see the flag in the darkness, de Gerlache decided he could no longer afford to wait. He lowered a boat and rowed to a nearby Chilean warship, leaving Lecointe and Amundsen alone to contain the rebellious Belgians.

A dinghy approached at dusk. As the boat neared the side of the *Belgica,* the officers made out an ominous figure. It was Warzée, returning from an unauthorized shore leave freshly soused, unrepentant, and itching for a fight. With Dom and Van Damme stewing in the forecastle and de Gerlache off the ship, Lecointe and Amundsen were now outnumbered by potential mutineers. To keep Warzée from joining them, Lecointe collared him, dragged him to the poop deck, and ordered him not to move. His eyes darting between Warzée and the forecastle, the captain kept his hand in his pocket, nervously fingering the trigger of a revolver. He was determined to "blow the brains out of the first man who flinched." Amundsen stood by on the bridge, ready to back up his captain. The minutes passed in gut-wrenching tension. Lecointe and Amundsen wondered what could be taking de Gerlache so long.

Finally, at midnight, a boat sidled up to the *Belgica* carrying the commandant and a detachment of Chilean troops. Two of them came aboard and stood guard outside the forecastle. Inside, Van Damme and Warzée packed their bags under Lecointe's supervision. Lecointe must have allowed himself to relax with the armed Chileans on board, because before he knew it Van Damme had grabbed a gun and started making his way to de Gerlache's quarters. The captain rushed to keep up with him.

A few moments later, Van Damme was face-to-face with the commandant, who surely had not expected to wind up essentially at gunpoint when he arrived back at the ship with a troop of Chileans. Van Damme spewed more insults and threats. He showed de Gerlache a diary in which he claimed to have documented everything that had taken place on board, and declared his intention to have it published back in Belgium, a notion that scared de Gerlache as much as, if not more than, getting shot to death. Meanwhile, Lecointe stood behind Van Damme, revolver at the ready, watching his every move.

When Van Damme had said his piece, he and Warzée were frogmarched to the port authority boat. As they passed before de Gerlache a final time, the commandant did something baffling: He put £1 sterling in each of their hands. Though he claimed it was a gesture of pardon, he was in effect buying their silence.

Order was restored by one-fifteen in the morning. The next day, Dom was given the choice to leave or stay on board and work. He chose the former, and he, too, was given a £1 coin.* De Gerlache took advantage of the purge to finally cashier the dangerously incompetent mechanic, Duvivier.

Four men were kicked off the boat on December 10, all of them Belgian. There were now more foreigners than Belgians on the *Belgica,* a scandal in itself. The firing of Van Damme once again left the expedition without a cook. De Gerlache entrusted kitchen duties to his personal attendant, the well-meaning but culinarily inept Louis Michotte, a move that would have severe consequences for the men's well-being once they were in Antarctica.

The crew had been depleted, but soon the population of the ship increased again. While anchored off Punta Arenas, the *Belgica* made fast against a coal ship called the *Martha.* Over the course of a few days, the men transferred one hundred tons of coal from the *Mar-*

---

* The money was wasted: when he finally made his way back to Belgium a few months later, Dom gave an interview to a Brussels newspaper in which he claimed that de Gerlache had fired every last Belgian crew member in Punta Arenas. The false accusation, which proved that the commandant's paranoia about the press had not been misplaced, seems to have been motivated purely by spite.

tha's hold to the *Belgica*. Coal dust turned their clothes and skin so black by the end of the day that the whites of their eyes seemed to emit light.

As the men slept, a faint squeaking pierced the silence of night. Shadows flitted on the deck of the *Martha*. They scampered up mooring lines and scurried along the gunwales. One of them bounded over the gap between the ships. Then another. And another . . .

CHAPTER 5

"Defeat Before the Fight"

THE *BELGICA* SAILED INTO THE LABYRINTH OF MOUNTAINOUS ISLANDS at the tip of South America on December 14 with nineteen men and an unknown number of rats aboard. Desertions and dismissals had the benefit of reducing the crew to its most dependable members just as the ship entered the most hazardous waters she had yet navigated.

But there was something else that concerned de Gerlache even more. The slow and perilous journey to Ushuaia—155 miles southeast from Punta Arenas as the albatross flies, but much more circuitous by sea—added to the many delays that had accumulated on the way down from Antwerp. It was becoming increasingly unlikely that the *Belgica* would have time both to explore Graham Land and to reach Victoria Land, on the far side of Antarctica, before winter set in. Failing to reach Victoria Land would mean that the entire expedition plan might have to be rethought.

The demands of science threatened to push the mission even further off schedule. For the naturalist Racovitza and the geologist Arctowski, the largely unstudied islands of southern Tierra del Fuego were sources of irresistible fascination. Every tide pool, every rock face, might contain a career-making discovery. Having sold the voyage as a scientific expedition, de Gerlache felt obliged to indulge their curiosity. One can imagine his frustration when Racovitza insisted on stopping for twenty-four hours so he could examine a bank of kelp or a rare breed of spider; or when Arctowski wandered deep into a moraine, picking up stones and losing himself in thought.

But if the delays vexed de Gerlache, they also offered opportunities for some of the other officers. As the scholars worked, Amundsen pursued his own calling, honing his skills as a would-be professional adventurer in the mold of Fridtjof Nansen and Jens Amundsen. He set daily challenges for himself, such as summiting the nearest snow-capped peak, walking across a vertiginous ridge no wider than a horse's back, or swimming across frigid mountain streams. The more exhausting the climb, the more miserable the elements, the more Amundsen enjoyed himself. He liked to imagine how he might appear to someone watching his exploits from afar, comparing himself to "a slinking panther" or, in one instance, to Ibsen's picaresque hero Peer Gynt. He would return to the *Belgica* cold, wet, tired, sore, muddied, lacerated, and happier than he'd ever been.

Dr. Cook, meanwhile, hoped to devote his time in Tierra del Fuego to the study of its three indigenous tribes, the Alacaluf, Yahgan (who called themselves the Yámana), and Ona (who called themselves the Selk'nam). As it had in Greenland, the native population fascinated him as much as the terrain. Though he had no academic training in anthropology—very few people had; the discipline was still in its infancy—the time he had spent among the Inuit had instilled in him a profound interest in traditional societies and qualified him to serve as the expedition's ethnologist. He had been eager to observe Fuegian rituals up close, despite intimidating reports. Charles Darwin, who had visited these waters in the early 1830s aboard the HMS *Beagle,* had described the natives as "cannibals" in a "miserable state of barbarism." The Ona, meanwhile, were said to be eight-foot-tall warriors who regularly raided European settlements. Since Cook had arrived in Tierra del Fuego, however, the only native people he'd interacted with had been the relatively Westernized refugees at a Christian mission near Punta Arenas who'd fled the genocidal brutality of white ranchers. Cook was told there were very few traditional Fuegian camps left but that he'd be more likely to find them in the wilds outside Ushuaia.

Steaming eastward down the Beagle Channel, the *Belgica* arrived at Ushuaia on the pitch-black night of December 21. The lighthouse indicated on the charts was nowhere in sight. The men sailed in darkness. Only in the morning did they see how dangerously close to the rocky shore they had dropped anchor.

Ushuaia, the capital of Argentine Tierra del Fuego, could hardly be called a village. It consisted of a scant twenty structures and a wooden chapel. De Gerlache rowed to shore. He walked to the regional governor's office to claim a load of free coal that an Argentine official had donated to the expedition as a token of his country's support—the only reason the commandant had sailed this far. Now he was told that the governor was away and the officer had no record of the gift. Yet in the most remote places on earth, favors are easily granted and rarely refused. The official arranged to have the *Belgica* pick up an additional forty tons of coal from a depot at Lapataia Bay, about an hour west. The ship left promptly, leaving behind Cook and Arctowski to study the Yahgan families living at a mission run by an Englishman named John Lawrence.

The *Belgica* spent the next few days coaling in Lapataia Bay, a picturesque inlet that reminded the Norwegians of the fjords back home. On Christmas Eve, Arctowski hiked to the ship from Ushuaia with two indigenous guides, who were invited to dine on board. During supper, a lookout saw smoke. The fire that Arctowski and his guides had built on the beach to alert the *Belgica* to their presence had been poorly extinguished and soon spread from the grass to the shrubs to the trees. De Gerlache sent the men ashore with axes and canvas buckets. He and Amundsen stayed behind and watched the ship's boats head toward the blaze across glassy water, slicing through the reflection of a flaming sky.

Luckily, there was no wind that evening. It nevertheless took the men nearly an hour to put out the fire. When they climbed back aboard, reeking of smoke, they found the ship utterly transformed.

The fire had provided de Gerlache and Amundsen with the perfect excuse to send their shipmates away as they decorated their quarters for Christmas. A tree stood in the middle of the forecastle, flags of every color were strung across the room, and gifts (many donated by Léonie Osterrieth) had been laid on each crew member's bunk: warm winter clothes, puzzles, and fine tobacco. The men were as children before the scene. The officers and scientists received presents as well—scarves, monogrammed books, and silver seals inscribed *Audaces fortuna juvat* (Fortune favors the bold).

Hot grog was served, music was played, patriotic toasts were offered, and a fraternal atmosphere reigned as never before, uniting officers and crew, Belgians and Norwegians. De Gerlache made the last toast of the evening, about the challenges they would soon face together: "My friends, we are not many, we will sometimes have a weighty task to accomplish, but I am convinced that you will do your duty. Let none of you come to me and say, 'I am tired!'—you are not allowed to be tired. When you are 'sick,' it will be different: I will give you rest."

De Gerlache reminded his crew of Belgium's national motto, plastered above the entrance to the ship's laboratories: "L'Union fait la force" (Union makes strength). Cheers drowned out his last words. It was an uncharacteristically stirring speech from the commandant. Since purging the crew of its troublemakers in Punta Arenas, de Gerlache had grown more confident.

They retired to their cabins shortly after midnight. Some kept their portholes open to let the mild sea air caress them to sleep. On the shore, patches had begun to smolder anew, sending thousands of sparks into the starry night.

On December 30, the *Belgica* returned to Ushuaia to pick up Cook. He climbed aboard along with John Lawrence, the missionary he'd been staying with, who asked to be dropped off at Harberton. This was the name of the estancia owned by a wealthy English missionary turned rancher named Thomas Bridges, to whom Lawrence owed a visit. Thirty-five miles east down the Beagle Channel, it was on the way out to the Atlantic. And since, as he'd learned, favors here were rarely refused, de Gerlache granted the request.

The sun set shortly after ten o'clock on the first day of 1898. It would soon become too dark to spot the underwater reefs. According to the rule de Gerlache had enforced since they'd entered the waters of Tierra del Fuego, the men should have dropped anchor at the first sign of night. But it was only a few more miles to Harberton, so they sailed on, relying on a compass and a chart they knew to be incomplete and outdated. The officer of the watch sent Tollefsen to sound the depth of the channel: twenty-eight meters, more than enough clearance. In the fading twilight, the Norwegian sailor squinted and made out a bed of seaweed beneath the ship. He dropped the sounding line again. *Seven meters!* he shouted in alarm.

Seconds later: *Six meters!* The helmsman spun the wheel around and the machinist reversed the engine, but the ship's momentum carried her forward until she crashed to a halt. Men stumbled on the deck and came rushing to the bow to see what had happened: The *Belgica* had run aground.

In an attempt to shake her free, de Gerlache called on the chief machinist, Henri Somers, to power the engine full steam ahead, then full steam astern, back and forth. The maneuver had no effect. Soundings established that the ship was perched atop a dome-shaped rock four meters below the surface. The channel's strong current kept the *Belgica* pinned against the rock. With any luck, de Gerlache thought, the rising tide would soon lift the *Belgica* off it.

Both dinghies and both whaleboats were put to sea to lighten the ship. Cook, Lecointe, Arctowski, and two crew rowed to the mussel-strewn shore to observe the movement of the tide. A cold breeze began to ripple the smooth surface of the channel. By early morning, the sea began to recede again. High tide had come and gone, and the ship had not moved. As the water level dropped, the *Belgica* slowly keeled over to her starboard side. If the water level dropped too low, the ship would tip over and not be able to right herself. Once she was on her side, water would pour in through the deck, and the ship would be lost.

De Gerlache's heart dropped. When he had imagined the kind of accident that might bring the expedition to an end, he had pictured a more glorious tableau: an apocalyptic sea, strewn with icebergs and crashing into towering white cliffs. He ordered the crew to prop spare yards—the transverse poles to which the sails are affixed, perpendicular to the masts—between the railing and the rock on the starboard side, acting as kickstands to brace the vessel.

They devised a plan to try to pull the ship back up. The men placed an anchor in each of the two dinghies and rowed as far as they could off the port side before dropping their loads into the sea. Back on the deck, the anchors' cables were reeled in—one around a large windlass, the other around a steam-powered winch—in an attempt to heave the *Belgica* upright and dislodge her. The men cranked at the windlass with all their might, and the pistons of the steam winch chugged, until the cables were so taut you could pluck a tune on them. Still, the 244-ton vessel didn't budge. The seagulls circling above seemed to cackle at the ship's predicament.

Just before dawn, Lucas Bridges, the twenty-three-year-old son of the Harberton rancher, looked out the window of his seaside house to see a sailing ship leaning on her side half a mile from shore, her masts at an unnatural angle. After watching the men struggle to kedge the ship against the anchors, Bridges pushed his small boat into the channel and rowed out to the *Belgica*. As he approached, a man on deck called out to him in American-accented English. "He was a smartly dressed, personable fellow," recalled Bridges, "not much over thirty and full of life; rather below medium height and slimly built. He introduced himself as Dr. Frederick A. Cook, surgeon and anthropologist."

Bridges offered to help lighten the *Belgica* so that she might float away come evening tide. He rowed back to shore with Cook and returned a few hours later with a flat-bottomed barge, accompanied by about twenty Fuegians who worked on the ranch. Over the next few hours, the natives and the *Belgica*'s crew off-loaded about thirty tons of coal and cargo. The transfer was a dangerous operation: By now the wind had picked up and was whipping the channel into peaks. Water began spilling over the boats and barges.

"Only two or three boat-loads were landed when a sudden storm rolled down the gullies from the high mountains to the northwestward, piling up a sea which made further communication with the ship impossible," wrote Cook, who had rowed ashore with Bridges and the Fuegians. The *Belgica* was on her own. Cook watched helplessly as powerful waves lifted the ship and slammed her back down against the rock.

On board, each blow against the hull sent chills down the men's spines. As the tide rose anew, de Gerlache harnessed every force at his disposal—steam power, manpower, wind power. He emptied the ship's precious freshwater reserves to lighten her further. But these extreme measures still weren't sufficient to free the keel. High tide came and went again; the *Belgica* righted herself only to slump back down, this time listing to port and falling fast. The crew rushed to gather every spare boom and yard and propped them between the rock and the ship. They looked on anxiously as the *Belgica* groaned against the wooden braces, then stabilized.

Minutes later, to the men's horror, every last pole snapped like a twig under the ship's weight. The *Belgica* smashed down against the reef with a shuddering boom. Men and debris and every unfastened thing slid down the steeply inclined deck. Books flew off shelves, and images on the wall swung a quarter turn. Waves dashed against the hull and washed in from both sides. The skies opened up and a heavy rain began to fall. The air was as wet as the sea. Water flooded into the cabins, poured in under doors and through fissures, finding its way down to the *Belgica*'s bowels.

By this point, de Gerlache feared more than the loss of the ship. The dinghies and whaleboats had gone to shore, and the sea was too furious to permit a rescue. Not even the ablest swimmers could survive these thrashing waters, and there were several on board who couldn't swim at all—he among them.

The commandant called Lecointe and Amundsen to his cabin. They scrambled across the slanted, sea-slicked deck, holding on to whatever fixed line or object was within arm's reach. In his quarters, dripping wet and ghostly pale, de Gerlache asked them whether they agreed that the *Belgica* was doomed, whether they should attempt an escape or throw every last case of equipment overboard in desperation. Before they could answer, de Gerlache's preternaturally calm façade fell away. He wept. The Belgian Antarctic Expedition would end before it had begun, he thought. "Defeat before the fight." The silence among the three men in the cabin accentuated the whistling in the rigging outside and the crashing of the hull against the rock, as slow and regular as a funeral toll. The *Belgica* was surely lost.

They clambered back into the storm. Lecointe solemnly ordered Arctowski to retrieve the expedition's largest Belgian flag, the one they had flown so proudly when entering the ports of Rio and Montevideo. If the *Belgica* was going to go down, she would go down with her colors. The scientist handed it to Danco, who hoisted the banner up the mainmast, tears coursing down his face and mixing with the rain.

As he watched the black, yellow, and red flag crawl up the flagpole, de Gerlache pictured the headlines back home. On the list of his many nightmares of disgrace and dishonor, this was near the top. He had succeeded in attracting the world's attention to his Antarctic endeavor; if he failed to clear even the tip of South America, he would forever be remembered as an embarrassment to his country and his family.

With nothing to lose, he decided against all odds to give salvation one last try. He raised the fore topsail, then sent every man on deck to the windlass to haul at the anchor—to lift an entire ship. "We pulled like madmen," Amundsen wrote. Using a telegraph-operated control board that connected the bridge to the engine room, de Gerlache ordered the machinists to build maximal pressure. The engineers fed the furnace, brought the water tank to a frenzied boil, and blocked off the valves to allow the steam no escape. Such an operation could easily destroy the engine, but then the engine wouldn't do much good at the bottom of the Beagle Channel.

When the tide could not rise higher and the steam engine's pressure had reached the breaking point, de Gerlache shouted out a string of commands: "Prepare the sail, raise the anchor—full speed ahead!" The sails swelled taut, the men at the windlass roared with effort, the pistons rotated the propeller's crankshaft at a rate the engine was not designed to sustain, and the barely submerged propeller spun as fast as it ever had. Under these combined forces, the Belgica lifted off for a few moments, then collapsed again. The tide was retreating now. The ship continued to rise briefly before falling violently back down. De Gerlache called for a final push.

The Belgica suddenly sprang back up. Her keel teetered off the rock, and the ship floated free.

The men erupted in triumph. Alone on the bridge, de Gerlache exhaled in quiet relief. Wiencke caught a glimpse of him: "The commandant stood with tears of joy in his eyes and stared out into deeper waters."

The ordeal had lasted twenty-two hours. Cook would later quip that the reef they'd struck had been "the Belgica's first geographical discovery."

. . .

It took several days to get the *Belgica* back in order, adding to the pileup of delays that had already pushed back the expedition's arrival in Antarctica by several weeks. Lucas Bridges, the *estanciero* who had helped off-load the ship, mentioned to Cook that "a party of Ona, real forest warriors with long hair, skin-robes and paint, were encamped less than a mile" away, and offered to introduce the doctor to them. Cook was thrilled at the chance to finally study and photograph the fearsome giants of Tierra del Fuego.

As he had in Greenland, the doctor gained the natives' trust by treating their ailments. In one case, he temporarily restored the sight of an Ona boy who suffered from gonorrhea and whose eye sockets had filled with pus. Bridges had warned the doctor that the Ona were suspicious of cameras, so Cook came prepared with a sockful of hard candy to mollify them. The images Cook captured through his custom-made Zeiss lens that day—a tribal leader posing regally in guanaco robes; a nude, pregnant woman staring defiantly into the camera; a hunter aiming an arrow at the sky—were some of the first ever taken of the Ona. They remain an invaluable record of a long-lost tribe and demonstrate Cook's flair for the dramatic. The doctor could already imagine the stir they would cause back in New York.

Another precious document of the endangered Fuegian people was a thirty-thousand-word Yahgan-English dictionary that Thomas Bridges had assembled over his three decades in the region. As the *Belgica* prepared to leave Harberton, Cook offered to take the only existing manuscript back to New York to have it published. But having watched the *Belgica* nearly sink right outside his front door, the senior Bridges decided to entrust Cook with his life's work only when the expedition returned from Antarctica. *If* it returned from Antarctica.

There was one last stop to make before crossing the Southern Ocean. All of the *Belgica*'s fresh water had been emptied into the Beagle Channel in an effort to lighten the load during the ship's near-fatal grounding. The closest accessible freshwater source on the way to Antarctica was on Isla de los Estados (also known as Staten Island), an Argentine penal colony twenty miles off the curled tip of Tierra del Fuego—the southernmost inhabited place on earth.

Convicts roamed more or less freely on Isla de los Estados. Escape by sea was inconceivable. Most of the jagged, rocky coast was accessible only to fur seals, penguins, and seabirds. During storms, monstrous waves would slam into the cliffs and send spray over their tops. Visiting ships were rare. Before the *Belgica* arrived at the mountainous island on January 7, it had been eighteen months since the last foreign vessel had moored in the harbor of San Juan de Salvamento. Soon after dropping anchor, the *Belgica* received a visit from two men who rowed out to greet her: a Mr. Fernández, the island's prefect, and the local physician, Dr. Ferrand. De Gerlache invited them to the wardroom for refreshments, and to entertain his guests he wound up the little music box in the corner, which played Charles Gounod's "Ave Maria." To de Gerlache's surprise, the delicate theme caused Dr. Ferrand to burst into tears: the last time he'd heard music was when his daughter sang that melody for him before he left Buenos Aires, months earlier.

One evening, as Argentine sailors filled the *Belgica*'s tanks with spring water, the explorers were invited to dinner at the subprefecture with the high society of this remote outpost on the fringes of civilization: Fernández, Ferrand, two lieutenants, a distinguished infantry captain who had been convicted of murdering his commanding officer and condemned to spend the rest of his life on the island, and the captain's beguiling wife, who had chosen to follow him. The three-course dinner consisted of mutton, mutton, and mutton, served on mismatched dishware salvaged, like the furniture, from the region's frequent shipwrecks.

When the *Belgica* left the island, at seven o'clock on the morning of January 14, Fernández and his servant stood on the shore to wave goodbye, the last human beings the explorers would see for a very long time. The ship tacked to the south, gliding over countless wrecks into the deadly waters beyond Cape Horn, where the Atlantic and the Pacific collided and the wind spun unimpeded around the planet.

CHAPTER 6

"A Body on Our Path"

ANTARCTICA WAS IMAGINED BEFORE IT WAS SEEN. THE ANCIENT Greeks, who already believed the earth to be spherical, reasoned that there must exist a great landmass on the far end of the globe to counterbalance the known continents of the Northern Hemisphere. This hypothetical land was given various names over the centuries, among them Terra Australis Incognita. The one that stuck—Antarctica—is an antonym of "Arctic," itself derived from the Greek word ἄρκτος, or "bear," because the northernmost regions of the planet lay squarely beneath the constellations Ursa Major (Greater Bear) and Ursa Minor (Lesser Bear).*

According to Polynesian lore, the great seventh-century navigator Ui-te-Rangiora ventured so far south in a canoe, made in part from human bones, that he saw "bare rocks that grow out of the frozen sea"—icebergs, presumably. If this story is true, it would be almost a thousand years before another man felt the Antarctic's chilling breath. That was the English privateer Francis Drake, who circumnavigated the earth at a time when cartographers populated the bottom of maps with chimerical monsters. Tasked with finding Terra Australis Incognita and claiming it for Queen Elizabeth (and keeping whatever Spanish treasure he could plunder on the way), Drake sailed the *Golden Hind*, one of the three galleons under his command, through Tierra del Fuego in 1578. As he exited into the Pacific, a terrible storm blew his ship into the uncharted waters south of Cape Horn.

---

*These are also known as the Big Dipper and the Little Dipper, which contains Polaris, the North Star.

"The winds were such as if the bowels of the earth had set all at liberty," wrote Francis Fletcher, a priest aboard the *Golden Hind,* "or as if the clouds under heaven had been called together, to lay their force on that one place." The five hundred miles that separate Cape Horn from the South Shetland Islands became known as the Drake Passage. Another sixty-five miles—the Bransfield Strait—lie between those islands and the Antarctic Peninsula, or Graham Land, the continent's oustretched tendril.

The *Belgica* took seven days to complete the stygian crossing between civilization and the planet's icy underworld. At first the ship enjoyed relatively calm seas, experiencing little of the fury described by Fletcher and many navigators since. De Gerlache was able to keep the *Belgica* steady enough for Arctowski to take a series of depth soundings, some of the first ever recorded south of Cape Horn.

The Polish scientist tested the proposition that the South Shetland Islands and the mountains that were known to ridge the Antarctic Peninsula were the continuation of the Andes, which run like a spinal column down South America and curve eastward to terminate at Isla de los Estados. Using a steam-powered sounding machine to drop a plummet and reel it back in, ticking away the fathoms, Arctowski measured a steep decline in the ocean floor, down to an abysmal depth of 4,040 meters.

Though Arctowski believed this disproved his proposition, his instinct was most likely correct: many contemporary geologists believe that the Andes and the Antarctic chain known as the Antarctandes were once linked. Fossils of reptiles and conifers remain in Antarctica as vestiges of a once temperate climate. The deep trough that Arctowski discovered was evidence of what would come to be known as continental drift, which pried open the Drake Passage about 50 million years ago.

As Arctowski worked, some sailors amused themselves by plucking albatrosses out of the sky. Their method was curious: They would bait a fishhook and cast a line in the air. A bird would swoop down to catch the bait before it hit the water, only to be yanked aboard and killed. The albatrosses' long, hollow wing bones, the men found, made beautiful pipes.

The crew had evidently forgotten their Coleridge. The *Belgica's* luck with the weather turned almost immediately. The next day, oil bags were required to settle the angered sea.

On January 19, a glimmer shone on the horizon, projected onto blackened skies. This was "landblink," a reflection of the snow-covered South Shetland Islands that lay beyond the curvature of the earth. Later that day, every man aboard rushed to the deck to see the first iceberg float by, a white speck several miles away. Curiosity soon turned to dread. The fog thickened on the night of the twentieth, and the *Belgica* proceeded at low speed into the darkness, out of which monstrous white masses, some taller than her masts, emerged with no warning, one after the other.

When Somers lowered the engine pressure to fix the malfunctioning condenser one morning, the men could suddenly hear the thunderous collision of ice in the distance, rumblings of the Antarctic beast. A large iceberg materialized out of the mist. Lecointe attempted to dodge it, but it was too late: the ship's keel slammed into the berg with a sickening crack. Fragments of wood floated to the surface.

Despite this warning, de Gerlache took the helm and powered ahead through exceptionally thick fog, anxious to reach his long-imagined destination. The cold and the danger seemed to invigorate him. Creditors, critics, mutinous sailors, and saboteurs were far behind—he was close enough to his destination to inhale its bracing air, and nothing would stop him from reaching it.

His boldness impressed Amundsen and even scared him a little. "The commander is not afraid. . . . The engine is still running at 75 revolutions," Amundsen wrote in his diary on the night of January 21. "I cannot help but admire his daring. Ahead always. I shall follow him cheerfully and try to do my duty."

Carl August Wiencke was at the helm shortly before noon on January 22 when sudden gale-force winds blew the sea into a frenzy. Penguins bounded in and out of the chop. Adjusting the wheel constantly for the yaw, pitch, and roll, Wiencke did his best to keep the ship steady and on tack, and to dodge oncoming icebergs. He was new to the job. Hired as a cabin boy, the twenty-year-old Norwegian had been promoted to sailor in Punta Arenas in recognition of his zeal and good cheer after the four unruly Belgians were dismissed.

Wiencke had grown attuned to the music of tempests, the way the winds "seemed to want to tear everything apart and screeched at the rigging with the highest treble right down to the deepest bass." He came alive in such storms, which reminded him of Beethoven's sonatas. Beloved by crew and officers alike, Wiencke had proven worthy of his leaders' faith. He volunteered for the most dangerous tasks, eager to show off his agility and all too often ignoring Amundsen's pleas for caution.

Now he faced his most difficult challenge yet. Icebergs threatened to assail the ship from every direction. It began to snow, further limiting visibility. Sheets of spray slammed into Wiencke's yellow sou'wester and oilskin coat.

Enormous waves broke over the *Belgica* amidships and flooded into the hold through the open main hatch. Wiencke heard Amundsen's voice slicing through the noise of wind, calling him down from the bridge to help. After handing off the wheel to the Belgian sailor Gustave-Gaston Dufour, Wiencke descended the ladder and splashed into the knee-deep water that now inundated the deck. Loose chunks of coal had blocked the scuppers and prevented seawater from escaping. As the ship rocked, the water sloshed from one side of the deck to the other. The pool grew deeper with every wave that crashed over the railings. Wiencke ran to Amundsen's side, struggling to keep his footing. The first mate ordered Wiencke to help his comrade Johansen unclog one of the scuppers. Various crew members had been jabbing at it with a wooden peg and had succeeded only in packing the coal more tightly. The two would have to get creative.

Johansen believed they had no choice but to go at the clog from the outside of the ship. He found a long iron rod, to which he lashed the wooden peg to create a mallet they could use to dislodge the coal. Wiencke would lie on the gunwale, hold the makeshift mallet over the railing, and align the peg with the scupper while Johansen, securely attached, would lean over the side of the ship and hammer at the peg.

Wiencke lay down across the wet gunwale in his slick yellow oilskin, gripping the railing with one hand. He held the mallet, and Johansen swung a large hammer at it, over and over, but the mass didn't budge. Johansen stepped away from the railing to think about what to try next. He turned his back to Wiencke.

An iceberg appeared out of the dense fog ahead of the ship, just meters away. As the *Belgica* swerved to starboard to avoid it, the wind caught her sails, causing the ship to jolt ahead. Simultaneously, another gargantuan wave smothered the ship. When Johansen turned around, Wiencke was gone.

Johansen jumped up on the railing and looked below—nothing. Then he looked astern and caught a terrifying sight: his friend, flailing in the frigid water, receding quickly.

Johansen ran to the officers' quarters, swung the doors open, and shouted at the top of his lungs: "Wiencke overboard! Wiencke overboard!"

At Johansen's cry, de Gerlache and Lecointe rushed out onto the decks.

"Quickly, the oil bags!" shouted de Gerlache.

Johansen scampered up to the bridge and instructed Dufour to steer into the wind in order to slow the ship down, but the Belgian helmsman shot him a quizzical look and turned his attention back to the onslaught of icebergs. For the first time, the language barrier aboard the *Belgica* had life-or-death consequences. Johansen resorted to hand signals, but Dufour still didn't understand. With every wasted moment, Wiencke fell farther behind the ship.

Even in calm waters, at this latitude a man could die of hypothermia within minutes. In a storm, when the risk of drowning was just as high, he would have even less time to get back aboard before the consequences were irreversible.

Without a moment to spare, de Gerlache scrambled onto the bridge. He shouldered Dufour aside, took hold of the helm, and hove to, all while keeping an eye on a looming iceberg. Amundsen telegraphed the machinists to throw the engine in reverse.

The log line—the thin knotted cord that trailed behind the ship to measure its speed—slithered past Wiencke. He swam frantically to grab its end and twisted it around his wrist. The momentum of the ship yanked him forward. Cook gripped the deck end of the line and began steadily to reel him in, fighting against the sea. He dragged

Wiencke through the waves, each one causing the boy's weight to jerk the log line like a two-hundred-pound fish struggling to swim free. Cook's arms and back quivered. The rope dug into the flesh of his palms. Soon it began to slacken a little: the doctor could feel the sailor's hands slipping. Johansen came to Cook's aid. By the time he arrived at the side of the boat, Wiencke could barely stay afloat.

Amundsen urged Lecointe and de Gerlache to lower a lifeboat, his voice straining above the roar of the tempest. But the commandant deemed the storm far too powerful and refused to risk the lives of four or five sailors to save one. Lecointe volunteered to go in himself. He quickly tied a rope around his waist in a bowline knot and asked de Gerlache's permission to jump.

In the moment, as the salt spray needled his face, de Gerlache hesitated: He couldn't abandon Wiencke, yet he couldn't afford to lose his second-in-command, whose navigational expertise was irreplaceable. Lecointe took the commandant's perplexed silence for a yes. In an act of unfathomable courage, he stepped onto the gunwale, timed his jump to the ship's swing, and threw himself into the sea.

The screaming of the wind and the shouts of his shipmates were muffled the instant Lecointe plunged underwater. He could hear only the swirl of the ocean. His boots and clothes dragged him down and slowed his rise to the surface. The sea was barely 28.4 degrees, the freezing point of salt water. At that temperature, the dominant sensation isn't cold but a burning pain.

Lecointe surfaced next to Wiencke and gasped for air. The younger sailor's eyes were wide open, staring into nothingness. He was paralyzed by the cold but breathing hard through his nose, expelling seawater. Lecointe wrapped his arms around Wiencke. Several men tried to hoist them back aboard. The captain had been in the water for just a few seconds, but he could already feel his own muscles seizing up. Tremendous waves lifted Lecointe and Wiencke almost to the *Belgica*'s gunwales before dropping them to the end of the rope, as if they had been hung from a gallows. Each time the rope snapped taut, Lecointe's hold on Wiencke loosened a little more. Wiencke was deadweight, and his waterlogged clothing made him even heavier. The rope flicked them two or three more times before Lecointe let go.

Lecointe dangled helplessly. Below him, the log line uncoiled itself from Wiencke's wrist, in which it had left deep, discolored furrows. The *Belgica* rolled so widely now that Wiencke came within reach of the deck with each wave. Johansen leaned over the railing, and with Danco and Amundsen holding him back, he was able to grab Wiencke's left hand. But as soon as the ship swung away to port, Wiencke's unbuoyed weight became too great to bear. Johansen's grip on his friend's limp, wet hand weakened. When the *Belgica* rocked back to starboard and slammed into the water, Johansen lost his hold. The sea fell away and took Wiencke with it.

Wiencke was now floating on his back. The men finally got a clear look at him. They were met with a ghastly sight: The young man they knew was no longer recognizable. His face was black and swollen, and he was foaming at the mouth.

A wave washed Wiencke farther away from the ship and he began to sink. His companions watched from the deck until they could no longer see the yellow of his hat.

In his laboratory, beneath rattling test tubes and beakers that he had had the foresight to lock away in cabinets, Racovitza was lying on the floor in an effort to stave off seasickness. A figure suddenly appeared at the door, and Racovitza turned his head to see Arctowski, pale and shaking.

"Wiencke is dead!"

"Dead?" Racovitza said, bolting to his feet.

"Yes, drowned, swept overboard by a wave!"

Racovitza hurried to the wardroom, where he found Lecointe. The captain had been helped back inside after the trauma of his failed rescue attempt. He was half-naked and trembling, and weeping uncontrollably. "*Raco*, I couldn't, he slipped from my hands."

The captain had to be soothed and dressed, as Racovitza later put it, "like a child."

Back on deck, there was no time to grieve. The tempest still raging, de Gerlache took control of the ship. He had to get out of this storm. He spotted land off the *Belgica*'s port bow. Consulting the fragmentary maps that were his only guides to the region—one from the British Admiralty, the other drawn a few years earlier by a German whaler named Eduard Dallmann—de Gerlache identified it as Low Island, the southernmost of the South Shetland Islands. He veered toward it to find shelter from the storm. With the wind pushing at her stern, the *Belgica* slalomed deftly between a gauntlet of icebergs to reach the lee of the island, where she moored.

The ship was becalmed at last.

That night, a suffocating pall was cast on the *Belgica*. In the cabins and the forecastle, the men replayed Wiencke's final moments in their minds. For many, this was their first experience with violent death. Even those, like the doctor, who were not strangers to the sight of a corpse, were unprepared for the nauseating vision of Wiencke's grotesquely disfigured face in his final moments.

Racovitza hadn't witnessed the accident, but he was haunted nonetheless. Unable to sleep, he went to his laboratory, sat in his chair, and thought about the sudden, tragic turn the expedition had just taken: "The endeavor had barely begun and already we'd left a body on our path. Who would be next to go among the eighteen that remained to struggle against the menacing unknown? . . . Nature always claims what she's owed." He was not the only one asking himself that question.

De Gerlache knew that Antarctica would be dangerous, that the continent was to be respected and feared, but he had lost a man, and a good one, before he even spied the mainland. The commandant wondered whether he had made the right decision not to lower a boat. He wondered what he would tell Wiencke's parents, who would surely blame him. If not for the *Belgica* expedition, their son would still be alive.

Cook could still feel Wiencke's weight on the other end of the log line. Wiencke was thrashing in the water when he had grabbed the cord. By the time Cook had dragged him back to the side of the *Belgica,* the sailor was alive but unresponsive. Could the doctor have reeled Wiencke in more quickly? Would that have made a difference?

Amundsen was tortured by the thought that it was he who'd ordered Wiencke to unclog the scupper. He eulogized his compatriot in his diary that night. "We will never forget him," he wrote. "Unfortunately he had one failing. He always wanted to go outboard without being secured round his waist. . . . I always called him back."

Amundsen told Wiencke countless times to tie a rope around his waist. But could he have told him just one more time?

Most troubled by the boy's death was the man who had done the most to save him. Lecointe had risked his own life by jumping into the frigid, raging waters. He had held the boy in his arms. But his heroic efforts had proven insufficient. The captain couldn't help regretting that he had not been able to hold on tighter. "I kept seeing Wiencke," Lecointe wrote, "his lifeless eyes wide open, washed away forever."

CHAPTER 7

Uncharted

AT FIVE O'CLOCK ON THE AFTERNOON OF JANUARY 23, A BLACK DOT appeared on the horizon, visible through a window in the fog. This was the men's first glimpse of the Antarctic continent. A few hours later, the mist dissipated and a mountainous land materialized around the ship. The *Belgica* had entered Hughes Bay, on the northwestern coast of Graham Land. It appeared to the explorers as a realm of myth. Where the water ended, the snow began, as if the ocean had risen halfway up the Himalayas.

For de Gerlache, it was a particularly electric moment, the culmination of his young life. Before him was the dreamscape he had yearned for so long to behold. He had conceived of the expedition, raised the money for it, endured arrows from the Belgian press and other naysayers, suffered delay after humiliating delay, and narrowly averted a mutiny and a shipwreck, and already he had lost one of the men under his command. But now, at last, his boyhood fantasy had been realized. Perhaps the only other man aboard who could understand his elation was Cook, who had himself spent years trying to get here. Despite the setbacks, neither man had ever relinquished the hope that he would see this day. Glory was finally within reach.

Proceeding cautiously through a flock of icebergs, the Norwegian and Belgian flags at half-mast in honor of Wiencke, the *Belgica* passed a number of small islands, few of which appeared on the map. The *chukka-chukka-chukka* of the steam engine propagated across the glassy water. At nine-thirty p.m., by the lingering midsummer light, the officers chose one of the islands on which to make their first landing: an unremarkable, uncharted hunk of basalt about 350 meters in diameter, swept mostly clear of snow, with an accessible coast. De

Gerlache would name the expedition's first contribution to the map after his father—Auguste Island.

De Gerlache, Cook, Arctowski, Racovitza, and Danco piled into one of the boats and rowed to shore. A cacophony of unfamiliar birds—skuas, petrels, penguins—protested their arrival. "Everything about us had an other-world appearance," wrote Cook. "The scenery, the life, the clouds, the atmosphere, the water—everything wore an air of mystery." The men explored the island for about an hour— Arctowski chipping off rock samples; Racovitza collecting lichen, moss, and seaweed specimens; Danco attempting to kidnap penguins. In that time, twilight had fallen and the tide had risen. Cook and de Gerlache went back in the boat to prevent it from smashing against the rocks and rested on the oars as their comrades worked on land. "We tried to follow them with our glasses as we rocked about in the boat," Cook wrote, "but soon lost sight of their movements in the darkness. We were able to locate Arctowski by the dull echo of his hammer, and we were able to trace Racovitza by the chorus of penguins which greeted him from rock to rock." The men returned to the *Belgica* shortly before midnight, Danco carrying a live, squirming penguin under each arm.

The next day, January 24, following a landing on a second uncharted island, the *Belgica* hugged the bay's shore in search of a passage that might cut east through Graham Land to the Weddell Sea. Such a watercourse never revealed itself, but a break in the mountain chain suggested the likelihood of a long channel leading southwest. The existing maps of Hughes Bay indicated only solid land in that direction, yet from the crow's nest the strait extended as far as the eye could see. The maps were evidently wrong. The *Belgica* had barely spent a full day in these waters before de Gerlache encountered what every explorer lives for: the possibility of a major discovery.

For three days, he resisted the temptation to enter the apparent channel so that the scientists could properly explore Hughes Bay and Captain Lecointe could chart its contours. The captain benefited on the twenty-fifth from a rare opening in the clouds that allowed him to mark the sun's altitude over the horizon with his brass sextant and enabled him to fix the ship's latitude. The fog that typically enshrouds Antarctica's shores helped explain why the few maps that existed were so inaccurate and incomplete: it was hard enough on most days to see the coastline, let alone the sun or the stars.

On the twenty-sixth, Amundsen joined the landing party on Two Hummock Island, one of the only islands that could be identified in existing charts, to test out his skis. He *shushed* blissfully across the glacier that covered most of the island, gliding past bemused penguins, confident that he was making the first-ever skiing trip on Antarctic terra firma. It was a minor exploit, to be sure, but it was his first *first,* the initial entry in what he hoped would be the long list of polar records he would accomplish in his life.

On the misty afternoon of January 27, de Gerlache at last steered the ship into the mouth of the southwestern channel that had been beckoning him for days. To mark the passage into virgin waters, de Gerlache flew the Belgian flag from one of the masts, knowing that he and his men and the wildlife would be the only ones to see it wave. The nearest ship was hundreds of miles to the north.

Or so they thought. As they cruised toward the channel, with humpback whales spouting to port and starboard, the men noticed a long, straight object floating ahead. It was a mast, yards still attached, and not yet bleached with salt—the vestiges of a shipwreck, and by the looks of it disturbingly recent. Had it taken place nearby, or had these remains drifted from a world away? Some on the *Belgica* read it as a warning. "Will this also be the fate of the *Belgica* to disappear forever," wrote Lecointe, "leaving no trace but a segment of yard or mast?"

The ominous sighting was soon forgotten, however, as the *Belgica* entered the strait under a fairy-tale light. The sun had dipped behind the mountains to the west but was still catching their peaks and illuminating the sparse clouds above, forming a golden canopy that stretched over the darkened valley and reflected against the blue-black water. Icebergs glided silently along, like "apparitions," Lecointe observed.

The men of the *Belgica* were the first humans to admire this sublime landscape. Steaming down the channel, they were cradled between five-thousand-foot mountains that shot straight out of the sea to either side of the ship. They were denizens of an icy Eden, giving a name to every island, coast, cape, and previously undiscovered species they encountered, every inch of progress extending mankind's knowledge of the world.

The Antarctic summer was a glorious period in which temperatures rarely dipped far below the freezing point (nor did they rise much above it) and night never fell in earnest. In its place was a drawn-out gloaming that cast a mother-of-pearl shimmer across the sea. "Twilight and dawn blend together," de Gerlache wrote, though darkness would soon wedge its way between them and persist a little longer with each rotation of the planet.

The fragments of rock that Arctowski, the geologist, chipped off indicated that this region consisted of igneous rock, primarily granite and basalt. All but the most vertical rock faces were blanketed in white. This was a landscape forged in fire and carved by ice. Glaciers didn't merely course through valleys like rivers, as they did in the mountain chains of more temperate regions. Rather, they covered every surface on which snow could gain purchase. It snowed most days, usually not for long and rarely in large flakes. But accumulating over thousands of years and never melting off in the summer, the snow compacted into a layer of ice up to several hundred feet thick that moved slowly but ineluctably toward the sea, where it would break off into icebergs, pulled down by its own weight or undermined by the lapping of the water beneath.*

Cruising through canyons of ice, Cook was struck by how much more dramatic this land was than what he'd seen of the Arctic. The expedition's designated photographer, he set his tripod on the deck and pointed the lens at every new marvel. "As the ship steamed rapidly along, spreading out one panorama after another of a new world," he wrote, "the noise of the camera was as regular and successive as the tap of a stock ticker." Cook's photographs were likely the first ever taken of Antarctica. They did justice to an environment that appeared even to the naked eye as largely black-and-white.

Among Cook's most frequent subjects were icebergs, in their infinite variety. They all had the same origin: when a chunk of glacier broke off and crashed into the water—a loud and violent process described as calving, as if the glacier were giving birth—but then took

---

* In other regions of the Antarctic mainland, the ice cap was more than a mile thick.

different journeys as the sea began to sculpt them. Ranging in temperature from slightly warmer to slightly colder than freshwater ice, the sea gradually smoothed out angles, deepened concavities, refined points. Eventually it might chisel off a large section, causing an iceberg's center of gravity to shift and the enormous mass to rise or reorient itself in the water. The sea could now carve away areas that had previously been above the waterline. Air bubbles rising to the surface left vertical grooves along the sides, like the fluting on ancient Greek columns. As the iceberg revolved in the water, the air would flee in a new direction, creating complex patterns.

The longer an iceberg remained in the water, the more distinct it became. Large bergs—some rose more than two hundred feet above sea level; others might be several miles long—could come to resemble arcaded palaces, the sea carving out deep grottoes and occasionally boring straight through them to form tunnels and colonnades. Smaller fragments looked like fantastical creatures. Watching them parade by, the men were like children seeing shapes in the clouds. "I heard Arctowski suggest the Egyptian Sphinx," wrote Cook, "but Racovitza insisted upon the likeness of a polar bear and some one shouted, 'It moves!' At once the picture became real, and the sailors refused to believe that it was not a living bear."

On windless days, when they posed no threat, icebergs were a source of endless fascination. But their beauty was in proportion to their danger. Because their submerged portions, known as bummocks, reached far below the surface, they were acted upon by deep currents that might run in a different direction from those at the surface or from the wind, causing them to move in unpredictable ways.* What in good weather could seem like a wondrous sculpture park could in a storm or in fog become a deathtrap.

While Cook's crisp black-and-white photographs were well suited to documenting the stark contrasts of the snow-covered mountains, they did not capture subtle pops of color visible only up close, like the yellow, red, and orange lichen that adorned the rocks, or the vibrant aquamarine of the submerged base of an iceberg. Nor did they

---

*On average, about seven-eighths of an iceberg's mass lies below the surface. A berg that reaches two hundred feet above sea level can have a fourteen-hundred-foot keel.

register the enchanting spectrum of blues that reflected off the ice and emanated from crevasses. The color was especially concentrated in the deep caverns that formed in icebergs, tempting sailors to venture into them.

Cook leapt at every chance to go ashore. The most agile of the expeditioners, he would stand on the prow of the rowboat and be the first to jump onto the slippery rock with a mooring line in hand. He lugged his cumbersome camera to precarious ledges and captured sweeping vistas of the *Belgica* cruising majestically down the channel. These images give an impression of stillness and serenity that is at odds with Cook's description of the sounds they heard: "Awe-inspiring and strangely interesting were the curious noises of the cormorants, the penetrating voices of the gulls, the coarse *gha-a-ah, gha-a-ah* of the penguins, the sudden and unexpected spouts of whales, the splash of seals and penguins, and the babyish cries of the young animals on the rocks before us." Every so often, the roar of a calving iceberg would echo across the mountains, the awesome sound of nature's raw power.

Racovitza, the first naturalist to set foot on the Antarctic continent, routinely put his life in danger in the interest of science. On the afternoon of February 1, on what would come to be known as Cuverville Island, he found himself at the foot of a vertiginous rock wall. Through his spyglass he saw a few blades of grass high up the cliff. It was like spotting a palm tree in the desert: since leaving South America, the only plant life he'd seen had consisted of seaweed, moss, and lichen. Racovitza was determined to collect a specimen of the grass despite the perilous climb it would require and his lack of experience as a mountaineer. He threw down his rifle and satchel and started climbing, clinging to small asperities of the rock with the tips of his fingers, jamming an ice ax into crevices and pulling himself up by its handle. The ascent was grueling, but adrenaline drove him on. Then, as he neared his goal, dizzyingly high above the pebble beach, two skuas—large, brown, gull-like birds—swooped in and began pecking at him and beating him viciously with their wings. They were evidently defending their two chicks, whose downy heads Racovitza could now see poking out from a nest on a nearby ledge. It was a terrifying moment—one wrong move could mean a fatal fall. His left hand gripping the rock, Racovitza swung wildly with his ice ax and succeeded in fending off the birds long enough to snatch the tuft of grass he sought before scrambling back down.

His prize was well worth the trouble: the southernmost flowering plant in the world, *Deschampsia antarctica,* a rare and especially hardy grass able to withstand the cold, the wind, and the paucity of soil. Antarctica is an unforgiving, inhospitable land, but by no means a sterile one. Life perseveres.

Under his microscope, Racovitza found an abundance of microorganisms, such as the plump, eight-legged tardigrade, which survives under the most extreme conditions on earth (and even, it's since been discovered, in outer space). He collected mites on the lichen-covered rocks and discovered the largest strictly terrestrial animal indigenous to Antarctica—a black, five-millimeter-long flightless midge that would be named *Belgica antarctica* in honor of the expedition. Antarctica's only native insect, it spends up to two years in a larval stage before living only a few days in the summer in adult form, just long enough to reproduce. That it evolved to lose its wings is a testament to the brutality of the winds that scour the continent.

As Racovitza observed, every animal in the ecosystem depended directly or indirectly on the sea. Birds survived mostly on krill and shellfish. A few, like the skua, ate penguin eggs and chicks. Others, like the Antarctic giant petrel, were voracious scavengers, sometimes loading up so heavily on carrion that they struggled to fly away when Racovitza approached to examine a carcass. But, as the zoologist learned, the giant petrel had developed a particularly repellent defense mechanism. "It hurls onto you the contents of its digestive tract and, when one is thus covered with matter that is more or less decomposed, one is not proud, I assure you," he wrote. "The odor is persistent and horrible, and . . . it is quite difficult not to give yourself over to similar expressions as that of the petrel."

Instead of the crystalline air the men might have expected to breathe at these frigid latitudes, the wind often carried less-than-agreeable aromas, from the mammalian pungency of seal colonies to the putrescent breath of whales, which Racovitza had the rare privilege, once again, of experiencing at point-blank range. He wanted at all costs to photograph a humpback whale as it surfaced to breathe.

When one day he spotted the submerged form of a cetacean slicing toward the side of the ship, he rushed to the bridge with a camera, ready to take the shot at the right moment. He had anticipated the whale's movement perfectly: the animal emerged immediately beneath him and exhaled through its blowhole, soaking Racovitza with a fetid spray infused with the odor of countless small animals that had gotten caught in its baleen and died.* "My nose was at this moment invaded by a stench so repulsive that I'm ashamed to admit that I forgot to press the shutter," he wrote.

Among the most pervasive smells was the rotten-seafood reek of penguin rookeries. These nesting colonies, slathered in guano that stained the snow blood red, could be detected hundreds of yards away by their acrid scent and the braying of their inhabitants. Of all the creatures the men encountered, none were as entertaining to them as penguins, with their comical waddle—reminiscent of the choppy way people walked in motion pictures, a technology that the Lumière brothers had demonstrated in Brussels just two years earlier—and their complex societies. Having evolved in isolation, Antarctic penguins had not learned to fear humans and would allow Racovitza to observe their rituals up close. A lively, frequently funny writer, the Romanian zoologist couldn't resist describing the two penguin species that dominated the channel, chinstrap and gentoo, in vividly anthropomorphic terms. The chinstrap penguin, he wrote, could be identified by "a thin black line that curls up on its white cheek like a musketeer's mustache. This gives the penguin a pugnacious air, which corresponds well to its character." Chinstraps were prone to bickering over small patches of territory. Dueling chinstrap penguins "looked from afar like two fishmongers questioning the respective freshness of the other's merchandise." More congenial and cooperative—and colorful—were the gentoo penguins. Racovitza described them as "slightly larger than the chinstrap and more sumptuously dressed," with their scarlet beaks and feet, and their black heads adorned with a white diadem.

While they were roughly alike in size and mating patterns, gen-

---

* Or so Racovitza surmised. Some biologists think humpback whales' rank breath must come from pulmonary bacteria instead.

toos and chinstraps were different enough in disposition that Racovitza compared their respective societies to the two major political
ideologies then clashing throughout the Western world (and subject
to passionate debate among the crew and officers of the *Belgica*): The
chinstrap penguin, he wrote, "is a strict individualist, constantly . . .
quarreling to defend its property." The "decent and honest gentoo,"
by contrast, "is a shrewd communist having nothing to defend against
its fellow citizens, having shared the land, and having simplified the
task of childrearing by establishing a communal nursery." So enamored were the men with gentoo penguins that they took three on
board as pets. Two died almost immediately. The third made itself at
home, ambling freely about the deck. His shipmates grew fond of
their pet penguin. They spoiled him and named him Bébé.

Racovitza's duties entailed more than mere observation. He was
expected to bring several specimens of every species he encountered,
botanical and zoological, back to Belgium, where they would join
various museum collections. The obligation required him to kill animals with sickening regularity, a necessary desecration of this white
paradise in the name of knowledge. Seabirds and penguins were easy
enough to dispatch with buckshot, a well-aimed bludgeon, or a quick
twist of the neck, but bigger game—notably leopard and Weddell
seals, with their dense layers of blubber—required heavier ammuni-
tion. Though Racovitza performed these executions with clinical ef-
ficiency, the gruesomeness of the violence often left him unsettled.
Finding a female leopard seal lounging on her side one day, he wrote
in his diary, "I shoot her behind the ear with a hollow-point bullet,
which exits above the eye. The animal expires on the spot, but jets of
blood as thick as a thumb spurt out of both orifices without cease for
5 minutes. The quantity of blood is truly terrifying."

After performing a few field measurements on the still-warm carcass, Racovitza and an assistant, usually Johan Koren, would prepare
it for conservation. In the case of vertebrates, they removed the flesh
and organs and scraped all tissue off the bones, which were labeled
and put away. If they found a fetus, it was cut out of its mother's
uterus and placed in a jar of alcohol. Some skins were dried and
treated with arsenic to guard against pests, so that they might be
turned into taxidermy upon their return to Europe. Smaller speci-

mens, such as larvae or microorganisms, were kept on slides. In three weeks, Racovitza collected specimens from more than 400 species of plants, animals, fungi, algae, and diatoms, 110 of which were unknown to science. His laboratory had taken on the look of a miniature museum. His only regret was having not captured a whale.

Emile Danco's work yielded less tangible results. He was responsible for conducting a geophysical survey of the region, which required him to determine precisely the local variations in the earth's magnetic and gravitational fields. Among the practical applications of such data was to help future navigators.* The data was also valuable from a purely scientific perspective, to better understand global magnetism. Unfortunately, Danco was no scientist. De Gerlache had hired him not because of his qualifications but rather out of friendship and loyalty, to have a trusted man at his side, and perhaps even out of pity. But he had struggled to find a role for him. Danco was an artillery lieutenant, a specialty of limited usefulness in Antarctic exploration. The commandant had at first put him in charge of meteorology, but after following courses at various institutions, Danco found the subject too difficult and asked to be assigned another discipline. De Gerlache then suggested geophysics, which Danco accepted. He studied for months with top experts around Europe, but he didn't have a technical mind. While he learned how to operate instruments like the Neumayer magnetometer competently enough, he didn't quite understand the phenomena they were measuring—certainly not enough to know what he didn't know, such as the external factors that might affect a reading. Nor could he perform the complex calculations involved. Danco could not remember simple yet crucial details about the expensive tools the expedition had purchased for him, nor about the standards to be followed. Much of his work turned out to be completely unusable.

Captain Lecointe, by contrast, was every bit the rigorous scientist that Danco was not. It was his job as navigator to situate the *Belgica*

* Throughout the nineteenth century, geographers were convinced that if they could establish a comprehensive chart of magnetic variations around the world, it would reduce the need for celestial navigation, which required clear skies, not always a given. Michael Palin, former president of Britain's Royal Geographical Society, has called this project "a nineteenth-century equivalent of GPS."

in space and time. The task demanded a thorough understanding of trigonometry and astronomy, and Lecointe excelled at both. The twenty-eight-year-old had inherited a love and aptitude for numbers from his father, a math teacher, and had published a respected and highly technical book on celestial navigation. Whenever the clouds would part long enough for him to sight the sun or the moon or a star through his sextant, Lecointe measured its altitude above the horizon, from which he deduced—after consulting celestial charts—the ship's latitude. Thanks to a marine chronometer set to Greenwich mean time, he could also fix her longitude. Based on those coordinates, Lecointe could then begin to chart the surrounding coastlines.

Yet the conditions he encountered in Antarctica seemed to conspire against navigation and cartography. Since most days were overcast, Lecointe was able to determine the complete coordinates of only five spots along the channel. Those coordinate readings were later found to be remarkably accurate—often within a minute of a degree. But to fill in the rest of the chart, he was forced to rely on other methods. One, known as dead reckoning, consisted of estimating a ship's coordinates and bearing based on variables including compass readings, local magnetic variation, and approximate speed since the last known position. While this approach was useful in tracking progress in open waters, it lacked the precision to allow him to draw an accurate map. As the discoverers of this new land, the explorers were duty-bound to attempt a more exacting method.

Lecointe proposed an alternative technique that would involve greater risk but possibly yield better results. It would require several men to climb to a high point of land that would provide a sweeping vista of the channel and its islands below. From there, measurements with a theodolite could indicate the angle of depression of the sight lines onto various points of interest below. As long as the altitude of the viewpoint was known precisely, these sight lines would form the hypotenuses of triangles that could then easily be solved, using plane trigonometry, to determine the distances of the points of interest. To attempt this method, it was decided that de Gerlache would lead a small party consisting of Cook, Amundsen, Danco, and Arctowski on a journey to a peak that might offer the requisite panorama. Lecointe would teach them how to use the theodolite.

On the stormy afternoon of January 30, the landing party rowed to one of two large islands that formed the northwestern side of the channel, a 680-square-mile mountainous landmass that would come to be known as Brabant Island. Lecointe and two sailors, Tollefsen and Knudsen, helped them disembark at the foot of a steep, slick rock on which sat a group of curious cormorants. Large waves rocked the boat and made the task all the more difficult. The men carried two sledges loaded with food and camping equipment to the island and hauled them through snow several feet deep, up an incline of 40 degrees. As a precaution, they carried provisions for fifteen days even though they planned to be on the island for no more than eight. Strapped to the overloaded sledges by ropes tied to their waists, the men played tug-of-war with gravity, struggling with every step. *The first sledge journey in Antarctica,* Amundsen thought as he trudged up the glacier, adding to his mental ledger of polar accomplishments.

It took them almost four hours to arrive at level ground, at an altitude of eleven hundred feet. Out of breath, their skin steaming from the effort, they paused to take in the splendor around them before snowfall began to obscure it. They bade goodbye to Lecointe, Tollefsen, and Knudsen, who let themselves fall freely down the snowy slope, laughing helplessly the whole way. For the next few days, in de Gerlache's absence, Lecointe would take command of the *Belgica* and continue to explore and chart the channel.

The snowstorm that had been building all day grew more severe. Frigid, swirling gales swept down from the peaks above, ruling out any further ascent. De Gerlache decided to set up camp for the night. (*The first night spent on Antarctica,* Amundsen noted in his mental log.) As the snow and wind whipped at them, three of the men dug out and patted down an area on which to erect their shelter—a tent made of oiled silk, shaped like a house, with four walls and a gable roof. It was an arduous task, made harder by the force of the elements. "A wind came out of the bed of a glacier above us, against which we could hardly stand," wrote Cook. "It took two men to hold up the tent, and the combined efforts of all hands to keep from having our effects scattered over the cliffs but a few yards away."

The party struck camp at nine the next morning and made for the peak they had spotted from the ship. Climbing through the thick fog that followed the storm, the expeditioners soon found themselves at the lip of a gaping crevasse that stretched across the landscape and blocked their progress to the peak. The men retreated to level ground to set up camp again. They had lost a day. The climb would not be nearly as straightforward as it had appeared from below. They were quickly learning that Antarctica's mountains could be as menacing as its seas.

The men sought an alternate route to the peak the following morning. De Gerlache and Danco, who had learned to ski together in Norway, decided to wear their skis that day to avoid sinking into the snow. Hitched to the same sledge, the two friends shuffled across the plain with difficulty, de Gerlache on the right, Danco on the left, each man keeping the other in his peripheral vision to coordinate their strides. The sound of their wooden skis brushing through fresh powder settled into a lulling rhythm. All of a sudden, Danco vanished. He had dropped into a crevasse that had been obscured by snow. By reflex, de Gerlache shot out his arms to reach for Danco. The commandant felt himself getting pulled down. "I would probably have been dragged behind him to the bottom of the abyss had his large skis not caught on the walls of the fault," de Gerlache wrote. After helping Danco climb out, the men discovered that the slopes that had seemed so uniformly white from the deck of the ship were in fact riddled with crevasses, some of them potentially hundreds of feet deep. Though he'd be able to chart the surrounding lands more accurately by reaching greater heights, de Gerlache deemed it impossible to proceed. Frustrated, the men again retraced their steps.

For the next few days, de Gerlache and Danco set up the theodolite on a lower promontory, a steep outcropping clear of snow, about a thousand feet above sea level. The first day, they found themselves in a cloud, their views of the channel below too rare and fleeting to take theodolite readings. The second day, the dissipating fog revealed the mountain-lined channel below in its full majesty, stretching from left to right, the water as seemingly still as a millpond, hulking icebergs reduced to specks. It was a panorama "even more beautiful," Cook wrote, "than anything we had seen since our first entrance into this new white world." Yet the few measurements de Gerlache and Danco were able to make were of little use: they had not climbed high enough for the distant islands below to stand out from the mainland. They were, however, able to determine from that vantage that there was no passage through the peninsula to the east.

Cook and Amundsen were not as easily dissuaded as the commandant. They had climbed this far and didn't know when they'd get another chance to ascend an Antarctic mountain. On February 4, they decided to make another attempt at the higher peak that had so far eluded them, not so much to meet the demands of science or cartography (they wouldn't bother to take a theodolite) as to satisfy an urge some men have to reach the top of things.

Sixty feet above Amundsen's head, silhouetted against the austral summer sky, Cook hacked into the mountainside with smooth, deliberate swings of his ax. Holding fast to the nearly vertical wall of snow, Amundsen watched the raining chips of ice fall past him. His face turned earthward, he caught a glimpse of what he'd been trying not to think about since they'd begun their ascent. He looked past the zigzagging path of footholds the doctor had cut for them, leading 150 feet down to the bottom of the ice wall, then continuing straight into a crevasse that could have been another 100 feet or more deep. The turquoise sheen at the surface of the ice gave way to darkness as the crack deepened. He couldn't see the bottom. Amundsen gripped the rope that connected him to Cook by the waist and coiled it taut. He concentrated on his breathing and the repetitive sound of the ax. His drooping blond mustache was flecked with snow. But despite the subzero temperature and a hissing wind that urged him to let go, he wasn't cold. If anything, he was uncomfortably hot, envious of Cook's light sealskin anorak and trousers.

In their time at sea, Amundsen had come to recognize Cook's expertise in polar matters and used each opportunity to study his approach. Amundsen admired the calm, methodical way in which the doctor climbed, a skill he'd acquired—like the sealskin clothes—in Greenland. His movements were precise and confident, as if he were performing surgery. He first chopped perpendicularly into the cliffside, and then, just as the blade entered the snow, he wedged it upward to widen the incision and prevent the ax from getting stuck. He then carved out a foothold wide enough to accommodate the Norwegian snowshoes both men had strapped to their boots. Those unwieldy contraptions, which looked like old wooden tennis rackets, were helpful over flat expanses of snow, distributing their weight over a larger area to prevent their feet from sinking in, but the snowshoes were far from ideal for such an ascent. They stuck out from the footholds, and the smooth wood they were made of provided no grip.

Nor did the rope offer much reassurance. Amundsen was far heavier than Cook. Were he to slip or the snow to crumble under his feet, he might pull his companion down with him. And if Cook missed a step and fell, the sudden whipping force he would exert on the rope as his weight snapped it taut would almost certainly yank Amundsen off the mountain and send them both plummeting into the icy chasm.

Danger loomed above as well in the form of protruding ice masses that teetered precariously past the cliff's edge like the crests of a wave, threatening to crash down on the climbers at any moment. They hadn't even been in Antarctica for two weeks, but already they'd seen how quickly the environment could transform and erode, how alive the ice was, especially at the height of summer.

Cook stepped into the foothold he had just carved out. Below him, Amundsen stepped up as well.

They clambered over the lip of the cliff and found themselves on a vast plateau. As they caught their breath, the men gazed upon a mountain range that looked like the black backbones of a dozen prehistoric monsters, piercing through the snow. *Highest altitude yet reached in Antarctica,* Amundsen told himself. From this vantage, Cook spotted what looked like a bridge arcing over the crevasse that yawned below them like a mouth waiting to be fed. But the only way to get there was down the same cliff they had just scaled. Once again, Cook led the way, which meant that there was nobody above Amundsen to hold the rope, but the first mate had freshly chiseled and stress-tested footholds to aid his descent. Already this was getting easier.

A little while later, they had looped around to the passage Cook had spotted from above, and up close they saw it was a marvel of natural engineering—a bridge made entirely of snow, spanning the emptiness as if built by an unseen hand.

Snowbridges were another of the Antarctic's wonderland features. The wind was their architect, picking up snow and depositing it at the lip of a crevasse. Little by little, a dusting accreted into an outcropping, which turned into a cornice, then a ledge that could—in the rare cases when it didn't break off under its own weight—reach all the way across. It was a beautiful sight, but one that held great danger. Because there was no way of telling how sturdy they were, these structures could be as treacherous as the pits that traditional hunters covered with loose sticks and leaves to ensnare an elk or a tiger. They were responsible for an inordinate number of deaths among polar explorers.

Cook instructed Amundsen to carve out a seat and footstools so that he could brace himself to support Cook's full weight in case the bridge—which consisted of nothing but snow—collapsed under him. He could test the ground with his foot, but the only way to determine whether it would support his weight was by placing his faith in it. He lay down on the thin top layer of ice to spread his body over as large an area as possible, like a human snowshoe. Feeling the slight, comforting tug of the rope at his waist, he crawled across.

It was now Amundsen's turn. The first mate had thirty pounds on the doctor. Cook had made it across, but could the bridge have weakened under his weight? The rope that tethered the men together was now level with the ground; it would not prevent Amundsen from falling at least some distance.

If he tried to cross quickly, Amundsen risked putting too much pressure on a single point or slipping off the ice and falling to one side. Then again, every second he remained suspended over the crevasse added further strain to the bridge. So he crawled as fluidly as he could, squinting into the windblown snow. The bridge held.

Finally, the two men had crossed the crevasse that had blocked their way for days. They continued on to the closest peak, a mercifully easy climb compared to what they had just endured. But just as they were taking in the view of the virgin landscape, a dense fog unfurled over it. Night wouldn't come for hours, and at this time of year wouldn't last long, but the fog prevented them from continuing on to a higher summit. Cook charted a course back to the ship that had appeared smooth from above when he'd surveyed it just before it became impossible to see more than a few dozen feet ahead. In fact, it was far more dangerous than the way they had just taken.

As Amundsen walked into the mist-choked valley through the sound-muffling snow, he kept his eyes on the rope that indicated the way forward and assured him he was not alone, even when he couldn't hear the doctor's footsteps or make him out through the fog. Suddenly, as if of its own volition, the rope pulled Amundsen violently forward. He caught himself after a few lurching, skidding steps and, by instinct, pulled back with all his strength. A few feet in front of him, the snow had given way under Cook. Digging his boots into the ice, Amundsen pulled at the rope, making full use of his muscular frame to keep the doctor's weight from dragging them both to their doom at the bottom of the crevasse.

Cook's feet were dangling over emptiness. With Amundsen's help, he clawed his way out and wiped the snow from his beard. For the second time in his career as an explorer, he had cheated death.

After likely sharing a nervous laugh, the two men continued on, but not as confidently as before. They now looked out over a landscape that held tremendous danger. It was clear that the smooth blanket of snow they had seen from above concealed a network of crevasses, similar to the one that had almost swallowed Danco three days earlier. Each tentative footstep on this island was an act of faith.

They moved gingerly across the snow, but with purpose. Within minutes, Amundsen broke through the ground. He experienced the nauseating sensation of falling faster than his guts, followed by a rush of adrenaline. The rope snapped taut. He peered at the darkness beneath him, into which the light that poured through the fresh opening gradually dissipated. His life now depended on the doctor.

Cook held on, and Amundsen pulled himself up to level ground. They made it back to the campsite eight hours after they'd left.

Perhaps no greater insight into the minds of Amundsen and Cook can be found than in their response to this ordeal. They had twice nearly lost their lives, and on an adventure justified by little more than thrill seeking. But rather than being humbled by the many ways the ice and snow might find to kill them, they were energized. And Amundsen's fascination with Cook had grown deeper. "The practical and calm way this man works is interesting to see," he wrote in his diary that night. "I hope that there are more of these wonderful trips to come."

They rejoined de Gerlache, Danco, and Arctowski at camp on a wretched night. Wind and rain slammed relentlessly into the tent's large, flat walls. The oiled silk fabric began to stretch, then to fray. Efforts to mend it using safety pins only caused new tears. Soon their shelter was no shelter at all. To salvage what was left of it, the men hastily confected a smaller tent out of the most intact fragments, built a wall of snow to protect it from the wind, and piled inside. The humidity—bad enough when the tent was full-sized—grew intolerable. Condensation from the breath of five closely huddled men beaded on the walls, dripped down onto their heads, and soaked their sleeping bags. Rain sprayed in through the tears in the fabric. The layer of snow beneath them turned to slush, and the tent gradually sank into it. By early morning, their snow wall had melted in the rain, and the wind redoubled its assault.

Nobody slept well that night. To pass the time, Cook and Amundsen, invigorated by their excursion and the thrill of budding friendship, batted around concepts for perfecting polar equipment, in particular for designing a tent that would offer better ventilation and less resistance to the wind. The two men were joined by a common purpose: both had ambitions of leading their own expeditions after the *Belgica*, and so treated every moment as crucial preparation.

The five men awoke to find their campground had turned into a puddle. The storm abated briefly, and to their relief they saw the *Belgica* in the distance below. They scaled a nearby rock on which they planted a small flag to signal that they were ready to return aboard.

Lecointe arrived with the *Belgica* off the coast of Brabant at five that afternoon. As they rowed back to the ship, the men reflected on the past few days. For de Gerlache, the mission had been a disappointment: the theodolite measurements had not yielded satisfactory results, and contributed little to the map of the channel. Amundsen, however, buzzed with excitement. Between his harrowing climb with Cook and the miserable final night in the shredded tent, his mind was brimming with lessons learned. As soon as he was back on board, he rushed to his cabin to jot them down in his diary. He made a diagram of Cook's idea—the doctor was never short of ideas—for a conical tent that would deflect a head-on assault from the wind. He sketched the sleeping bag that Cook had designed for himself, with a hood that could be cinched around the face to keep the rest of the body warm and, more important, dry. Among the other lessons: "Dress lightly, wool everywhere. Always use the lightest kind. Ensure you have a large and a small waterproof box for matches. Snow goggles are indispensable."

Amundsen made no secret of his admiration for Cook's practicality and polar experience and considered his time with him an apprenticeship of sorts. Delighted to find someone so receptive to his ideas, Cook wasn't insensitive to the flattery. Long after the rope that linked them on the cliffside was untied, the bond that formed between Amundsen and Cook that day would remain unbreakable.

CHAPTER 8

"To the South!"

"Hurry up, Arctowski!"

On the morning of February 10, the Polish geologist sprinted up a moraine to collect rock samples and was soon swallowed by the fog. Waiting on the rocky beach by the rowboat, de Gerlache called after the geologist to remind him he had only ten minutes before they needed to head back to the *Belgica*.

There was an urgency in the commandant's call that went beyond the particular circumstance of Arctowski and this moraine. De Gerlache was starting to worry about how much time the expedition was spending in the channel, on the tip of Graham Land. According to the initial plan, the ship should by now have been hundreds of miles closer to Victoria Land, the presumed site of the South Magnetic Pole, on the other side of the continent. But never mind the pole, the *Belgica* was still far north of the antarctic circle, which sits at a latitude of approximately 66°30′ south.

And the clock was ticking. Since the expedition's first landing in Antarctica, just three weeks before, nights had gone from virtually nonexistent to several hours long. Soon a depthless cold would sweep over the surface of the water and freeze it into an impenetrable mass of sea ice, blocking everything in its path and trapping any vessel unfortunate enough to be caught in it. If the *Belgica* could not reach the antarctic circle—which was not even virgin territory, having first been crossed more than a century earlier by Captain James Cook—before the sea ice set in, de Gerlache could expect savage treatment in the Belgian press when he returned. His fears of squandering his chance at glory returned with full force, and each day found him eager to cover more ocean. Yet he recognized that he would also face criticism if he gave the scientific program short shrift. So when Arc-towski observed a "pyramidal mountain of red rock, very different in appearance from the surrounding scenery," and begged for the chance to examine it, de Gerlache relented as he had many times before—but insisted on rowing the geologist ashore himself to keep him on schedule.

The landing, on the shore of what is now known as Paradise Bay, was the expedition's eighteenth. On the morning of February 12, the expedition passed what would later be named Cape Renard, a loom-ing tower of dark basalt soaring straight out of the sea, so steep that it was clear of snow on all sides. The rock, which looked to Lecointe like "the spire of a cathedral," stood at the southern end of the chan-nel. Lecointe, Racovitza, Arctowski, Danco, and Cook rowed to its base, bringing the total number of landings to twenty, more than all previous expeditions to Antarctica combined.

The *Belgica* rounded the cape and arrived shortly at the mouth of a narrow, winding canyon flanked by walls of rock that dwarfed the ship and cast her deck in shadow. Intent on moving forward at all costs, de Gerlache decided to sail between the cliffs despite poor vis-ibility, incipient dusk, and unknowable depths. The commandant was as daring in confronting the dangers of the sea as he had been timid in confronting a defiant crew earlier on. What could be described as courage when all ended well—such as when he'd sped through the iceberg-strewn Bransfield Strait—could just as easily be character-ized as recklessness when it didn't, as was the case when he'd allowed the *Belgica* to sail by dimming light into the shallows of the Beagle Channel.

The ship advanced into the darkened gorge, her hull gliding over unseen rocks. It became difficult for the crew to distinguish the shore from the sea. Proceeding farther down the unknown strait was mad-ness, but so was staying in place as night fell. By the time the *Belgica* exited the waterway, the men could tell by the rocking of the deck and the sound of breakers crashing onto the surrounding rocks that they had reached the open ocean.

It was a bittersweet moment, marking the successful passage through a perilous canyon but also the end of the *Belgica*'s dreamlike period of discovery. The ship dropped anchor for the night, and when the sun rose and the fog cleared, a strikingly new landscape unfolded across the horizon. Hundreds of icebergs floated through a seemingly infinite expanse of loose sea ice. "The entire mass—icebergs, sea-ice, and the ship—rises and falls with the gigantic heave of this South Pacific," wrote Cook.

De Gerlache was desperate to push south to where the map of Antarctica was blank again. But a vast icefield blocked access to the coast. The *Belgica* sailed along its fragmented edge, probing for a lead, but the ice only shoved the ship farther and farther away from the mainland.

A favorable wind propelling her south, the sturdy *Belgica* plowed through bands of drift ice, leaving a long black trail in her wake. Now that the scientists could no longer clamor for landings, de Gerlache was at last unbound, and the ship was making rapid progress.

Amundsen was on watch on the evening of February 13 when the fog descended and the *Belgica* was suddenly encircled by reefs, rocks, and ice-covered islets. The ocean began to swell, squalls to blow, and powerful currents to swirl around the ship. Waves exploded against the surrounding rocks, sending chunks of sea ice flying through the air. Gulls and penguins looked down from perches all around, as if from the bleachers of a coliseum. The *Belgica* was trapped. Despite his rank as first mate, Amundsen was still relatively green as a sailor. Had he had time to think, he might have been able to figure a way out of this predicament, but the elements didn't afford him that luxury. Deadly obstacles lay in almost every direction, yet the water was too deep to anchor, and the wind and the ocean were too forceful for the ship to stay in place.

De Gerlache took control with his typical poise. To scope out an escape route, he flew up the rigging to the top of the mainmast, which swung wildly in the wind, like an orchestra conductor's baton.

"Starboard!" he shouted in warning. The helmsman frantically turned the wheel to avoid the long, flat reef that appeared in that direction. The maneuver saved the *Belgica* but put her on course for a small island, separated from the reef by little more than a ship's length.

"Straight ahead!" de Gerlache bellowed from above. Amundsen understood that the commandant intended to sail between the reef and the island, a waterway so tight it made the canyon passage they had just navigated look like a mighty river. The first mate ordered the helmsman to steer the ship as close as possible to the island, whose steep slope indicated that the water immediately around it was probably deeper there than by the flatter reef. But there was no way of knowing for sure. To avoid being caught in the current, or sideswiped by a wave and slammed into the rocks, de Gerlache ordered the firemen to force the steam. "The engineer," recalled Cook, "urged on the engines as he had never done before."

The *Belgica* sailed six meters from the rock. The water was barely deep enough for the ship to pass: despite the onset of night, Amundsen could clearly see the reef extending below when he peered over the bulwark. He felt the spray from huge breakers that crashed to port and starboard with the sound of heavy artillery. He was certain that, after so many narrow escapes, the *Belgica*'s time had finally come.

At the end of this corridor were two 100-foot-tall icebergs that had run aground, one to each side, forming what Amundsen called a kind of "triumphal arch for this menacing place." As the *Belgica* steamed toward the icebergs, Amundsen had no choice but to trust his commandant—as well as a higher authority. "I started to think of something else and looked calm and indifferent," he wrote in his diary afterward. "Inside I prayed to You, God. You may steer us as you will." To Amundsen's amazement, the *Belgica* slipped between the rocks and through the iceberg portal without a scratch.

The *Belgica* maintained her southwesterly course into the Bellingshausen Sea. There hadn't been a clear night sky since the ship left the channel, so Lecointe was unable to establish her coordinates precisely, but by his dead reckoning they would cross the antarctic circle on the evening of February 15.* The Belgian flag was flown to mark the occasion. It was a moment of relief for de Gerlache. While glory

---

* The antarctic circle marks the latitude beyond which the sun remains in the sky for twenty-four hours straight at least once a year (and, conversely, remains below the horizon for a full day as well).

was not yet his, the milestone would save him from total humiliation back home.

Yet the farther south he sailed, the greater risk he ran of not even making it back home. The thickening texture of the pack could be discerned by the noises that resonated inside the ship as she sliced through. The blunt knocking of loose floes against the wooden hull gave way to the slow rumble of pancake ice, then to the gravelly crunch of brash ice. The sound of the sea gradually freezing around the ship was alarming to several of the men on board, particularly the scientists. Each day, entrapment grew more likely.

No human being had ever wintered south of the South Shetland Islands—let alone south of the antarctic circle—and the dangers of doing so in the sea ice were obvious. De Gerlache was well aware of the fate that could befall an icebound expedition. He had read enough polar history to know that it was far easier to enter the pack than to break out of it. Such was the case with the Franklin expedition of the 1840s: after the *Terror* and the *Erebus* succumbed to the pack in the Canadian Arctic, all of their men were left to die of cold, starvation, and disease.

De Gerlache knew that the ice could destroy a ship as a boa constrictor kills its prey, crushes its bones, and swallows it whole. He was a teenager, already enraptured by polar narratives, when in 1882 newspapers around the world published the sensational story of another doomed American vessel, the USS *Jeannette*. Under the command of the naval officer George W. De Long, who set out in 1879 to reach the North Pole via the Bering Strait on the mistaken assumption that there existed a channel of relatively warm, open water leading straight to the top of the planet, the *Jeannette* was entrapped a few hundred miles north of Siberia. The ship drifted across the Arctic Ocean for almost two years before the ice released its grip. This brief reprieve was no mercy: the buffer of open water around the ship allowed the pack to gather momentum when pressures renewed the next day. The ice smashed the *Jeannette* from all sides and punctured her hull below the waterline. De Long and his men evacuated onto the ice and watched their home sink slowly, agonizingly, into a narrowing hole. Cables snapped, lines slackened, and the horizontal yardarms bent vertically as the vessel was sucked into the opening.

After the ice closed its jaws, there was nothing but a residue of paint and splinters to indicate where the *Jeannette* had been. Only a third of the castaways survived, thanks to native Siberian hunters, who found them half-dead, fed them, warmed them, and guided them to safety.

De Gerlache tried not to let such stories blunt his courage as he sailed on south. The dangers of the ice, after all, were precisely what made the poles such coveted prizes.

The drift ice around the *Belgica* was a labyrinth whose design changed hour by hour, depending on wind, currents, and temperature. To find his way through, de Gerlache would regularly climb to the crow's nest and scan the pack for leads and clearings, black veins in a field of white. Though the coast of Graham Land was out of sight, de Gerlache saw a persistent iceblink to the southeast—a milky glimmer over the horizon where the solid pack ice reflected against the clouds. To the seasoned polar explorer, the sky could be as informative as it was to the astronomer, but not for the same reasons. In fact, it helped if it was overcast. It then became a canvas on which an image of the sea was projected by reflection, like an inverted map. In addition to iceblinks, dark blots called "water skies" indicated the presence of open water beneath.

But the sky could just as easily deceive in the Antarctic. In his log entry for February 21, de Gerlache reported an astonishing sight on the horizon that afternoon. At the edge of the pack, to the south, he spied what looked for all the world like "a city by the sea," complete with a lighthouse. He soon recognized that the city was a strange type of mirage, and the lighthouse a "spire-shaped piece of ice," elongated by refraction, whose peak scintillated in the setting sun. The vision was known as a Fata Morgana, caused when a layer of uniformly cold air rests beneath a warmer layer, bending and distorting the light from distant objects. Icebergs could look like mountain ranges with impossibly steep peaks, or seem to hover over the horizon, or hang upside down from the sky like Edgar Allan Poe's heavenly cataract in solid form. Such mirages contributed to a general sensation that the pack was a weird, ever-changing, untrustworthy place, as if under a dark enchantment.

Sprawled across the open ocean, the icescape through which the men were navigating was strikingly different from what they had experienced in the channel. Though there were still scattered icebergs, much of the surrounding waters were covered in sea ice. Aside from both icebergs and sea ice consisting of frozen water, the two have little in common. Icebergs are born on land from fresh water; sea ice is formed in salt water. Freshwater ice is rigid and brittle; saltwater ice is relatively flexible. Icebergs can reach monumental proportions and rise high above (and extend even farther below) the surface; sea ice remains more or less flat. Icebergs frequently give off a bluish tint; much of the sea ice the men saw here appeared yellow, especially near the waterline. The *Belgica*'s scholars proposed various explanations for this color before Racovitza examined a chunk of sea ice and discovered it to be covered in phytoplankton—photosynthetic microorganisms that bloom in the water in midsummer, dye the water yellowish green, and coat the underside of the ice. The fauna, too, was different. The gentoo and chinstrap penguins had been left behind on the shores of Graham Land, and now two other penguin species abounded: the Adélie, a small black-headed breed with cartoonish white eyes, and the four-foot-tall, dignified emperor.

The officers and crew were starting to wonder where exactly de Gerlache was leading them. They were sailing through an empty map. The rare occasions on which Lecointe was able to glimpse the stars and fix the ship's position were greeted with joy. This was a disorientingly alien environment, neither sea nor earth, and to be able to point out their coordinates on a chart, even an empty one, made the men feel temporarily less lost. "In reality, however, we are as hopelessly isolated as if we were on the surface of Mars," wrote Cook, "and we are plunging still deeper and deeper into the white antarctic silence."

De Gerlache's log for this period is a chronicle of slow but inexorable constriction. On February 20, he noted, "The ship is caught between several large 'pans' that grip it and make all progress impossible." The ice would ensnare the *Belgica* for an hour or two before loosening its stranglehold.

On these occasions, some of the men would venture down onto the ice, but its firmness was not to be trusted. "The pans are closely packed," Cook wrote, "but in some places there are soft buffers of pulverised ice and snow, and these are dangerous to the traveler."

Such patches might look solid, and might even hold up to a few tentative stomps of the boot, but still give way under a man's weight. Falling into 30-degree water was an easy way to die. The body's instinctive response to cold shock is to gasp for air; if the head is submerged, the inhaling reflex might instantly fill the lungs with water. If a man survived the initial plunge, it was possible for the hole he fell through to drift away faster than he could catch up to it, leaving him clawing at the underside of the ice, staring helplessly at the faint light that filtered through the pack, until everything turned black.

On February 23, de Gerlache accompanied Cook on a short trip across the seemingly solid pack. The excursion was especially risky for the commandant, who'd never learned to swim. They walked unsteadily at first, probing every suspicious patch of snow. But the longer they traveled, the more confident their strides became. They had almost forgotten they weren't walking on land when the commandant stepped onto snow-covered slush and fell straight through into the frigid ocean. With feline agility, Cook snatched de Gerlache by the coat collar before his head reached the surface. The doctor jerked him out of the water. "I tore his collar, and disturbed his buttons, but I had the satisfaction of keeping him from a complete bath at a temperature six degrees below zero," wrote Cook.*

To avoid being trapped in such a treacherous environment, de Gerlache kept his ship on the periphery of the expanding pack, making tentative inroads when a lead opened up. The *Belgica,* which Cook had found so awkward and graceless beside the elegant yachts and ocean liners in the port of Rio de Janeiro, here impressed him with her feistiness. This was what she had been built for. If the ice closed in around her, she would fight and wriggle her way out, leaving behind flecks of wood as she scraped through. "She complains and groans and cracks and shivers," Cook wrote, "but she goes on cutting great pans of ice five feet thick, and pushing aside floes two hundred feet in diameter. She is ploughing the ice-littered sea like something animate."

---

* Either Cook here is referring to the air temperature or he is guilty of embellishment. Seawater freezes around −2 degrees Celsius, or 28.4 degrees Fahrenheit, so it could not have been much colder than that.

De Gerlache was tempting fate by continuing to push forward as winter approached. As the days grew shorter and colder, he found fewer and fewer openings into the pack. The idea of leaving Antarctica a day too soon tore at him. Despite the advantage of steam power, the *Belgica* was still short of Captain James Cook's southernmost latitude of 71°10′ south, reached more than a century earlier, in 1774, to say nothing of the standing farthest-south record of 78°09′30″ south, which James Clark Ross set in 1842. Both of those achievements had taken place on the other side of the globe. De Gerlache had already traveled farther south in the Bellingshausen Sea than any whaler or explorer before him. Yet that was no substitute for the irrefutable glory of a record latitude.

The commandant kept his eyes fixed on the horizon. Water skies to the south suggested that vast clearings lay in that direction, beckoning de Gerlache to stay just a little longer in hopes of reaching them.

Yet with each passing day, the ice seized the *Belgica* more frequently and for longer periods of time, to the distress of most of the men on board. On the night of February 23, de Gerlache canvassed the officers and scientists about their feelings regarding the possibility of wintering in the ice. According to Cook, "Everybody is opposed to it." Long ago, it had been Cook's plan to lead the first expedition to winter in Antarctica, but that would have been on the continent itself, not trapped in a seemingly limitless expanse of ice drifting aimlessly around the sea. Cook didn't believe that any good would come from getting stuck in the pack. Yet as the only man aboard to have endured a polar winter (in Greenland with Peary), Cook was also the only one remotely prepared for one.

Petrified at the prospect, the scientists objected most vehemently. None of them had signed up for a winter in the ice. They claimed to be concerned primarily for the preservation of their work: if the *Belgica* were to be crushed by the ice, they argued, Arctowski's collections and Racovitza's miniature museum would go with her to the bottom of the sea. But truly it was their own lives they were afraid of losing. They grew incensed at what they considered de Gerlache's foolhardy pursuit of glory.

"Unfortunately the scientists are very frightened," Amundsen

wrote that evening. The first mate was among the few who supported de Gerlache's determination to push as far south as possible
before turning back; he had contempt for those who cowered at the
thought, particularly Racovitza and Arctowski, who, in his mind,
should have been eager to study new lands. "They do not want to sail
further into the ice any longer. Why did we come here then? Wasn't
it to discover unknown territory? That cannot be done by staying at
the edge of the ice and waiting."

As long as the pack remained closed beyond its outer fringes, de Gerlache's deliberations about whether to winter in it had been largely
hypothetical. But on the morning of February 28, a violent storm
shattered the edge of the pack. Floes parted and leads opened up, in-
viting the *Belgica* in and presenting de Gerlache with a fleeting opportunity to pierce deep into the heart of the Antarctic sea ice.

The commandant was forced to make a decision. The ship had just
passed the 70th parallel, and the newly formed avenues offered him
the chance to blaze a southern course and perhaps set a new record.
But penetrating this far into the pack this late in the year meant almost certain entrapment, not for hours or days but for months or
possibly years. As the *Belgica* rolled among the jostling floes and gale-
force winds skirled through the rigging, de Gerlache mulled over his
options.

The stories of the *Terror*, the *Erebus*, and the *Jeannette* weighed on
his mind as he contemplated entering deep into the pack. To be ship-
wrecked in the Antarctic was an altogether more daunting proposition. Unlike in the Arctic, there would be no passing ships to rescue
them. Even if the *Belgica*'s whereabouts were known, which they
couldn't have been, the closest vessel was surely hundreds of miles
away. Nor would the men be likely to survive the journey across the
Drake Passage in the *Belgica*'s small, uncovered boats. And, since de
Gerlache had planned for only four men to winter over in Victoria
Land, the expedition had only four sets of clothes designed for extreme cold. If left to haul boats across the pack without the proper
apparel, many men would die.

But the safety of his men was not, in this moment, at the forefront of de Gerlache's mind. The commandant did not relish suffering for its own sake the way Amundsen did, had not familiarized himself with its clarifying grip. Yet he understood that glory followed risk, and that risk and suffering were generally inextricable. In addition to the grim stories of ships lost to the ice, he would have remembered the happier tales of captains who had wagered their men's lives and triumphed. On January 5, 1841, a few years before Franklin would lead the *Erebus* and the *Terror* to their doom in the Canadian Arctic, James Clark Ross had steered them into the pack at a similar latitude on the other side of Antarctica. Over the course of four days, the vessels forced their way through 134 miles of pack ice and emerged into open water on the other side, allowing Ross eventually to discover Victoria Land. What would the world make of de Gerlache if he was afraid to attempt what Ross had accomplished almost sixty years earlier?

The *Belgica* awaited orders, battered by waves, wind, and ice. As the intensifying tempest fractured the edge of the pack, it became too dangerous to remain in place. De Gerlache would have to either seek refuge from the waves by advancing deep into the ice or escape the storm-tossed floes and icebergs by retreating into the open ocean. His decision couldn't wait much longer—the expedition had already lost a man in less hazardous conditions.

Yet underneath all the rational arguments de Gerlache considered for leaving or remaining in the ice was a deep current of anxiety that his chance at glory was slipping away. The endless delays had already forced a cascade of changes to the expedition plan with which he remained profoundly uncomfortable. All told, the expedition would now have to take three years, rather than the two de Gerlache had first envisioned. The extension had become necessary because delays in South America—dismissals and desertions; the scientists' insatiable curiosity in Tierra del Fuego; the near shipwreck in the Beagle Channel; an unplanned detour to Isla de los Estados to refill their freshwater reserves—now prevented the *Belgica* from reaching Victoria Land before the winter sea ice blocked off all access. But the extra year posed its own problems. The expedition's 300,000-franc budget was barely sufficient for two years; in fact, there were only 16,000 francs left in the coffers. Considering how long it had taken de Gerlache to raise the sum, it was foolish to expect to raise another year's worth of funds in just one winter in South America. It would be hard enough to convince the expedition's financiers or the Belgian government to give him more money after he'd failed to reach one of his main objectives. Doing so from Chile or Argentina would be nearly impossible. Likewise, given his struggles in assembling, retaining, and disciplining his crew, de Gerlache could expect several of his men to jump ship at the *Belgica*'s first port of call rather than wait around all winter for the vessel to depart again.

The commandant could see it all falling apart. Without the money or the men to continue the expedition, de Gerlache would have to call an end to it, which would represent a national, personal, and familial humiliation. Scholars might be impressed by the *Belgica*'s scientific discoveries in the channel, but rocks, lichen, and a flightless midge were hardly enough to satisfy a Belgian public thirsting for national glory and vicarious adventure. Were the *Belgica* to retreat to South America, the reaction in the newspapers would likely be brutal and could influence what few financiers were still willing to back the expedition.

Despite its dangers—rather, *because* of its dangers—an imprisonment in the ice would solve each of those problems. It wouldn't cost any more money, de Gerlache wouldn't lose any men—at least not to desertion—and it would make for a dramatic story. If the *Belgica* expedition couldn't reach the South Magnetic Pole (not that year, at any rate), her men could establish another record by becoming the first to winter south of the antarctic circle. The perils involved were not a deterrent but rather an inducement: the more harrowing the story, the more people would want to read it, and the more publishers would pay for an exclusive account.

If this factored into de Gerlache's internal deliberations, it didn't make him any more cynical than other explorers. It was customary for expedition leaders to publish memoirs upon their return. This was in large part how they made their money, how they paid off creditors, and how they financed future expeditions. In the absence of easily accessible natural resources to exploit, stories were what polar explorers extracted from these barren icescapes. And the best stories weren't the ones in which everything went well.* While de Gerlache knew that trapping his men in the ice could lead to terrible suffering, he also had to have known that this suffering could be a down payment on future returns, financial and otherwise.

A swollen sea lifted floes up and sent them hurtling into one another and against the sides of the *Belgica*. Snow swirled upward to the tops of the masts. The commandant walked across the deck, adjusting his step to the swaying of the ship. He climbed the ladder to the bridge, where he found Lecointe. He took the captain aside, so the helmsman couldn't hear their exchange, and explained his intentions. The freezing wind muffled their voices. But when the commandant was done talking, the captain smiled. The two men shook hands vigorously, their grip loaded with meaning, an assurance that each would assume responsibility for the momentous decision.

Lecointe turned to the helmsman and shouted, "To the South!"

With sixty-mile-an-hour winds in her sails, the *Belgica* careened into the pack, speeding down rivers and lakes of open water. Horizontal torrents of sleet stung the sailors' faces. The visibility was so poor and the ship was going so fast that it was often necessary to maneuver at the last second to dodge icebergs or to avoid crashing too violently into the opposite bank of a clearing. At other times, a violent crash was required: if a barrier of ice blocked the way to further leads and clearings, de Gerlache called on the engineers for extra power in order to ram it. The *Belgica* tacked south into the night, the sound of ice striking wood growing ever more frequent.

"We enter, it seems, into another world," de Gerlache wrote. "Like

---

* Publishers of adventure narratives were bloodthirsty types. They tended to be more interested in expeditions that went awry than ones in which nobody suffered excessively. This is part of the reason James Clark Ross's groundbreaking voyage to Victoria Land in 1841 took years to be properly recognized. Upon his return, Ross submitted an account of his discoveries to the *Gazette*, the journal of the British Admiralty, which had championed the expedition. The submission was declined, as one of Ross's allies at the Admiralty explained, due to one member's "extraordinary crotchet that because there had been no bloodshed your despatch ought not to be in the Gazette." While de Gerlache never explicitly cited this logic as a rationale, it helps explain why explorers like him took so many risks, and why they tended to write in such a florid, unscientific style.

heroes of Scandinavian sagas, the terrible gods put us through super-natural trials."

Only de Gerlache and Lecointe knew that there would be no turning back. Everyone else was under the impression that they were entering the ice temporarily in order to seek refuge from the storm. It takes only a few miles for the force of waves traveling under dense ice to dissipate. Yet in the twenty-four hours since she had entered the pack, the *Belgica* had sailed almost eighty nautical miles, reaching latitude 71°31′ south, a record in the region and more than twenty miles beyond the 71°10′ south attained by Captain Cook. Nobody suspected that de Gerlache had decided, against everyone's wishes, to sail south at all costs, even if it meant condemning the expedition to imprisonment.

By the morning of March 1, the storm had abated and a clear sky revealed 360 degrees of whiteness. The *Belgica* plowed through this field with difficulty. The pathways of open water that allowed the ship to reach this far had closed behind her. Small clearings that appeared when the wind picked up in the afternoon offered no outlet. The ship struggled to make a few more miles of progress on March 2. The next few days were cold and calm, allowing young ice of a deep ochre color—rich with blooming phytoplankton—to form in the space between the floes, soldering the pack together.

Unable to proceed south, de Gerlache made a few half-hearted attempts to return to open ocean in the north, but it was too late. The pack was impenetrable. He surely knew the effort would be futile. If he'd had second thoughts about wintering in the pack, the time to turn back would have been just after the storm clouds parted, when the ice was still navigable.

De Gerlache's log entry for the afternoon of March 5 is poetically succinct: "Unfurled all the sails. The ship doesn't move." The *Belgica* was stuck fast, this time for good.

PART II

But not yet have we solved the incantation of this whiteness, and learned why it appeals with such power to the soul. . . . Is it that by its indefiniteness it shadows forth the heartless voids and immensities of the universe, and thus stabs us from behind with the thought of annihilation, when beholding the white depths of the milky way? Or is it, that as in essence whiteness is not so much a colour as the visible absence of colour, and at the same time the concrete of all colours; is it for these reasons that there is such a dumb blankness, full of meaning, in a wide landscape of snows—a colourless, all-colour of atheism from which we shrink?

—HERMAN MELVILLE, *MOBY-DICK*

CHAPTER 9

Icebound

WHEN THE SKIES CLEARED ON THE AFTERNOON OF MARCH 6 AND THE
sun shone on the solid pack, the *Belgica* found herself marooned in a
white Sahara, with just a few scattered oases of clear water. In his log,
de Gerlache described the pack as an "immense field of ice through
which not even the most powerful ship could force its way." Snowdrift had softened every protuberance, rounded out every hummock
and pressure ridge, forming mounds that mimicked dunes. The wind
had painted wavelike undulations in the snow, as it does in fine desert
sands. Icebergs strewn throughout the pack, locked in as tightly as
the *Belgica*, resembled distant rocks and mesas. This was, as Racovitza
phrased it, "a parody of terra firma," a landscape in eternal motion,
composed entirely of water.

There was no way of knowing how large the pack was. To find its
limits, the men would have to travel far from the ship, but to do so
would be to risk never finding the *Belgica* again. Also unknown was
the distance to land. A week earlier, Lecointe had estimated that the
coast of Graham Land had been about four hundred miles to the
east. But the ship had traveled more than a hundred miles south since
then. The map of Antarctica in that region remained blank: it had not
been determined whether there even *was* land to the south.

After dinner, nearly all of the men ventured onto the ice—some on
skis, some on foot—to explore their new surroundings. As they
strayed from the ship, they no longer heard the creaking of the timbers, the chug of the engine, the endless bustle of sailors in close
confinement, the thumping of floes against the hull, the whistling of
the wind, or the sloshing of waves. Aside from the crunch of their
own footsteps, they heard only the strains of the ice itself. "It emits

cries resembling human moans," Lecointe wrote. "This is the voice of young ice forming, the child saying its first words."

Seeing the ship held fast in the pack, the men realized—if not that day then slowly over the following days—that this was not an accident. The men were awakening to the fact that a decision had been made, one that had not been part of the expedition's original plan, and which filled them with trepidation.

Cook was alarmed, both in his capacity as physician and as the only man with experience of a monthslong polar night. He had implored de Gerlache not to risk an icebound wintering. Even Cook's wretched winter in the Arctic with Peary, during which he had almost died, was bound to seem pleasant by comparison with what he and his shipmates were about to confront. At least the Peary expedition had been able to build a comfortable cabin on a bed of solid rock that never threatened to split open or to crush the house to splinters at a moment's notice. The *Belgica*'s winter would be far more perilous.

If Cook was deeply critical of de Gerlache's decision, the scientists went further, accusing de Gerlache of outright betrayal. An enraged Arctowski reminded him that prior to the *Belgica*'s departure from Europe, the commandant had explicity assured them that he would not seek to winter in the ice and argued that he had no right to make such a consequential decision on behalf of the others.

Arctowski's misgivings were now shared by the majority of the men. "Most of us have assumed the responsibility of criticizing the management, and blame the director for entering the main body of the pack at the season's end," wrote Cook. The men's only hope was that there might still be a chance to escape. De Gerlache and Lecointe, sensing perhaps that they would need some plausible deniability of their intentions to quell the anger growing on board, did everything they could to make them believe that.

A few days into the *Belgica*'s imprisonment, de Gerlache convened the officers and crew and shared news of an encouraging development: according to Lecointe's celestial observations, after having reached latitude 71°19′ south two days earlier, the ship was now at a latitude of 71°18′ south, which meant that the pack was drifting north. With luck, it would push the *Belgica* toward its edge and eventually release her back into the open ocean. The gathering sighed with relief: disaster might yet be narrowly averted.

Shortly afterward, however, de Gerlache and Lecointe took Amundsen aside and informed the first mate that the coordinates they had just shared with the men had been false, "invented for the occasion," Amundsen wrote, "to keep up spirits." Lecointe had in fact observed a latitude of 71°26′ south, which meant that the *Belgica* was drifting to the *southwest* at a speed of three miles a day. Amundsen kept the secret to himself but made note of the dishonesty in his diary. "At present only the commander, Lecointe and myself are aware of this. The commander does not yet want to tell the others because they are already afraid of spending the winter here."

By keeping the fires burning in the engine room and pretending that the ship was drifting north, de Gerlache could assure them that he stood at the ready should an escape route to the north open up. But even this was a ruse. If de Gerlache and Lecointe kept the engine running, it was only in hopes of pursuing the *opposite* course: a dark water sky loomed over the southern horizon, suggesting that a vast open sea lay in that direction. Desperate to push even farther south, no matter the cost, de Gerlache nonetheless wondered how he and Lecointe would conceal the ship's bearing from the increasingly vocal critics of an icebound wintering. In jest, Lecointe offered to tamper with the compass so that "the helmsman would think he's heading north when, in reality, he will be sailing south."

In the end, however, all parties were disappointed. On March 8, the water sky disappeared from the horizon and the ice tightened, causing popping sounds to resonate across the pack. There would be no going south and no going north.

It took a week for the men to resign themselves to their predicament. In that time, the pack relaxed and contracted, like the heart of a living organism, but never fragmented enough to allow egress. De Gerlache endured the panicked outrage of his shipmates, who were by now convinced that he'd never had any intention of heading back north and had in fact consigned the *Belgica* to the ice on purpose.

Lecointe defended himself and the commandant vociferously against that charge. "It is *certain* that we *honestly* tried to return toward the north, but it is certain as well that de Gerlache and I were happy about the failure of our attempt."

And yet it would have been difficult for de Gerlache and Lecointe to dismiss entirely the omen that marked the imprisonment of the *Belgica*. On the very first day the ship was trapped in the ice, Bébé, the gentoo penguin picked up a month earlier, who had become a beloved presence on deck, stopped eating. Despite his shipmates' tender care, he died the following night "in horrible convulsions."

There was too much work to do for the men to wallow long in resentment and anguish. In the rapidly diminishing daylight hours of March and April, the crew went about preparing the *Belgica* for winter. The sails were furled and stored away, the propeller was lifted out of the water to protect it from the pressures of the ice, and the fires of the engine were allowed to die down. Among the most urgent tasks was to build a massive snowbank around the ship to insulate her against the cold. This encasement, sloping up to the gunwales, kept the interior of the *Belgica* at a comfortable 50 degrees despite a precipitous drop in the mercury outside. In mid-March, the thermometer indicated an exterior temperature of −5 degrees. Ice formed around the ropes in the rigging, lending it the look of a silver spiderweb.

At this latitude, by Lecointe's calculations, the sun would set for good by mid-May and night would last almost three months. Temperatures were sure to drop further in the coming weeks, though nobody knew by how much, since no man had ever lived through winter this far south. All the expedition could do was prepare for the worst.

On the morning of March 16, de Gerlache, Lecointe, and the third officer, Jules Melaerts, descended into the hold to reorganize provisions and equipment. They advanced into the obscurity carrying candles on small wooden planks. Their feeble glow caught the shadows of rats scuttling across the walkway, accompanied by the occasional squeak. The two-level hold, in the ship's midsection, was piled high with crates containing thousands of cans of food, hundreds of bottles of wine, a wide range of intricate scientific instruments, reservoirs of benzine, several barrels of alcohol for the preservation of zoological samples, construction materials, and other cargo.

The contents of the ship had been jostled around during the many storms and mishaps on the voyage down, and it took several days to rearrange them. The engine room lay between the main hold and another storeroom at the back of the ship. De Gerlache, Melaerts, Lecointe, and the crew worked in the storeroom by open candlelight, which was a remarkably dangerous proposition: the room was a fireworks display waiting to happen. In addition to the half ton of tonite sticks that de Gerlache had onboarded as his anti-ice insurance, which had already been tossed about, there were damaged cases of rifle shells and harpoon-gun cartridges, some of which had torn, releasing a carpet of gunpowder onto the floor. Since the slightest spark could quickly lead to a conflagration that would leave them without shelter, the men sawed a hole in the ice beside the ship to provide ready access to water and worked every day to keep it open.

Ensconced in ice and snow, stripped of her sails, the *Belgica* had ceased to be a functional ship and became simply a home for eighteen men. "We are no longer navigators," wrote de Gerlache, "but a small colony of prisoners serving their sentence." The crew's quarters were more comfortable than when the expedition had left Antwerp, now that there were fewer sailors sleeping in the bunks along the walls of the snug, V-shaped forecastle. Nestled belowdecks at the nose of the vessel, the room was illuminated by a square opening in the roof that cast a pillar of light onto a central table, and was frequently enlivened by Johansen's fine accordion playing and Van Mirlo's poor cornet playing. Farther sternward, still belowdecks, were the kitchen on the starboard side and a storeroom on the port side. Beyond those was a washroom in which the men were required to bathe once a week.

On the deck level amidships were Arctowski's and Racovitza's adjoining laboratories—facing port and starboard, respectively—each with an array of delicate glassware and instruments and a large window that flooded the cramped space with light. In March, the crew erected a shelter over the deck between the laboratories and the officers' quarters at the stern of the ship, using wood, sailcloth, and tar paper that had been reserved to build huts for the four-man party originally expected to winter on Victoria Land. The sound of hammering echoed across the pack. The structure served as a hangar in which the crew installed a blacksmith shop, as well as hooks and shelves on which to dry outdoor gear. It also contained a boiler— made out of parts taken from the now unnecessary steam engine—to melt snow for drinking water. To conserve coal, since the fires would have to burn continuously, Cook and the second mechanic, Max Van Rysselberghe, worked out a system to combine briquettes with seal blubber, which filled the ship with an acrid aroma that the men soon grew accustomed to.

There were two doors leading from the deck into the officers' quarters. The one to starboard opened onto de Gerlache's cabin, the largest and most comfortably appointed on the ship, with a carpeted floor, books piled neatly in the corner, a sizeable desk by the rectangular window, and a curtain separating the working area from the bed, forming a kind of suite.

The door to port opened onto a hallway that led to the wardroom, at the very back of the ship. Along the hallway were two cabins. One was shared by Amundsen and Melaerts, who quickly ran afoul of each other. (That the Norwegian Amundsen, as first mate, ranked higher than the Belgian Melaerts, the third officer, surely did not make for the most harmonious cohabitation.) The neighboring cabin was Lecointe's. The captain's space was so stuffed with scientific instruments, maps, reference books, and rolled-up charts that there was no room for furniture. When Lecointe needed a desk to write on, he lowered a piece of cardboard onto his bed. In lieu of a chair, he sat on a trapeze-like swing that he hung from the ceiling.

The wardroom, at the end of the hallway, was the most convivial space on the *Belgica*. The officers and scientists spent most of their leisure time around the large rectangular table at the center of the room, arguing, laughing, reading, or listening to the mechanical organ known as a coelophone; each man had his favorite tune. The walls were decorated with colorized photographs of Belgian cityscapes and an image of Fridtjof Nansen's glorious return to Kristiania aboard the *Fram*, in 1896. Cabinets on the port side contained a set of custom dishware and napkins decorated with a red anchor and a scroll spelling out "Belgica." (The officers and scientists made a pact that the dishware would be a wedding gift for the first of them to be married.) A long banquette ran along the back wall, next to the gun rack and beneath a bookshelf that held the expedition's small library. The collection included polar narratives, scholarly journals, popular magazines, and novels, but, as the Methodist-raised Cook noted, "only one Bible (which is kept under cover) and no prayer book." The absence of religious texts was deliberate. "The Belgians were Roman Catholic. The others were nominally protestant," Cook wrote, yet "there was no religious conflict. De Gerlache did all he could to encourage harmony with religious behavior, but in effect it was a non-religious assemblage."

On the starboard side of the wardroom was a door that led to the scientists' quarters. The cabin was long and narrow, with two sets of stacked bunks in line along the side of the ship. Cook and Arctowski shared the smaller set. Racovitza and Danco had to have their bunks extended by ten centimeters. The four men contorted themselves to squeeze through the space: there wasn't room to pass broadside between the bunks and the wall, and it was impossible to sit up in the morgue-like beds without hitting one's head. (To reduce the frequency of such impacts, Cook had progressively removed his bedding, his pillow, and his mattress, and preferred in the end to sleep in his reindeer-skin sleeping bag directly on the hardwood bunk.) There were two comically small sinks and a jug of fresh water, which the men drank out of test tubes. The cabin was dimly lit by two small portholes, only one of which could open, and the ceiling was black with soot from every candle the men had lit. The lack of ventilation exacerbated the stale stink that accumulated in the room over time, as did Danco's incessant pipe smoking and Cook's reluctance to bathe and to launder his clothes.

A solid wall separated the scientists' cabin from de Gerlache's personal water closet. Between the water closet and de Gerlache's quarters was the darkroom, in which Cook spent much of his free time developing photos.

He devoted the rest of his time to observing the behavior of his shipmates, more as an anthropologist, for the moment, than as a doctor. His experience among the Inuit and, more recently, the Fuegians had instilled in him a profound curiosity about his fellow man. Here, on board the *Belgica,* the only tribe for him to study would be his own. He was particularly keen to chronicle the way humans respond—physically and mentally—to extreme isolation, cold, stress, and fear. "Shipwreck, starvation and ultimate death by frost extreme was for us ever in the foreground," Cook wrote. In taking an interest in the well-being of every man aboard, crew and officers alike, Cook soon became the most popular member of the expedition.

The immediate outskirts of the *Belgica* took on the appearance of a small village. Cook, Amundsen, and Lecointe built two huts with corrugated metal roofs to serve as observatories for astronomical and meteorological research. Danco and his assistant, Dufour, erected one in which to conduct magnetic measurements, far enough from the ship that the metal on board would not influence the instruments' needles and skew the results.

At first the little colony bustled with activity, a constant coming and going, as the men sought comfort in work and routine. Scientists darted between the ship and their observatories. From morning to night, crew members cut blocks of snow to melt for drinking water. Over time, they had to travel farther and farther from the *Belgica* to find snow that hadn't been tainted by coal dust, animal carcasses, and the other detritus that accumulated around the ship.

The scientists pursued their daily observations, making the best of their predicament. With the help of the crew, they erected a kind of tripod made of three poles tented over the hole they'd made in the ice, on which they affixed a pulley that allowed them to lower a sounding lead or a fishing line. Racovitza dredged up a rich variety of sea life from deep below the ice: plankton, diatoms, krill, and a number of nightmarish fish, several of which were unknown to science and later named after members of the expedition, such as *Racovitzia glacialis, Gerlachea australis,* and *Nematonurus lecointei.* After each successful fishing session, Racovitza was occupied for days cataloging and preserving his catch.

Together with Amundsen, Racovitza experimented with various new designs for deep-sea ice-fishing tackle. For Amundsen, in particular, this was a period of learning. He had embarked on the *Belgica* not just to see the Antarctic but also to acquaint himself with all aspects of polar exploration. If he was to mount his own expedition, as he planned, he would need to acquire a functional understanding of zoology, meteorology, oceanography, magnetism, and astronomy— or at least learn how to gather data in these fields. In studying with the *Belgica*'s scientists, he was motivated less by curiosity than by ambition. He had been a mediocre student when confined to the classrooms of Kristiania, but he excelled in the university of the pack.

Arctowski, meanwhile, performed regular depth soundings and discovered that the ship was drifting over the lip of a shelf, which led him to conclude, correctly, that Antarctica consisted of one massive continent. He had been adamantly against wintering in the ice, but he now realized it provided him with the singular opportunity to study the pack ice and the long Antarctic night, both of which were as mysterious as the shape of the continent itself.

Together with his Polish assistant, Dobrowolski (who bunked with the sailors in the forecastle), he made hourly meteorological measurements, keeping a detailed log of ocean temperature, air temperature, barometric pressure, snowfall, and wind direction. Dobrowolski spent much of his time with his neck craned toward the sky to study cloud formations.

Every night, he and Arctowski hoped for the clouds to part so they could observe the aurora australis, or southern lights. While the aurora borealis, or northern lights, had been well documented by Arctic explorers and inhabitants, their antipodal counterpart had rarely been observed from such a high latitude. The twin phenomena were poorly understood at the time. In the late nineteenth century, the prevailing theory was that the luminous sheets that rippled through the polar night sky were akin to lightning—that is, they were caused by a buildup of electricity in the atmosphere.

A few fizzling glimmers had appeared earlier in the month, but the southern lights revealed themselves in their full splendor on the gloriously still and cloudless night of March 14, about a week into the *Belgica*'s imprisonment. The men spent hours in awe at the otherworldly spectacle, admiring the ribbons of undulating light as they grew in intensity. Arctowski and Dobrowolski, who had only read of such things, scrutinized the auroras, notebooks in hand.

Seeking a moment of solitude as well as a chance to test his resistance to the cold, Cook decided to view the aurora from off the ship, out on the ice about fifty yards away. Despite the temperature of -4 degrees, he thought the distance would help to "better see the new attraction." Trudging out around midnight, he found what looked like a good spot. He stripped off his clothes, quickly slipped into his reindeer-skin sleeping bag, and cinched its hood tightly around his face. Once he'd squirmed into a suitably comfortable patch of snow, he lay on his back and fixed his eyes on the heavens. "At first my teeth chattered and every muscle of my body quivered," he later wrote, "but in a few minutes this passed off and there came a reaction similar to that after a cold bath."

Cook described the aurora as "a trembling lace-work, draped like a curtain, on the southern sky. Various parts were now dark, and now light, as if a stream of electric sparks illuminated the fabric. The curtain seemed to move in response to these waves of light, as if driven by the wind which shook out old folds and created new ones, all of which made the scene one of new interest and rare glory."

Oddly, by invoking wind and waves of light, Cook's poetic description came closer to an accurate explanation of auroras than most scientific theories of the day. These phenomena are, in fact, driven by solar wind, a flow of charged particles ejected violently from the sun. This fast-moving plasma, especially intense during periods of heightened solar activity, travels through space until it slams into the earth's magnetosphere, whereupon it follows the lines of the planet's magnetic field down to the poles. When the particles collide with oxygen and nitrogen atoms in the earth's upper atmosphere, the agitated atoms emit radiation that we perceive as streamers of red, green, violet, or white light.

Lying on his bed of snow, watching the light dance, Cook let his mind drift. He likely thought of previous times he had witnessed such a spellbinding display, as a member of Peary's 1891–92 expedition to northern Greenland. Back then, on a night illuminated by a magnificent aurora borealis, Cook strolled along the rocky seashore with an Inuit elder named Sipsu and asked his companion what he thought caused the northern lights.

"These dark lights," Sipsu offered in response to Cook's question about the aurora, "are Eskimo lights, indicating the movement of the people who have passed beyond the earth. Perhaps they are trying to talk to us. What do you think about it?" Six years later, at the opposite end of the world, Cook might have thought of the dead in his life. Could his late wife and child be leaving behind these spectral trails? Could it be Wiencke?

At around two in the morning, Captain Lecointe was on deck pointing a telescope at the sky—not toward the aurora, which had begun to fade, but in the direction of Jupiter. Within the next half hour, he expected to observe an eclipse of Io, the planet's first moon. Discovered by Galileo in the early seventeenth century, the four Jovian satellites that became known as the Galilean moons had long served as a kind of celestial clock. The timing of their eclipses was predicted so precisely that navigators could set their chronometers by them and thereby determine a ship's longitude. (Such periodic adjustments were essential: an error of just a few seconds in an astronomical observation could throw off one's geographic positioning by miles.) Aiming a telescope at such a minute target was virtually impossible from the rocking deck of a ship at sea, but the icebound *Belgica* was as stable as land. Through his eyepiece, Lecointe could see a small white dot approach Jupiter's massive, marbled face. As soon as the dot disappeared behind the planet, Lecointe would alert Dobrowolski, who sat inside the ship by an open window with the chronometers, awaiting the captain's signal.

Lecointe could feel his extremities go numb. He took his eye off Jupiter for a moment and paced the deck to warm himself. As he looked out onto the pack through the cloud of his own breath, he noticed a dark, oblong shape writhing on the ice just fifty yards from the ship. *An adventurous seal,* he told himself. Lecointe had a hunter's instinct. He rushed into the wardroom and returned with a rifle, loaded it, and prepared to shoulder it.

Cook was unable to sleep. He had turned on his side, and a glacial breeze was blowing in his face, caking his beard with frost. His perspiration had turned to ice and fused his head and neck to his hood.

The entire mass was frozen solid, and the slightest movement caused him shooting pain. When he tried to swivel away from the wind, it felt as if someone were yanking his hair out. He was comfortable enough as long as he remained motionless on his back, even if this allowed the helmet of ice to harden around his head. Staring at the Southern Cross directly above, he lost himself in the night sky, unable to see in his peripheral vision that his captain was watching him carefully while raising a rifle and getting ready to fire.

Before pulling the trigger, Lecointe decided to quickly check on the eclipse. The seal looked to be in no hurry, after all, and the moon would enter Jupiter's umbral cone imminently. He put the gun down and looked through the telescope—just in time to watch the satellite vanish. The captain called out to Dobrowolski to set the chronometers, and was so happy to have successfully performed the observation that his instincts became "as peaceful as they had been bellicose a few minutes earlier." He unloaded the rifle and ordered a sailor to place it back in the rack. "I continued to quietly observe the last vestiges of the polar aurora, all while occasionally casting a protective glance towards the seal, now immobile on the pack."

Cook was awoken a few hours later by a band of curious penguins, pecking at the shell of ice around his head. When he stirred, they brayed and scattered. He shuffled off his sleeping bag and hood at the cost of a few clumps of hair, threw on his clothes, and returned to the ship. It was only then that Lecointe learned how close he had come to shooting the expedition's doctor, and that Cook discovered how narrowly he had avoided being killed for his hide and blubber.

Whenever a new lead would open up in the ice, the officers and crew would hunt seals and penguins. Dispatching a seal was ugly business, typically requiring multiple bullets. Massacring a penguin was particularly difficult, and not just because the birds looked so endearingly human. "One day, it happened that four of us pursued one [penguin], who was courageous to the point of heroism," Lecointe recounted. "The hunt lasted more than an hour, and when the poor creature finally fell, it had endured three bullets from a revolver, two bullets from a rifle, without counting numerous blows with a cudgel. We were, ourselves, exhausted." Van Mirlo would later discover a less tiring method: blaring his cornet from the prow of the ship, he had the effect of an Antarctic pied piper. More enthused by his horn play-ing than his shipmates were, Adélie penguins waddled right up to the *Belgica,* where they were brutally ambushed. "It seems that penguins are musical animals," Amundsen observed.

Given that few on board had the stomach to try the meat of either animal, hunting served for the moment primarily as exercise. But while it kept their bodies active, the campaign of killing weighed on the men's souls. Troubled by the cruelty of the endeavor, the hunters reassured themselves that it wasn't for naught: every kill provided Racovitza with fresh study material.

"One must see Racovitza, after these days of carnage, the apron around his neck, a large knife in his hand, eviscerating the still-warm cadavers to examine their stomachs, their intestines, even remnants of food!" Lecointe wrote. "And what joy when he discovers an em-bryo! He takes it away as if it were a priceless treasure."

Animals were stripped of their blubber and hides, organs were left out for the petrels to feast on, and muscle was carved out and covered with snow, as an emergency food cache. With temperatures averag-ing around 15 degrees throughout the austral autumn, the entire pack functioned as an icehouse.

In late March, the winds blew without end. "We are indescribably tired of these seemingly ceaseless storms," Cook wrote. For several days toward the end of March, Lecointe wrote, "snow fell almost constantly in a fine powder that the gusts swept with violence and that penetrated everywhere, under clothing, in the observatories through the tiniest fissures, in the cabins through the smallest joints of doors and windows."

Fresh precipitation piled up on the snowbanks that the crew had built to insulate the *Belgica.* Soon a massive white mound engulfed the ship. When the clouds finally dissipated, the pack was unrecognizable. "The topography about has changed much under the influence of the drift-snow during the last storm," Cook wrote. "About the ship there are huge drifts of snow which make it difficult to disembark. The old hummocks are reduced to little rounded hills, the small crevasses are filled with new ice and snow, and the entire pack of restless floes near the bark seems more like one homogeneous mass. Everything is restful and motionless, and covered with the white silence of death."

The comings and goings slowed as the men tired of outdoor work. De Gerlache began to worry that his idle crew would once again grow restless and resentful. Cook, meanwhile, became concerned about the pernicious physical and mental effects of inactivity. He led regular skiing excursions across the pack, usually to a nearby iceberg and back. But de Gerlache had established a firm rule: the men were forbidden to stray more than a few miles from the *Belgica* lest they lose sight of her masts and fail to find their way back. In the constantly shifting ice, cracks could suddenly form and floes could break off into small, enclosed clearings at any moment, casting wandering expeditioners adrift. "Landmarks" could not be relied upon: a hummock that one noticed on the way out could be obscured by snow or fog or otherwise transformed by ice pressure by the time one returned. This limited range of movement only worsened the oppression of monotony and confinement that was starting to set in as, day in and day out, the men saw the same faces at the same table, played the same songs on the coelophone, performed the same tasks, and looked out over the same field of ice.

The intellectual stimulation the scientists derived from their work kept them from sombering into apathy, but the cold was making their work difficult. Sitting motionless for hours on end in their poorly insulated observatories, Lecointe and Danco were starting to feel the pinch of frostbite and endured other cold-related mishaps. Danco returned to the ship one day with, as Cook described it, "a frosted foot, and with a piece of skin, torn from his eye, frozen to the metal of the eye-piece of his instrument." Lecointe, having lost a few eyelashes in the same manner, would from then on cover the metal parts of his sextant with flannel.

The cold hampered the scientists' work in other ways, making their world smaller and smaller with each passing day. The mercury bath in Lecointe's artificial horizon—a device that allows for sextant measurements even when the horizon is obscured—occasionally froze solid, indicating a temperature below −37 degrees. Tools with rotating parts, such as sextants and telescopes, would seize up as the grease that lubricated them thickened and hardened; kerosene lamps would go out in the slightest wind, and oil lamps wouldn't work at all, making it impossible to read instruments' indicators in the darkness of the observatories. Snowdrift infiltrated every crevice, rendering useless some of the more sensitive instruments, such as the hair hygrometer (which relies on the moisture-retaining property of human hair—or occasionally horsehair—to measure ambient humidity). The marine chronometers that Lecointe relied on to time his celestial readings were likewise too delicate to transport from the ship to the hut, or to withstand the extreme cold of the captain's observatory. To solve this problem, Cook, Amundsen, and the Norwegians Tollefsen and Johansen installed a telegraph line between the hut and Lecointe's cabin on the *Belgica*. When Lecointe performed his observations, Dobrowolski sat by the chronometer and wired time signals to the observatory. The system, hooked up to a small battery, functioned remarkably well and established a minor record: the southernmost electrical communication in history.

But the most damaging effect of the cold was to keep the men confined inside the ship. As harsh as the deep cold could be, it was preferable in many ways to slightly warmer temperatures. The men's favorite temperature was around a crisp −15 degrees, when all the moisture was frozen out of the air. As the thermometer crept up from there, humidity seeped into every fiber of clothing and bedding, with the paradoxical effect of making the men feel colder. "We try in every possible way . . . to eliminate moisture," Cook wrote, "but our success is small." When the men reached their hands under their beds, they chipped off icicles that tinkled to the ground. "If the mattress is removed every nail is found to be covered with ice," Cook wrote.

These discomforts added to a swell of complaints: about the cold, about the wind, about the stultifying monotony. In the darkening days of autumn, crew members began shirking their duties, some sleeping in, others flatly refusing to work, in defiance of de Gerlache's Christmas pronouncement: *You are not allowed to be tired. When you are "sick," it will be different: I will give you rest.* The men were now somewhere between sick and tired.

De Gerlache was nervous about another breakdown in discipline. This time, he wouldn't be able to kick unruly sailors off the ship or pay them off with £1 sterling. He felt there was little he could do to address their grievances. Just as he had largely delegated disciplinary duties to Lecointe and Amundsen, he left it to Cook to confront the growing malaise.

It was a wise decision. Cook could read human beings as adroitly as the commandant could read winds and currents. When he listened, his transfixing gray-blue eyes exuded empathy. While some of the other officers and scientists tended to look down on the residents of the forecastle, Cook developed a profound respect for the crew, a sense of kinship grounded in American egalitarianism and his own hardscrabble youth. "We are inclined to believe that the volume of brain substance and the volume of brain work of a highly cultured man is far in excess of the common worker," he wrote. "But my observations on the Belgica proved to me that this was not true. . . . The common laborer who cuts snow blocks or lays bricks has passing through his brain in each day as many, perhaps more individual impressions than the professional man."

He earned the affection and gratitude of all on board and, in turn, felt for them something like the love of a protector. The doctor was determined to keep his shipmates from falling into a depression and took it upon himself to keep their spirits up and their minds occupied. In late March, Cook interviewed every man on the *Belgica* at length to ferret out the sources of growing discontent. Working his way around the ship, he asked each sailor and officer a series of questions—"What do you miss most from home?" "Whom or what do you dream about most often?"—and jotted down their answers diligently in his notebook.

The doctor's survey ingratiated him further with his shipmates, his very concern providing a measure of relief. Cook's inquiries revealed two main complaints. One was the absence of female companion-ship. From the breathlessness of his report, one gets the sense that Cook was not a dispassionate observer. "We are hungry for letters from mothers, sisters, and other men's sisters," he wrote, "and what would we not give for a peep at a pretty woman?" Sexual frustration was a ship-wide affliction. Even members of the crew, less likely to speak frankly of such matters with an officer, were candid with Cook: "Two or three, in lone dark corners and in tears, slyly admit that a few moments with the girls of their hearts would be more to their liking."

The other, more urgent cause of dissatisfaction was the canned food the men now depended on almost exclusively. Although not of poor quality by the canning standards of the late nineteenth century, it had after many months become offensively insipid to most palates. The soft, colorless gobs the men found on their plates every night bore little resemblance to whatever dish was promised on the can's label. Particularly revolting to most were *kjøttboller*, the spongy meat-balls that de Gerlache had purchased in Norway when the *Belgica* was docked in Sandefjord, and which formed a substantial part of the ex-peditioners' diet.

The men "desire first some substantials for the stomach," Cook discovered. "Fresh food, such as beefsteaks, vegetables, and fruits are their foremost wants." Even de Gerlache, who had personally picked out each item in the larder to ensure the greatest variety of foods, admitted that "this variety resides largely in the names." The men blamed the unappetizing food not only on de Gerlache's selections but also on his hardworking attendant, Louis Michotte, who had gamely taken on kitchen duties after two cooks had been forced to disembark in South America. (Van Mirlo had briefly filled the role in the interim.)

Despite having cited cooking—alongside fencing and sharp-shooting—among his skills in his application, the former legionnaire was hopeless behind a stove. "He prepared almost every dish in the same manner," Lecointe complained: "with a little water or with a lot of water, depending on the desired consistency." Worse still, de Ger-lache acknowledged, "Michotte was ambitious." He was particularly proud of his "tarts"—inedible slabs of unleavened dough onto which he emptied a pot of jam—and would look on eagerly as his shipmates attempted to masticate them. "His soups are full of 'mystery,'" wrote Cook, "and the 'embalmed meats' are on every tongue for condemnation." In an effort to vary the flavors, Michotte would often mix the cans together into a nondescript stew, which was somehow less than the sum of its parts. De Gerlache, having himself been assigned to the kitchen as a young sailor, had a soft spot for the lad. "Poor Michotte!" he wrote. "He was so full of zeal that we closed our eyes to his lack of culinary aptitude."

Though the men made nightly jokes about the contents of their plates, the general disgust for the food soon turned into a serious crisis. Life in the pack offered very few things to look forward to. Mealtimes should have been among them. Instead, they were dreaded. Eating the equivalent of prison food was to the men a nightly reminder that they were trapped, and it had an incalculable effect on morale.

Longing for something fresh, fibrous, and toothsome, several of the men resolved to try the penguin meat they had been stockpiling. They thawed out the penguin steaks that Racovitza had carved out and entrusted them to Michotte. They weren't the first explorers to try penguin meat, but reviews by previous adventurers were decidedly mixed. In Tierra del Fuego in the late sixteenth century, Francis Drake and his men gorged on Magellanic penguin, which they considered "a very good and wholesome victual." James Clark Ross tasted emperor penguin in 1841 during his expedition to Victoria Land. "The flesh is very dark," he reported, "and of a rank fishy flavour." Penguin was not added to the menu.

In Michotte's inexpert hands, the meat was perhaps even more offensive. It tasted somehow like both fish *and* fowl, with a gamey tang. "If it is possible to imagine a piece of beef, an odoriferous codfish, and a canvas-back duck, roasted in a pot, with blood and cod-liver oil for sauce," Cook wrote, "the illustration will be complete." For a full impression, one must also imagine the tenacious reek of guano that clung to the birds. Most of the *Belgica*'s men vowed that their first morsel of penguin would be their last. De Gerlache, who according to Cook felt insulted that his men would even consider eating such a repugnant meat as an alternative to the canned food he had so carefully picked out, refused to touch it. Danco, the commandant's loyal friend, said he'd rather die than eat it.

Only one man seemed to be not merely scraping along but fully enjoying himself. For Roald Amundsen, the deprivations of the pack were a source not of pain but of elation. "The food is excellent in every way," he wrote in his diary. As a Norwegian, he was well acquainted with *kjøttboller* and devoured them with relish—even as he jokingly assured his fellow officers that they were made of cat meat, complete with ground-up hair, teeth, and bone. He also took a liking to their yet more reviled cousins, *fiskeboller,* fish balls, which were served on Fridays but were typically eaten only on a lost bet. As for penguin meat, Amundsen pronounced it "the most delicious steak you could wish for." He recommended simply searing the cutlets in a pan with oleomargarine. He genuinely enjoyed the taste, but he must also have savored the nauseated expressions on his shipmates' faces as he scarfed the meat down. Since his adolescence, when he held the doomed explorer John Franklin in reverence, Amundsen had equated suffering with accomplishment, to the point where it didn't feel like suffering anymore. From that perspective, bad food was a mere trifle.

Nor did the absence of women cause him terrible grief. He doesn't seem to have had much of a romantic life before embarking on the *Belgica.** Sexual conquests were of less interest to him than geographical ones. He found little use in activities that didn't help him fulfill his polar ambitions. Every second he spent in the pack brought him closer to his goal.

"It is my greatest desire, when spring comes, to head southwards with a kayak for two and a sledge," he wrote in early April. (He doesn't specify who the other man in his kayak would be, but after

---

*One of Amundsen's biographers, Tor Bomann-Larsen, suggests that Amundsen had an affair with his landlady in Antwerp—until he came home to find her dead of an apparent suicide. But Bomann-Larsen provides no evidence for this.

their experience on the cliffs of Brabant Island, he would surely have preferred Cook, if it wouldn't have meant depriving the expedition of a physician.) His plan—more like a daydream—was to travel south for six weeks, hauling provisions in a sledge over the pack ice and transferring them to the kayak whenever water blocked his progress, before making his way back to the *Belgica*. Underscoring the audacity of what he contemplated, he added, "With such a venture you have to be prepared that you may not find the ship again."

That realization only emboldened Amundsen. Within the same diary entry, as if goading himself on, he revised his plan: "Well, in that case we will travel southwestwards, as long as the season permits. As winter approaches we will establish ourselves in the best possible way on top of a suitable iceberg. . . . Once we have set up camp we will stock up for the winter: penguins and seals. The following spring we will once again travel southwestwards until we find land. If all the land we find is South Victoria Land then we will sail northwards from there with the kayak and from the northern islands we will then try to reach Australia. This would of course take a number of years but I do not doubt that it is possible."

Never mind that traveling by kayak from Victoria Land to Australia was assured suicide, or that camping on an iceberg was at best illadvised. Scrawling furiously in his cabin by candlelight, Amundsen was more focused than ever on writing his own legend. When, a few weeks later, an iceberg in a nearby clearing suddenly flipped on its side with a tremendous roar, Amundsen wrote, "I will not allow my plan to spend the winter on an iceberg to be influenced by this."

Amundsen's spirits were raised even further when his cabinmate, the churlish third officer, Jules Melaerts, requested to be transferred to the forecastle, among the sailors. "We did not get on well together so I shall not deny that I am pleased about this," Amundsen wrote. Melaerts's departure not only left the Norwegian first mate with his own cabin, but also improved the atmosphere in the wardroom considerably. "He did not have a good relationship with anyone aft," Amundsen wrote. "There are now seven of us. I do not know six other people who are as friendly and pleasant. I feel good here." As he wrote that line, Amundsen caught himself. If suffering was tanta-

mount to accomplishment, then pleasure was a form of compla-
cency. He added: "Almost too good."

Amundsen could surely tell that his high spirits made him an exception on board. And even he had little idea of what to expect in the
coming weeks. Only two things were certain: it would get colder, and
it would get darker.

CHAPTER 10

The Last Sunset

As the days stretched on, the view from Cook's soot-blackened porthole hardly changed. The same distant icebergs remained more or less in the same positions relative to the ship, as stable and reliable as the church steeples of neighboring towns. Yet this reliability was an illusion. The whole pack was moving erratically at the rate of several miles a day. The *Belgica* was no longer sailing, but she was still roaming the ocean on a course beyond her control. "There has been no fixed point to indicate our drift, and we cannot see that we pass through the water because the entire horizon, the countless fields and mountains of ice, slide with us at the same rate of speed," Cook wrote. The doctor began to worry that the men's minds would likewise come untethered and drift into fear and insanity.

Not only was the pack moving, but the shape and solidity of the ice itself were ever fluctuating. The pack looked like land but behaved like water—only more slowly. The forces that affected it, that subtly changed its topography over time, were the same forces that stirred the ocean: wind and current. Neither of these forces was consistent. When they came from contrary directions, they pulled at the ice with the violence of a medieval torture device. Underwater currents had more of an effect on deep-keeled icebergs than on surface ice and could send these hulking masses plowing recklessly through the pack.

Sea ice, typically only a few feet thick, was more easily influenced by wind, which determined nearly every aspect of the *Belgica*'s surroundings. "Our first question in the morning," Cook wrote, "is 'how is the wind?'" Even a light breeze could gain purchase on the pack and set the whole thing in motion. A storm could crack it up, creating a web of thin, treacherous crevasses and a few small clearings, but never enough to allow the ship to escape. A reprieve from the wind could cause the ice to relax and old fissures to suddenly open up again. Conversely, wind that blew from any direction for a sustained amount of time compressed the pack, pushing floes together with such force that barricades of rubble ice shot up along their seams. These pressure ridges rose so quickly and violently they seemed alive, and the sounds caused by the grinding of ice on ice—from deep, ominous moans to high-pitched squeals—only confirmed that impression. A ridge could within hours reach two stories high—a vast wall of ice springing into existence from nothing but the movement of air. Every creak of the *Belgica*'s timbers caused the men to shudder and reminded them that they were at the mercy of the wind.

Incessant, shrieking Antarctic gales threatened to obliterate the men's shelter and shatter the very ground they walked on. "This polar underpart of the world is decidedly unfit for human life," wrote Cook, "for it is seemingly the part which receives the kicks of the angered spirits as the globe passes through space." The relentless wind hounded the men, screamed their fate back at them. With few obstacles in its way, it frequently blew so hard across the icy plain that the expeditioners were confined to the ship for days on end.

Aside from wind and current, there was a third element that could dramatically alter the shape of the pack, or at least men's perception of it: light. On the rare clear days, color exploded across the blank, white canvas. Such brief delights inspired florid descriptions.

"The plain, as if powdered with diamonds, sparkles in the clear sun," wrote de Gerlache. "Icebergs and hummocks flaunt their silver crests and project behind them diaphanous shadows, of a blue so pure they appear to have been stripped from the sky. Channels trace winding paths of lapis-lazuli, and, on their shores, young ice takes on an aquamarine tint. Towards the evening, imperceptibly, the shadows change, turn a tender pink, a pale mauve, and, behind each iceberg, it seems that a passing fairy has hung her veil of gauze. Slowly, the horizon is colored in pink, then in yellow-orange, and, when the sun has disappeared, a crepuscular glimmer persists, fading deliciously into the dark blue sky in which countless stars scintillate."

The pack was a playground for light. The sun's rays glanced off the earth at a low angle, bent and twisted through the atmosphere, and refracted in the icy air. Mirages, fogbows, sun dogs, mock moons, and other tricks of the light were so common the men learned not to trust their eyes. On windless days, when suspended ice crystals drifted slowly through the air, they formed prisms that refracted light and made it seem as if there were multiple suns in the sky. The most spectacular such illusion, known as a parhelic circle, caused four false suns to appear at the cardinal points of a halo around the real sun. When conditions were perfect, two perpendicular lines of light, vertical and horizontal, connected these illusory orbs, intersecting in the center to form an enormous, talismanic cross. The sight filled even a man as scientifically inclined as Lecointe with reverential awe. "You feel that there is something else besides the earth," the captain described. "This sort of religiosity makes you sense a God, not a specific God, but a vastly superior being."

Antarctic light deceived in less enchanting ways when the sun was out of sight. In cloudy or foggy weather, which is to say most of the time, the pack was a monochromatic wasteland. The gray of the sky melded into the gray of the ice, blurring out the horizon. As daylight waned, distances became particularly hard to gauge. Without shadows to delineate contours, "nearly all irregularities were obscured or distorted," Cook wrote. "Huge hummocks, ten to twenty feet high, were not observed until we stumbled against them. Small elevations, with sharp angles, sometimes produced a mirage like that of an iceberg at a great distance. We would glide along leisurely on *ski* and suddenly find that we had crossed this huge obstacle,—in reality only a few inches in height."

Whether truthful or deceptive, light defined the contours of the men's world, yet each day a little more of it slipped away. As nights lengthened and temperatures dropped with the approach of the winter solstice, the elements that brought color and variety to the *Belgica*'s surroundings were quickly vanishing. Leads and clearings froze over completely, and the pack became a formless sprawl. The men heard the exhalations of whales less frequently, penguins stopped visiting, and the ice would soon grow too thick for seals to carve out breathing holes or to see their prey in the darkness underwater. Life seemed to be following light on the way out.

. . .

De Gerlache was keenly aware of the dangers the encroaching monotony would visit on the men's souls, as days and nights bled together and scrambled their sense of time. In an effort to stave this off, he established a calendar of special occasions for the men to look forward to. Every conceivable cause for celebration—birthdays, anniversaries, national holidays from the many countries represented on board—was fêted as lavishly as food stocks permitted. "It is a slow week," wrote Cook, "when we have not succeeded in having at least one day set aside as a period of special feeding, followed by a flow of champagne." (Among the rare advantages of pack life was that the champagne was chilled to perfection.) The men eagerly awaited these events—if not for Michotte's overambitious feasts, at least for the merriment.

Another beloved monotony-breaking ritual was the presentation of Racovitza's daily cartoon. In addition to his skill at anatomical drawing, the zoologist was a scathing caricaturist with an eastern European fondness for the absurd and a scatological streak. Though bawdy and puerile, Racovitza's pencil sketches were an unfiltered take on life aboard the *Belgica,* a chronicle of the men's frustrations and inside jokes.

Taken together, Racovitza's cartoons formed a kind of serialized farce, an opera buffa on ice. Its main character was the expedition's geologist and meteorologist, Henryk Arctowski. Racovitza imagined his fellow scientist as a buffoonish magus named Artocho, with a long beard and a bulbous backside that became a character in its own right. (Sample cartoon: Artocho's posterior acts as a barometer, inflating in wind, sagging in rain, shriveling in dry weather, and flatulating wildly in a storm.) The twenty-six-year-old Arctowski was the most self-serious man on board, which made him an irresistible target to Racovitza.*

The cartoonist showed Artocho solemnly observing a magnificent

---

* Racovitza would routinely pull pranks on Arctowski. In one instance, he switched out lard for petroleum jelly at the dinner table and watched with glee as Arctowski absent-mindedly swallowed several pieces of bread slathered with it.

aurora borealis that spells out M-E-R-D-E (shit), or pontificating to a band of indifferent penguins, one of whom sprays him with guano.

Aside from Artocho and the odd *kjøttboller* joke, the salient theme of Racovitza's cartoons was sexual frustration. In a cartoon titled *The Pleasures of Mechelen,* he shows Danco lying in a gutter in his hometown, looking up the skirt of a urinating woman. Racovitza even created a mock-up of the front page of an imaginary newspaper about life on the *Belgica* called *The Ladysless South.*

Surprisingly, the man who had the hardest time adjusting to the ribaldry and sexual banter was Cook. As the lone Yankee, he might have been expected to have a taste for vulgarity, but in the beginning Lecointe considered him "the most rigid American the New World had ever birthed." Having grown up penniless, Cook had long ago adopted a genteel affect to better fit into the social circles he hoped to join. And unlike the Belgians, he rarely drank excessively and always kept his wits about him.

Cook had been particularly put off by his fellow officers' penchant for awful, salacious, trilingual puns—in part, presumably, because he didn't understand them. "Never show yourself in New York with such manners," he had huffed. But here on this lost ship, thousands of miles from polite society, his refined airs gradually fell away. The doctor understood that humor—coarse as it may be—was an invaluable defense against gloom. "Cook got offended less frequently," Lecointe noted. He "enjoyed some of our jokes, became himself rather amusing, and in the end fully took part in our silliness." Soon enough, he was making atrocious puns of his own, barreling heedlessly through the language barrier.

Nevertheless, despite his own healthy libido, Cook discouraged the unending discussions of sex around the wardroom table, deeming it unhealthy for the men to fixate on something they couldn't have. Determined to "wet-blanket this talk about girls," he warned the officers and scientists one day that the polar night could have on them "the same effect as castration has on the steer"—that it might render them sterile and impotent. As his shipmates listened aghast, Cook claimed that the sooner they abandoned all residual thoughts of women, the better off they would be. "Amundsen and I have passed this icy phase of sex inhibition," he added. The Norwegian first mate, who was perfectly comfortable with the monastic life of a polar explorer, played along.

If Cook had simply intended for the men to change the subject, his plan backfired dramatically. On April 7, while rummaging through papers, one of the men unearthed several volumes of an illustrated magazine, donated by an Antwerp patron, containing pinups of famous Parisian socialites, actresses, and cabaret performers. The discovery inspired the organization of an elaborate beauty contest in absentia. "Nearly five hundred pictures were selected," Cook wrote, "representing all kinds of poses and dress and undress, and anatomical parts of women noted as types of beauty." Categories ranged from the chaste—"Irreproachable character," "Grace, personified," "Shapely hands (tapering fingers)"—to the mildly libidinous— "Mouth (Cupid's bow)," "Supple waist," "les jambes" (legs). There followed three days of heated electioneering among the officers and scientists (the crew was not invited to participate). Arctowski was tapped to officiate, under the mocking title of "Artocho the First, King of the Ice."

The winners were announced after a well-lubricated dinner on April 10. The two frontrunners were the dancer and muse Cléo de Mérode (immortalized by Toulouse-Lautrec among other artists) and Clara Ward (the Detroit-born heiress who married a Belgian prince and left him for a penniless Hungarian violinist). A boisterous argument ensued. Lecointe, an advocate for Ward, sought to wrangle Cook's support for the American candidate, since the doctor had the deciding vote. "Cook is utterly befuddled," wrote Lecointe. "He doesn't understand a word of what we're saying; it's a great advantage for me: it makes him incorruptible! What's more, sparing neither his efforts nor his lungs, he yells out over and over, '[Number] 209, Clara, first prize!'" Her supporters cheered in triumph, de Mérode's in outrage. Playing the role of peacemaker, de Gerlache popped open some champagne, and the gathering toasted vigorously: "To all the beauties!"

Lecointe stumbled to the coelophone, inserted the roll for the Belgian anthem, and began cranking. When an odd, unrecognizable tune rang out, he realized he'd drunkenly loaded the roll backward. The wardroom exploded with laughter as "La Brabançonne" reso-

nated in reverse across the dark and desolate pack, a fitting coda to
this celebration at the bottom of the world.

It was one of the last happy evenings.

The days grew as short as they did in wintry Belgium, but then they
grew shorter, as the latitude mercilessly shaved off up to twenty-five
minutes of light every day. In two weeks, nights lengthened by more
than three hours. De Gerlache feared that order would break down as
darkness took hold. The increasingly sunless days were thus regulated by a strictly enforced routine, dictated not by the light but by
the clock. Work began at eight in the morning and continued until
five in the afternoon, with breaks for lunch and exercise. Supper was
served at five-thirty, and evenings were spent at leisure by the steady
light of oil lamps: playing cards, mending clothes, reading. A bright
moon might invite the men outside for an evening stroll on the pack.

On Sundays and holidays, crew members were each given a grog
and fifteen centiliters of Bordeaux wine, as well as a morning glass of
port if de Gerlache was satisfied with the cleanliness of their quarters. Keen to avoid another liquor-fueled uprising, as happened in
Punta Arenas, de Gerlache forbade alcohol outside of these occasions, though officers had special privileges.

Perhaps inspired by the socialist movements taking hold in Europe
at the turn of the century, de Gerlache instituted an eight-hour work-
day. On the *Belgica*, however, overwork was not a concern. With the
ship encased in ice, de Gerlache's more pressing worry was finding
eight hours' worth of work for the sailors to do in a day. Their primary duty was merely to survive until the ice relinquished the ship.
Other than occasionally assisting the scientists, their responsibilities
consisted of little more than gathering blocks of snow to melt for
fresh water and keeping their stations clean. Hunting had been the
one job that consistently provided any excitement, and now even that
activity slowed nearly to a halt as wildlife grew scarce.

And so despite the commandant's best efforts, by late April a ship-
wide apathy had set in, particularly in the forecastle. Several crew
members wouldn't perform their few remaining daily tasks or take

their weekly sponge bath unless formally ordered to do so. Some refused to leave the ship, despite Cook's insistence that they exercise at least once a day. The hint of mutiny was back in the air. If anything, the crew's desperation was worse than in Punta Arenas, where at least deserters could escape to bars or brothels, or try their luck at gold digging.

The men's daily rations of canned sludge fueled their growing discontent. Crew and officers blamed the metastasizing onboard malaise on the bad food, and they blamed the bad food, in turn, on Michotte and de Gerlache. "The arrangement of the menu is condemned, and the entire food store is used as a subject for bitter sarcasm," Cook wrote. "Everybody having any connection with the selection or preparation of the food, past or present, is heaped with some criticism. Some of this is merited, but most of it is the natural outcome of our despairing isolation from accustomed comforts." Complaints became less jocular, more urgent. Not only was the food barely edible, crew members protested, but it was also insufficient. Cook described the growing resentment as a "food insurgency."

The griping became so insistent that after dinner on May 2, Lecointe took de Gerlache aside and communicated the crew's concerns to the commandant, adding that he believed they were right to object. It would be unwise, he said, to let their grievances go unanswered. He would never have questioned de Gerlache's decisions in front of his shipmates. But perhaps because he had been forced to swallow the same tasteless slop, he was in a combative mood himself. The captain demanded to know whether there were enough provisions to last the winter.

"Certainly, we have provisions," de Gerlache replied. "But what will the 'press' say when, later, they will speak of us? Won't they accuse us of having abused the situation by eating too well?"

Lecointe could hardly believe his ears. Once again, the commandant seemed to be more concerned about his reputation back home than about the welfare of his men. This had been an ongoing obsession: de Gerlache was fixated on the notion that journalists would accuse him of having stocked the Belgica's hold with too many fine foods and imply that he and his men were gorging themselves unpa-

triotically on the public dime. It was as if the commandant had lost
sight of the fact that they were not in Belgium but ten thousand miles
away, fighting for their lives on a drifting sheet of ice.

As quick-tempered as de Gerlache was even-keeled, Lecointe
raised his voice, saying he couldn't care less about the press, "especially the Antarctic press," and urged the expedition leader to provide
sufficient rations "without worrying about the rags from temperate
zones."

De Gerlache did as Lecointe advised and increased daily rations.
He even worked out a rotating monthly menu—plotted out on a
grid—that ensured no single item was served too often. But if the
men now had enough to eat, they were far from satisfied. "Now we
are tired of everything," wrote Cook. "We despise all articles which
come out of tin." No amount of permutations in the menu could
make up for the canned food's unbearable softness—weekly staples
like beef tongue, blanquette de veau, game pâté, and stewed hare,
were virtually indistinguishable in texture or in taste. Marinated her-
ring was no less bland. Vegetables were uniformly green-gray and
offered no resistance.

"The stomach demands things with a natural fiber, or some tough,
gritty substance," observed Cook, who believed that after several
months the human body would stop drawing nutrients from preserved food. "At this time, as a relief, we would have taken kindly to
something containing pebbles or sand. How we longed to use our
teeth!"

Cook's observations were no longer those of a curious anthropologist but of a concerned doctor. In early May, alarmed by the general
dyspepsia he observed around him, Cook began conducting regular
medical checkups in both the wardroom and the forecastle, weighing
his shipmates, taking their temperature, monitoring their heart rate,
examining their mouths and eyes. Pulses had become erratic after
months of confinement and inactivity, and the men "entered the long
night somewhat underfed," Cook reported, "because of our uncon-
querable dislike for such [food] as we had." But aside from "a few
light attacks of rheumatism, neuralgia, and some unimportant trau-
matic injuries, there had been no complaint."

For the most part, Cook kept his medicine cabinet closed. "If you were my *paying* client in New York, I would give you medication," he told one patient. "But out here, it's not worth it: you will get better just as well without it!"

At first, symptoms of unease were less physical than psychological. With no prospect of deliverance anytime soon, the ship-wide mood swung between boredom and anxiety, a poisonous combination. A series of alarming events during the fall temporarily shook the men from their ennui and reminded them of the precariousness of their situation. At one point, the woodwork behind the pipe of the cabin stove burst into flames. While everyone else scrambled about the deck in a frantic search for water and a working pump, Amundsen calmly removed the stove from the wooden panel and smothered the fire with snow.

And in mid-May, even as the *Belgica* drifted down to latitude 71°35′ south, the persistent northern winds that had pushed her there also brought several days of thaw, cracking up the pack that had seemed so dependably solid. Fissures formed under the men's feet. These were deadly enough when visible, but soon snow covered them, creating a landscape of lethal traps like the one Cook and Amundsen had barely survived back on Brabant Island. "In these storms it is not prudent to venture outside over the pack," wrote Cook. "We have already had several cold baths by sliding through these soft drifts, and a fatal accident might easily occur."

The ice could kill not only by opening up but also by closing back together. In this way, it was like a predator lying in ambush, lulling its prey for weeks before suddenly striking. On the calm night of May 13, the watchman looked out over the pack and saw something startling: Lecointe's small astronomical observatory hut was being swallowed by a newly opened crevasse, sinking at a perceptible rate. He cried out for his shipmates, who rushed to the deck and watched in disbelief as suddenly the crevasse began to clamp back together before their eyes, crushing the hut between its jaws. The planks began to split one by one. In a matter of seconds, the observatory and all the precious instruments it contained would be lost to the deep.

Lecointe, Cook, and Amundsen jumped down onto the ice and ran to the crumbling hut. Parts of the floor were gone, and some of Lecointe's equipment had already tumbled into the sea. The three men threw a rope around the four walls and pulled with all their strength, but the hut was too heavy and the grip of the ice too strong. Their feet were sliding toward the crevasse. Soon nine crew had joined the effort. Struggling against the forces of the pack, they succeeded in saving the structure "in the nick of time."

The men were able to salvage some of Lecointe's instruments and enough of the construction materials to rebuild the observatory, this time closer to the *Belgica,* where the ice remained intact, still several feet thick. Yet it was not lost on the expeditioners that what happened to the hut could easily happen to the ship itself. Indeed, it was precisely how the *Jeannette* and so many other icebound ships had been devoured.

For weeks, the growing darkness had been measured by the amount of time it was still possible to read without candlelight. In the days leading up to the sun's final bow, this was down to an hour or so. "Our noonday is not now brighter than our twilight of a month ago," Cook wrote.

According to Lecointe's calculations, the sun would dip below the horizon on May 16 and not reappear for seventy days, presuming the ship didn't drift too far to the north or south. Yet he predicted that refraction, the bending of light through the atmosphere, would afford the men one last illusory sliver of sunlight the following day.

The expeditioners looked forward to May 17 with dread. For the fiercely patriotic Amundsen and his Norwegian comrades in the crew, there was some consolation in that the date was a national holiday, marking the signing, in 1814, of Norway's constitution (which remained in effect even as the country fell under the authority of the Swedish king following a war that same year). But out on the ice, at the far end of the world, the vicissitudes of the sun took precedence over the distant drama of human history, of politics and war. However much champagne would flow in the wardroom and the forecastle at lunchtime to toast the anniversary, it would be a day of mourning.

With a thick haze masking the horizon on the expected morning, it didn't seem as if the sun would show up for its own funeral. Just before breakfast, Lecointe burst into the wardroom and announced that he had seen a different, far stranger kind of light. Instead of a fleeting sunrise in the north, as he hoped to see in a few hours, the captain had spotted a blue glow in the west that seemed to turn on and off, as if sending a message. He called his fellow officers to the snow-covered bridge to witness it for themselves. At first they saw nothing and ribbed their companion for his failing eyesight and over-eager imagination. "We accused him of having had too early an eye-opener," wrote Cook. They stamped their feet to keep warm and were about to return indoors. Then they saw it: the light appeared again, flickering like a torch. The men's already excitable pulses quickened—they were not alone on the continent after all!

"Soon all hands were on deck and all seemed to think that the light was being moved towards us," Cook wrote. "Is it a human being? Is it perhaps some one from an unknown south polar race of people?" Could the doctor have been onto something when, a few years earlier in Brooklyn, he had led his audience to believe that he might discover "an isolated tribe of men"? Could this light be a signal from the creators of those mysterious spheres of sand and cement that Captain Larsen had discovered five years earlier on Seymour Island, which he deemed to have been made by human hands? Someone would have to leave the ship to find out.

It is telling that, faced with the possibility of a diplomatic summit— or a more hostile confrontation—the men turned not to the expedition's commandant or to the *Belgica*'s captain but to the most natural leader among them. "Amundsen, who was the biggest, the strongest, the bravest, and generally the best dressed man for sudden emergencies, slipped into his *annorak*, jumped on his *ski* and skated rapidly over the gloomy blackness of the pack to the light," wrote Cook.

A short while later, the officers and crew made out Amundsen's figure, torch in hand, striding back to the ship. He climbed aboard, sheepishly, to report that the light had come from a patch of snow on a bobbing iceberg, illuminated by a coating of bioluminescent algae. The discovery was greeted with amused relief at first, but soon a profound disappointment settled over their minds. It was almost as if the men had hoped some supernatural event would save them from the cosmological inevitability of a monthslong night. When none did, it only deepened their sense of isolation.

At around ten o'clock, the fog lifted suddenly, setting the stage for the final sunrise. As noon approached, Cook, Amundsen, and de Gerlache skied across the pack, which had closed up again after a cold spell, to view what Cook called "the last signs of the departing day." They turned their eyes to the northern horizon, where a cream-colored light pushed back valiantly against the night. Behind it flowed a wash of orange. "Precisely at noon half of the form of the sun ascended above the ice," wrote Cook. "It was a misshapen, dull semicircle of gold, heatless, rayless, and sad. It sank again in a few moments, leaving almost no colour and nothing cheerful to remember through the . . . long days of darkness which followed. We returned to the ship, and during the afternoon laid out the plans for our midwinter occupation."

The Antarctic night wasn't uniformly black. The rotations of the earth were marked by a gloaming that lasted for a few hours. Every morning set up a climax that never came, a promise made and tantalizingly denied. "We could feel that this pale dawn was powerless to give birth to the day," wrote de Gerlache. "Soon it renounced its efforts to triumph against darkness; in an imperceptible transition, it became dusk."

The disappearance of the sun deprived the pack of life. Almost all carbon-based life forms are sun-eaters. Man eats the cow that eats the grass that draws energy from the sun to absorb minerals from the earth with which to build organic matter. The scavenging petrel eats the carcass of the leopard seal that eats the penguin that eats the krill that eats the phytoplankton. Like grass, phytoplankton is photosynthetic: it employs the molecule chlorophyll to convert the sun's light and heat into chemical energy. It is the basis of the Antarctic food chain, forming what Racovitza described as "an immense floating prairie." But when light can't reach it, because the sea ice is too thick or because the sun never rises, phytoplankton withers, dies, and sinks down to the ocean floor. The zooplankton that feasts on it directly under the ice is left to turn on its own kind. Through his microscope, Racovitza witnessed the cannibalistic carnage. With nothing to eat in the depleted ocean beneath the pack, swarms of krill drifted away or became less active, their metabolism slowing to a standstill. Requiring light to hunt by, the larger animals that depended on them fled to the brighter northern fringes of the pack, taking the rest of the ecosystem with them. Below and above the ice, the pack became, in de Gerlache's words, "a dead world."

CHAPTER 11

The Southernmost Funeral

SHORTLY BEFORE THE START OF THE LONG NIGHT, COOK HAD BEGUN to notice increasingly disturbing changes in the men's behavior. "It is not difficult to read on the faces of my companions their thoughts and their moody dispositions," he wrote. "Around the tables, in the laboratory, and in the forecastle, men are sitting about sad and dejected, lost in dreams of melancholy from which, now and then, one arouses with an empty attempt at enthusiasm." Repeated "perhaps for the fiftieth time," the stories and jokes that had elicited peals of laughter just weeks before had turned as stale and unpalatable as the food. "All efforts to infuse bright hopes fail."

Cook expected a downward turn in the general mood, but he was surprised by the depth to which it fell in the days following the last sunset. The men walked the *Belgica*'s decks seized by despair—when they could even be roused to walk at all. The primordial gloom that all humans feel in darkness—what Victor Hugo described as the "deep, dark anguish that might be called anxiety for the absent sun"—was here compounded by total isolation and the ever-present fear that the ice could crush the ship or open up beneath one's feet. "The curtain of blackness which has fallen over the outer world of icy desolation has also descended upon the inner world of our souls," Cook wrote. "Physically, mentally, and perhaps morally, then, we are depressed."

The explorers complained of dizziness and headaches. They grew irritable and coveted solitude, hard to come by in the *Belgica*'s cramped quarters. "If we could only get away from each other for a few hours at a time," wrote Cook, "we might learn to see a new side and take a fresh interest in our comrades; but this is not possible. The truth is, that we are at this moment as tired of each other's company as we are of the cold monotony of the black night."

Even Nansen the cat was suffering. Whether preening on deck, purring against crew members' legs at dinner, or curling up on their chests at night, Nansen had been a source of comfort and amusement. As the men grew weary of one another, the black-and-white cat remained an object of unguarded affection. But she was not immune to the contagion of despondency. "Altogether 'Nansen' seemed thoroughly disgusted with his surroundings and his associates, and lately he has sought exclusion in unfrequented corners," wrote Cook, who, like the sailors who had named the cat, assumed she was male. "His temperament has changed from the good and lively creature to one of growling discontent." To Cook, Nansen's hostility portended similar changes in the men's behavior. Her deterioration was a sign that boredom alone couldn't account for the ship-wide affliction. More-sinister forces—both physical and psychological—seemed to be at play, and the doctor was determined to find out what those were.

Although none of the men was spared from the mental and physical ravages of the long night, some suffered more than others. Cook and Amundsen, who had expected some amount of psychological strain and even considered it essential preparation for their own future expeditions, had so far fared among the best. Especially concerning to Cook was the man who seemed to be suffering the worst from the mysterious malaise: de Gerlache. The commandant's spacious cabin afforded him a solitude unavailable to his shipmates, and he spent most of his waking hours holed up inside it, leaving only for meals. "After supper, we stay together several minutes on the bridge, then he retires again until the next morning," wrote a worried Lecointe. "His health is not good: he endures constant violent pressure in his temples."

Cook couldn't explain de Gerlache's condition. Lecointe, for his part, believed that exhaustion was partly to blame. Whatever the cause, the commandant spent innumerable hours alone at his desk. The infinite darkness outside and the flickering candlelight within turned his rectangular window into a mirror, and de Gerlache stared at his gaunt reflection, superimposed on the Antarctic night. For years he had dreamed of visiting the southernmost regions of the earth, of claiming glory for himself and for Belgium. But now that he had finally reached this place, he felt nothing of the triumph he'd hoped for. He felt only pain and sorrow. One man had already died, and the lives of eighteen others were at stake.

De Gerlache had a depressive nature, never more pronounced than when he remained inactive. His condition on the *Belgica* recalled the health problems and bouts of melancholy he had experienced as a teenager when he returned from a journey at sea, only far more acute. Something was breaking in him. For a man as enamored with the open ocean as de Gerlache, to be at the helm of an icebound ship was to be robbed of purpose. The pack had taken control of the *Belgica* from him. The rudder was frozen solid, the helm was immovable, and the sails had no role to play. Nor, de Gerlache was beginning to feel, did he. He was seen less and less frequently on board. His shipmates presumed that he spent the hours in his cabin updating the ship's log. Yet throughout this period, page after page of his log lay all but empty, as barren as the view from his window.

Those who fared the best tended to be those who kept busy, and no one made more of an effort to stay active than Cook. Between his photographic work, his writing, his rigorously maintained exercise schedule, and his perpetual tinkering with polar equipment, Cook didn't allow himself to sink into boredom. Among other contraptions, he designed a wind-propelled sledge, crafting a splendid array of sails out of bedsheets. It kept tipping over in the first test rides on the pack, but that only gave Cook more reason to keep tinkering.

The doctor's preternaturally cheery disposition helped inoculate him against despair. His remarkably solid constitution kept him largely healthy. And with the distress of his shipmates now requiring his constant attention, Cook was suddenly the busiest man on board.

The deadening effect of winter took a visible toll on the men's bodies, which had started to atrophy for lack of exercise. (Aside from moonlit nights and a few minutes of twilight around noon, nobody walked outside in the dark, for fear of disappearing into a crevasse.)

"All seem puffy about the eyes and ankles, and the muscles, which were hard earlier, are now soft," Cook noted. "The skin is unusually oily. The hair grows rapidly, and the skin about the nails has a tendency to creep over them, seemingly to protect them from the cold." Over time, he wrote, "we became pale, with a kind of greenish hue; our secretions were more or less suppressed. The stomach and all the organs were sluggish and refused to work."

All signs pointed to a gradual, generalized breakdown of the body. "About half of the men complain of headaches and insomnia," Cook noted. "Many are dizzy and uncomfortable about the head, and others are sleepy at all times, though they sleep nine hours. All of the secretions are reduced, from which it follows that digestion is difficult. Acid dyspepsia and frequent gastric discomforts are often mentioned. There are also rheumatic and neuralgic pains, muscular twitchings, and an indefinite number of small complaints."

Most surprising to Cook were the "cardiac symptoms." The men's heart rate shot up with the slightest effort. "If we walk hurriedly around the ship the pulse rises to 110 beats [per minute]," Cook observed. A half-hour stroll on the ice caused hearts to pound at up to 140 beats per minute, and the men to pant for air. At other times, a man's heartbeat would drop suddenly to an equally worrisome 40 or 50 beats per minute. These swings mirrored similarly wild fluctuations in the men's mental state. "There was a failing control in about all functions of the body," Cook observed. "From dull periods of depression, they suddenly rose to semi-hysterical excitement."

Nothing Cook had learned in medical school could explain this alarming ship-wide phenomenon. Since it coincided with the onset of the long night, the doctor hypothesized that it was related to darkness. "The sun seems to supply an indescribable something which controls and steadies the heart," he wrote. "In its absence it goes like an engine without a governor."

These cardiac symptoms caused serious discomfort for all of the men aboard, but they led to an especially rapid deterioration in Emile Danco, de Gerlache's trusted lieutenant. "He has an old heart lesion," Cook observed, "a leak in one of the valves, which has been followed by an enlargement of the heart and a thickening of its walls." Under regular circumstances, Danco felt no strain. But the effects of the Antarctic night caused his heart to exhaust itself. By early May, he complained of shortness of breath after leisurely twilight walks. Upon the slightest effort, "Danco would frequently stand still and gasp." A few weeks later, Cook started to fear for his shipmate's life. "The hypertrophied muscular tissue is beginning to weaken," the doctor wrote. "Atrophy of the heart is the result, dilating and weakening with a sort of measured step, which, if it continues at the present rate, will prove fatal within a month."

When he informed de Gerlache, the commandant was crushed. He felt personally responsible, having known from the beginning that Danco's solid physique belied a frail constitution. De Gerlache feared that enlisting him on a two-year journey to one of the most taxing environments on earth would pose an unacceptable risk to his health. But when de Gerlache initially refused to let him join the expedition, Danco made a threat: he was set on adventure, and if he couldn't go to the Antarctic, he'd head to the Congo instead. Deeming the sterile polar climate to be at least more sanitary than the malarial jungles of central Africa, de Gerlache finally relented. Now he was racked with guilt over that decision.

Danco, however, took the news in stride. He had already known more excitement in the past six months than in the first twenty-eight years of his life, spent largely under the watchful eye of a tyrannical father. Moreover, he did not seem to anticipate the worst—in fact, he was looking forward to recovery. Cook monitored him closely and prescribed rest. The lieutenant lay on the wardroom's banquette, the most comfortable spot on the *Belgica,* and remained there for days on end. Cook forbade him to leave the ship in this debilitated state, lest he catch pneumonia. Dutiful as ever, Danco despaired at having to abandon his magnetic and gravitational work. Lecointe secretly took over his schedule of observations and looked forward to surprising him with fully updated notebooks as soon as he got better.

Regular, restful slumber might have helped mitigate the effects of the ship-wide malaise. Yet the perpetual night wreaked havoc on the men's sleep patterns. De Gerlache's so-called socialist regime divided the twenty-four hours of the day into eight hours of work, eight hours of leisure, and eight hours of sleep, but few were capable of adhering to that timetable. Without the regulating influence of the sun, some slept for nine hours or longer, too lethargic to rise. Others lay suspended in torturous insomnia.

There was no such thing as a silent night. Those who lay awake in their bunks were tormented by the squeaks coming up through the floorboards. The only creatures seemingly unaffected by the oppression of obscurity were the rats. "It was as if the absence of the sun's indiscreet rays favored their amorous passions," wrote Racovitza, "and at each instant one could hear the indignant, piercing squeals of Mademoiselle Rat being embraced by an overeager gentleman." The Romanian's sense of humor disguised a deep anxiety about the infestation. Rats are mostly nocturnal; darkness is their element. Since they'd embarked in Punta Arenas, the rodents had already produced several generations. After Nansen the cat lost interest in hunting, there was nothing to stop their proliferation. Their cries resounded across the ship and in the minds of the men trapped in the semiconscious limbo between wakefulness and sleep. It was as if the rats were scurrying through their brains.

Arctowski was among the insomniacs. "Often . . . lying in my berth, I put my ear to the wall and listened to hear what was happening a long way off," the scientist wrote. If the pack was a living organism, the *Belgica* was its central nervous system, receiving signals of pain from miles around. The ice was particularly active in the last days of May. Although the surface temperature dropped down to double digits below zero, the sea was never colder than 28 degrees or so; the large temperature differential strained at the half-meter-thick ice from both sides, causing it to crack. The sounds that reached Arctowski's ear through his wall were chilling: sometimes a resonant metallic clang, like a tightly wound spring suddenly snapping; sometimes something more organic, like the gurgling stomach of a ravenous beast.

Even more maddening were the deep, booming sounds of the terrible pressures convulsing the pack during this period. "We hear them coming from afar like the rumble of field artillery galloping towards us," wrote Lecointe. The pressures, more violent than any the men had yet witnessed, squeezed the *Belgica* like a vise.

Had he looked out his cabin's starboard window at the right time on May 28, de Gerlache would have seen the ice suddenly rip open, leaving a wide crack that ran parallel to the ship. The next day, May 29, the new crevasse clamped shut with tremendous force. Its two sides didn't stop after they crashed together but continued grinding into each other relentlessly, forming a massive ridge, just as the collision of tectonic plates will give rise to a mountain range. It would have taken just a few minutes for the ridge to grow nearly as high as the deck of the ship. De Gerlache would have seen it form with his naked eye. Because the pressures moving in from starboard were greater than those resisting them, the ridge began advancing inexorably toward the ship.

In his cabin, the commandant listened powerlessly to the *Belgica*'s agony. She emitted long, baleful groans as her timbers bent and quivered when the ice threw sudden, vicious blows to her ribs, each one threatening to stave in the hull. Until now, the ice had been relatively tame. De Gerlache had been lulled into assuming that his gamble would pay off; that, being mostly unconstrained by land, the pack would be incapable of crushing the *Belgica* the way it had the *Terror,* the *Erebus,* and the *Jeannette* in the Arctic. But the sounds he was hearing now made it clear that the ice of the Bellingshausen Sea could be just as destructive.

The commandant watched the giant pressure ridge close in on the hull like a slow-moving tidal wave. Boulders of ice weighing as much as several tons each were pushed to its crest before rolling back down like pebbles. The *Belgica* had surprised de Gerlache with her resilience before, but this was different. It was not like sailing through a storm. He could not negotiate his way out of trouble. The ice would do what it would do. It didn't care that there was a ship in the way.

Then, at half past ten on the morning of May 30, the creaking of wood and the roar of moving ice suddenly ceased. Out of the silence came, of all sounds, the peaceful babble of water. Looking over the side of the ship, the men saw something that gave them a start: a few centimeters of black between the hull and the ice. They followed it around the perimeter of the vessel and realized that, for the first time in months, the *Belgica* was floating freely.

But this was not escape, not nearly. Rather it was the prelude to a final attack. The ice was merely gathering strength, drawing back before ramming the hull with redoubled force. "Now we would be able to see how strong our old ship was," Amundsen wrote in his diary. At eleven, the pressure ridge threw itself into the starboard bow, a brutal haymaker of ice. "We suddenly felt the whole ship shudder and move and there was a strange hissing noise."

As the ridge slammed into the hull, the ice piled up against the back of the ship and spilled over the gunwales, like a crashing breaker. At the prow, meanwhile, an enormous slab of ice that had ducked beneath the pack slid under the stem and hoisted the 244-ton *Belgica* by several feet, making her pitch backward as if tackling an oncoming wave.

The assault of the ice lasted through the night. The men waited in anguish, helpless to aid the ship in her struggle. To everyone's amazement, the *Belgica* held strong, and by the next day, as if out of begrudging respect, the ice relented. It resumed its quiet, smothering embrace of the ship. From that day forth, however, the vessel remained at a slight incline, such that her masts formed an acute angle with the horizon and a walk from the stern to the prow would be uphill.

De Gerlache, already rattled by depression and migraines, would from then on live in constant fear that the pressures would be back. Destruction could come at any moment, as sudden as a change in the weather. He drew up a plan in case the ship was lost: the men would load as many provisions as they could into two lifeboats, drag them possibly hundreds of miles to the edge of the pack, and then sail in the direction of the South Shetland Islands. He put their chances of surviving the Drake Passage at a hundred to one.

On the clear and frigid evening of June 3, Cook left the ship with his camera and tripod on his shoulder and walked about a hundred yards across the pack under a dazzlingly bright moon. By its light, even the most distant icebergs stuck out neatly from the horizon. The doctor cut through a maze of hummocks and ridges caused by the previous week's pressures. He planted the tripod in the ice, turned his camera toward the *Belgica*, and opened the shutter. A spectacular image filtered through the Zeiss lens and began to impress itself on the light-sensitive silver salt emulsion that coated the camera's glass plate.

Cook paced vigorously to keep warm, unable to return to the ship lest his movement ruin the exposure. A self-taught photographer, he wasn't sure how long to wait; all he knew was that the ship had never looked more beautiful and there would likely never be a better chance to capture her at night. As fear and anxiety took hold of the *Belgica*, Cook's curiosity and passion for polar work were undiminished. It was as if he could fly at will above the concerns of the pack, much like a cartoon Racovitza had drawn, depicting the doctor as a winged, angel-like savior.

After an hour and a half, Cook delicately closed the shutter, hurried back aboard, and stomped the snow off his boots. Impatient to see the photograph, he walked through de Gerlache's cabin and into the darkroom. In the chamber's dim red glow, Cook plunged the clear glass plate into a vat of developer. The specter of a ship gradually appeared as the exposed silver salts darkened in the chemical bath. When he was satisfied with the image, he dropped the plate into acetic acid to stop the development process. Next, he would fix it, eliminate all remnants of silver salts, and render the negative impervious to light. During this step, he moved slowly and tried not to breathe, aware that the slightest false movement could prove deadly. Having used up all of the sodium thiosulfate—a fixer commonly known as hypo—in the early part of the voyage, when he was still getting used to his equipment and to the subtleties of photographing in polar light, the doctor had improvised a solution. He had read in an old issue of a British magazine lying around the ship that hydrocyanic acid, an extremely toxic poison, was once used as a fixer for daguerreotypes. Conveniently, Racovitza had brought twenty gallons of it on board to kill animals for specimens. ("One drop on the tongue," Cook wrote, "and it was all over for the animal.") After experimenting with various dilutions, Cook had found a formula that did the trick. He poured a bath of the stuff, which smelled faintly of almonds, and daintily submerged the negative plate. "Needless to say," Cook wrote, "nobody remained in the darkroom during fixing." The poisonous fumes eventually escaped the unventilated darkroom through the door to de Gerlache's cabin.

Once the cyanide was washed away, Cook could finally contemplate his work in unfiltered light. The doctor was a gifted photographer. His candid snapshots of his shipmates have a painterly touch. His anthropomorphic images of animals betray a sense of whimsy. But the portrait he took of the *Belgica* on that cloudless, moonlit evening is undoubtedly Cook's masterpiece. In the foreground, hummocks appear as a choppy sea frozen in place. In the background, an ethereal luminescence, a trace of twilight, emanates over the horizon. The *Belgica*'s skeletal rigging, shorn of sails and sheathed in ice and snow, traces clear white lines against the black, star-dotted sky, as if illuminated by a flashbulb. (With a white sea and a dark sky, the photograph looks like a negative, and the negative that Cook was admiring looked, conversely, like a picture of a ship in the daytime.) The crispness of the image was evidence of how still the windless evening was. The long exposure registered no human activity, giving the *Belgica* the air of a ghost ship.

In this respect, Cook had captured not just the exterior of the vessel but also the mournful mood within. It is even possible that he had ventured out that night as a distraction from a specific circumstance: back on the ship, his sickest patient had taken a terrible turn for the worse.

After supper, Danco lay on the wardroom banquette as the officers and scientists played a lively game of whist. The once strapping lieutenant had grown cadaverously thin. Too tired and weak to participate, he offered occasional advice to the cardplayers and forced himself to laugh at the wisecracks volleyed across the table. The men put up a merry front, both to buoy their ailing shipmate's spirits and to conceal their own anguish. Yet the sound of Danco's belabored wheezing cut through the forced pleasantries. He had lost his appetite days before, and it had become obvious to everyone that his condition was deteriorating by the hour.

Obvious, that is, to everyone but him. Watching the card game from his banquette, the twenty-eight-year-old Danco claimed to be feeling better, almost like his former self. His good cheer may have given his colleagues hope, but Cook harbored no illusions that this apparent improvement was anything but "the calm before the storm": not only was Danco's heart wearing itself out, but a buildup of protein in his urine revealed that his kidneys were failing as well.

When the doctor informed de Gerlache, the commandant was

shattered. "None of my companions was dearer to me," he wrote, "nor, I believe, more devoted." He also knew how fond the other men had grown of Danco. Seeing the lieutenant jump to obey every order, refuse special treatment, and address his childhood friend as *"mon commandant"* galvanized the crew and helped solidify its esprit de corps. Though his scientific contributions were questionable, he had become a beloved and passionate member of the expedition, in many ways its standard-bearer.

On June 4, Danco was too sick to swallow anything but a few drops of lemon juice. Cook, taken with the notion that light gave life and darkness took it away, insisted that two candles be kept constantly aflame in the wardroom, which created an unintended and premature funereal effect. "We have the sad impression of already keeping vigil in a mortuary chamber," wrote Lecointe.

Danco expressed his gratitude for the little his shipmates could do for him. Defying their tearful, pitying looks, he spoke eagerly of the return voyage. He would climb to the crow's nest, he said, so he could be the first to see land. "Is this sweet illusion sincere?" Lecointe wondered. "Or, in an exquisitely tactful consideration inspired by his generous soul, is he deceiving us in order not to sadden us further?"

Danco's agony on the morning of June 5 was so acute that Cook gave him an injection of morphine. After Danco fell asleep, the doctor found de Gerlache and announced the news in a shaky voice.

"Commandant, it will be today."

Word spread from stem to stern. Sailors kept their voices down and muffled their footsteps. A churchlike silence fell upon the ship.

At around four in the afternoon, Danco awoke. His breathing was strained and shallow. The lieutenant could no longer speak but smiled softly at all who approached his bedside, consoling those who had come to console him. At five, Cook gave him another dose of morphine. In order not to disturb him, the officers and scientists ate their supper in de Gerlache's quarters that evening, while Cook remained at Danco's side. The doctor entered the commandant's cabin at seven to inform his colleagues—de Gerlache, Lecointe, Amundsen, Racovitza, and Arctowski—that the end had come.

Slowly the five men rose and filed into the wardroom, gathering around the banquette in a solemn tableau. Cook asked Lecointe, who had been Danco's classmate at the military academy, to talk to his dying friend. The devastated captain was speechless. Waiting for the right sentiments to arrive, he could only hold Danco's hand. "Every so often, he opens his eyes wide then closes them slowly," wrote Lecointe. "A long death rattle escapes from his chest."

Speaking softly, Lecointe brought up pleasant memories of their old regiment, which, since Danco's parents had died, was the closest thing he had to family back home. "I felt, at a slight pressure from his hand, that these remembrances still touched his heart," recalled Lecointe.

With his friends huddled over him, Danco forced out a few halting words.

"I feel better, thank you."

Almost immediately, a frightening pallor washed across his face, his features tightened, and he closed his eyes for the last time.

All continued to stare at Danco for a moment, as if death wouldn't come until they looked away.

As soon as he could collect himself, de Gerlache asked that the body of his friend be draped in the Belgian flag and invited the crew to come pay their respects. That night, de Gerlache, Lecointe, and Amundsen took turns keeping vigil in the wardroom. On his watch, de Gerlache could not keep his eyes off Danco's bearded face, enlivened by the flicker of a solitary candle.

He was feeling something worse than guilt—a deep, painful loneliness. With his general reserve, de Gerlache counted few intimates in his life, and almost none he had known so long as Danco. On the *Belgica,* he had a loyal ally in Lecointe and a cordial relationship with Cook and Amundsen, but Danco had been his close friend, someone in whom he could confide despite their difference in rank. His loss left de Gerlache feeling even more isolated and despondent. The commandant again interrogated his conscience. *Had I done well to cede to his solicitations?* he asked himself. Cook had told him that Danco might have lived just a year or so longer had he stayed in Belgium; at least he got to live his dream of adventure. De Gerlache wondered if this was true.

The wardroom was glacially cold. For reasons of hygiene, the sky-light had been cracked open, and the Antarctic air poured in. De Gerlache watched his breath condense into puffs of fog. He thought of the rest of his men, all of whom were ailing—not yet as sick as Danco, but worsening day by day. *We are all threatened now. Were we to disappear, who would bring the fruit of our labor back to Belgium?* He shuddered not from the cold, but from the thought that they might lose their lives for nothing. He had hoped that steering into the ice would solve all of his problems, but not this way.

The commandant gave all the men the next day off except for Knudsen, who sewed a sailcloth bag in which to place Danco's body. By the time the sailor had finished the job, the corpse had begun to rot. Cook, Amundsen, and Lecointe lifted Danco off the banquette to enshroud him. Van Rysselberghe, the nineteen-year-old second engineer, diffidently entered the wardroom with a bouquet of dried flowers. He told the men that his mother had given them to him just before he embarked and had requested that he keep them until they met again. But he wanted to bury them with Danco. Touched by his gesture, the officers let him place the flowers on the lieutenant's chest before the bag was sewn shut.

The body was placed on a sledge on the ice. "One man who carried him out onto the pack did complain he stank too much," wrote Dobrowolski. The scientist conducted his meteorological observations from the poop deck that evening, one of the coldest nights he'd yet experienced. Dobrowolski was supposed to be studying the clouds, but there were few in the sky that night. His gaze was fixed on the sledge bearing Danco's body. "The crescent moon illuminated the pack ice with deathly paleness," he wrote in his diary. "The firmament glistened with stars. My eyes were riveted to the sled, which reflected darkly off the snow. I wanted to see something through the dark, shapeless shroud. What, I do not know, but I was long unable to pull my gaze away. Finally my tired gaze slipped from the sled on its own and involuntarily turned toward the stars. Yet the stubborn sled followed it, white, as if cleansed of earthly filth, ghostly. It soared, flitted among the stars. Finally it dissolved in the dark firmament. . . . An ordinary afterimage, of course. I knew of them very well, yet this phenomenon made a strange impression on me: I don't know why, right then I wanted to forget that optical illusions existed."

Danco's body remained on the pack overnight. By morning, it was as hard as stone. The funeral was set for that day. It would be the southernmost burial in history. The Belgian colors, adorned with a black ribbon, rippled in the wind. Since the masts' halyards were frozen stiff by a chill of −31 degrees, the flag had to be tied in the rigging, halfway up the mast. Sailors struggled for several hours to cut a hole in the ice a hundred yards from the ship, through which to commit Danco's body to the sea. They chiseled and sawed to little effect. Then, as if by some unknown intelligence, an old crevasse abruptly parted beneath their feet. A gateway to the deep had opened of its own accord.

Around eleven a.m., in the feeble light that now passed for day, four men harnessed themselves to the sledge and hauled it to the edge of the opening, Danco's feet pointed toward the crevasse. Dressed in their finest clothes despite the cold, the officers formed a procession behind the sledge, followed by the scientists and the crew. All removed their hats as de Gerlache stepped forward to give a eulogy. His throat tightened with emotion, and he couldn't emit a sound. The men waited in silence as the wind blew bitterly into their uncovered ears. "After several moments," wrote Lecointe, "he was able at last to deliver the sorrowful regrets and the eternal adieu."

Weights were tied to Danco's feet. Several men had started to tip the sledge into the crevasse when the lip of the ice broke off under Jules Melaerts's feet. Before he knew it, he was in the water. The men dropped the sledge and reached toward the opening. Melearts gasped in shock, splashed frantically back to the edge, and pulled himself up with his left hand gripping the sledge and his right on Dobrowolski's shoulder. The water was as cold as water could get, and still it was far warmer than the wind that now lashed at him on the ice. Melaerts would soon die if he didn't get back to the ship. But the funeral was not yet over.

The men again tipped the back of the sledge and pushed the weights into the water. As they plummeted, Danco's body slid feet-first into the crevasse. Pivoting against the edge, the corpse shot up suddenly as it hit the water. For a moment, it stood fully vertical, as if possessed. Danco's shipmates recoiled in horror at the sight of this revenant standing at attention, stiffened by rigor mortis and the freezing night. They watched him sink slowly into the black water.

"Nom de Dieu!" shouted one of the Belgian deckhands.

Danco disappeared. The ice closed back up.

CHAPTER 12

Madhouse Promenade

DANCO'S DEATH DRAGGED THE MEN'S SOULS TO ABYSMAL DEPTHS, AS IF the weights had been attached to them, too. After visiting the forecastle that evening, Cook reported to de Gerlache that the sailors were demoralized and recommended that the commandant lend them the coelophone, along with rolls for religious hymns that might give them solace. Preferring to distract them from their sorrow rather than indulge it, de Gerlache sent them a round of grog instead.

Night after night, the men were haunted by visions of Danco suspended above the ocean floor, in absolute blackness, his corpse eerily preserved in the cold water. "We are constantly picturing to ourselves the form of our late companion," Cook wrote, "floating about in a standing position, with the weights to his feet, under the frozen surface and perhaps under the *Belgica*."

The men's grief was compounded by a fear no one dared utter out loud. "Who among us will come after him?" Arctowski wrote in his diary. "When we were all in silence and listening to his breath getting weaker, I do not think I was the only one who asked himself these questions."

Dobrowolski, who had inherited Danco's expensive winter coat, expressed a similar anxiety: "Goodbye, goodbye Lieutenant Danco! You are not the first and you are not the last. Maybe we will 'meet' again! Maybe even this winter!"

It took only three weeks for the Antarctic to claim its next victim. Nansen the cat had been sick for a month. Her illness seemed to mirror Danco's. But unlike the lieutenant, who had maintained his grace and equanimity until his dying breath, Nansen showed signs of mental degeneration. Once sweet and affectionate, she had grown vicious and saturnine and avoided her shipmates. "His mind has wandered and from his changed spiritual attitude we believe that his soul has wandered too," Cook wrote on June 26. "A day or two ago his life departed, we presume for more congenial regions. We are glad his torture is ended, but we miss 'Nansen' very much." The cat's death affected the men deeply, not least because she had been, as Cook put it, "the only speck of sentimental life within reach."

Nansen's mental decline presaged the cognitive impairment that affected the men as winter wore on, what Cook referred to as "cerebral symptoms." He and his shipmates found themselves listless, unmotivated, incapable of concentrating on anything for more than a few seconds. Some grew hostile, even if, unlike Nansen, they mostly managed to keep a civilized façade. Everyone experienced these symptoms to some degree. In his diary, Arctowski described the turmoil behind his placid exterior: "Yes, I have peace, but only around me, because in my head there is always uncertainty and unrest. I have no confidence in the future."

The combination of fear and fatigue, depression and disorientation, darkness and isolation, the risk that the *Belgica* might be crushed in the ice at any moment, a slanted floor that had never leveled out after the formidable pressures of late May and seemed to skew reality itself, an infestation of rats, and a ship-wide illness with no obvious cause made most of the men feel as if they were losing their grip on sanity.

The expeditioners did their best to conceal their inner torment for fear of being ostracized or sparking a panic on board. Yet for some the anguish was too excruciating to contain. Amundsen was reading in his cabin one afternoon in early July when he "suddenly heard three or four long, terrible screams." He threw open his cabin door and found Cook. The doctor had also heard the chilling shrieks, as had the sailor Johan Koren. The three men rushed to the afterdeck, where the noise seemed to originate. But they found no one there. "There was nothing to be seen," reported Amundsen. "Then we ran to the engine room but there was nothing to be seen there, either. Everyone was inside. The commander was walking on the deck and had heard nothing. Lecointe and Racovitza were on the ice and had not heard anything either while Arctowski was asleep. The doctor,

Koren and myself were the only ones who heard the terrible screaming. I do not know what it was but I have recorded this event as accurately as possible for a number of reasons."

The source of the screams was never discovered. They might as
well have been the expression of collective angst. Dark thoughts were
inescapable during the polar night. "Murder, suicide, starvation, insanity, icy death and all the acts of the devil, become regular mental
pictures," Cook observed.

Arctowski put it more succinctly: "We are in a mad-house."

It tortured de Gerlache to think that the suffering around him, like
his own, was the direct consequence of his decision to sail the *Belgica*
deep into the pack ice at the end of summer. It was the sort of self-
doubt he would ordinarily have admitted only to his closest friend,
but since Danco's death, de Gerlache had nobody in whom to confide. One July evening, while speaking with Amundsen in the wardroom, he could no longer keep his misgivings to himself and made a
remarkable admission.

"As a Belgian I had to go further south with a steamship like the
Belgica than [Capt. James] Cook with only a sailing boat," de Gerlache told his first mate, unprompted. "I am very sorry that we are
stuck fast as a result, that Danco died and that everyone is now ill but
I had no choice. I readily admit that my officers, Messrs. Lecointe and
Danco, pointed out to me that the year was already nearing its end
but, as I said, I had no choice."

Amundsen was stunned by the commandant's candor. "I do not
understand why he told me all this, particularly as I had not asked any
questions which could have elicited such an answer," Amundsen
wrote in his diary. "I will not record my opinion of this."

The first mate had until then held de Gerlache in the highest regard as a sailor and a leader. What likely surprised Amundsen about
the confession was not that de Gerlache admitted to having deliber-
ately sailed the ship into the ice in an attempt to break a record.
Amundsen already suspected as much, and the presumption had only
increased his respect for the commandant's daring. Instead, it was de
Gerlache's need to justify his decision, and the impression he gave of

regretting it, that dismayed Amundsen. If de Gerlache wasn't pre-pared for such dire consequences, then why had he done it? In the Norwegian's young mind, it was a leader's duty to project unwaver-ing resolve. The exchange marked a turning point in the first mate's attitude toward the commandant. Soon Amundsen's mentions of de Gerlache in his diary became frequently critical.

Amundsen's diary throughout this period is a clearheaded account of the anguish swirling around him, as if he were in the eye of a storm. Although he felt just as sick and physically weak as everyone else, and his heartbeat was just as prone to alarming fluctuations, he did not lose his mental composure. If anything, he thrived.

"I will, of course, be very happy when [the sun] has returned but I must say that I have felt good the whole time and have not missed it at all, on the contrary," he wrote in his diary. "This is the life I have always wished for. It was not a childish whim which made me do it. It was a mature decision. I have no regrets and I hope to be able to retain my strength and health in order to complete the work I have started."

Amundsen, who dreamed of being a world-famous polar explorer in the mold of Fridtjof Nansen, approached the expedition as train-ing. The more grueling the conditions, the more he felt he was get-ting out of it. Experiencing the tribulations of polar travel provided him with a sense of purpose, even as the scientists and sailors felt they were being driven mad by monotony and idleness. Survival was the point. It might as well have been his job.

Cook's obligations as physician likewise kept him sane, albeit in-creasingly concerned for his colleagues, and uncertain how to treat them. Like a medical detective, the doctor now dedicated all of his time to determining the causes of the general malaise that plagued the ship during the long night. He gave it the name "polar anaemia." He had witnessed a far milder form of it during his winter in Green-land, when he and the other members of the Peary expedition be-came sullen and fatigued. But their heartbeats did not rise and fall so precipitously, and they did not look so sickly and pale. Nor did they report the cognitive symptoms now affecting the men of the *Belgica*, including a shortened attention span, confusion, and the tendency to stare blankly and unresponsively into the middle distance.

The *Belgica* anchored at Antwerp, on the River Scheldt, before her August 1897 departure. LIMBURGENSIA COLLECTION OF BIBLIOTHEEK HASSELT LIMBURG

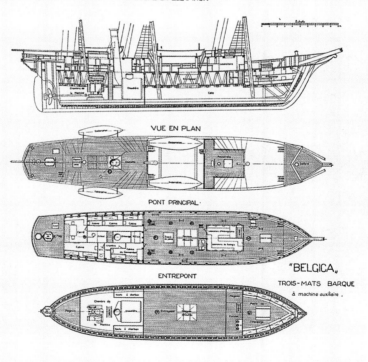

COUPE EN ELEVATION

VUE EN PLAN

PONT PRINCIPAL·

ENTREPONT

"BELGICA„

TROIS-MATS BARQUE
à machine auxiliaire .

The layout of the *Belgica,* with officers' quarters at the stern, laboratories amidships, and crew quarters in the forecastle, belowdecks. FROM "FRAGMENTS DU RÉCIT DE VOYAGE," BY ADRIEN DE GERLACHE DE GOMERY, PART OF *RÉSULTATS DU VOYAGE DE LA BELGICA EN 1897-99 SOUS LE COMMANDEMENT DE A. DE GERLACHE DE GOMERY,* 1936

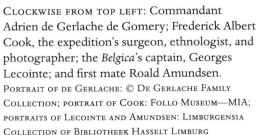

CLOCKWISE FROM TOP LEFT: Commandant
Adrien de Gerlache de Gomery; Frederick Albert
Cook, the expedition's surgeon, ethnologist, and
photographer; the *Belgica*'s captain, Georges
Lecointe; and first mate Roald Amundsen.
PORTRAIT OF DE GERLACHE: © DE GERLACHE FAMILY
COLLECTION; PORTRAIT OF COOK: FOLLO MUSEUM—MIA;
PORTRAITS OF LECOINTE AND AMUNDSEN: LIMBURGENSIA
COLLECTION OF BIBLIOTHEEK HASSELT LIMBURG

The equator-crossing ceremony aboard the *Belgica,* on October 6, 1897. Albert Lemonnier, the expedition's cook, wields a wooden "razor" to shave initiates. FOLLO MUSEUM—MIA

Three Ona women, photographed by Cook in Tierra del Fuego. LIBRARY OF CONGRESS, FREDERICK A. COOK SOCIETY

Norwegian sailor Carl August Wiencke, age nineteen.

The *Belgica* anchored in what would come to be known as the Gerlache Strait, in the first few weeks of 1898. © DE GERLACHE FAMILY COLLECTION

The view from the foremast shows the pack ice tightening around the *Belgica* in February 1898. © DE GERLACHE FAMILY COLLECTION

The *Belgica* caught in the Antarctic pack ice, 1898. LIBRARY OF CONGRESS, FREDERICK A. COOK SOCIETY

The scientists in their labs. ABOVE: Romanian naturalist Emile Racovitza. BELOW: Polish geologist and meteorologist Henryk Arctowski. ABOVE: © DE GERLACHE FAMILY COLLECTION; BELOW: LIBRARY OF CONGRESS, FREDERICK A. COOK SOCIETY

Racovitza's cartoons lampooned life on the *Belgica*. Here, Arctowski admires an aurora australis that spells out *shit*. National Library of Norway

Second engineer Max Van Rysselberghe melts snow for drinking water under the shelter built amidships. © De Gerlache Family Collection

Lecointe on wash day.
FRAM MUSEUM

De Gerlache and an emperor
penguin captured on the pack ice.
© DE GERLACHE FAMILY COLLECTION

Amundsen on skis, with
freshly slaughtered Adélie
penguins. NATIONAL LIBRARY
OF NORWAY

Sailor Johan Koren dissects an emperor penguin in the wardroom. © DE GERLACHE FAMILY COLLECTION

An excursion to an iceberg caught in the pack not far from the *Belgica*. COURTESY OF THE NATIONAL LIBRARY OF NORWAY

The forecastle, seen from the nose of the *Belgica*. Above: From left: Engelbret Knudsen, Jan Van Mirlo (looking at camera), Gustave Dufour (far end of table). Next page: Ludvig Johansen plays the accordion and Adam Tollefsen (far right) sits at the table. The other three men have been identified as Jules Melaerts, Antoni Dobrowolski, and Johan Koren, though their unkempt, post-wintering appearance makes it difficult to say who is who. Both images © De Gerlache Family Collection

Cook's "masterpiece," taken by moonlight on June 3, 1898, with an exposure time of an hour and a half. © De Gerlache Family Collection

Lieutenant Emile Danco, de Gerlache's childhood friend and the expedition's magnetician. © De Gerlache Family Collection

De Gerlache in his cabin, where he spent much of his time as sickness took hold of him. © De Gerlache Family Collection

Frequent fellow travelers Cook and Amundsen.
Library of Congress, Frederick A. Cook Society

Sledging and camping equipment, including Cook's ingenious design for a wind-deflecting conical tent. National Library of Norway

Dinner in the wardroom. From left: Arctowski, Amundsen, Lecointe, Racovitza, and de Gerlache. Fram Museum

The toll of the long winter night. LEFT: De Gerlache, his face bloated with scurvy. RIGHT: Cook, who refused to cut his hair during the expedition. LEFT: © DE GERLACHE FAMILY COLLECTION; RIGHT: NATIONAL LIBRARY OF NORWAY

The madman Adam Tollefsen.
NATIONAL LIBRARY OF NORWAY

The expedition's desperate escape plan called for sawing through about a mile and a half's worth of ice more than a meter thick. © DE GERLACHE FAMILY COLLECTION

Amundsen, left, and Arctowski, preparing sticks of tonite explosives in the *Belgica*'s wardroom. © De Gerlache Family Collection

Clearing what the men hope to be a way out of the pack. Some pans of ice weighed several times as much as the ship herself. Library of Congress, Frederick A. Cook Society

Cook suspected that the stress due to confinement, isolation, boredom, and fear contributed to the phenomenon. But he believed the most critical factor was the disappearance of the sun. "Oh, for that heavenly ball of fire!" Cook wrote. "Not for the heat—the human economy can regulate that—but for the light—the hope of life." In its absence, he observed, the men became pale, and their hair turned gray and grew quickly, "like plants in a hot-house." Cook was convinced that human beings were no less dependent on sunlight than photosynthetic plants. This belief stemmed from his clinical observations of the Inuit in Greenland during the winter of 1891–92. "During the whole of this long Arctic night the secretions are diminished and the passions suppressed, resulting in great muscular debility," he had written in *The New York Journal of Gynaecology and Obstetrics* in 1894. "I should judge from this that the presence of the sun is as essential to animal as it is to vegetable life."

Cook's belief in the life-giving properties of the sun was also informed by his understanding—or possibly misunderstanding—of Inuit metaphysics. During Cook's beachside stroll with Sipsu in 1892, under the green shimmer of the northern lights, the Inuit elder had told him, "There is light in all life—in your body and mind. Can you see this? You feel life but can you see the light stored in your body?" Even assuming that Cook's command of the language was firm enough to comprehend such a subtle thought (doubtful) and that his recollection of the conversation was accurate, Sipsu was not voicing any well-established Inuit dogma. Perhaps he was describing the animistic concept of a spirit in terms Cook could relate to, by translating it as "light." Or perhaps he was simply philosophizing with a new friend. But what Cook gathered from the encounter—regardless of whether he faithfully recorded Sipsu's statement—was that light is as essential to life as blood. The condition of the *Belgica*'s men seemed to confirm this notion. Their weakness and pallor and mental atrophy and irregular heartbeats were in his mind akin to the etiolation of plants deprived of sunlight.

Cook knew for certain that if he did nothing, more men would die. Since he couldn't bring the *Belgica* to the light, he attempted to bring light to the *Belgica*. He ordered the most severely affected men to stand naked in the glow of a blazing wood or coal fire, "the best substitute" for the absent sun. The "baking treatment," as Cook came to call it, appeared to improve the men's moods and even some of their physical symptoms. "I have stripped and placed men, before the direct rays of heat, whose pulse was almost imperceptible, and in the course of less than an hour had a heart action nearly normal," Cook wrote. The main benefit of the treatment, in the doctor's estimation, was not heat but light. "From an oil stove it is quite impossible to get this effect."

Cook's intervention is the first known instance of light therapy, regularly used today to treat seasonal affective disorder and other conditions. The doctor's intuition about the psychological benefits of light may have been correct, but the flames from the wood and coal burning in the *Belgica*'s stove weren't nearly as bright as the full-spectrum light typically used in modern phototherapy. It's unlikely the direct action of light could fully account for the apparent benefits of Cook's baking treatment. Other factors may have been just as important: Cook's patients found relief in the warmth and dryness of the fire. More important, they took comfort simply in being taken care of. The doctor had a soothing effect on almost everyone he met.

Yet however temporarily beneficial it might have been, the baking treatment was not sufficient to reverse the damage of the Antarctic night. Nor did it solve the riddle of what was ailing the men. By mid-July, many were bedridden, showing signs of grave degeneration of both body and mind. To keep them active, Cook mandated that those who could stand on their feet walk on the ice around the bark for an hour a day—an exercise regimen nicknamed the " 'mad-house' promenade." During these interminable loops, "the men easily freeze parts of the face, the fingers and toes, without knowing it," Cook wrote. The doctor initially attributed this blunting of the senses to "enfeebled circulation." But he was beginning to suspect a more serious ailment.

He considered the growing list of physical symptoms suffered to some extent by every man on board: lethargy, weakness, anemia, discolored and waxen skin, and "dropsical effusion"—a buildup of liquid—under the eyes, around the ankles, and in other parts of the body.

Cook recognized these as the unmistakable signs of an unmentionable disease, one whose name struck fear in the heart of every sailor. The doctor was shocked to discover that the *Belgica* was in the grip of scurvy.

By the turn of the twentieth century, scurvy was thought to have been largely an affliction of the past. It is estimated to have claimed the lives of two million seamen between the time of Columbus and the 1800s, making it by far the most common cause of death on the seas in the age of sail. It became accepted as a cost of doing transoceanic business, leading navies and merchant marines to recruit—often forcefully—many more men than they needed for long journeys, on the assumption that a high percentage of them would die of scurvy.

Symptoms typically appeared a few months after a ship left port. Early signs included sluggishness, edema (what Cook called "dropsical effusion"), foul breath, and papery skin, which would gradually become mottled with sores and lesions. The disease grew excruciatingly painful over the course of a few weeks, causing gums to rot, teeth and joints to loosen, limbs to gangrene, long-healed wounds to reopen as if by sorcery, and, at last, a merciful death usually brought on by a heart attack or cerebral hemorrhage as blood-vessel walls liquefied. It was a vicious and inexorable disease. Nobody ever recovered without intervention.

"Scurvy had a thousand remedies," Cook wrote, "which in itself is the best evidence that it was not understood." The early study of scurvy generated several fanciful theories about its causes and treatments that did more harm than good, revealing the medicine of the day to have been a hybrid of modern empiricism and ancient quackery. Many physicians, mistaking one of scurvy's first symptoms, lethargy, for its cause, concluded that the disease affected the lazy and indolent. To combat it, they increased the workload of the afflicted, weakening them even further and speeding their demise. Others presumed that scurvy was a disease of putrefaction that occurred in damp, insalubrious, vermin-infested quarters belowdecks. (Plenty of maladies, such as yellow fever and malaria, thrived in such conditions, but scurvy was not one of them. It could affect officers in their clean and spacious cabins as indiscriminately as lowly deckhands sleeping cheek by jowl in the hold, as long as all were eating the same food, which, in truth, they often weren't.) The prevailing medical theory of the time, inherited from antiquity, was that almost all diseases were caused by an imbalance in the four bodily "humors"—blood, phlegm, yellow bile, and black bile—and could thus be cured by restoring the balance. In the case of scurvy, doctors frequently prescribed bloodletting, at best a counterproductive treatment.

A number of astute physicians, noticing that the disease tended to appear only once reserves of fresh fruit and vegetables, meat, or sauerkraut had run out, suspected that nutrition might have been a factor. But it was difficult to tell the nostrums apart from the effective treatments—that is, until 1747, when a young Royal Navy surgeon named James Lind conducted one of the first controlled clinical trials in the history of medicine and demonstrated the powerful antiscorbutic properties of oranges and lemons.

It took almost half a century for the conservative British Admiralty to accept Lind's conclusions and act on them. In 1795, a year after Lind's death, it began issuing a daily ration of lemon juice to sailors. As surely as water douses fire, rates of scurvy dropped dramatically. A few decades later, however, the Royal Navy tried to cut costs by switching out Mediterranean lemons for cheaper limes from the British West Indies. Limes were not nearly as effective as lemons in fighting scurvy, and attempts to preserve lime juice for long voyages—typically by reducing it into a concentrate—rendered it even less potent. In the second half of the nineteenth century, rates of scurvy began creeping back up. But since the advent of steam-powered shipping, which cut the duration of ocean voyages, fewer sailors were spending enough time at sea to show symptoms, blinding the Royal Navy—and all the fleets that emulated its practices—to the ineffectiveness of lime juice concentrate as an antiscorbutic. The hard-won cure was again in danger of being forgotten.

The *Belgica*'s reserves of lime juice were evidently not doing the trick. Cook found himself in much the same predicament as the first physicians to encounter scurvy. His only advantage over them was that he knew, thanks to Lind, that scurvy was directly related to nutrition. But without access to proven remedies like fresh citrus fruit or sauerkraut, nor to any indigenous populations who might point him to antiscorbutic local plants (as the Iroquois did for Jacques Cartier in sixteenth-century North America)—nor, indeed, to any local plants—Cook was forced to improvise.

While Antarctica had never been inhabited, its conditions were not fundamentally different from the Arctic's, Cook reasoned. Living among the Inuit in northern Greenland during the winter of 1891–92, Cook had observed that they exhibited none of the symptoms of scurvy. And if the Arctic was able to sustain human life despite its lack of vegetation, then Antarctica must be able to as well. Cook's hunch, then, was that the Inuit diet, consisting of almost nothing but fresh (or frozen and thawed) meat and blubber, frequently eaten raw, was sufficient to ward off scurvy, even if it led to other health complications.

Even as he avoided naming the dreaded disease he was attempting to treat, the doctor prescribed a daily diet of fresh meat, most often penguin but occasionally seal, to every man aboard. In keeping with Inuit culinary tradition, Cook recommended that the penguin steaks be as rare as the men could stomach. He preferred his lightly seared. Amundsen, whose health had taken a bad turn in early July, valued the doctor's opinion so highly that he forwent cooking altogether and ate his penguin raw, without bothering to wait for dinnertime. Remarkably, after just a few days of guzzling down the cutlets, which had the consistency of fatty, uncooked chicken, Amundsen was almost back to normal.

Cook could not explain why fresh meat seemed to work, but then nobody would for nearly four more decades. Vitamin C, otherwise known as ascorbic acid, is crucial to the formation of the protein collagen, the key component of the connective tissue that binds the body together. Collagen is found in everything from bones to tendons to skin. Without it, the body comes undone, which is what was beginning to happen to the men of the *Belgica*. They had gone virtually without vitamin C since they'd left Tierra del Fuego in January. Whatever fresh fruit they might have bought in South America would have gone bad by the winter. The ascorbic acid in the lime juice that de Gerlache had bought in Europe would have oxidized during the bottling process. Nor did the canned food that formed the basis of the men's diet contain any vitamin C.

Science would later explain how the Inuit remained scurvy-free despite consuming almost no fruit or vegetables. Variety of foods isn't as important as variety of nutrients, and the oils in caribou, fish, walrus, seal, and other meats the Inuit ate contain all the vitamin C humans require. The same goes for penguin, on the other side of the earth. This is because most animals, with scarce exceptions like guinea pigs, humans, and a few other upper primates, synthesize their own ascorbic acid. Almost any meat has an antiscorbutic effect, as long as it is eaten in sufficient quantity and not overcooked, since heat breaks down the fragile compound. Cook's insight was aided to some extent by the fact that the frozen penguin and seal meat the expedition had collected that autumn was the only underutilized source of fresh food available on the pack, aside from rat meat (which we now know also would have been effective against scurvy) and human flesh (which would not).*

But healing the men of the *Belgica* would not be so simple. Despite Amundsen's speedy recovery, most of the men were reluctant to follow the doctor's orders, so thoroughly disgusted were they by the smell, taste, and texture of penguin. De Gerlache's adamant refusal to eat penguin meat gave the men cover to resist Cook's recommendation as well. When Cook confronted the commandant and insisted on the importance of his proposed treatment, de Gerlache stood fast.

"The British Navy has used lime juice against scurvy for fifty years," he huffed. "What is good for them is good for us."

Cook responded, astutely, that "bottled lime juice, like tinned food, has had its vital substance destroyed in the system of preservation." De Gerlache wasn't swayed.

The commandant attributed his stubbornness on this matter simply to his revulsion for penguin meat, but it seems likely that he also doubted Cook's judgment. If he had been convinced that his life and the survival of his expedition depended on eating it, he would surely

---

* Cook evidently did not remember the likely embellished passage from one of his favorite polar narratives, Elisha Kent Kane's *Arctic Explorations*, in which Kane and his icebound party overcame a scurvy epidemic during the winter of 1854–55 by eating rats, which they supposedly killed with bows and arrows.

have stifled his gag reflex. Yet he remained determined to abstain from Antarctic game, as if he were bound by principle to stick to the supposedly more civilized foods in the *Belgica*'s larder. Perhaps he felt he owed it to the expedition's backers to consume the provisions he had purchased with their money. In the months since the officers and crew had begun grousing about meals, de Gerlache had grown defensive. So when Cook urged the men to eat widely despised seal and penguin instead, de Gerlache took offense. "To him, this was an insult because with it there went the condemnation of his selection of food," Cook wrote.

"This argument on the evil effects of canned food had been so tiresome to our commander that it peeved him for days every time the question was raised, so we delayed farther entreaties," he continued. Nevertheless, the doctor and Amundsen saw to it that "an ample supply of seal tenderloin and penguin breasts were on hand when the time of urgent need should arrive. And that time arrived quickly."

The proof was in the eating. Those who listened to Cook and ate daily servings of penguin soon saw their symptoms improve. Those who followed de Gerlache's example, meanwhile, continued tumbling down the scorbutic slope, of which death was the inevitable end. The only uncertainty was who the next victim would be.

Cook's approach to scientific inquiry was fundamentally at odds with that of fellow scientists. Whereas Arctowski, Racovitza, Dobrowolski, and Lecointe were strict empiricists, deriving conclusions from methodical observation, Cook valued intuition over data and was particularly drawn to the wisdom of "primitive" civilizations, which he believed contained truths inaccessible to Western science. That feeling was bolstered by the apparent success of his Inuit-inspired antiscorbutic diet. "The Eskimo had for me shattered much of my preconception about the wonder realm of civilized intelligence," he wrote. "Now I was to unlearn and distrust about all taught in our schools as dependable knowledge."

As much as he relished the animated wardroom debates with his fellow scholars—conducted in an unholy mishmash of languages, and a regular source of entertainment for their shipmates—Cook found a more receptive audience for his unconventional ideas in Amundsen. "I implicitly believe what [Cook] says because he is a very experienced polar explorer," the first mate wrote in his diary. "As a result of his contact with the North Greenland Eskimos and his in-depth study of everything to do with polar life he undoubtedly has a deeper insight than other people. If you add to this the fact that he can be regarded as a very competent doctor and that he is specialized in all ailments which occur at the poles then such a man cannot be valued too highly." Amundsen had submitted himself wholly to Cook's baking treatment and penguin diet, and he credited both with his recovery. As far as he was concerned, the doctor could do no wrong.

Cook recognized in Amundsen a man whose conception of the possible was as vast as his own. Both men had ambitions of polar glory that extended beyond the *Belgica* expedition. (Cook had his sights set at that time on the South Pole. Amundsen hoped to be the first to sail through the Northwest Passage, which had eluded his childhood hero John Franklin.) In the *Belgica*'s darkest days, the two became inseparable, forming what Cook described as a "co-partnership . . . to make new and more perfect traveling equipment," including anoraks, penguin-skin boots, sledges, and a tent that could be erected in a few minutes even in the fiercest windstorm. They tested out and improved designs by other polar explorers, such as a pair of wolfskin suits cut to a pattern recommended by Fridtjof Nan-sen. The suit was indeed warmer than any Cook had worn before, but when he and Amundsen returned from a short skiing trip drenched in sweat, he concluded that its greatest shortcoming was a lack of ventilation—a potentially fatal flaw in a polar climate, where perspiration can quickly freeze. The doctor suggested adjustments in line with Inuit methods. "Finding Nansen's improvement a failure," he wrote, "we have reduced the suits as nearly as possible to the ab-original style."

Cook and Amundsen spent much of their free time lost in conver-sation, whether working side by side on their designs or skiing to-gether across the pack. Amundsen peppered Cook with questions and hung on his every word as if it were scripture. Cook, for his part, considered the Norwegian "the most interested, and most interesting man" he'd ever met. "He was cold in manner but alluring and friendly in every act. When his profundity could be grasped in our long isolation . . . we dreamed dreams to remake this old world—for the good of the generations to come. No idea was too big—no inspiration too small to elicit attention."

The pragmatic businessman in Cook—the one who'd cornered much of Brooklyn's milk-delivery market in his early twenties—saw opportunity in the barren wastes of the continent. He conceived of moneymaking schemes that would have made his prospective backer Andrew Carnegie proud: establishing whaling stations and fishing ports in the South Shetland Islands, for example, or relaunching the dormant fur trade in the region.* The dreamer in Cook had less-practical plans in mind, such as harvesting all the penguin guano on the continent to fertilize the world's crops and feed its hungry.

The ideas Cook and Amundsen hatched together were even grander than those Cook conceived on his own. Having seen sheep grazing across the once wild plains of Patagonia—to say nothing of the fortunes amassed by the ranchers—they wondered what other underexploited regions of the world could be so fruitfully transformed. "Said we, the desert of one age is the grainery of the next. Why not plant the Sahara and make the African sands become a new empire of wealth?" Cook wrote.

Another of their fixations entailed nothing less than the reorganization of life on earth. Cook referred to it as "a new ark"—a project to redistribute the world's animal populations more rationally than nature had done, to benefit both man and the creatures whose habitats had been spoiled by human development. "In this Ark dream," Cook wrote, "we planned to take the penguin, the seal, the guanaco and the llama to the North and from there we would bring the bear, the musk ox, the reindeer, the eider duck, the trout, the seal and walrus to the Southern hemisphere and transfer the big useful creatures

---

*Fur seals were thought to have been largely exterminated by the 1830s, but the *Belgica* encountered several colonies of them on Isla de los Estados.

from Africa to South America. Broad oceans, continents, temperate and torrid zones should not separate a better future food supply for man and his animal wilds."

Cook's and Amundsen's musings were all the more outlandish and wide-ranging for having originated in the minds of captive men. They were as vivid as the pack was bleak, as sunny as the night was dark. Lecointe and Arctowski dismissed these plans as "crazy," but they were never meant to be acted upon. They instead served the concrete purpose of keeping Cook's and Amundsen's minds active and focused on something other than their plight. In "the dark icy prison of the crystal hell," Cook wrote, such fantasies offered "redress in dreamy extremes." Whereas so many of their fellow expeditioners were falling prey to illness and despondency, Cook and Amundsen hoped to come out of the "soul-withering Antarctic with mental magazines loaded with brain buck shot."

Just before midnight on July 10, Lecointe pulled off his covers and slid out of his bunk to start his four-hour watch. The floor felt different beneath his feet. He noticed that his legs had become hideously engorged. His left hand was also beginning to swell. Since Cook hadn't dared to utter the name of the disease that was now eating away at the men, Lecointe didn't realize that these were signs of advanced scurvy. He dismissed his concerns and finished dressing. Duty was duty. As sick as he had gotten over the previous few weeks, he had never missed a watch. He limped outside to perform his meteorological and celestial observations. It was a calm, clear night, and the stars shone brightly. Lecointe normally savored these moments of solitude, these silent exchanges between him and the sky. But on this morning, he was so fatigued and in such pain that he could barely make it to the end of his watch. He struggled back into his bunk and found that his legs and hand had ballooned. Despite his exhaustion, the captain was unable to sleep. He remained in a delirious torpor, staring at the rolled-up maps he had strapped to the ceiling for want of storage space in his cabin.

An hour or so later, in a half sleep, he tried to adjust his position. To his horror, his legs and his left arm did not respond to his commands: he was paralyzed. He wanted to scream for help but was wary of panicking his shipmates. At around six a.m., he managed to grope his way out of bed and crawl across the darkened wardroom to Cook's cabin, his legs dragging uselessly behind him.

Cook awoke to a nightmarish apparition, bloated and grotesque and stricken with terror.

"Doctor, I am going—I will follow Danco," Lecointe rasped, clinging to Cook's bedside. "Death is creeping up to me from my feet. See my ankles. It's all over."

Cook looked down at Lecointe's legs and felt a cold shiver rush down his spine. To give his bleary brain time to react, Cook began mechanically performing examinations on the captain. He feared not just for Lecointe but for the entire expedition. With de Gerlache in critical condition and frequently holed up in his cabin, Lecointe was, in the doctor's mind, "the most commanding figure among us." Were he to succumb, the rest of the men, already teetering on the brink of insanity, would surely give in to despair.

He took Lecointe's vitals: his heart rate was high, his pulse was weak, his face was swollen, his skin was cold, waxy, and "shockingly pale." Had Danco ever looked so ill? That Lecointe claimed to have lost the use of his limbs indicated either a terminal stage of scurvy or a hysterical fear reaction. Neither boded well.

"Men are not yet dead until the doctor closes the eyes," Cook said, attempting to conceal his alarm. "If you come under my orders will you do exactly as told?"

"Yes," said Lecointe. "I am at your mercy."

Cook gave the captain a pill—most likely strychnine—and helped him back into his bed to rest, with hot bricks at his feet to aid circulation. With the doctor at his side, Lecointe calmed down, but began making "irrational remarks." To the extent that Cook could understand anything he said, Lecointe was confronting the likelihood that he would not live another day.

When, shortly thereafter, Lecointe heard breakfast being served in the wardroom next door, he summoned what was left of his strength to call Amundsen into his cabin. He told the first mate where he kept all his documents as well as a chest containing letters destined to his loved ones, and offered his final recommendations concerning the expedition. Amundsen listened in silence, attempting—unsuccessfully—to hide his emotion.

Given that de Gerlache was in the throes of scurvy and that his chances of surviving the ship's imprisonment were not much greater than Lecointe's, it seemed all but inevitable that Amundsen, a twenty-six-year-old Norwegian who had never captained his own ship, would inherit command of the Belgian Antarctic Expedition. This was a scenario de Gerlache had hoped desperately to avoid: he believed his backers and the Belgian press would sooner forgive his death than that kind of national embarrassment.

But such concerns did not burden Lecointe at this moment. He faced his destiny with a strange sense of peace. He gazed out of his porthole at the darkness of the pack, which blended with the darkness of the sky. By his estimation, the sun would not rise for another two weeks. It occurred to him that he would never see it. He drifted off to sleep, half thinking, half dreaming that death was not such a terrible thing.

He was surprised to open his eyes a day later. On Cook's insistence, he forced down a small penguin fillet, then fell back asleep for a few more hours. Lecointe woke up feeling slightly better. The doctor took his pulse and was pleased to note that it had dropped. But at 98 beats per minute, Lecointe's resting heart rate was still worrisomely high, approaching tachycardia.

"His case seems almost hopeless to me," Cook wrote in his notebook on July 14. The unfavorable prognosis has sent another wave of despair over the entire party."

Though the doctor harbored little hope for the captain's recovery, he issued strict instructions. "In the future your usual food and drinks will be stopped," he said. "You will eat raw meat, drink hot water and be baked before a hot blaring fire three times daily."

"I will sit on the stove for a month and eat penguins for the rest of my polar life if that will do me good," Lecointe replied.

Cook smiled and assured him that if he followed this regimen, he would be back on his feet to see the sun rise. Cook didn't believe it. Lecointe didn't either, but he nevertheless obeyed the doctor's orders fanatically, eating nothing but penguin, drinking nothing but water, and spending hours naked in front of the fire.

With each passing morning, the swelling in Lecointe's limbs and face decreased. Little by little, his symptoms improved. Against Cook's expectations—but in line with what he had optimistically told the captain—Lecointe was well enough by July 18 to perform his observations.

Word of Lecointe's miraculous recovery spread throughout the ship, and soon almost everyone was coming to Cook, seeking treatment for "real or imaginary troubles."

For many, Cook discovered, the troubles were all too real. He issued a report to Lecointe on the direst cases: "De Gerlache is seriously threatened; Knudsen's legs are very swollen, especially around the ankles; Melaerts counts a hundred and fifty heartbeats per minute." Racovitza, Arctowski, and Dobrowolski were "in a bad way," and Cook admitted to being concerned about his own heart rate.

The doctor prescribed the same regimen to all: "I prohibit all food except milk, cranberry sauce, and fresh meat, either penguin or seal steaks fried in oleomargarine," he wrote. Cook also called for the baking treatment and—for those well enough to get out of bed—daily exercise, albeit nothing too taxing on the heart. The patient's "bedding is dried daily, and his clothing is carefully adjusted to the needs of his occupation. Laxatives are generally necessary, and vegetable bitters, with mineral acids, are a decided help." He recommended total abstinence from alcohol: "We have been accustomed to take light wines at meals, but the wine has a bad effect upon the heart and kidney functions, so much so that we have stopped its use altogether," Cook wrote, though in practice there were enough special occasions to warrant plenty of exceptions to this rule.

Cook's treatment did not eradicate suffering on board, but those who submitted themselves fully to it saw undeniable improvement. Most swore off nearly everything but seal and penguin and came to crave the meat. Acknowledging the severity of his illness, even de Gerlache pinched his nose and ate the occasional penguin fillet, but he could keep it down only if it was charred to a crisp, which nullified much of its antiscorbutic effect. For the most part, the commandant stuck to the menu he had meticulously designed and ate the food he had purchased for the expedition at no small cost.

Cook's air of optimism was the keystone of his treatment plan.

"When at all seriously afflicted," he wrote, "the men felt that they would surely die, and to combat this spirit of abject hopelessness was my most difficult task." The doctor turned his shipmates' eyes away from the dark chasm of anguish into which they stared throughout the night and toward the light at the horizon, which lingered a few minutes longer every day, heralding the sun's imminent return.

CHAPTER 13

The Order of the Penguin

DAYS BEFORE THE SUN WAS EXPECTED TO RETURN, EVERY MAN ABOARD had picked out a spot from which to greet it. Some would climb to the crow's nest or hang in the rigging; others would spread out across the pack. On the morning of July 22, Cook, Amundsen, Lecointe, and de Gerlache marched with difficulty to the summit of a nearby iceberg.* What should have been an easy ascent took an hour in the men's weakened state. They stopped to catch their breath every hundred steps or so, their heaving exhalations cutting through the silence. The effort was especially draining on de Gerlache, who by then was in far worse shape than the others, and yet the commandant persevered in anticipation of seeing the sun for the first time in seventy days—or at least a fragment of it. According to Lecointe, the sun wasn't expected to rise in earnest for another twenty-four hours, but the men hoped that by climbing to a high enough elevation, they might peek just beyond the curvature of the earth and catch an early glimpse, if only by refraction.

When they reached the top of the iceberg, the four men turned to the north and focused on where the dawn was brightest. As the noon hour approached, the cirrus-strafed, pale-yellow sky turned pink, then exploded in an ever-shifting multicolored conflagration. "There were spaces of gold, orange, blue, green, and a hundred harmonious

---

* Strangely, while all primary accounts of the sun's apparent return note that it marked a critical turning point in the ship-wide mood, they don't agree on the date it took place. According to Cook and Amundsen, it was July 22; for Lecointe it was the twenty-third. Racovitza, who was not among the iceberg-summiting party, recorded the date as the twenty-seventh. De Gerlache, meanwhile, reported that it was July 21, Belgium's national day commemorating Leopold I's ascension to the throne following the 1831 revolution.

blends," wrote Cook, "with an occasional strip like a band of polished silver to set the colours in bold relief."

Just before twelve o'clock, the haze that hung over the horizon parted as if on cue. A sliver of fire burst into view and reflected in the men's tired eyes. "We could not . . . have found words with which to express the buoyant feeling of relief," wrote Cook, "and the emotion of the new life which was sent coursing through our arteries by the hammer-like beats of our enfeebled hearts." The oppression of the long polar night had been so overwhelming that even though they knew, logically, that the sun would be back, its appearance felt like nothing short of a miracle. Its rays didn't yet reach the pack, but skimmed the crests of the tallest icebergs and shone for a few instants on the Belgian flag that flew from the top of the *Belgica*'s mainmast, which in the commandant's mind lent the occasion an added, auspicious symbolism.

"Our eyes were dazzled by this radiant vision," de Gerlache wrote. "One must be deprived of the sun to know how beneficial it is for the body and the soul. One understands then the sentiment of savage peoples who have, since time immemorial, made it their first divinity."

Just as abruptly as it had risen, the hint of sun disappeared. But it left a lasting afterglow.

The sun lingered about twenty minutes longer every day. Its stark, naked light revealed the damage of the long night. The winter had taken something from the men that they could never fully recover, had warped their minds and visited grotesquerie on their bodies, compressing a lifetime's worth of torment into a single dreadful season. "We are bloated and yellow," wrote de Gerlache; "mutually we find one another to have aged; our features are tired, drawn, and our faces have retained, from the suffering of winter, a sad and worried expression." Several of the men had gone gray in just three months, as if the winter night had distended time itself, like the terrible vortex in Poe's "A Descent into the Maelstrom." "We have aged ten years in thirty days," wrote Cook.

Photographs of the men around this time confirm de Gerlache's and Cook's descriptions, especially when compared to the bright, hopeful portraits taken before the *Belgica*'s departure. In Antwerp, Lecointe smolders with youthful vigor in a finely tailored uniform; five months into the *Belgica*'s imprisonment, he seems worn-out, sickly, bloated, a decade older than his twenty-nine years. In a promotional image taken in Belgium, de Gerlache strikes a glorious pose, gazing upward as if at the peak of a mountain he means to conquer; his goatee is lush and neatly trimmed, his mustache curled just so; he wears an elegant fur hat at a jaunty angle, with a fur cape draped over the shoulders of a dashing winter coat. This fantasy of a polar explorer contrasts poignantly with a photograph Cook took of the commandant after the long night: de Gerlache, in a coarse sweater, looks mournfully toward nowhere, his face haggard and puffy and overgrown with hair that creeps from just below his bulging eyes to halfway down his neck. Not that his shipmates were any more presentable. The explorers emerged from the night looking like wild men. Weekly (at best) baths were not enough to wash the seal grease or the coal residue out of their tangled manes.

But with the sunrise came a desire for renewal. The men gathered to have their hair and beards cut. As the resident surgeon, Cook was deemed skilled enough with a pair of scissors to serve as the officers' barber, though he proved less conscientious than some might have preferred. Reported one dissatisfied customer: "Sometimes . . . much like a shopkeeper who, having no competition, has little fear of losing his business, [Cook] trims the hair on one side and refuses to trim on the other . . . and has a good laugh at our expense!" Such pranks were not idle tomfoolery. They were part of the doctor's strategy to lift the men's spirits and focus their attention on something other than their bleak surroundings.

Two people managed to avoid Cook's shears: Racovitza, who preferred to cut his own unruly thatch, and Cook himself. The doctor grew his fine, straight hair down to his shoulders and kept it out of his face with a ribbon tied around his forehead. With his voluptuous beard, he had taken on a messianic appearance. His fervid, half-crazed slate eyes were those of a fanatic. Indeed, the Antarctic night had turned him into a kind of zealot—a devotee of the sun. He conceived of it as one might conceive of God. It was the origin of all life, and its absence was a kind of damnation. With its return, he was born again.

"How that great golden ball of cold fire incites the spirit to expressions of joy and gratitude!" he wrote. "The sun is, indeed, the father of everything terrestrial. We have suddenly found a tonic in the air, an inspiration in the scenic splendours of the sea of ice, and a cheerfulness in each other's companionship which makes the death-dealing depression of the night a thing of the past."

Cook's faith in the power of the sun led him to ascribe to it properties that defied science. Just as he had come to believe that living things store light, as the Inuit elder Sipsu had suggested, he became convinced that the ice itself captured the sun's rays. "The snow in the night now assumes a noticeable brightness after a day of sharp sunshine," he wrote a few weeks later, when daytime started gaining on nighttime. "[This] phosphorescence I have ascribed to a kind of latent retention by the snow of the light of the sun. I have taken much interest in this phenomenon, and have recently made certain tests which seem to confirm my theory."

To demonstrate his hypothesis, he stretched black fabric over a smooth patch of snow while the sun was shining. At night he removed the cloth "and invariably there has been a dark spot," he reported. "This, in my estimation, proves that the snow absorbs and retains for a time certain rays of light."

He was wildly wrong. A charitable interpretation of Cook's observation suggests that the black cloth absorbed more of the sun's heat and caused the snow beneath it to melt faster than the uncovered snow around it; the slicker texture might have reflected moonlight or starlight differently. But it's more likely that Cook's romantic side got the better of the scientist in him.

With the advent of day, the *Belgica* colony churned slowly back to life. The men scurried in and out of a warren of tunnels and paths they had built in the embankment of snow around the ship. The sound of hammer striking anvil resonated once again from the forge amidships as Somers built spare parts for the sounding device and other machinery. The scientists were back at their posts—sounding, dredging, fishing, measuring, observing. July was the coldest month yet, and since the expedition had not brought enough clothes suitable for such extreme temperatures, the crew spent several days stitching anoraks out of red wool blankets, which they lined with wolf fur. (Cook had brought a number of furs along with him.) To Amundsen, the contrast of the bright-red coats against the blindingly white snow "certainly produced a bizarre and theatrical effect."

Since the adoption of Cook's regimen, onboard health had improved, even though several men remained in poor condition, notably the baby-faced Norwegian sailor Engelbret Knudsen and Commandant de Gerlache. Cook had correctly deduced that a penguin and seal diet would stave off scurvy, but the winter had drawn down the ship's store of Antarctic game. Just as animal life had been slow to flee beyond the northern horizon heading into winter, it was slow to return. Penguins were nowhere in sight, which meant that the men were in danger of running out of the one thing that could keep death from scurvy at bay.

Day after day, Cook continued to peer out over the bulwarks in the hope of spotting dark forms against the ice. Now and then, small geysers erupted out of freshly carved breathing holes, signs that seals were gradually returning. Before long, penguins could be heard braying in the distance—*kaah . . . kaah . . .* —but not seen. Getting to them soonest would require traveling beyond sight of the ship.

At the end of July, Cook, Lecointe, and Amundsen received de Gerlache's permission to embark on an extended journey to hunt for penguins. The goal they had set was a massive tabular iceberg about seventeen miles east-northeast. Though it looked like a straight shot to the berg, this was no simple journey; it would be crucial to keep their eyes fixed on a prominent visual marker at all times, lest they get lost in the ever-fluctuating icescape. That the iceberg lay slightly to the north presented an added advantage: since the penguins had followed the light to the edge of the pack for winter, they would presumably be returning from that direction.

It would take them at least two days to get to the iceberg and back. For Cook and Amundsen, the excursion would also provide the chance to test out the travel equipment they had designed together, including the sail sledge and the conical tent—a trial run for an evacuation from the ship by foot, should that become necessary, as well as for their own future expeditions. The hunting trip would present, moreover, a welcome change of scenery after months of imprisonment. "We were tired of the 'mad-house' promenade about the bark. The little mountains of tin cans, ashes and other *debris,* which decorated our immediate surroundings, were wearisome," Cook wrote. "We felt that if we could get away for a few days and pitch our camp upon the bare bosom of the sea of ice near some iceberg, we might make some studies worthy of record, and we would certainly come back loving the *Belgica* and our companions better."

Amundsen, for his part, looked forward to logging another record: the first sledge journey over the Antarctic pack ice.

The departure of this expedition within an expedition, on the cold, clear morning of July 31, was met with a sort of pastiche of the ovations that had accompanied the *Belgica*'s push-off from the Antwerp dock the year before. Lecointe, Cook, and Amundsen were giddy with excitement; they formed, as schoolboys might, an Antarctic society they called the Order of the Penguin, and appointed Amundsen as chairman and the other two as mere knights. Max Van Rysselberghe, the second engineer, made medals for the order from the bottoms of empty tin cans, on which he carved an image of a royal penguin and the words "Speed! Deprivation!" Lecointe solemnly hung the medals around Cook's and Amundsen's necks, as well as his own, by their red ribbons.*

The three travelers loaded the sledge with camping equipment, rifles, and ten days' provisions for what was meant to be a two-day trip. Amundsen and Lecointe donned skis and harnessed themselves to the sledge, hauling it as Cook, wearing snowshoes, walked behind to stabilize it. They unfurled the sail Cook had stitched out of bedsheets, which ballooned in the light southerly breeze, providing the propulsive force of one extra man. Despite his condition, the ailing

---

*In Lecointe's recollection, the brotherhood was called the Order of the Kjøttbollers, and it was Cook who was named its leader. The discrepancy could be chalked up to the unreliability of memory or perhaps to the utter silliness of the ceremony. It might also be due to the three-way language barrier between the members of the order. Lecointe's English was as hopeless as Cook's French, and neither spoke Norwegian. Amundsen, a quick study with language, was left to translate.

de Gerlache accompanied the men partway before seeing them off with a firm handshake.

Still recovering from the illness and muscular atrophy of winter, Amundsen and Lecointe paused frequently to rest. They sweated profusely despite a temperature of −30 degrees and the well-ventilated fur suits Cook had designed. The party advanced at a fraction of the speeds Cook had achieved running dogsleds in Greenland, and it soon became obvious how fundamentally inefficient manhauling was as a means of conveyance over snow. But if progress was laborious, it was steady at first. The sledge glided smoothly across a relatively flat crust of hard ice, and its heavy load acted as ballast, allowing the wind to fill the sail without tipping the contraption over.

When the travelers had surveyed the ice from the ship, the path to the distant iceberg had appeared largely white, flat, and unbroken, with just a few thin streaks of water along the way that seemed easy enough to bypass. But as they advanced into it, they found the topography to be distinctly more complex and disorienting. What had seemed from afar to be tiny hillocks were in fact impassable ridges, and the streaks of water were vast clearings. The trio stopped every so often to take compass bearings of the ship shrinking behind them, the hummocks around them, and the giant iceberg ahead of them, keeping in mind that the pack was in constant motion and that their map could quickly become outdated. No matter how far they progressed, the berg appeared to be "within gunshot." This was an illusion, as its base was in fact beyond the horizon. The Antarctic light was back to its old enchantments. A setting sun and a full moon occupied the same sky, twin medallions of gold and silver. "The scene here was a picture for the gods," Cook wrote.

That afternoon, the three men came to a halt at the edge of a vast lake of new ice barely three inches thick that blocked their path to the iceberg. The sheet was so thin they could see the darkness of the ocean through it. Yet some distance ahead of them, the ice took on a yellowish tint, suggesting the return of photosynthetic organisms and thus the possibility of larger animal life. Though they had learned that ice of this color was rarely strong enough to bear a man's weight, Lecointe, Amundsen, and Cook nevertheless decided it was worth investigating. They stepped gingerly onto the slick surface, which offered little purchase for their skis and snowshoes, and struggled to drag the overloaded sledge across it. The combined weight of the travelers and the sledge approached half a ton. With every step, the thin surface beneath their feet felt as if it was oscillating. It was like walking directly on the water. Each pop of the ice sent chills down the men's sweat-drenched backs. They couldn't help but imagine what it would be like to fall through. It would take a few seconds for the water to soak their heavy fur suits before shocking their skin. Their waterlogged clothes and boots would make it nearly impossible for them to stay afloat, and the two men attached to the sledge would have little time to free themselves before being dragged to the deep.

As they advanced toward the middle of the lake, the ice ahead of them began to separate into tightly packed floes. They hadn't traveled far before they saw an abundance of whales and seals, as well as a few penguins, splashing about in a band of black water ahead. But the ice was too thin and broken up to proceed any farther. To reach the animals, the men would have needed a boat. Even if they'd had one, penguins are as quick and agile in the water as they are lumbering on foot and would have been nearly impossible to catch. The sledging party retreated carefully to the older, thicker ice and attempted to circumvent the lake.

As they walked along its banks, the lake narrowed into a mile-wide channel of open water. When they decided to pitch their tent at nightfall—around three p.m.—they had the impression of camping alongside a river. They looked across it to the giant iceberg, still far in the distance. "We were, apparently, no nearer our destination after the day's march of seven miles than when we started," wrote Cook.

"The tent Cook and I had worked so hard on was erected quickly and easily," Amundsen wrote with pride, from the comfort of his reindeer-skin sleeping bag. "It is sturdy and able to stand up to any wind but it is too small for three people. We have to get changed one by one." It took six hours to thaw the evening meal on a small, ethanol-burning stove wedged between two sleeping bags.

Cook's conical tent stood fast in the strong wind sweeping across the ice that night. The patter of snow against the canvas lulled the knights of the Order of the Penguin to sleep. It snowed inside the tent as well: the condensation from the sleepers' breath froze against the walls and floated back down in flakes.

The next morning, the three men awoke, shook off a coating of frost from their sleeping bags and beards, and ate a breakfast of cocoa and alpine biscuits. At around eleven (they relied on the sun to tell time since their watches had stopped working in the cold), they peered outside the tent to find a different landscape than the one they had seen at sunset. Mist billowed across the ice, and the dark water skies—indicating newly opened leads below—suggested that the wind had caused the pack to fan out overnight. If the ice continued to break up, the campsite might soon be surrounded by water, floating freely through an expansive clearing in the heart of the Antarctic pack.

After breakfast, Cook, Amundsen, and Lecointe made a short reconnaissance trip without the sledge to look for a way around the channel that still blocked their access to the iceberg. There was none to be found. "The lead before us . . . extended as far as the eye could penetrate to the east and to the west, a great polar river in the mid-polar sea of ice," wrote Cook. "In it were hundreds of whales, finbacks and bottlenoses, and countless seals, Weddell sea-leopards, and crab-eaters, but strangely enough no penguins." The three might have been tempted to bring back seal meat instead of penguin, but depending on the species, Antarctic seals could easily weigh more than a thousand pounds. Even if they could have captured a swimming seal—which, without harpoons, they could not—it would have been far too heavy to drag back to the *Belgica* across miles of unreliable ice.

With the temperature dropping to −31 degrees, the river was quickly freezing over. It looked like it might soon be possible to find a way across. But if the new ice was barely sturdy enough to support the weight of a man, it certainly would be too thin to support the sledge. Shortly before sunset, the travelers returned to the tent and decided to camp at the same spot for a night or two in the hope that another shake-up in the pack might reveal a solid path to the iceberg.

As Lecointe prepared the evening meal, Cook and Amundsen built an igloo, which, as the doctor learned from his travels among the Inuit, "is always preferable to a tent for a long stay." Cook showed his apprentice how to saw crescent-shaped blocks of snow, stack them in circles of diminishing size to form a dome, and fill the gaps with fist-fuls of snow. Three hours later, the structure was finished. Compared with the tent—to say nothing of the damp and rat-infested ship—the igloo was the pinnacle of comfort. It was warm and spacious and free of condensation, thanks to a flow of air running from the low-slung door to small vents in the encasement of snow. The light of a single candle bounced around the white walls and shone as bright as day.

It was warm enough in the igloo that night for Amundsen to write in his diary with an ungloved hand. The laconic Norwegian indulged in a rare burst of lyricism: "I have never seen a more beautiful sight than this evening. The moon was in the north, there were large cir-cles round it and there was a great deal of light beneath it. In the southwest the red trail of the sun, with black clouds which sail quickly by. On the ice between the hummocks a small, illuminated tent can be seen and a bit further on a brilliantly illuminated Eskimo palace." Keen as ever to set a polar record, he couldn't resist adding: "This must be the first time that the Antarctic pack ice has been honoured with so many strange things."

The travelers spent two blissful nights in the igloo, reading, playing cards, and shooting the breeze as they waited for the pack to reas-semble itself. Although the hunting trip had so far proven to be a failure—they had not yet caught a single penguin—it had the benefit of uniting the three men in friendship. They found that they traveled well together. Amundsen and Cook welcomed Lecointe into their polar alliance, which until that point had been based less on the vicis-situdes of the *Belgica* than on their shared dreams of future journeys on which they would call the shots. Now, with Lecointe, they began to think of what might happen in the months or years ahead on this expedition—should the *Belgica* ever break free of the ice. Their mus-ing led to a potentially seditious notion: since de Gerlache did not appear to be in any shape, physically or psychologically, to lead a dash to the South Magnetic Pole in 1899 as he had planned, perhaps, they thought, that mission should be entrusted to the Order of the Pen-guin.

The suggestion that they might claim for themselves the expedi-tion's most prestigious objective represented a shift in the *Belgica*'s balance of power, one that Amundsen and Cook had to navigate delicately with the ever-loyal Lecointe. Such thoughts had been brewing in their minds for weeks. Ever since de Gerlache had expressed misgivings about having entered the pack, Amundsen had harbored doubts about his leadership. Cook, meanwhile, remained frustrated by the commandant's stubborn objection to eating penguin, which Cook considered irrational and irresponsible.

Lecointe, however, would tolerate no bad-mouthing of de Gerlache. If he had any reservations about the commandant's decisions—as he occasionally did—he would address them with de Gerlache privately. He was forever de Gerlache's protector. Still, he could not ignore the severity of the commandant's condition; perhaps deep down he, too, questioned de Gerlache's resolve or his fitness to see the expedition through to the South Magnetic Pole. In any case, he promised Cook and Amundsen that he would write up a proposal for the three of them to make an attempt at the pole by dogsled the following year. He would deliver it to the commandant as soon as they returned to the *Belgica*.

On the morning of August 3, they found that the mile-wide lead—their river—had narrowed to a trickle as they slept, such was the strength of the winds and currents that had moved the ice overnight. It seemed that a path to the iceberg had at last revealed itself. Or so the men assumed—the fog was growing so thick they couldn't quite make out the berg. When they looked in the opposite direction, they discovered a far greater problem: they could no longer see the *Belgica*, either. Just as worrisome were the dark water skies that stained the clouds in every direction, reflections of a pack now evidently riddled with leads. Though there might not be a better chance to reach their goal and potentially stumble on a waddle of penguins, the men decided it would be wiser to head home before the pack shifted even further and cut off their route to the ship entirely, leaving them hopelessly stranded in an archipelago of floes. For all they knew, that had already happened.

Around midday, they struck camp, said goodbye to their "beloved igloo," and headed into the disorienting swirl of snow and fog. Cook and Amundsen, on skis, hauled the sledge while Lecointe, wearing snowshoes, attempted to navigate using a compass attached to the back of the sledge. Lecointe was relying on compass bearings he'd previously taken of the ship, the iceberg, and a few standout hummocks, but all of those landmarks were now obscured. Even had they been visible, it was likely they would have moved in relation to one another given the forces that had transformed the pack the previous two nights.

It was necessary to stop every twenty meters for the compass needle, which vacillated wildly with each jolt of the sledge, to come to a halt. Each of these stops brought the possibility of error: the slightest adjustment in the sledge's direction might, over several miles, lead them dangerously off course. A discrepancy of just a few hundred feet, Lecointe feared, would be enough for them to pass by the *Belgica* without seeing her. Fresh snow made for smooth traveling, but visibility was so poor that Cook and Amundsen failed to notice obstacles—bumps, hummocks, ridges, crevasses—until they stumbled into them. The sledge tipped over frequently.

Several miles into their trek back to the ship, the travelers heard the sound of frolicking whales. Ordinarily these were enchanting noises. But now, coming through the fog from every direction, they indicated that the men's fears had come true: the pack had cracked up behind them. They were surrounded by bands of open water, cut off from the large floe that held the ship.

The ice on which they walked had fractured into loosely interlocking pans. The three men tried at first to jump from one to the next, hoping in this way to reach solid ice. But as evening fell, the wind changed direction and floes spread out across the water. The sledging party was suddenly cast adrift. All around them, pans hurtled and ground chaotically into one another, getting smaller with every collision. By nighttime, the men managed to reach a square floe no wider than twenty meters and found a reasonably solid area on which to pitch their tent. They had no choice but to spend the night on an island of ice. "I cannot imagine a position in the polar pack more hopeless," wrote Cook.

Afraid that the ice would break up beneath them overnight and that they would not awake until they fell into the water, Lecointe, Cook, and Amundsen took turns keeping watch. Not that any of them got much sleep. They were kept up by the screeching wind; the sound of ice bumping, cracking, and crumbling; and a symphony of grunts, barks, and exhalations. "Our floe was little by little reduced in size until we could hear the seals in the water as plainly as if they were under the tent," wrote Cook.

"The sole candle flickering inside the tent gave it a funereal aspect," Lecointe wrote. "Whales surfaced right by us, as seals found refuge on the narrow ledge that remained free around our shelter."

Amundsen was on watch when, around five in the morning, the floe suffered a sudden, violent convulsion. He looked toward the sound and saw the ice split within a few meters of the tent. The Norwegian thought about waking his comrades, who had finally managed to drift off, but concluded that they would be no safer if they moved to another part of the islet.

Morning light revealed how desperate the men's situation had become. Their floe had grown so small that they could not spend another night on it. Their only escape was to a single adjacent pan. "Our journey was limited to moving from our ice floe to the one next to us," Amundsen wrote later that day, after the tent had been erected on the neighboring slab. There was "water on all sides," he wrote. The three men were "trapped like birds in a cage." Fog eclipsed everything but the narrow belt of water immediately surrounding the floe. The "mainland" of the pack was out of sight.

The castaways busied themselves as best they could during the daylight hours. Lecointe thawed out breakfast while Cook, as usual, found something to tinker with, a problem to solve. Amundsen, usually the very picture of sangfroid, paced back and forth outside the tent. The trip had already lasted twice as long as they'd planned, and their provisions were beginning to run out. They had only a few days' worth left. The ice played a long game, and the men began to wonder what they'd do for food and fresh water if they remained stranded. There were no good answers.

Amundsen stared into the fog for hours, willing it to lift. He became attuned to the most minute variations in its texture, every wisp of gray on gray. When he saw it start to thin in the afternoon, his heart leapt at a familiar sight, and he let out a cry of joy. Lecointe and Cook came rushing out of the tent. They squinted at a ghostly form that appeared in the distance.

"There is an iceberg!" exclaimed Lecointe. Its contours were as familiar as the face of an old friend. It was the same iceberg they had skied to many times for exercise, caught in the pack no more than a half hour's journey from the ship. The fog continued to lift, and before long the men were relieved to make out the dim outline of the *Belgica* herself. "We decided to prepare a festive meal for the occasion," wrote Amundsen.

As pleased as they were to see the ship again, the travelers were no closer to the other side of the clearing. They retreated to the tent and hoped for the wind to shift.

Later on, Cook happened to peer through a ventilation hole in the tent and saw two men approaching the edge of the water on the far side of the channel. In a burst of excitement, he alerted his tentmates. The castaways soon recognized the men as Van Mirlo and Tollefsen. When they got within shouting distance, the new arrivals explained that the rest of the expedition had begun to worry that the sledging party had been lost for good and described the relief they all felt when the fog cleared and de Gerlache spotted the tent from the crow's nest: a dark triangular speck on a sea of white. The sailors bounded nimbly from floe to floe and pussyfooted across translucent new ice in an effort to rescue their shipmates. Yet every conceivable path to the tent ended at the unbridgeable moat surrounding the floe. In a desperate effort, Van Mirlo attempted to jump onto a pan but lost his footing and fell into the glacial water. Cook, Amundsen, and Lecointe watched in horror as the panicked Belgian flailed back to his side of the channel, where Tollefsen hoisted him onto the ice. Van Mirlo was chilled to the bone and had to be rushed back to the ship. Tollefsen vowed to return the next day.

Torn between hope and despair, the castaways returned to their tent and made a hearty meal out of their dwindling provisions. They would have to endure at least another night on their island. One slight comfort was that the temperature had dropped again. The ice would not break so easily, and slushy new ice forming on the water would cushion the floe against knocks and pressures. Nevertheless, the three men each slept with a knife at the ready in case the ice split beneath them and they needed to cut their way out of the tent while holding their breath in the pitch-black water.

They awoke on August 5 to a gloriously clear day but a terrifying sight: the banks of the channel had drifted apart, and their islet was now drifting in a lead wider than the river Scheldt. They could barely make out the *Belgica*.

Around midday, they saw three men arrive at the channel's opposite edge, too far for the castaways to recognize them. Lecointe, Amundsen, and Cook saw the men walk eastward along the water to an area where the ice was thicker. They watched the leader of the rescue party with particular admiration as he leapt athletically among the floes. *Who can it be?* they asked themselves. When he arrived close enough to salute them, "we quickly recognized the rigid greeting," wrote Amundsen. "It was Tollefsen." Amundsen took pride in seeing his fellow Norwegian show such initiative. Tollefsen and the other two, Van Mirlo and Johansen, marched eastward along the channel in hopes of finding a way across, but the gap between the campsite and the rest of the pack remained too wide. Soon the castaways would run out of food. It was possible they would die within sight of their shipmates.

All of a sudden, the ripples on the surface of the water changed direction, like a school of minnows fleeing a predator. The wind was turning. The castaways could now feel it at their backs. Almost imperceptibly at first—in what Lecointe might have interpreted as a stroke of blind luck, Amundsen as divine intervention, and Cook as a vindication of his optimism—the channel began to close. This was their chance. As their island sailed toward the agglomeration of floes pushed up against the old ice, the men packed their last day's worth of food onto the sledge and left the rest of the equipment inside the tent. They would have to travel lightly to have any hope of making it across the fragile ice. Using the sledge as a bridge, they managed at last to pass over leads and crevasses and rejoined their shipmates. Once on firm ice, the six men made rapid progress. By two o'clock, they were back on the *Belgica*. They had returned without a single penguin, and only barely with their lives. It would take nearly two weeks for the pack to consolidate enough that Amundsen and Cook could retrieve their tent.

The nearness with which the travelers had avoided catastrophe— the sheer luck of their safe return—ruled out any further excursions on the treacherous pack ice beyond sight of the *Belgica*. Despite the jubilation that accompanied the end of the long night, and the prospect that a summer thaw would soon liberate the ship, the expeditioners felt more confined and isolated than ever. Everyone had placed their hopes on the sun to undo the harm done by the darkness and cold, but the suffering continued. Rather than lift the men's spirits, the return of daylight had, perversely, deepened their despair.

CHAPTER 14

Insanity

As the forecastle was coming to life on the morning of August 7, Van Mirlo, his eyes glistening with fear, handed a note to Max Van Rysselberghe:

I can't hear, I can't speak!

Van Rysselberghe was flabbergasted. He at first suspected a hoax—Van Mirlo was notorious for his histrionics—and asked him a series of questions. When his fellow Fleming failed to respond, Van Rysselberghe took him straight to Cook's cabin.

After examining the patient, the doctor concluded that there was nothing wrong with Van Mirlo's ears or vocal cords. The problem was with his mind. He was experiencing a hysterical crisis that Cook thought was likely to get worse in the next few days. He ordered Van Mirlo's crewmates to discreetly keep an eye on him, in two-hour shifts, even at night.

The deckhand recovered his speech and hearing within a week, but not his reason. Among the first things he said when he found his voice was that he was going to murder his superior, chief engineer Henri Somers, as soon as he had the chance. Cook's photographs of the twenty-one-year-old, light-haired Van Mirlo around this time suggest madness. In one portrait, the sailor's eyes are almost entirely white. His pupils are thrust all the way to the side, fixed on something just off camera that appears to frighten him. His downy lip begins to curl into a smile.

Van Mirlo's insanity struck his shipmates at their core. It was one thing to be depressed, to suffer from despair, or even to be worn down by physical maladies like Danco. But Van Mirlo's unraveling escalated the sense of terror that had been simmering on board for months. He was simultaneously an augury of the worst that the men feared for themselves and a vector of fear. If he said he would murder Somers, what was to stop him from changing his mind and killing someone else? Now the expeditioners had to worry not only about "the elements conjured against us," wrote Lecointe, but also "this man who was irresponsible for his actions." The sailor's condition was a particularly extreme manifestation of the generalized panic that most were barely managing to keep contained.

Instead of recovering with the end of winter, as all had hoped, the expedition seemed to be coming undone. Cook was alarmed to discover a ship-wide relapse of the various physical and mental symptoms that had plagued them during the long night—what he had collectively labeled "polar anaemia." De Gerlache continued to experience debilitating headaches, which Cook associated with "nervous troubles." The crew members Johansen and Knudsen were stricken with alarmingly swollen legs and resting heart rates of up to 150 beats per minute. Arctowski, ever the contrarian, saw his pulse drop to an equally disconcerting 46 beats per minute. The weakest among the men—including Melaerts, Van Rysselberghe, and Dobrowolski, all three of whom were soon bedridden—were those who resisted eating penguin or seal meat. But that couldn't explain everything, as even the committed penguin-eaters Amundsen and Cook were unwell. Around the same time, Tollefsen had begun exhibiting strange, paranoid behavior, avoiding the company of his shipmates and quaking in fear at the slightest creak of the *Belgica*'s timbers.

After relenting slightly in August, the cold returned with a vengeance in early September. At four a.m. on the eighth of that month, the thermometer registered −45.6 degrees. At that temperature, the lowest the men had yet experienced, eyelashes froze, teeth and eyeballs cringed, and even regular breathing became painful, triggering coughing fits. The cold confined the men to the ship and locked the *Belgica* even more firmly inside the ice. Seawater turned overnight into a layer of ice ten centimeters thick. There was not a trace of liquid water to be seen from the crow's nest.

Cook looked out onto this unbroken expanse of ice and saw a vast white shroud. Its stillness belied how deadly it was. He realized that the men's survival depended on freeing the ship this summer. Fridtjof Nansen and his hardy Norwegian shipmates aboard the *Fram* may have somehow survived multiple winters in the ice, but it was clear the men of the *Belgica* would not. In the doctor's estimation, several on board were unlikely to last just one more winter in the pack. Nor were they in any condition to march hundreds of miles to land, even presuming the officers knew where land was. (They didn't.) The thickness of the ice that had built up around the ship—reaching several meters in places—led many to doubt whether it would ever melt away on its own at a latitude where temperatures rarely rise above the freezing point, and never for long. Yet Cook was struck by the fatalism that seemed to grip de Gerlache and Lecointe, the sense that the ice would either free the ship or it wouldn't, and there was nothing the men could do about it.

In an attempt to impress upon them the gravity of the situation, Cook informed the officers that the *Belgica* would have to escape the pack by summer, or many men would die. They could not wait to find out whether nature would be cruel or kind. It was no longer the time to worry about whether the expedition would reach its goals, whether it would be remembered as a triumph or a failure; its only objective now was to survive. The *Belgica* threatened to become one of the great disasters in the history of exploration, destined to be mentioned in the same breath as the *Jeannette,* the *Terror,* and the *Erebus.* The point of no return, Cook insisted, was just a few months away.

De Gerlache and Lecointe hadn't until then been overly worried about the prospect of a second wintering. From the beginning, they had placed their faith in the half ton of explosives they had loaded on board back in Belgium, on the day of departure. Should it not be possible for the ship to leave the ice as she had entered it, they thought, the tonite would enable them to blast away a passage. Yet Cook's warning planted a doubt in their minds. It prompted them to put their emergency breakout plan to the test in the frigid early days of September.

Trained as an artillery officer, Lecointe volunteered to conduct the first experiment. He descended into the hold to take stock of the tonite. He opened one of the crates of explosives and took out a single cartridge, shaped like a long, thin brick. When he pinched it, the charge frittered away in his fingers. Its waterproof paraffin casing had melted and no longer sealed off the whitish powder, nearly equal parts guncotton and barium nitrate. Lecointe picked up another, which also proved unusable. His heart dropped. Frantically, he inspected stick after stick and found that a large number were ruined. The melted casings indicated that the tonite had first been damaged long ago in the extreme heat of the tropics. The extreme cold of the Antarctic had also had an effect: many of the fuses had become so brittle they snapped off like twigs.

Lecointe rummaged through the crates and picked out 160 relatively unharmed sticks. He climbed out of the hold, descended onto the ice, and placed the charges delicately on a sledge to transport them a long distance from the ship. After bundling them together and nestling them in the ice, the captain rigged the bomb with three mercury fulminate detonators and rolled out a long fuse. He ordered the officers who accompanied him—Amundsen, Cook, and Arctowski—to move to safety behind a hummock several hundred yards away. The explosion, he warned, would shake the entire pack and send massive chunks of ice sky-high. Then he lit the bomb and hurried away.

Five minutes passed. Then ten. Twenty minutes later, the men had still not heard the expected detonation. They peeked nervously around their hummock and just then saw a small flame, like a matchbox catching fire. Then came a column of thick black smoke, but no explosion. Fearing that the tonite could go off at any moment and perhaps shatter the pack so completely that they would be unable to reach the *Belgica*, the four men cautiously skied to the edge of the bomb site. What they found dismayed them. The tonite *had* gone off. The crater left behind was dishearteningly puny, a sooty concavity about ten feet in diameter and just four feet deep. The explosives had done little but melt the snow on top of the hard layer of sea ice.

Lecointe tried again the next day, this time bundling five hundred sticks of tonite—enough, under normal conditions, to blow a ship like the *Belgica* to smithereens. The mercury fulminate detonator hissed as it deflagrated. Then the tonite ignited. But instead of blowing up, it merely burned beneath the snow. "We saw a beautiful white light, which turned yellow, green, and then nothing, not the slightest explosion!" reported Lecointe. "It was humiliating in the extreme." (Recalling that tonite was said to be "more powerful than dynamite and much safer," Cook quipped that it was "decidedly safer.")

Lecointe refused to abandon hope. He concluded that the cold must have compromised the charges.* They would need to be thawed before he could properly test them. Just days after handling the charges with surgical care, for fear that the slightest false movement would set them off, Lecointe now impatiently stuffed 160 sticks of tonite into his bed to warm them against his body overnight. But when he ignited them the next day, the result was no more encouraging than in the previous two attempts.

"I've thus lost all confidence in the tonite," Lecointe wrote.

The failure of the explosives wasn't just embarrassing. It was a devastating blow to the expedition's hopes of salvation. The tonite on board had reassured the men that they had at least a chance of influencing their fate should the ice not relinquish the ship on its own. But now that the charges appeared to be duds, the *Belgica* no longer had any say in the matter. The fail-safe had failed. There was no escape plan.

The realization that their lives now depended entirely on the whims of the Antarctic ice pack sapped the men's already dismal morale and immediately impacted their physical and mental health. Aside from fresh meat, bright light, and exercise, hope was the crucial fourth prong of Cook's prescribed health regimen, and it, too, was now in critically short supply.

In one important aspect, nature was merciful: animals were returning to the vicinity of the ship. The men's mandated diet of antiscorbutic fresh meat required that they slaughter the seals and penguins

---

* As it happened, one of the reasons the officers chose tonite over dynamite was that, aside from its greater explosive power, tonite was said to be more resistant to extreme temperatures, but its makers likely weren't counting on the bottomless cold of an Antarctic winter or the torrid heat of the tropics.

for which they had developed profound gratitude, even affection. Survival was a demoralizing, stomach-wrenching affair. The men killed on a daily basis, spattering blood across the white pack. Most written accounts elide the brutality of the hunt, but Amundsen's diary chronicles the violence in unflinching, clinical detail. For the Norwegian, putting an animal to death was just another skill to master.

Amundsen and Cook were skiing on the pack one day in late September when they encountered a seal and gave pursuit. "It was a very intelligent animal," Amundsen wrote. "We attacked from two directions, the doctor with a ski, me with an ice pick. After the seal had been gashed with the ice pick he became very afraid of it. The doctor's ski, on the other hand, did not worry him. It turned into a very difficult hunt. . . . It was interesting to see how quickly the seal could distinguish between the dangerous ice pick and the harmless ski." Such a battle could take hours before a seal breathed its last.

Guns were the preferred method of execution. But if the process was quicker, it was no less gruesome. "The first shot penetrated deep into its right lung," Amundsen wrote, describing the killing of a crab-eater seal. "The animal did not seem to be hindered much by this because he calmly continued on his march which had been interrupted by the shot. The crab-eater only gave up a quarter of an hour later when a second shot penetrated its larynx and aorta. Even after that fatal shot the animal still fought for its life for five minutes. Some seals have had five or six bullets in their head before finally giving up." He and Cook eventually discovered a more humane technique: "We shot them through the bottom of the neck, through the larynx, into the brain. It worked almost immediately."

Not every sailor could muster Amundsen's composure. One afternoon in late August, Van Mirlo, who had only recently begun speaking again and was still considered dangerously unstable, was asked to help haul back the carcasses of five seals that had been killed and butchered on the ice that morning. The sailor was carrying a twenty-pound piece of meat when he shouted in terror.

"Captain, it lives! It lives yet!" he stammered.

Van Mirlo ran to Lecointe, who was standing nearby, and showed him the section he was carrying, cut from a seal's back. It was still convulsing. Versed in science, the captain understood the disturbing phenomenon to be a cadaveric spasm, known to occur in lifeless tissue following a violent death in which the victim experienced intense emotion. But the mentally fragile Van Mirlo could not be convinced that the animal was no longer suffering.

At six p.m. on September 20, de Gerlache retired to bed before supper. Violent migraines gripped his temples with renewed force, as if in concert with the constricting action of the ice around the ship. Incapacitated by pain, he rarely left his cabin during the following weeks. "He is sad and taciturn, seeking solitude," wrote Lecointe.

De Gerlache absorbed the toll of everything that had gone wrong: the death, the suffering, the hopelessness that followed the failure of the tonite. Adding to his depression was a crippling sense of guilt. In mid-October, Cook informed the commandant and the captain that two of the men, Melaerts and Michotte, had reached an advanced stage of scurvy, at last speaking aloud the name of the affliction he had been combating for months. He urged de Gerlache and Lecointe not to tell the crew. "The commandant is so shaken," wrote Lecointe, "that he asks himself, in anguish, whether his conscience might not be responsible for all these ills!"

After examining de Gerlache a few days later, Cook announced that he, too, was severely affected by scurvy. The commandant received the news with a resigned calm—his own poor prognosis troubled him less than that of his men. He had gradually come to terms with the likelihood that he would die on the pack. That evening, he strode arm in arm with Lecointe, who steered the conversation to pleasant subjects relating to life in Belgium, as he had done with Danco in his final hours. "This awakening of memories seemed to have done him some good," Lecointe wrote. "We decided that each day we would spend two hours together."

The commandant's weakened state left more responsibility on the shoulders of Lecointe, Cook, and Amundsen, but de Gerlache never ceded command of the expedition, and his position at the top of the hierarchy was never in doubt. Nevertheless, tension had begun to form between de Gerlache and the self-styled knights of the Order of the Penguin over plans for the future of the expedition.

Even as Lecointe provided friendly succor to his ailing commandant, consoling him during their daily strolls, the two were engaged
in an extended, increasingly heated cabin-to-cabin correspondence,
exchanging long letters related to the third year of the *Belgica* campaign. In Lecointe's regimented mind, there was no contradiction
between the two impulses: His loving support and his unvarnished
criticism were merely two facets of duty. Both were necessary, he felt,
to help de Gerlache recover and finish what he started.

The correspondence had begun months earlier, on July 22, the day
the sun returned, when de Gerlache had shared his revised plan with
Lecointe to seek his opinion. Like most of the officers, de Gerlache
had hoped that the pack would break up by summer, perhaps even as
early as mid-November. (This was before the fizzling failure of the
tonite experiments had made an escape less likely.) Once free, the
Belgica would, under his plan, pursue a southern course in order to
determine whether a landmass existed in that direction and perhaps
to capture the farthest-south record that had previously eluded him.
Before temperatures dropped again, he would sail the ship north,
around the tip of the Antarctic Peninsula, and head back to Tierra del
Fuego, arriving by mid-March. De Gerlache then mapped a frenzied
itinerary up the west coast of Chile, across the Pacific to French Polynesia, and finally, by late November 1899, to Melbourne, where the
expedition had been initially expected to winter in 1898 and where its
mail and remaining funds awaited it. The *Belgica* would then return
to the edge of the Antarctic pack ice and sail westward along it all the
way to the Weddell Sea, essentially circumnavigating the continent.
In mid-February of 1900, the ship would return to the mountain-
flanked channel the expedition had discovered in the first few weeks
of 1898 (which the explorers now called the Belgica Strait), to allow
the scientists to complete their observations in the region. After that,
the ship would sail home to Belgium.

Conspicuously missing from de Gerlache's new plan was any mention of reaching the South Magnetic Pole, presumed to lie somewhere in the vicinity of Victoria Land on the other side of the
continent, immediately south of Australia. The magnetic pole had
been among the principal goals of the expedition as pitched to the
Royal Belgian Geographical Society, one that had galvanized the pub-

lic and the press, and that astronomer Charles Lagrange had called the mission's raison d'être. Conquering it would secure de Gerlache's legacy and guarantee the triumph of the expedition. The commandant had fantasized about it in detail and imagined that both he and Danco would be among the four-man landing party.

But this was before the ice had trapped the *Belgica* in the Bellingshausen Sea, before de Gerlache had fallen ill, before Danco had died. By midsummer, such a journey had become unthinkable. Even assuming he could stretch the expedition's nearly depleted budget, the commandant was not confident he would survive the winter of 1898, let alone a strenuous overland journey the following year. And so he had quietly dropped it from the plan.

Three weeks later, on August 15, Lecointe responded with his counterproposal, written in close consultation with Cook and Amundsen after they returned from their long camping trip across the ice. With the blunt honesty that de Gerlache had come to appreciate in him, Lecointe methodically outlined his objections to the commandant's itinerary. "The plan to head south is not justified," he wrote. Lecointe argued that attempting to reach a higher latitude in the Bellingshausen Sea would be to risk another winter in the ice and more casualties. The captain reminded de Gerlache of the crew's frail condition. "My judgment is based on the information I gather daily from the physician of the Expedition [Cook]. Not only are none of our men able to make any effort, but none of them are able to provide the work of an ordinary man. This situation will certainly improve, but I understand that the doctor feels that a single incident would set it back, and even exacerbate it.

"Dobrovolski [sic], Johansen and Knudsen are seriously affected; we can no longer rely on Van Mierlo [sic], whose mental state is too shattered; what will happen if the other sailors buckle under the weight of strains too violent for their weak forces?"

Lecointe proposed that instead of pushing south, the expedition should sail north as soon as the ice would let them. The *Belgica* would return to the Belgica Strait, then proceed without delay to Punta Arenas, where Cook insisted the men be allowed to recuperate for at least a month and enjoy "total freedom," despite the risks of another breakdown in discipline. The expedition would then make a straight shot for Melbourne. Lecointe suggested cutting out the proposed stops in Valparaiso and the archipelagoes of French Polynesia, for which he considered the ship ill-suited.

But where Lecointe's proposal differed most drastically from de Gerlache's was in its plan of action for the third year. Intuiting that de Gerlache no longer felt capable of leading a mission to the South Magnetic Pole, Lecointe volunteered to make the attempt himself, alongside Amundsen and Cook, his fellow members of the Order of the Penguin. The itinerary he proposed was based on an idea the doctor had described to him, which itself closely resembled the expedition Cook had initially intended to lead, back when he was seeking support from American scientific societies and the likes of Andrew Carnegie.

According to this new proposal, de Gerlache would sail the *Belgica* to the Ross Sea at the end of the spring of 1899 and drop Cook, Amundsen, and Lecointe off as close as the ship could get to Cape Gauss, on the shore of Victoria Land, with provisions for one hundred days. From there, the three men would travel overland on skis and by dogsled, following the needles of the magnetometer to locate the magnetic pole. Cook had convinced them that the Inuit-style dogsleds he'd seen in Greenland were the most efficient means of locomotion across the ice. Dogs were light, powerful, and naturally insulated against the cold. They would cut down on the cost and the weight of provisions and would allow the men to conserve their energy—essential considerations on a mission where every centime, every ounce, every second, every calorie, and every mile would count. Indeed, each dog could be considered an ambulant food source. In his letter to de Gerlache, Lecointe outlined the plan's ruthless logic: "Once the dog food runs out, the animals will be eaten and the sledges pulled by the men."

This was a radical proposal. Several Arctic explorers, including Nansen, had understood the advantages of dogsleds. But dogs had never been used in the Antarctic, and no previous explorer had eaten the animals as a matter of strategy.

As the landing party searched for the magnetic pole, the *Belgica* would spend the summer in Melbourne and sail back to Cape Gauss at the beginning of the winter to pick up Lecointe, Amundsen, and Cook.

The captain concluded: "It would be useful for us to receive your reply soon because we consider that preparations and tests of all kinds, as well as the establishment of the calculation tables, will be so time-consuming that it is necessary to begin work as soon as possible."

That night, as he awaited de Gerlache's response, Lecointe had reason to wonder whether he had overstepped his role in rejecting the commandant's plan and in claiming the most glorious aim of the Belgian Antarctic Expedition—the magnetic pole—for himself and two foreigners. Given de Gerlache's fragile state, it was hard to know what the repercussions of such audacity might be.

The following afternoon, Lecointe, Amundsen, and Cook met with de Gerlache to discuss the proposal in person. The commandant thanked his fellow officers for their ideas but did not say whether he agreed with the plan for the South Magnetic Pole. He let them stew for five more weeks, until September 22, when he convened an official meeting of the *Belgica*'s officers and scientists to determine the course to follow if ever the ice liberated the ship. All agreed on an itinerary back to South America along the lines Lecointe had suggested in his letter.

Cook blurted out the question that was weighing on his, Amundsen's, and Lecointe's minds: did de Gerlache approve their proposed journey to the South Magnetic Pole or not? The commandant, torn between his duty to deliver the prize he had promised and the recognition that he was in no shape to pursue it himself, had still not made a decision. Instead, he put it up to a vote. He asked the gathering, first, whether it would be justified for the expedition to dedicate a third year to locating the pole, and, second, whether each man would commit to remaining with the *Belgica* through 1900. Though both Racovitza and Arctowski felt their studies of the Belgica Strait had been cut short, neither was keen to extend his time in Antarctica, and both abstained. De Gerlache, for his part, was no longer certain he had the strength to command the *Belgica* for another year, whether or not he joined the landing party at Cape Gauss. Yet he believed he could not in good conscience oppose the pursuit of a goal that he had established in the first place. Faced with the unified front of Lecointe, Cook, and Amundsen, de Gerlache voted in favor of their proposal, relinquishing to the Order of the Penguin the potential glory that should by all rights have been his. All six men signed the official minutes of the meeting.

The following day, having decided he needed to appear more committed to the goal of locating the pole, as he had proposed to his Belgian backers from the outset, de Gerlache requested Lecointe's permission to amend the written record of the meeting. He had no desire to let posterity know how tentative he had been. Rather than opening the discussion by asking his fellow officers for their thoughts on the matter—which, he feared, came off as pusillanimous—de Gerlache wanted to replace the first question with a bolder statement, more fitting of a leader: "I am formally determined to undertake a third year of campaign and to direct it towards the Ross Sea and the austral magnetic pole. Who among you can, from this moment, agree to take part in this voyage?"

Before the beginning of the expedition, Lecointe had vowed to respect de Gerlache "always and forever" and pledged his undying devotion, telling him, "You will find in me a 'second you.'" But the dynamic between the two men had changed. In Lecointe's mind, the commandant's latest request had gone too far. A stickler for protocol, Lecointe told de Gerlache that nobody had the right to alter the record. The captain was fiercely loyal, but he had his limits. De Gerlache had just found them.

A sudden thaw in late September loosened chunks of ice from the ship's rigging and sent them crashing onto the deck. It wasn't long before the warmer temperatures began disintegrating the pack itself, well ahead of schedule. Crevasses split open, floes fanned out, and a large clearing formed just six hundred meters from the ship. Liberation was closer at hand than it had been since the beginning of the expedition's imprisonment. To everyone's surprise and delight, it seemed likely that the pack would break up after all, perhaps even before the end of the year.

To see if they could speed its fragmentation, the men carried out two more experiments with the tonite. Although the charges didn't do much damage, at least they exploded this time. Humidity and warmer temperatures were thought to make the explosives more potent, but also more volatile; as a precaution, the crew moved the nearly half ton of tonite to a hummock a few hundred yards from the ship. "It started to get rather uncomfortable keeping them on board any longer," Amundsen wrote. On top of everything the men were already struggling with, no one thought it wise to add the ever-present possibility of suddenly being blown up.

In preparation for departure at the earliest opportunity, the few able-bodied members of the crew dismantled the shelter that had been built over the deck amidships. Yet the *Belgica* was far from ready: equipment was still scattered across the ice, sails were stowed away, the engine was cold and its pipes were colonized by rats, the hold was in disarray, and the majority of the men were gravely ill.

Just as problematically, there was once again confusion as to where the *Belgica* would be heading if she did break free. On October 24 and 26, right around the time he learned he was severely stricken with scurvy, de Gerlache wrote Lecointe two perplexing letters that upended the plan they had agreed on. Though de Gerlache didn't explicitly say it, his missives made it clear he was too sick to contemplate taking part in a third year aboard the *Belgica*. He now wanted to disembark as soon as the ship reached South America, take the *Belgica* out of commission, and return to Europe. He saw little upside in ferrying Lecointe, Cook, and Amundsen to Cape Gauss and waiting around so they could achieve the glory he'd reserved for himself. If the three of them wanted to search for the magnetic pole, de Gerlache now proposed that they make their own way from Europe to Victoria Land in January of 1900 and establish wintering quarters there. He suggested, bafflingly, that they first stop in New York to purchase a small schooner. The trio, he said, could hire a crew in America to sail the ship to Melbourne and then to Cape Gauss. To help pay for the schooner and the crew, de Gerlache offered to put Lecointe in touch with an Australian newspaper with which he had been in contact—perhaps one to which he had originally planned to sell the story of the expedition to the pole, when he still expected to lead it.

This time, Lecointe responded with undisguised exasperation, bordering on insolence. De Gerlache's change of heart—justified as it was, given the gravity of his condition—struck the captain as an abandonment of duty. "For my part, I cannot subscribe to the plan you propose," Lecointe wrote in a long letter dated October 26, largely devoid of the deferential language that usually graced the men's correspondence. Lecointe seems to have surmised that scurvy, depression, and fatigue had worn down de Gerlache's resolve and clouded his thinking. The letter was an attempt to shake some sense back into him. Lecointe went through de Gerlache's suggestions one by one, pointing out the absurdity of each. He concluded his letter on a cold note: "I cannot accept your proposals . . . because, in the contract signed by the officers, you freely expressed your willingness to take part in the voyage to the Ross Sea and to command the vessel that would take us to Cape Gauss." Having refused to amend the agreement as de Gerlache had requested, Lecointe was now rubbing it in his face.

Throughout the unseasonably warm days of early October, even as the pack was cracking up around it, the two-mile-wide floe that held the *Belgica* remained stubbornly intact. The window of opportunity closed in the second half of the month, when temperatures dropped again, newly formed leads froze over, and it began snowing. Snow fell for a week, then two weeks, then three.

In the end, it would snow for twenty-five consecutive days. The view from the crow's nest was nothing but unblemished whiteness, stretching from the horizon all the way to the foot of the mainmast, directly below. Snowdrift buried the deck under several feet, sloped up from the pack to the level of the bulwarks, and blanketed a pressure ridge that had risen above the poop deck. "Nothing but the masts are visible," wrote Cook.

The *Belgica* had been prepared to sail free by mid-November. Instead, when that time came, the ship had disappeared into the pack, her masts and yardarms sticking out of the snow like three crosses marking graves. "If this continues," Arctowski wrote in his diary, "it will be swallowed up by the snow altogether."

CHAPTER 15

Darkness Under the Sun

LATE IN THE EVENING ON NOVEMBER 16, THE SETTING SUN GRAZED the horizon before swinging back into the sky, where it would remain for more than two months: from endless night, the *Belgica* now entered endless day. The event that marked the occasion would have been a momentous spectacle had a persistent cloud cover not prevented the men from witnessing it. Instead, an unchanging gray light emphasized the deadening monotony of life on the pack.

"Could there be a more melancholy, a more maddening, or a more hopeless region than this?" wrote Cook. "Storms, tempests, and steady howling winds with snow are our constant lot. . . . The sky is always cloudy and dirty; the air is always wet, cold, and agitated; under such circumstances the human mind assumes a like attitude."

Dismal weather, suffocating quarters, widespread illness, teeming rats, and the receding prospect of deliverance provided ideal conditions for misery to ferment into hostility. Around this time, Somers wrote a letter to de Gerlache complaining about the abuse he sustained from his younger shipmates in the forecastle, particularly his assistant Max Van Rysselberghe. "I have always restrained myself from committing violence," Somers wrote, "but I'm always afraid that one day or another my patience will come to an end and in a burst of anger I might not be able to control myself."

Meanwhile, open dissent against de Gerlache now spread beyond the Order of the Penguin, as Arctowski, the headstrong meteorologist, accused de Gerlache of undermining him. Following a general meeting on November 13 to determine the allocation of the expedition's scientific specimens and observations, Arctowski took exception to de Gerlache's order that all meteorological data be consigned to the commandant so he could transfer it to the ship's log and eventually deliver it, as had been agreed upon with the Royal Belgian Geographical Society, to the Belgian meteorological service. Implying he didn't trust de Gerlache's good-faith assurances that the Belgian government would allow him access to his own data, Arctowski refused to hand over one of his notebooks. Since he didn't have a diploma, his observations from the *Belgica* and his analysis of them would be among the few concrete accomplishments he could show for himself.

Over the next few weeks, a flurry of increasingly antagonistic letters traveled between de Gerlache's cabin and Arctowski's laboratory. (It is remarkable that men who lived in such tight quarters would so often communicate with the commandant in writing. They did so partly to maintain a paper record of contentious exchanges, but also because de Gerlache had become so withdrawn since the onset of his illness.) With each reply, the scholar grew more unhinged and insubordinate. The expedition had been poorly conceived and organized from the start, he claimed, and, like its leader, was geared more toward adventure than rigorous science. "The goals we pursue [are] unfortunately too different," he wrote, adding that de Gerlache would, in any event, not be capable of understanding the data. In response to what he considered de Gerlache's tyrannical demands, he wrote, "I will seek to remove myself from [your] command as soon as I will have an opportunity to do so."

In his final retort, a defensive de Gerlache reminded Arctowski that, "though a mere sailor without scientific pretension," he had been the one from the outset who had insisted that the expedition be scientific in nature. But de Gerlache's unflappable poise had been shattered. The draft of his letter was written in an uneasy hand. The right words, which ordinarily flowed so easily from his pen, weren't coming to him. He second-guessed himself and made mistakes, squeezing in numerous corrections and frantically scratching out passages.

But at that moment, de Gerlache was less worried about Arctowski than about a new and far more dangerous enemy he had made at that same November 13 meeting. In the course of the gathering, Amundsen had discovered evidence of what he considered to be an unpardonable betrayal. In discussing the future obligations of the expedition, the officers consulted the contract de Gerlache and Lecointe had signed with the Royal Belgian Geographical Society. Amundsen had not been shown the document before, and when he read article five, it became obvious to him why:

> *In the event that during the expedition I am no longer the commander of the ship and if Mr. Lecointe is unable to take over command then I will decide who succeeds me. My successor will be selected from among the Belgian officers or members of the scientific staff unless absolutely necessary to deviate from this rule. In the latter case command may be transferred to a foreign seaman.*
> *Brussels, 19th March, 1897**
> *[Signed] Adrien de Gerlache*

Amundsen was too stunned to speak. He could feel the anger coursing through his veins. According to maritime custom and the *Belgica*'s established hierarchy, he, as first mate, would by all rights take command of the ship in the event of its leaders' deaths. Given the strong possibility of such a circumstance—both de Gerlache and Lecointe would soon write their testaments—the question of succession was more than theoretical. Yet the stipulation that the helm must pass to a Belgian national "unless absolutely necessary" meant that Amundsen would be skipped over for the next Belgian in line. Since Danco had died, the captaincy would fall to the third officer, Jules Melaerts, Amundsen's detested former roommate, who had banished himself to the forecastle. This was the ultimate humiliation. The document had been countersigned by every other officer and scientist except for Cook (who had joined the expedition at the last minute). Amundsen was convinced it had been kept out of his sight on purpose.

After the meeting, he took Lecointe aside and held his friend to account. *Why had this been agreed to?* When the captain couldn't pro-

---

*De Gerlache claimed that this contract had been backdated and that he and Lecointe had in fact signed it on August 12, 1897.

vide a satisfactory answer, Amundsen confronted de Gerlache and informed him that he would *"never* have taken part in this expedition if this contract had been shown to me in Belgium."

Amundsen's rage boiled throughout the day. As word spread of his discontent, the other officers rallied to his side. Cook declared that "the Geographical Society had drawn a line between the honest Belgians and the dishonest foreigners." Racovitza agreed. Even Lecointe conceded the point.

The next morning, Amundsen demanded to speak with the commandant. Unnerved by the first mate's wrath, de Gerlache asked him to take two days to carefully think through what he had to say. When that time came, Amundsen entered the commandant's cabin and didn't mince words: unlike Arctowski, he wouldn't wait until he could leave the ship before resigning from the expedition.

"I wish to make my plans clear to you in a few words, Commander," he told de Gerlache. "Since learning of the contract between yourself and the Geographical Society I consider my position on this ship as no longer existing. For me this is no longer a Belgian Antarctic expedition, the Belgica is an ordinary ship, stuck fast in the ice. It is my duty to help the handful of people here on board. For this reason, commander, I will continue my work as if nothing has happened, I will do my duty as a human being."

De Gerlache was taken aback. He wasn't sure what Amundsen was implying, whether he intended to follow orders or not. All that was certain was that the first mate now represented a serious threat to his power. Again at a loss for words, he told Amundsen that he saw no way to settle the matter while they were stuck in the ice.

Amundsen replied that he agreed, but the *Belgica*'s predicament made for an awkward exit. He would not have the satisfaction of slamming the door and walking away for good. The two were bound together until the end. He would be sitting at the breakfast table across from the commandant the next morning, even if, having resigned as an officer of the ship, he had no business remaining in the officers' quarters.

Cook advised Amundsen to put his grievances in writing. The first mate did so in a long letter, in Norwegian, that he delivered to de Gerlache on November 19. "Commander, if you know that the contract was sent to . . . everyone except for me," Amundsen wrote, "then you confirm the contents of it even more. I.e. my position means nothing to you. I came to you voluntarily, to work for a project of general benefit. It is not a question of money but a matter of honor. However, you have violated this honor by robbing me of my rights."

Immediately after reading the letter at his desk, de Gerlache pulled out a sheet of the expedition's official stationery, dipped his pen in his inkwell, and held it over the blank piece of paper, pondering his response. He was already entangled in bitter exchanges with the expedition's captain and one of its scientists. Now he had lost the trust of his first mate. On the one hand, if he upheld the contract, he would stoke the ire of a young and physically intimidating officer who counted the doctor as a faithful ally, who had formed a close bond with the captain, and who commanded the allegiance of the Norwegian crew members. Though de Gerlache did not believe it to be in Amundsen's character, mutiny was not out of the question. On the other hand, if de Gerlache violated the contract to allow a foreigner to take over the expedition, as Amundsen was demanding, he would be betraying his supporters back home, to whom he had until this moment accorded his utmost loyalty.

De Gerlache had forever feared the judgment of his backers and the press, but the *Belgica*'s ordeal had clarified his priorities. The ice had already claimed his ship and his health. Without the support of his men, he had nothing. There could be no doubt in his mind that Amundsen was the rightful heir to the helm. It was obvious to all on board that he had the makings of a larger-than-life polar explorer in the mold of Ross, Nansen, or even the fictional Captain Nemo, the kind of hero a young de Gerlache had hoped one day to become. The notion that Melaerts would ever come to command the ship instead of Amundsen certainly gave the commandant a start, because in that event there was a high likelihood that no one would hear from any of them again. In the end, de Gerlache decided that whatever concessions he had made to the Royal Belgian Geographical Society in the name of nationalism were secondary to the cohesion of the expedition. The *Belgica* was his country now. He would appease Amundsen. He could deal with the harrumphing of Belgium's armchair explorers when he returned. In fact, however, he wouldn't have to; if they ever learned of a tacit amendment to article five of the contract, it would mean that he had died.

He began his response by deflecting blame onto the Royal Belgian Geographical Society. "I did not propose the drafting of the contract in question," he wrote, underlining the sentence. He claimed not to have known that the organization had failed to provide Amundsen with a copy of the document. And he assured the first mate (whom he referred to as second officer) that Melaerts would never leapfrog him in the hierarchy: "It never occurred to me that the 3rd officer—were he Belgian—would take command of the expedition ahead of the 2nd officer, and it is beyond doubt that this circumstance is among those the authors of the contract would consider a case of 'absolute necessity.'"

De Gerlache ended his draft of the letter with the following line: "The only satisfaction I can grant you, Mr. Amundsen, is to offer you . . ." He paused as he thought of how to end that sentence. Then he scratched it out. He realized he had nothing left to give. The damage was done.

On November 20, the day after Amundsen had sent his letter of resignation, the *Belgica*'s hull sprang a leak. A sudden constriction of the pack earlier in the month had heaved the prow onto the ice and dropped the stern into the water; the vessel now listed yet more precipitously backward and to starboard. As snow kept falling onto the slanted deck, its tremendous weight pushed the ship even deeper down, squeezing her through the encasement of ice until the sea licked her bulwarks. Water seeped through weather-weakened planks, ran down the hold's inner walls, and pooled at the rear of the ship, rising at an alarming rate. By the next day, it had filled the bilge and risen above the engine deck. The *Belgica* was slowly sinking.

Amundsen kept his word to de Gerlache and continued to perform his duty as reliably as ever, as he soon had a chance to prove. He joined in the general effort to pump the water from the bilge—the process took six hours—and over the next few days worked tirelessly to help dig the ship out from under several tons of snow.

Polar exploration, to Amundsen, was not a job but an almost chivalric calling. He had volunteered to serve without pay because money was secondary to glory. Amundsen cultivated the image of a modern Viking and followed a code of honor that often conflicted with the nuances and compromises of life at lower latitudes. Just as he remained fiercely loyal to his closest friends—a small group that now included Cook—he rarely forgot a slight. He would never forgive de Gerlache. His confrontation of the commandant, whom he had once so admired, was practically Oedipal in nature. It marked the end of his polar apprenticeship and his coming-of-age as a leader in his own right.

The skies finally cleared on November 27, revealing the midnight sun for the first time. Crew members greeted the awesome sight with impromptu festivities. Somers, the chief engineer, bellowed a rousing version of "La Brabançonne" from the deck. His forecastle nemesis, Van Rysselberghe, joined in with his dulcet voice. The long-suffering Knudsen sang along, and Johansen brought out his accordion. Soon all the men emerged from the ship except for de Gerlache. Too sick to leave his cabin, the commandant nevertheless ordered that several bottles be opened. Rivals harmonizing together, Belgians and Norwegians arm in arm, sailors and officers clinking glasses—such was the unifying power of the sun. Music played through a night indistinguishable from day. In the bright wee hours, Cook and Amundsen went for a delightful ski on the pack and took photographs of the ship. Meanwhile, the rest of the men kept drinking, and the euphoric atmosphere gave way to maudlin daydreaming. Some spoke of home. Somers—the only family man aboard the *Belgica* and a born raconteur—told stories of his young daughter. He teared up at the thought of her, wondering when he would see her again, whether she would remember him, whether she imagined he was lost at sea.

However much the men had looked forward to it during the winter, constant light proved no less unsettling than perpetual dark. When the sun was out, there was no shade to be found on the ice. The assault of the sun came from above and below, reflected off the pure white of the pack. Even on overcast days, those who didn't wear goggles complained of snow blindness. The unrelenting brightness pierced through the black cloths the officers hung over the portholes. It left the men tossing and turning in their bunks and forced them to face their deepest anxieties in broad daylight. "There is too much light, causing sleepless nights," Arctowski wrote in his diary.

Yet it wasn't only the light that kept the men awake. Just as nerve-racking, for Arctowski, was "the fact that we have begun to discuss the eventuality of a second wintering, because the ice does not seem to want to separate." With every day that the pack remained unbroken—despite favorable winds and the constancy of the sun—liberation became that much more unlikely. The men had finally come around to what Cook had been warning them about for months: the ice was not letting go, and a second winter aboard would prove fatal to many. This realization—on top of ineradicable illness and a simmering crisis of leadership—could drive already unstable men over the brink.

Cook had believed the return of the sun would clear away the "mental symptoms" that had bedeviled the ship during the winter. He was wrong. In a few men, they had become far more serious. "Nearly every one is suffering, more or less, from insomnia," Cook wrote, "and the cases which have been mentally deranged before show new signs of disturbance."

Though Cook doesn't mention him by name, he was thinking in particular of one sailor, Tollefsen. The boatswain was among the most experienced and dependable seamen on the ship. He was accustomed to the cold and dark, having worked in the Arctic, and had performed his duties with skill, intelligence, and zeal. Amundsen was especially fond of Tollefsen. But in his diary on November 28, the first mate acknowledged that his fellow Norwegian "displayed some very strange symptoms today which are indicative of insanity." That night, Tollefsen had asked him if he was truly on the *Belgica*. When Amundsen answered that he was, Tollefsen looked perplexed and said he had no memory of embarking on the ship.

Tollefsen's paranoid behavior had begun to trouble his shipmates earlier that month. His protuberant eyes darted nervously at every creak of the hull, every pop in the ice. He experienced ferocious headaches and kept his thickly bearded jaw clenched at all times, as if bracing for imminent disaster. Tollefsen grew so suspicious of his fellow crew members that he retreated to dark corners of the ship, much as Nansen the cat had before her death. He avoided the fore-castle at night and slept instead in the freezing hold, among the rats, without a bedcover or proper winter clothes. "His spirit is troubled by delusions of grandeur and mad terrors," observed Lecointe. "Odd mystery: the word 'chose' [French for 'thing'] infuriates him. Since he doesn't speak French, he imagines that 'chose' means kill and that his companions have given each other the signal to execute him."

A frightened man is a dangerous man. Tollefsen had to be watched at all times, lest he attempt to strike first against those he believed meant to harm him. His friend Jan Van Mirlo, still reeling from his own bout of hysteria, volunteered to be his guardian. Van Mirlo noticed that Tollefsen had begun to act bizarrely after Danco's death, back in June. "He became shy," recalled the Belgian deckhand, and "was continuously writing letters to his beloved 'Agnes' in which he wrote about all his misery here on the ice and about his persecution at the hands of his shipmates." According to Van Mirlo, Tollefsen would place these letters in a small hummock that resembled a mailbox. "To give him pleasure, we went to retrieve the letters and told them they were on their way to Agnes."*

Tollefsen's mental state deteriorated drastically during the month of November. "He doesn't speak, his eyes look vacant, and the only task we can entrust him with is to scrape sealskins," wrote Lecointe. "Even then, he barely progresses in this work: after ten minutes, he drums on the skin with his knife, looking with a bewildered air in the direction of distant pressure ridges." Whenever anyone approached him, Tollefsen would shudder and instinctively bow his head, "as if to receive the coup de grâce."

On the splendid afternoon of December 12, Cook and Amundsen embarked on a long skiing trip. Their destination was the same massive tabular iceberg Cook, Amundsen, and Lecointe had set as a goal for their excursion in early August. (Due to the constant movement of the pack, it had shifted closer to the ship.) They hadn't gone far before they encountered Tollefsen wandering the ice "like a lost

* There is reason to doubt the accuracy of Van Mirlo's recollection, since Tollefsen's fiancée's name was not Agnes but Alette.

soul." Figuring the exercise might do him some good, they invited him along.

When they left, at four p.m., there wasn't a cloud in sight. Because the iceberg appeared to be less than three hours away across a flat, solid pack, they didn't bother to pack food or water. At first their skis glided smoothly on the sun-softened powder. Striding with ease, Tollefsen was enjoying himself for the first time in weeks.

On the way, they ran across a large, curious Weddell seal. Without thinking much about it, Cook pulled out his revolver and shot it in the head at close range. In case the trip took longer than expected, the doctor thought it prudent to kill the animal and leave it behind as an emergency food supply. To Tollefsen, seeing the gun and the cold-blooded ease with which Cook dispatched the seal was terrifying, and only reinforced his belief that his shipmates had taken him far from the ship in order to murder him. What had begun as a pleasant outing suddenly took on a palpable tension.

At the foot of the iceberg, Cook, Amundsen, and Tollefsen removed their skis, carried them over their shoulders, and climbed without difficulty to the top. Beneath the sun's unobstructed rays, they felt, in Amundsen's words, "wonderfully warm." Sweeping their eyes across the pack, they saw a small black dot in the distance: the *Belgica*. As the doctor took a series of photographs, a cold wind began to blow. Amundsen glanced at the sun to the north. At this time of year, it traced tight circles in the sky, as if around the dial of a twenty-four-hour clock. Judging from its position, Amundsen figured it was about ten p.m. The excursionists had lost track of time and suddenly felt desperately hungry and thirsty. They could see from the top of the iceberg that the wind was already starting to change the shape of the pack. Leads were appearing between the floes, giving rise to isolated plumes of mist as seawater evaporated. It was time for the men to leave, or risk not finding their way back. They rushed down from the berg and strapped on their skis.

After skiing for about ten minutes, Cook, Amundsen, and Tollefsen were enveloped by a dense fog. The *Belgica* vanished from sight. To find their way back, the men had to follow their ski tracks in reverse. But soon those tracks led straight into the sea. In the hours since they'd crossed it, this area of the pack had been transformed beyond recognition, its floes broken up and rearranged. The first mate pulled out a pocket compass and led the way in what he assumed was vaguely the direction of the ship, keeping in mind how fickle magnetic readings could be at these latitudes.

Cook and Amundsen refused to panic; they had lived through similar circumstances before, on the Order of the Penguin's first attempted trip to the iceberg. Their companion, however, had not. As they skied, the doctor and the first mate turned around occasionally to keep an eye on Tollefsen. He was visibly terrorized, his jaw clenched more tightly than ever.

The three kept going well into the following day without any indication that they were nearing the ship. They were growing faint with thirst and hunger. All of a sudden, Amundsen spotted parallel markings in the snow.

"Here are our tracks!" he shouted with relief.

"And there is a seal!" Cook said, pointing to the Weddell seal he'd shot near the start of the journey.

Without hesitation, Amundsen dropped to his knees, slashed his knife across the animal, lay down alongside the carcass, and placed his mouth against the laceration, sucking warm blood from the wound. Even though the seal had been killed hours earlier and left on the ice, its thick coating of blubber had kept its insides from cooling down. Once he had drunk his fill, he offered his place to Cook, who let the metallic-tasting substance trickle down his parched throat. His beard dripping with gore, the doctor turned to Tollefsen. Aghast, eyes darting between the knife and his bloodied shipmates, the boatswain said that he would prefer to die of hunger than to partake in such a hideous feast.

Still famished, Cook and Amundsen carved out slices of meat, which they devoured raw and which the first mate declared "delicious." Tollefsen then watched in disbelief as Amundsen cut off the seal's head to keep as a trophy. He was surely convinced that *they* were the madmen.

It wasn't until four in the morning that the ice closed up and a clear passage back to the ship presented itself. Seeing his chance to escape his shipmates, Tollefsen made a frantic dash, skiing so fast that Cook and Amundsen could hardly keep up. When they reached the *Belgica,* Tollefsen appeared to be on the verge of passing out. To revive him, Cook asked Amundsen to give the man a shot of cherry brandy, which Tollefsen downed in one gulp. Amundsen told him to go to bed and promised to bring him a cup of hot chocolate. As Cook and Amundsen waited for the water to boil, Tollefsen stormed into the kitchen, his face twisted in fright.

"What did you give me?" he shouted. "I feel so ill I think I'm dying."

Before they could answer, the boatswain ran out and trudged across the snow-covered deck to the officers' quarters. He skulked down the silent hallway to Lecointe's cabin. Tollefsen pushed the door open, padded up to the bed, and extended a hand toward the captain's sleeping form. Lecointe jolted awake and gasped at the sight of the mad sailor at his bedside, shrouded in shadow. *Cook and Amundsen have tried to poison me!* Tollefsen raved. It took a few minutes for Lecointe's racing heart to slow down. Becalmed at last, the captain told Tollefsen to stay put and went to the doctor and the first mate in the kitchen to find out what had happened, leaving the boatswain huddled in a corner. Lecointe returned a short while later with a piece of buttered bread, which Tollefsen consented to eat, and assured him there was nothing to worry about. The Norwegian returned to his bunk.

But as Cook and Amundsen were preparing to leave the kitchen, they turned around and found Tollefsen standing motionless behind them, in his underpants, staring into space. "He looked very confused," wrote Amundsen.

The boatswain's condition only worsened with time, to the distress of his shipmates. "[He] was a strong man who had spent many years on the sea and had not believed he would be unable to endure imprisonment in the ice," Arctowski would later observe in his diary. "I am of the opinion that many cases of madness have occurred on polar voyages but have been concealed with great care."

Cook attributed polar madness to a combination of fear, uncertainty, monotony, confinement, and extreme isolation. All of those emotions were heightened with the passing of the summer solstice, December 21. Even at its apex, the sun was powerless to break the pack. Now, Cook warned, it would begin "sliding down the hillside of winter." Marooned aboard a motionless ship, at the mercy of the ice's pressures, stuck fast in an indestructible floe, just one among the many millions that formed a seemingly limitless band of white around a desolate continent at the bottom of the globe, the men of the *Belgica* had little left to hope for.

CHAPTER 16

Man Against Ice

THE SECOND CHRISTMAS ABOARD THE *BELGICA* WAS A GRIM AFFAIR.
Illness, anguish, and enmity traversed the ship. Every attempt at merriment felt forced, a half-hearted pantomime of happier days past.
Long forgotten were the boisterous games of whist, the bawdy tomfoolery of the beauty contest, the giddy thrill of discovery. At dinner
the men sat sullenly around the wardroom table as they ate their veal
roulade and sipped their brandy. "We have long since worn out all
social enthusiasm," wrote Cook, "and can unearth nothing new to
infuse fresh life into the desired good cheer of our Christmas dinner. . . . The doubt of our future was pictured on every face."

From this dark perspective, the significant movement in the ice
over the previous week seemed like a cruel joke. Looking out from
the crow's nest, one could see new leads crisscrossing the pack. A
clearing had formed a few hundred meters from the ship. Yet the
two-mile-wide floe that held the *Belgica* remained intact, seemingly
unbreakable. On Christmas Eve, Arctowski had bored a hole downward through a pressure ridge that stretched across the floe and
found the ridge to be more than eight meters thick. The ice that had
accumulated around the ship was also several meters thick; it would
never break up on its own. Nowhere was the floe thinner than a
meter. The prospect of wintering in the ice once again grew more
certain with each day.

Adding to the men's worries was the madman lurking among
them. "Tollefsen's mental state is getting worse," de Gerlache wrote
in his log. "This man suffers from delusions of persecution. He barely
sleeps and, seeing only enemies around him, flees the company of his
comrades." On one occasion, after a panicked, daylong search across

the pack, the men found him crouched behind a hummock. Even as it inspired pity, Tollefsen's condition was a source of constant, simmering dread—of where he might be hiding, of what he might do, of who might follow him into madness.

Few were in the mood to ring in the New Year. Shortly before midnight on December 31, the *Belgica* was eerily quiet. De Gerlache, still in severe pain, retired to his cabin early after a cup of cocoa. Some crew members lay in their bunks, while others sat despondently around the forecastle. Racovitza and Lecointe went to bed around eleven o'clock. Cook retreated to his corner, and Arctowski sat at his desk in the sun-drenched laboratory, looking over old notes.

Suddenly, his door swung open. There stood Amundsen, brandishing a bottle of cognac that he had saved for a special occasion. Since this might be the *Belgica*'s very last special occasion, the two men cracked the bottle open and poured out a nip to lift their spirits. A few minutes later, Lecointe appeared in the lab, complaining that he couldn't sleep, only to discover this unexpected scene of good cheer. Cook soon joined the party. Before long, a dismal night had grown into a celebration. Amundsen then invited the crew to help them finish the bottle. Once it was empty, the gathering migrated to the forecastle. Lecointe brought out ham, cheese, biscuits, and several bottles of wine from the hold. Johansen pulled out his accordion. By midnight, a wave of genuine gaiety had washed over the ship, the first in a very long time. "The crew received us with song and music, and then told us stories which were new to us, but had been told a hundred times in the forecastle," Cook wrote. "We in return did some speech-making, and a little story-telling too." That night, the *Belgica* grew so warm that the men almost forgot that they were prisoners of the ice.

The officers left the crew's quarters at half past one and staggered across the deck back to their quarters. The temperature was −8 degrees, and a stinging wind blew across the ship, but a drunken glow insulated the men from the cold. In their jovial state, they found the *Belgica*'s surroundings particularly resplendent. "The entire ice was a mass of quivering blue," Cook wrote. To the north was a pale-white moon. To the south was the sun, dipping lower than it had the day before, and higher than it would the following day. It wouldn't set until later in the month, but after it did, night would quickly regain the upper hand.

The only wish anyone had for the New Year was the breakup of the floe. The heat of the summer sun was proving insufficient: whatever melted at high noon refroze by early morning. It had been assumed that since a violent storm had allowed the ship to break into the ice, only an equally powerful storm would allow her to leave. Most of the *Belgica*'s men, therefore, consigned their fate to the Antarctic winds.

Yet it had become increasingly clear that even they wouldn't be enough. Since entering the ice the previous February, the *Belgica* had drifted more than thirteen hundred nautical miles. But driven by variable winds and currents, the pack had taken her on a circuitous loop.* On New Year's Eve, Lecointe had fixed the *Belgica*'s position at latitude 70°03′ south and longitude 85°10′ west—almost exactly the same spot where, the previous February, de Gerlache had decided to enter the pack. Nearly a year later at those coordinates, the ice extended as far as the eye could see. Its edge might have been just beyond the horizon, or it could have been hundreds of miles to the north. The floe that encased them now appeared far thicker and sturdier than the ice through which they had forced their way the previous March.

"I think it highly unlikely that we will get out of here the same way as we came in here," Amundsen wrote. Lecointe and de Gerlache seemed to agree. Robbed of the surety the tonite had given them, they saw no other choice but to think ahead to surviving the winter.

For Cook, however, surrender was out of the question. He believed more fervently than ever that a second wintering would have disastrous consequences. In the previous few days, he had run through the muster roll in his head and identified at least four men who would die right off the bat, and more who were at grave risk.

---

* Plotted on a chart, the itinerary was a knotted tangle, twisting back on itself and revealing no clear pattern in the movement of the pack. The ship had gone as far south as latitude 71°36′ south (May 31), as far west as longitude 92°22′ west (April 25), as far east as longitude 80°28′ west (October 22), and as far north as latitude 69°38′ south (October 29).

Many of those who would survive would surely go insane. If his fellow officers didn't grasp the urgency of escaping the ice before the end of the summer—or didn't think it was possible—Cook felt bound by his Hippocratic oath to convince them.

At a meeting of the officers in the wardroom on January 4, Cook grew enraged, which shocked the other officers. For all the hot tempers on the ship, they had never before seen the doctor lose his. Cook insisted on the absolute necessity of exiting the pack. He demanded that all scientific work cease until a strategy could be devised. The other officers' surprise at Cook's anger soon gave way to disbelief. They "hooted at the idea," Cook wrote. He might as well have suggested that they flap their arms and fly home. Even Amundsen, his loyal student, found preposterous the idea that they might somehow break free of the ice. The expedition, Cook's colleagues assured him, no longer had a say in its own fate.

But Cook refused to be cowed. A few days later, he presented de Gerlache with a spectacular idea. Having come to revere the sun, the doctor proposed to harness its power to hasten the melting of the ice. His plan was to dig two long, meter-wide trenches in a V formation that branched out from the prow of the ship all the way to a clearing approximately four hundred meters ahead of it. They would shovel out the top layers of snow and slush so the sun's rays could reach the foot-deep layer of fresh water immediately above the hard sea ice. Cook believed water retained heat more efficiently than snow and could thus transfer that heat to the underlying ice. He also counted on the albedo effect, by which darker surfaces absorb more light— and thus more heat—than paler ones. The sea ice at the bottom of the trench and the compact layers of slush and snow along its walls formed a bluish gutter that would reflect less sunlight than the pure white granular snow, or firn, on the surface. Pouring black soot into the trench would accelerate the effect. Eventually, the melting would weaken the ice and form two fault lines. If a storm did shatter the pack, the floe would be more likely to break along those lines than somewhere farther away from the ship, where it would be of no use. The *Belgica* could then sail through the newly formed passageway into the small clearing.

The plan's flaws were obvious to de Gerlache and Lecointe from the start. First, while the sun didn't set, it remained low in the sky; for much of the day, its rays struck the pack at too oblique an angle to illuminate the bottom of the trench. Second, they believed the soot was unlikely to absorb much heat, since sunlight would first have to travel through frigid snowmelt to reach it and water is far less efficient than air at transferring heat. Third, the doctor hadn't considered that the gutter's walls would not be hermetic. The layer of slush at the bottom of the trench wouldn't prevent water from spreading out evenly over the floe. Whatever heat it absorbed while it coursed through the trench would quickly dissipate.

Cook had had enough of their relentless fatalism. Perhaps his escape plan was imperfect, but what else were they to do? Just accept the likelihood of their own death? Even doing something pointless, he insisted, was less harmful than doing nothing at all. Finally, Cook broke through. "Inaction has become dangerous," de Gerlache agreed. "It would lead in the short run to discouragement, which would carry the gravest consequences for the health of all." And so the men would try to dig themselves to freedom.

Work on the trenches started on January 7 but had to be stopped almost immediately due to a ship-wide case of food poisoning from a tainted seal liver. While the men recovered, Lecointe decided to give the tonite another chance. He was the only member of the expedition who still had any faith in the explosives to help break the ice, but then he was also the only one with munitions training. The captain thawed out more sticks of tonite and meticulously scraped off the damaged parts. To his delight, they blew up. Triumphant, Lecointe enlisted Amundsen, Melaerts, and Johansen to help him build an "infernal machine," a bomb consisting of 535 sticks stuffed into an empty oil barrel, which was then sealed and lowered beneath the ice. Lecointe hoped that the blast would not only blow away the ice immediately above the barrel but also cause a wave so massive that it would make the entire floe ripple and shatter.

Once the device was in place more than two hundred meters from the *Belgica*, Lecointe lit its five fuses, which were connected to twenty-five mercury fulminate detonators. He uttered a quick prayer to Saint Barbara, patron saint of artillerymen, and sprinted back to the ship for cover. The fuses were so cold that the flames went out. Lecointe had to return five or six times to reignite the ever-shorter lengths.

The explosion was superb. Blocks of ice shot up to great heights and rained back down like an apocalyptic hailstorm. The shock wave could be felt on the *Belgica*. Lecointe was certain that it had caused a web of fault lines to spread across the floe. When he went to inspect the damage, however, he was crestfallen: the hole where the bomb had been was no more than ten meters in diameter and filled with rubble that soon froze back into a solid mass. There was not the slightest crack in the ice beyond the hole. Lecointe's experiment might have more thoroughly shattered a floe of freshwater ice, but sea ice is far less brittle. The captain was forced to acknowledge that if tonite had any role to play, it would be marginal.

In the meantime, the rest of the men had begun attacking the ice with pickaxes and shovels. "For three days we have worked, not like men, but like dogs in chase of game," Cook wrote on January 12. Yet his trenches seemed to have no effect. The mountains of shoveled snow lining the trenches had fooled the men into thinking they were making progress toward their liberation. But in the end, even Cook agreed that their labor was nothing short of Sisyphean. "The sun at midnight is now so feeble that it permits the formation of new ice to such a thickness that the heat of the following day is barely sufficient to melt it," Cook wrote. "Had we done this in December, the result might have been more satisfactory, but now it is too late." It was soon obvious to everyone that the plan would never achieve its goal. Worse, they had squandered a week of precious summer heat on it. The days ahead would only grow darker and colder, the chances of extraction slimmer.

Cook's plan may have failed, but it did succeed in one very consequential way: It shook the men free of the resigned lassitude that had prevented them from even contemplating escape. It got them thinking of other approaches. Breaking out of the ice no longer seemed like a ridiculous proposition.

No one on board was more transformed by the experience than the commandant, who now believed in the possibility of escape with the zeal of a convert. On the evening of January 11, de Gerlache convened a meeting of the officers and outlined a new plan, one that dwarfed Cook's in its ambition. Instead of praying for a storm to fracture the floe, the men would in effect create their own tempest.

There were four old ice saws on board, left over from the *Belgica*'s days as a whaling ship. The commandant proposed that the men use them to cut out a full-fledged canal leading from the ship to one of the nearby clearings.

De Gerlache's plan was the most audacious idea he'd had since conceiving of the expedition itself. The breakout would have no precedent in the history of ice navigation. It would require sawing all the way through several feet of ice, for hundreds of meters, to form two banks, then sawing and removing the ice in between to clear passage for the *Belgica*. It would entail doing this with ice saws, which were designed to be used on a much smaller scale, typically to carve out blocks for refrigeration, or at most to cut out a small harbor for a whaleboat. It would demand an almost inconceivable amount of labor from every man aboard, the sick and the healthy alike. And it would have to be completed in a matter of weeks, before the coming of winter.

Had de Gerlache himself lost his mind? The men had reason to doubt his judgment. It was the commandant, after all, who had condemned them to this prison in the first place. For de Gerlache, however, this was precisely why the plan had to work. He did not expect to survive another winter; Cook had made that clear to him. More important, he felt responsible for the *Belgica*'s predicament and for the lives of everyone on board. Despite his illness, he would do everything in his power to redeem himself, even if he died in the effort.

As he laid out the plan, he displayed an assurance and a sharpness of mind that had eluded him for months. His newfound energy galvanized his fellow officers, who all agreed the canal was worth attempting. (All, that is, except Cook, who at first couldn't countenance a plan that wasn't his, though he soon got over his wounded pride and took credit for having inspired de Gerlache.)

The closest edge of the floe, to which Cook's trenches had been leading, was about four hundred meters ahead of the ship's prow. But a patch of intervening ice had been too thick for the men to saw through. De Gerlache suggested that they now saw in the opposite direction—from the stern, along an area where, during the winter, a lead had briefly split the floe. The lead had long since frozen over, but the commandant reasoned that the ice there would be thinner than the multiyear ice around it.

The next day, Arctowski drilled a series of holes through the floe and confirmed de Gerlache's hunch: the hard sea ice was thinnest over the frozen lead, where it ranged in thickness from one meter to a little over two. He staked out a path for the canal that ran from the stern of the ship to the former channel, then curved toward starboard and continued on to a large clearing of open water. In all, the canal would cover almost three times the surface area of a hypothetical canal along the lines of Cook's trenches. It would be seven hundred meters long, one hundred meters wide at its mouth, and only about ten meters wide near the *Belgica*. Creating both banks would demand cutting through almost a mile of solid ice, work that could begin only after the men had cleared the top layers of ice, snow, and slush over that same distance using pickaxes and shovels. Crisscrossing the area in between to slice it up into extractable pans would bring the total to about a mile and a half, not counting the areas that would have to be sawed twice because they had refrozen in the meantime.

The amount of work required of so few men in such a little time would rival the greatest construction projects in human history. It was all the more daunting given the pitiful condition of the laborers. But inspired by their reinvigorated commandant, the men threw themselves into it with abandon.

The first saws hit the ice on January 14. To prevent the cut sections from fusing back together overnight, the men would have to saw around the clock, under a never-setting sun. They formed two teams to ensure the saws would almost never stop moving. De Gerlache led the day shift, which included Melaerts, Racovitza, Van Mirlo, Johansen, Koren, Van Rysselberghe, and the madman Tollefsen. They sawed from eight in the morning to six in the evening, with breaks for lunch and for coffee on the pack. Lecointe's team, whose shift went from seven p.m. to four a.m., consisted of Cook, Amundsen,

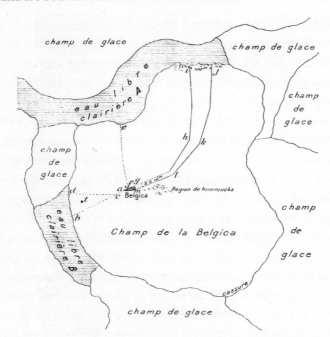

A diagram of the *Belgica*'s two attempted paths out of the floe that
contained her, from Georges Lecointe's *Au pays des manchots* (1904).
The dotted lines branching out from the prow of the ship—defined by
the points *a, b, c,* and *d*—mark the trenches proposed in Cook's plan.
The solid lines leading from the stern to the clearing at the top of the
map designate the banks of the canal proposed by de Gerlache. The
dotted line between the points *e* and *f* indicates the crevasse that opened
up on January 30, 1898.

Arctowski, Somers, and Dufour.* The one man exempt from sawing
was Michotte, who kept the kitchen going day and night, and blew
the cornet from the deck when meals were ready.

Somers combined two of the four saws, using sheets of iron, to
form a double-long, seven-foot saw. Men worked in groups of three.
Those using a small saw took turns, each man sawing for five minutes
straight before passing the tool to his shipmate. (Cook and Amundsen partnered with Arctowski and were content to listen to the ab-
sentminded scientist prattle on as he sawed for ten or fifteen minutes

---

* The record isn't clear on which team Dobrowolski belonged to, but the junior scientist worked as hard as anyone else. Knudsen was at this time too sick to leave his bed, but
he eventually joined the effort as well.

straight, in no rush to remind him his turn was over.) For the double saw, one man would hold on to a horizontal wooden bar that ran through the handle, while two others heaved at a rope to lift the saw and let its weight pull it back down. By the end of the day, the men could barely lift their trembling arms.

The first day, the men sawed forty meters along what would become the canal's banks, beginning at the edge of the clearing. The following day, they cut the ice between the banks into enormous interlocking triangles. At the mouth, where the canal was widest, these sections were each about the size of half a football field. The men affixed ropes to them and hauled them toward the clearing, like horses drawing a barge along a river, as Dobrowolski led a chant of "Song of the Volga Boatmen." To pull one of these sections, which weighed several times as much as the *Belgica*, away from the bank and get it moving before inertia took over demanded an almost inconceivable amount of effort by many men at once.

The backbreaking labor had the beneficial effect of uniting a fractious group. All distinctions of class, rank, and nationality evaporated in the pursuit of a common goal. De Gerlache, ill as he was, sawed as hard as any crew member. Crucially, the task gave the men a sense of agency in their own deliverance. In general, spirits were higher than they'd been in months.

One notable exception was Amundsen, who remained the most pessimistic—or perhaps realistic—of the group. "I do not think we can get the ship out this way," he wrote. "The final role in the story of this expedition will probably be played by the sloops," added the first mate, referring to the *Belgica*'s whaleboats.

Even to those who believed wholeheartedly in de Gerlache's plan, it was evident that saws alone could not free the ship. There were two spots in the proposed path where the ice was several times thicker than the double saw was long. One was at the edge of the floe along the clearing, where a ridge of hummocks stretched across what would be the mouth of the canal. The other was immediately around the ship herself, where a year's worth of snowdrift had hardened into a block of ice as high as the bulwarks in some places and almost as deep as the keel. Lecointe, keen as ever to put the tonite to use, argued that these areas would have to be blasted away. Such a course of action would risk blowing a hole in the ship, of course, but the expedition would be lucky to face that possibility. It would mean that the canal had been nearly completed.

On the morning of January 15, the explosives at last delivered the kind of satisfaction that Lecointe had long hoped for. The captain picked out a bundle of charges, cleaned them diligently, and placed them in the ridge of hummocks at the future canal's mouth. All of them exploded. Previous experiments with the tonite had failed in part because the bomb sites had been surrounded by ice. But since the hummocks were at the edge of the water, there was nothing on that side to absorb the shock, and the hills of ice were reduced to slush.

Buoyed by this success, Lecointe's team rushed to prepare the rest of the explosives during their hours of rest. "This task is undertaken with truly foolhardy imprudence," Lecointe wrote. "The packets of tonite are brought *close to the fire* to thaw. Then with kitchen knives we scrape off all the damaged parts. . . . We find explosive residue in our plates!" The wardroom was transformed into what Arctowski called "a bomb factory." Once the sticks had been thawed and scraped clean, they were stuffed into tin cans, along with a fuse and a detonator, then covered with wax to keep the device watertight. "Never has there been a conspiratorial gang of anarchists or nihilists as passionate as Lecointe, Amundsen, Cook, and me," Arctowski wrote.

Yet as valuable as it had finally proven to be, the tonite was no substitute for sawing. While the explosives had succeeded in blowing up the hummocks, the wind blew the floating rubble back into the channel, where it formed a thick porridge that soon fused with the pack, plugging the indentation that had just been created. The tonite would never be the miracle solution Lecointe had imagined. It would have to be used strategically, in small quantities, to help dislodge tenacious fragments of ice after they'd been sawed. Escape still depended on luck and the atrophied muscles of exhausted men.

The first few massive triangular fields of ice were successfully coaxed into the clearing, but early on, one of them got wedged between the banks and wouldn't budge. Several bombs were required to break it up, which only further clogged up the canal with debris, costing the men a day's work. Soon they realized that the shape of the sections was fatally flawed: one side would always be pinched between the banks. Unless the configuration of the subdivisions was rethought, the canal would never be finished in time. The solution to this problem would depend not on luck or labor but on logic.

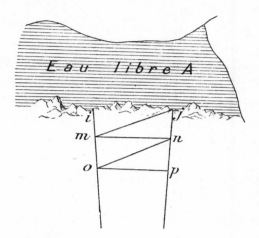

At first, the ice between the canal's banks was cut into enormous triangles, which were to be moved into the clearing above.

Ideas came from the forecastle as well as the officers' quarters. Some suggested sawing the ice in a random crisscross pattern. This would have the advantage of creating pans that were easy to move and too small to get stuck, but it also would demand far more time and manpower than the expedition had at its disposal.

Another proposal called for cutting the ice into roughly square segments, with evenly spaced cuts perpendicular to the canal's banks, and then planting a small charge of tonite in the middle of each to shatter it. While this shape would minimize the amount of sawing required, someone pointed out that the friction along three of each pan's four sides would prevent easy removal and blunt the effect of the explosives.

Each new proposal encountered one or both of these difficulties: too much friction or too much time and effort.

Fittingly, it was the ship's great idea man who figured it out. After all the men's suggestions had seemingly been exhausted, Cook presented an ingenious design to his colleagues.

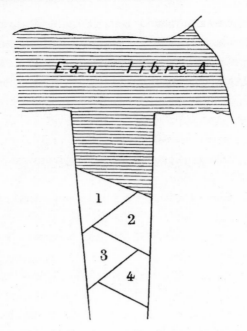

Cook's improved sawing pattern.

Cook's pattern of asymmetrical quadrilaterals immediately struck his shipmates as so simple and practical, it should have been obvious from the beginning. The shapes were not so wide that they would get stuck between the banks, and the angles of the sides allowed each subdivision to gracefully slide away from its neighbors with the aid of a tonite blast.

The doctor's plan allowed the men to clear out the seven-hundred-meter canal at an astounding rate of about sixty meters a day. As the work progressed, the sections grew smaller and required fewer men to guide them to the clearing. Every once in a while, a sailor would have to jump onto a freshly cut fragment of ice and use a long pole to steer it into the clearing, like a gondolier. The trickiest part was leaping back onto the main floe at the last second, or risk drifting away. Cook, who grew up rafting on the Delaware River, "excelled at this kind of sport," according to Lecointe. The doctor would run from one side of the icefield to the other, mimicking his fellow officers and shouting orders to himself to keep the men amused. "He . . .

often comes close to falling into the sea," Lecointe wrote, "but, with the agility of a monkey, always manages to catch himself in time."

The herculean effort didn't sap the men's energy but, on the contrary, replenished it. Their health improved with labor, thanks in large part to the astounding amount of antiscorbutic seal and penguin meat they ingested to supply the required calories. On average, the expeditioners ate seven meals a day. (By now, animal life had returned to the pack, and whichever men weren't sawing or sleeping were hunting.)

For the better part of a year, they had been mired in a listless torpor, starved for light, fresh food, and hope. With his baking treatment and his penguin regimen, Cook had sought to provide the first two of those missing elements. By giving the men the courage to attempt an escape, he had provided hope. Now that all three abounded, everything was falling back into place. "I'm eating a lot, at least twice as much as before," wrote Dobrowolski, who not so long before had been unable to leave his bunk. "Unbelievable appetite. . . . I no longer feel any fatigue. I sleep perfectly and a lot. I shit regularly."

Two weeks of digging Cook's trench and sawing de Gerlache's canal under unrelenting sunlight began to transform the men's bodies. "Everybody is being hardened to the work and developing ponderous muscles," wrote Cook. "Our skin is burnt until it has the appearance of the inner surface of boot leather. Our hands . . . are more comfortable if not washed, especially with soap, because then they crack and become painful. The result is that we all have a more savage physical appearance than most Indians. But this is of little consequence to us. There are no ladies here to arouse the sleeping vanity which we all once possessed." Collectively, the men formed an odd and incongruous sight: a dandy back in civilization, Arctowski wore a tattered overcoat and a frayed top hat, like a polar hobo; others sported snow goggles and slathered their faces with petroleum jelly to soothe their sunburned skin, looking to Dobrowolski like a "group of divers."

By January 20, the canal was halfway complete. At five o'clock that afternoon, the men witnessed something that lifted their hopes even further: a curious bottlenose whale ventured into the partially cleared canal. The visit felt like a blessing from the Antarctic. It was one thing to watch an avenue of dark water slowly lengthen as the ice was cleared away, but it was another to see an animal swim in it as in any other lead. It made the men realize how much progress they'd made. All of a sudden, the canal felt real, as, for the first time, did the possibility of freedom.

But that night, all work came to a sudden halt. At around nine p.m., Tollefsen got out of bed and left the forecastle without telling anyone where he was going. (He had long since stopped speaking, and his paranoia had only deepened.) Three hours later, he was nowhere to be found. His prolonged absence worried his colleagues, who dropped everything to search for him. He was in none of his usual hiding spots. They looked in the hold, in the machine room, in the netting along the bowsprit, in the trunks, even in the hole of the privy. "Fear, uncertainty, perplexity among the men. . . . It seems he was suspected of a suicidal mania," wrote Dobrowolski. Perhaps, his shipmates thought, he would go after one of them instead.

Tollefsen did kill that night, but not a human being. The madman returned around two in the morning, skiing in with three freshly slaughtered penguins trailing behind him.

On January 21, the nine-week-long day came to an end. "Today the midnight sun is leaving us," Amundsen wrote in his diary, by the dimming blue-gray light that trickled in through his cabin's porthole. Night eats into day far faster toward the poles than in temperate regions. In less than a week, it would be impossible to read in the evening without a candle. By mid-March, darkness would dominate once more. Temperatures were dropping fast. Although the men were finally making progress, the first mate was convinced they had started too late.

He had been pessimistic about the canal from the beginning. Since the ship had first entered the ice, Amundsen had climbed to the crow's nest more often than anyone else to survey the state of the pack. "With the exception of the months of August, September and October there have not been any possible ways of going anywhere," the first mate wrote. "Very long channels, completely free of slush and small pieces of ice, appeared in August, September and October but unfortunately during these three months we were too weak to start the sort of work we are doing now."

The most physically powerful of the men, Amundsen sawed perhaps harder than anyone else. But he never believed the canal, even if it was finished in time, would lead the *Belgica* to open water. "Even if we try to do *everything possible* I do not think that this time will have much influence on our escape." He knew that where they were sawing, over the old channel, where the ice was the thinnest, would be the easy part.

As he expected, progress slowed to a standstill when the teams reached the vicinity of the *Belgica*. Saws became blunted as they began cutting into the older, thicker ice by the ship, and then—with grating, screeching sounds and nauseating smells—into objects other than ice. Saw teeth broke off against a year's worth of tin cans and other refuse that had been thrown overboard and incorporated into the pack. This ring of detritus—which included animal carcasses and human feces—had absorbed the sun's rays and melted the top layer of snow beneath it, forming a vile swamp atop the hard, thick sea ice.

"What a sight! We've grown used to it, but it's still terrible. Surrounded by heaps of trash and shit, which form puddles under the influence of the strong sun," wrote Dobrowolski. "The ship sits in a foul-smelling puddle, which has spread wide around the upper layer of the pack ice." The men continued to saw, knee-deep in putrid slush, advancing less than two meters in eight hours.

There were just a few more meters to go. The laborers looked back on what they'd accomplished. Vast amounts of ice had been cleared, and the long, open lane of water stretching out before them cheered them immeasurably. They had made de Gerlache's mad vision a reality.

The men estimated they were three days away from finishing the canal when the ice began fighting back. The first sign of trouble occurred early on January 30, as pressures around the ship increased to such a degree that the double saw got stuck in the ice, and it became impossible to pull it out.

Then came the ice's devastating counterattack.

At nine o'clock that morning, when the canal was just meters away from completion, thunderous cracks reverberated through the floe, sounding like a series of explosions. Before the men's disbelieving eyes, a fissure formed at the prow of the *Belgica* and shot almost instantly to the clearing, running more or less parallel to the canal. For nearly a year the explorers had wished the ice would split. It had finally done so—at the worst time, and in the worst way imaginable.

Had the crevasse been larger, it would have meant freedom. Instead, it threatened the ship with annihilation.

The crack now formed one side of a giant, roughly triangular field of ice, bordered on another side by the clearing and on the third side by the canal. The field remained attached to the floe by its point, at the level of the *Belgica*. Under the influence of the wind, the crevasse began to widen, pushing the new icefield toward the opposite bank of the canal. The rocking movement of the field put intense pressure on the ship, whose timbers keened with agony. The men watched in shock as the two banks of their canal slowly clamped shut, like monstrous jaws, with the *Belgica* at their hinge. Weeks of work disappeared before their eyes in a matter of moments. Not even a whaleboat could get through. Nor was the new fissure wide enough to allow passage.

The undoing of a month's worth of excruciating labor dealt a crippling blow to morale. The explorers were in a worse position than they would have been had they done nothing. Not only had their escape route been closed off, but the *Belgica* was now in more severe danger of being crushed than she had been since she first entered the pack. As long as the ship had been stuck fast, the solid ice had formed a protective belt around her. Now she was caught between two huge, interlocking fields of ice, like an almond in a nutcracker.

"The ice is even more close and sometimes we feel the ship shudder after the movement of the ice," wrote Amundsen on February 1. "It is starting to get dark early. It is now ten o'clock in the evening and there is only just enough light to write by."

The first mate's defeatism had been vindicated. The canal project was doomed, and so, quite likely, was the *Belgica*.

CHAPTER 17

Last Ditch

IT STRUCK ROALD AMUNDSEN AT THAT MOMENT THAT THE EXPEDITION's leaders had not proposed a backup plan in case the ship was crushed by ice. He put down his pencil and went to find Lecointe to point out "how wrong and how unforgivable it was that we have no fully-equipped sloops and sledges ready." Conveniently, he had come prepared with his own plan, which he outlined to the captain.

It all seemed simple to Amundsen. He recommended that the men transfer the most necessary provisions and equipment onto two sledges and two small whaleboats, harness themselves to them like sled dogs, and drag them in a northeasterly direction across almost eight hundred miles of sea ice back to the Belgica Strait, where the expedition would set up camp on firm ground. From there, a party would sail the more seaworthy of the two whaleboats across the Drake Passage to Cape Horn and seek rescue.

For Amundsen, this was the obvious course of action not just because the canal appeared to be leading nowhere, but also because, in his mind, this was what true polar heroism looked like. This kind of grueling overland march pitting man against the naked elements was what he had been preparing for all his life, from the days he had slept with his window open in the winter to his harrowing trek across the Hardangervidda with his brother Leon, in which he'd come several breaths short of death. This was what his apprenticeship with Cook had been building to, what their adventures across the pack had been about. It was almost as if Amundsen wished the ship would be destroyed so that he could put his plan into action, lead the expedition to safety, and prove to de Gerlache that he had been deserving, after all, of the *Belgica*'s command.

After some back-and-forth, Lecointe and the officers agreed to Amundsen's plan, despite how insane it seemed. Its flaws were clear. First, preliminary traction tests, in which the crew hauled the empty whaleboats across a short distance, revealed the craft to be heavy and unsteady over ice. It was hard to imagine how even healthy men could pull the fully loaded boats for hundreds of miles to the Belgica Strait. Second, the trip across the sea ice would not be a straight line across a flat surface; it would require long detours around obstacles, such as hummocks and pressure ridges, too steep to pull the boats over. Third, ever since early January, the region of the pack that contained the *Belgica* had been drifting consistently to the west. (The average westward drift had recently accelerated to about ten miles a day.) If the pack continued in its course, it would cancel out much if not all of the expedition's daily progress to the east. Even in the best conditions, it was understood that many of the men would not survive the journey to the channel, let alone the 650-mile trip by whaleboat to Cape Horn, across some of the most perilous waters in the world.

But if Amundsen's plan had little to recommend it, so did the idea of remaining on their floe without shelter, drifting helplessly to their deaths, were the *Belgica* to be crushed. Cook, Amundsen, and de Gerlache took charge of preparing camping equipment: tents, sleeping bags, sealskin outerwear, kit bags, and snowshoes crafted from broken skis. The crew reorganized the hold to provide easy access to the most necessary provisions and equipment.

In the process, they made a bloodcurdling discovery: the rats had reduced the expedition's reserve of winter clothing to threads. Even with the proper clothing, a monthslong march across the ice during the Antarctic winter would kill the weakest men. Without it, such a journey would almost certainly wipe out the entire expedition. The rats had chewed through any hope the men might have had to escape Antarctica without the *Belgica*. The explorers' survival depended on hers.

That revelation was followed two days later by an equally spine-chilling sight. The canal—rather, the narrow passage that had once been the canal—had vanished. Its surface had frozen over and disappeared under a blanket of snow that by the night of February 3 had turned into hard ice.

The commandant was forced to concede defeat. "It no longer seems that we can avoid a second wintering," he wrote.

De Gerlache was confronted with a choice between two deadly courses of action: a march across the ice, with no shelter or sufficient winter clothing and no realistic prospect of reaching land; or another winter on board, which Cook had assured him would lead to several fatalities, perhaps to the death of every member of the expedition should the ship founder. The commandant decided to remain on the *Belgica*, which at least contained a stock of provisions. There was enough for three more months. To make it last, de Gerlache reduced rations. Each man's daily allotment would consist of 150 grams of butter, 150 grams of sugar, a small loaf of bread, and a biscuit. The drastic measure would in theory allow the *Belgica*'s men to survive the winter, as long as the ship held strong—and as long as fresh meat could regularly be procured, which was far from guaranteed. As they had discovered the previous year, animal life fled the pack during the long night.

Despite his conviction that escape was no longer possible, de Gerlache refused to order an end to the work on the canal, which had proven beneficial to the men's health and for the moment kept them from total despair.

Yet by the second week of February, the expeditioners were locked in a seemingly unwinnable battle against nature, sawing up the sheets of ice that formed overnight and attempting to widen the ever-shrinking passage by carving away the ice on its banks. Over the previous few days, an insistent wind had pushed fragments of ice from the clearing back toward the mouth of the canal, where they clustered and froze into a solid barricade. Though the cut sections were smaller now, the men weren't able to guide them into the clearing as they had before. Instead, they had to break up the sections into even smaller pieces, each nevertheless weighing several hundred pounds, and pry them out of the water with the aid of an inclined plane.

The labor that had at first invigorated the men began to weaken them. They now had to work even harder on less food. Their diminished rations did not provide enough calories to fuel their efforts, and their bodies were starting to feed on themselves.

With the continual grinding of the ice against the *Belgica*'s hull and the reshuffling of the hold's provisions, the rodents in the ship's underbelly grew as hungry and agitated as the men. "As long as we were generous, they left us in peace," Arctowski wrote. "But now that all of our boxes of food have been carefully arranged and nothing is left in the ship's hold, the rats begin nightly raids to our beds." The *Belgica* was assailed from without and from within.

At first it seemed like an illusion, another Antarctic mirage: from the crow's nest, the entire pack appeared to rise and fall ever so subtly, as if it were breathing. Then the deck began to sway. For the first time in nearly a year, the men felt the swell of the ocean. The discovery was a source of both fear and hope—fear because the movement of the ocean increased the pressure of the ice against the ship, hope because it meant they couldn't be more than a few dozen miles from the northern limit of the pack. With any luck, the rolling waves might destabilize the floe and reopen the canal.

As they sawed, the men heard cracks propagating from the rear of the ship. The pack was breaking, shifting unpredictably. They kept their eyes on the ice for any sign that the ship might be under attack or, more hopefully, for any possibility of release. They did not have to wait long.

At three in the morning on February 12, under the influence of the ocean and the wind, the banks of the canal suddenly began to part. In a short time, the waterway grew just wide enough to allow the *Belgica* passage. A jolt of excitement electrified the ship as the men scrambled to take advantage of the moment. De Gerlache ordered Somers to fire up the engine.

Then, as abruptly as it had opened, the ice began to tighten anew. It was now or never. The lane was almost clear. And yet one major obstacle remained: the ship herself was still held back by the massive block of ice that gripped her stern like a claw.

Tonite alone could break its grasp. But setting off explosives so close to the ship could easily puncture her hull and let seawater rush in, condemning her to the ocean floor almost a mile beneath their feet. Lecointe, as the resident artilleryman, was left to quickly determine the precise amount of tonite required and the exact distance at which to place it, in order to blow up the ice without harming the *Belgica*. Lecointe had been experimenting with various amounts each time he tested the tonite, but never this close to the ship. There was no more time for testing. The men's lives depended on the accuracy of his calculations.

Lecointe planted the charges in the ice mass and, after likely whispering another prayer to Saint Barbara, ignited them one after another. The men on the ice hurried away to a safe distance and braced themselves.

The detonations shook the entire vessel, making a sound unlike any the men had yet heard. Windows shattered. Lab equipment rattled. The onboard barometer registered sudden increases in air pressure, followed immediately by equally strong dips as wind was sucked back into the vacuum caused by the explosions. Cinder-block-sized pieces of ice were thrown high into the air, only to rain back down on the deck, along with chunks of dead animals and human waste. Each successive blast unleashed a new wave of damage and an accompanying hail of falling ice. Each blast risked blowing off the rudder, shattering the hull, or setting off the remaining crates of tonite on board.

The reverberations of the final blast faded, leaving behind a scintillating haze made up of tiny, suspended ice crystals that danced in the air. A silence settled over the pack, broken only by the gentle swishing of the canal. The men moved toward the ship, uncertain of what they would find. They pulled away remaining chunks of ice, examining the greenheart cladding of the ship and fearing the worst—large holes or major sections torn away, water already seeping into the hold.

In a few moments, it became evident that Lecointe's bombs had been perfectly calibrated. The ice was pulverized, but the hull was intact. For the first time since March 1898, the *Belgica* could set sail.

By the next day, the canal was finally clear, or as clear as it would ever be. The barricade of ice still stretched across its mouth. De Gerlache knew he had no choice but to ram through it, despite the risk this would pose to the ship. Yet there remained another problem:

Since the canal began at the *Belgica*'s stern, she was pointed in the wrong direction. And the passage was not wide enough for her to turn around.

Over the following twenty-four hours, the men redoubled their efforts, sawing and blasting away a small harbor at the elbow of the canal to allow the *Belgica* to reorient herself. As soon as the harbor was ready, the *Belgica* reversed into it in order to swing her prow toward the ice barrier.

But just as she was halfway through the maneuver—a tight three-point turn aided by hawsers and kedge anchors—a sudden change in the wind's direction pushed the banks closer together and wedged her lengthwise across the canal. The ice was not giving up. So soon after breaking free, the *Belgica* was caught once again, and this time in a far more precarious position. Her vital organs—the propeller and the rudder, without which she was no more able to direct her course than was a piece of driftwood—were bearing the brunt. With any more pressure, they would be smashed. This time, though, there was nothing to be done but seek the blessing of a higher power. Some of the men invoked God and some didn't, but all of them prayed as the sound of bending wood and metal grew louder.

"Anxiously, we watch," wrote Captain Lecointe. "All of our thoughts, all of our souls, call for release."

Suddenly, as if exhausted by battle, the ice loosened its grip ever so slightly, just enough for the *Belgica* to complete her turn. De Gerlache wasted no time: he pointed the prow toward the mouth of the canal and, with a clear path ahead, attempted a final charge. Somers built a full head of steam, making the most of his nearly depleted reserves of coal. The *Belgica* huffed like an angry bull. On de Gerlache's command, the ship barreled toward the wall of ice four hundred meters away, sails taut, pistons churning at maximum capacity.

The men held their breath as the *Belgica* launched herself at full speed into the barricade. There was no going back: either the ship or the ice would prevail. The stem slammed into the mass and crushed it to bits under her weight. "With no further obstacle, [she] sails triumphantly into the grand clearing," Lecointe reported.

"No body of men was ever happier than the officers and crew of the *Belgica*," Cook wrote, "as the good ship thumped the edge of the ice which had held her a prisoner for nearly a year."

Relieved of much of her coal and food reserves, the *Belgica* floated high on the water, bobbing and bucking like an animal let out of its cage. But she was not yet free from the pack. From the crow's nest, it was apparent that the clearing into which the ship had escaped was totally enclosed. So were all the leads and clearings beyond it. A dark smudge in the clouds above the horizon—a distinct water sky—seemed to indicate that the open ocean was about a dozen miles to the north, but there was no obvious way to reach it. Throughout the pack, leads were oriented east to west, perpendicular to the direction of the wind. The *Belgica* had no choice but to sail westward within the drifting ice and take every opportunity to wend, wedge, and batter her way from one lake to the next in an effort to reach the pack's northern limit.

Once her tanks were ballasted with seawater, she thrust her stem into isthmuses of ice, sliding up onto them and crushing them under her weight. This was what she had been built to do, and she threw herself against her captor with a vengeful élan. If the ice was young enough, she could split vast fields with a single well-placed blow. By the first of March, she had muscled her way to within five miles of the open ocean. The men worked day and night to avoid recapture, but soon the ship was threatened once again.

The view from the top of the mainmast revealed the thinnest of black lines beneath the horizon. Through his spyglass, de Gerlache could see the spray of the sea crashing against the edge of the pack.

"The danger has not disappeared," wrote the commandant. "It has been modified." The *Belgica* was trapped no longer in a single sheet of ice but in a dense mosaic of floes jostling in the swell. They were now close enough to the limit of the pack that each wave sweeping in from the ocean drew the ice chunks back before hurling them against the vessel. If the ice could no longer squeeze the *Belgica* to death, it was now bent on battering her open.

"The ship suffers one telling blow after another," Amundsen wrote in his diary. "Fortunately there is still enough slush and small pieces of ice between them to absorb the impact but the bigger blocks are coming closer and closer."

On March 5, when the ocean had settled down, Amundsen and Cook climbed down onto a pan of ice. The floes were pressed tightly enough together that a man could step between them. Amundsen and Cook made a two-mile trip across the gently undulating pack to a nearby iceberg, from which they hoped to survey the ice and perhaps find open water. Cook had brought his camera to document the scene.

As they walked, they heard a distant rumbling from the north, like the sound of a waterfall. Then suddenly they saw a seven-meter-tall wave advancing toward them, closing in like a charging cavalry. It hit the floes in its path with tremendous force and cracked them up, the fragments shooting up to the wave's crest before dropping out of sight behind it. The wave would be on them in seconds.

With no time to think, Cook and Amundsen turned around and bolted in the opposite direction. Jets of spray shot from cracks in the ice, getting nearer and nearer. The roar swelled at their backs as they bounded desperately from floe to floe. The wave was gaining on them; they'd never get to the ship in time. They stopped only when they'd reached a floe of old ice and clung to it for dear life as the enormous wave rolled beneath. Cook never let go of his camera.

Fists of ice weighing several tons each pummeled the *Belgica* day and night. "The ship is shaken hard," wrote Amundsen, "and trembles like a leaf." Each blow left paint chips and splinters on the jagged floes. If this beating continued much longer, the planks would crack. Resourceful as ever, Cook devised an effective, if gruesome, method to cushion the hull. He hung penguin carcasses from the gunwales and dangled them in front of spots where the ice was striking the wood. The fleshy fenders helped blunt the impact of the floes until they were crushed to a pulp. Months after Cook had discovered their scurvy-fighting properties, the birds were still saving the men's lives.

They did little, however, to protect the rudder from the repeated assaults of a large pan of ice at the ship's stern. Without the rudder to direct her, the *Belgica* would be unnavigable, her passengers as good as dead. Several crew members descended onto the pan and sawed out a notch for the rudder to fit into. They worked with furious intensity, refusing to let the pack claim the ship for another winter. They fought back like medieval soldiers defending a besieged fortress, swinging axes at the ice to round off sharp angles and blowing up the most menacing floes with tonite. The explosives reduced the ice to soupy brash, which formed a buffer against the larger chunks.

Little by little, the *Belgica* wriggled her way to the scattered fringes of the pack, aided by a steady southern breeze. On the evening of March 13, the wind picked up and pushed the entire pack northward, and the ship along with it. Hemmed in by fast-moving floes, the *Belgica* was driven helplessly toward a phalanx of enormous, deep-keeled icebergs that guarded access to the ocean. Being less susceptible to the wind, they remained in place, like a giant's teeth.

By morning, the *Belgica* was heading straight for a gargantuan molar of ice, a tabular berg many times the size of the ship. A deadly collision seemed inescapable. Large floes flanked the vessel, and the southerly wind was pushing her from behind. A relatively open lane of water lay ahead, but it led directly into the iceberg. To make matters worse, the space between the icebergs was clogged with floes that had gotten caught attempting to escape to the open sea.

De Gerlache took the helm, seemingly rejuvenated by the excitement of high-stakes navigation. The men counted on him, after all this time, to do what he did best. In order to build enough momentum that the ship could graze past the iceberg without being slammed into it by a sideswiping wave, he would need a longer stretch of water. He ordered Somers to throw the engine in reverse. The maneuver could wreck the engine, de Gerlache thought, but if it worked, it might buy the ship just enough space to make a final dash.

Her propeller rotating backward, the *Belgica* fought against the drift with every last unit of horsepower. At de Gerlache's command, Somers, the chief engineer, flipped the engine's direction, and the ship shot forward at top velocity.

Somers then forced steam into the two cylinders. The pistons yanked madly at the propeller's crankshaft. The pressure dials hit their maximums. Bolts loosened and joints rattled under the strain.

Somers climbed to the deck to tell de Gerlache that the engine couldn't take it anymore, but when he saw how close the ship was drifting to the iceberg, he ran back down and pushed it to the breaking point. He "made the engine steam as it had never steamed before," wrote Amundsen, "and probably will never steam again."

Everyone but Somers was on deck as the *Belgica* sped toward the iceberg and into the mass of surrounding floes. Time slowed down. Six meters to impact, five meters, four meters—the engine hyperventilating all the while. When the expected crash didn't happen, the men realized that they were free.

At two in the afternoon on March 14, they passed the northernmost piece of sea ice. Soon the only remaining trace of their white prison was an iceblink on the southern horizon.

CHAPTER 18

Strangers in the Mirror

"What multiple sensations we feel in succession, during these first moments of deliverance!" wrote Lecointe. "Something infinitely happy, yet laced with sadness, with regret, stirred in the bottom of our hearts: Goodbye to the pack with its attendant suffering and grief, but which has given us, amid the bitter joy of discovery, a feeling of pride that never again we shall experience! Goodbye to our poor companions, Danco and Wiencke, who paid the ransom of our salvation! Hurrah for the limitless Ocean, which takes us far away, to the home country, to everyone we love. Ah! Will we see them all again?"

The ship's late escape from the pack, as well as the poor health of the men, ruled out extending the mission for a third year. The South Magnetic Pole would remain unclaimed, a prize for future explorers, and the bad blood between de Gerlache and the Order of the Penguin over plans to reach Victoria Land was mostly forgotten. Now that the *Belgica* was leaving Antarctica for good, it was time for de Gerlache, as leader, to give names to the places the expedition had discovered, all of them in the Belgica Strait. His first considerations were for the two men who had lost their lives. The *Belgica*'s earliest victim was honored with the twenty-three-kilometer-long Wiencke Island. To his childhood friend, the commandant assigned a vast stretch of the Antarctic continent now known as the Danco Coast.

He continued down the list of people and places of importance to him and the expedition, such that the map of the channel now reads like a map of the Belgian countryside (if Belgium had a far more dramatic topography): Anvers Island, Brabant Island, Flanders Bay, the Solvay Mountains (named after his first and most generous financier, Ernest Solvay), the Osterrieth Range (named after his patron and confidante, Léonie Osterrieth, aka "Mother Antarctica"). He named a spectacular bay after Queen Wilhelmina of the Netherlands, in tribute to her gracious gesture of sending a ship to accompany the Belgica through Dutch waters on the day of the expedition's departure from Antwerp. The only reward de Gerlache could offer his supporters was immortality in the form of a distant spit of land they would likely never see.

When he had run out of people to thank, de Gerlache allowed the officers to name what minor geographical features remained, as a way of adding their signature to the landscape. Amundsen chose to honor the late Norwegian explorer Eivind Astrup. Cook named small islands after New York's first mayor, Robert Van Wyck, and his own hometown of Brooklyn.

Albatrosses and giant petrels escorted the ship as she crossed back over the Drake Passage. De Gerlache had intended to reenter Tierra del Fuego from the south, via the storm-battered, reef-strewn Cockburn Channel. The passage was more hazardous than entry points on the Atlantic and Pacific coasts, and every chart warned against sailing through it. That was the point: the danger meant the Belgica would be less likely to pass a ship that might recognize her and prematurely announce her safe return. De Gerlache had Wiencke first in mind: he would risk further danger to be able to properly inform the young man's family of his death. (Danco had no living relatives.) Yet consistently overcast skies prevented Lecointe from fixing the Belgica's position, and dead reckoning could give the men only a vague idea of where they were. De Gerlache decided at the last minute to play it safe by overshooting the continent, rounding Cape Horn and doubling back through the calmer waters on the Argentine side of the Strait of Magellan.

Ludwig Johansen was at the helm on the afternoon of March 26 when a cormorant flew across the ship's bow, heading north. The sailor followed the bird with his eyes as it dissolved into the fog off the port side. Where it had vanished, the faint contours of a craggy island soon appeared through the mist.

"Land!" Johansen cried out to his shipmates, who gathered at the port bow to marvel at the first piece of solid earth they had seen in more than a year.

A few minutes later, the ship passed a jagged spear of black rock that soared out of the frothing welter. It was covered with cormorants. De Gerlache and Lecointe consulted the British Admiralty map and searched for a corresponding formation around Cape Horn. There was none to be found. Confused, they examined the chart closely, running their fingers along the fragmented coast of Tierra del Fuego, and determined that the black steeple had to be one of the Tower Rocks, at the southern tip of Noir Island—more than three hundred miles to the west of where they expected to be. Such was the strength of the currents where the Pacific and Atlantic oceans swirled together. They had arrived at the embouchure of the treacherous Cockburn Channel after all.

Evening would soon obscure the network of reefs guarding the channel's entrance, so the commandant decided to drop anchor in the lee of Noir Island. Several of the men were desperate to plant their feet on solid ground, but de Gerlache, worried about the rising wind and the unfamiliarity of the terrain, preferred to wait until daylight before considering a landing. Throughout the night, westerly gusts of increasing violence juked around the rocks and sideswiped the *Belgica,* each blow causing her to list at a steep angle and her masts to teeter toward the water. Before dawn, the wind had veered to the southwest and hit the ship directly.

Thus began a storm more powerful and terrifying than any the men had experienced before. In Dobrowolski's description, it was a tempest worthy of J.M.W. Turner's most chaotic seascapes:

> Under a black sky so low that the waves could seemingly
> spray it with foam—they were a diffuse regiment of mighty
> pyramids of fluid iron colors with dribbling streams of foam.
> Their peaks, sliced by the gale, steamed with water and
> smoked with dust. Between them in vast valleys, sudden
> *staccata* of wind flung thick dust in the air, which was then
> promptly seized by the dense, spinning coils of vortexes of
> air. This procession of hazy vortexes, this dance of monsters

first clustering together, then again leaping apart, amid the
smoking volcanoes of waves—it was truly something from
a fairy tale!

Hurricane-force blasts sent wave after wave slamming into the
prostrate ship and pushed her ever closer to a line of breakers that
betrayed a submerged reef downwind, just four hundred meters
away. The storm overwhelmed the restraining force of the anchor,
which dragged along the sandy bottom as the *Belgica* slid toward the
menacing reef. Even with her engine at full steam, she couldn't make
enough headway against the wind to slacken the chain and allow the
men to haul the anchor back aboard. Instead of keeping the ship
from drifting into obstacles, the anchor—by preventing her escape—
was now all but ensuring her demise.

When it seemed impossible that the wind could blow any harder,
a squall of biblical magnitude walloped the *Belgica* on her port side
and shoved her viciously toward the reef. The commandant had only
seconds to avert catastrophe. He decided to abandon the anchor, and
as soon as it was released, its cable whipped across the deck and disappeared into the ocean. Unleashed, the *Belgica* careened even faster
toward the reef. Gripping the gunwales, drenched in spray, shouting
over the wind, de Gerlache ordered the crew to unfurl the fore-
topmast staysail, fire the engine at full steam, and swing the wheel to
port.

Thus arrayed, the ship harnessed the very forces that an instant
earlier had threatened to destroy her. The wind snapped the sail taut
and sent the *Belgica* past the reefs, flying to the northeast in the direction of the Cockburn Channel. According to the available charts, the
only way into the corridor was through a narrow passage between
rocks known as the West Furies and the East Furies. Yet as the ship
advanced, it quickly became apparent that the charts were dangerously unreliable. The commandant saw islands that didn't appear on
the maps and encountered areas of open water where land was indicated. He would have to sail blindly into an unknown, fog-shrouded
constellation of rocks amid a raging storm, guided by nothing but
providence and his reawakened navigational instincts.

That evening, the lookout spotted shapes ahead that fit the de-

scription of the West Furies, on which, according to the commandant's log, "the heavy seas crashed *furiously*" (emphasis de Gerlache's).
The *Belgica* sailed past the gateway to the Cockburn Channel miracu-
lously unscathed. As she glided through the fog into the sheltered
waterway, those on deck felt the wind gradually die down. Soon they
caught their first glimpse of green. It was enough to make some of
them cry.

The *Belgica* sailed into the port of Punta Arenas at sunrise on March
28, 1899. There were far more and far grander ships at anchor than
the men remembered. The arrival of the battered whaler caused little
commotion at first. The officers and several crew rowed to shore.
One by one, they set foot on land for the first time since at least February of the previous year.

The sensation left some of the crew giddy. "A few of the sailors
who came ashore remained on the beach, kicked about in the sand,
and tossed pebbles," Cook wrote. "So much were they interested in
this first touch of solid ground that they continued to play in the sand
for hours, with the delight of children on the seashore."

While the crew prepared the ship for a long stay in port, several of
the officers and scientists waded back into civilization. "Our walking
attitudes, as we strolled up these streets, were a study in alcoholism,"
wrote Cook. "We had travelled on *skis* and other snowshoes so long,
and had been tossed about on the sea so much, that we had forgotten
how to walk normally. We spread our legs, dragged our feet, braced
and balanced our bodies with every step, and altogether our gait was
ridiculous." On the way to their hotel, they were astounded by how
much Punta Arenas had changed since they'd last seen it. It felt as if
they had traveled through time. Dirt roads had been paved and were
now bustling with crowds and lined with fancy shops. Wires snaked
overhead, electric lights abounded, and ringing telephones could be
heard through windows and open doors. If the town had grown, it
seemed that the world had gotten smaller.

Strolling among the sheep farmers, pioneers, and gold diggers
were well-heeled gentlemen and ladies dressed in the latest fashions
from Paris. To the *Belgica*'s hirsute, "love-starved" explorers, the rus-

tling of silk underskirts was akin to "music and poetry." The sight of two comely young women had the electrifying effect, wrote Cook, of "a Faradic battery" and awoke the men's dormant vanity. "Somehow we all, at the same time, unconsciously brushed aside the year's growth of hair from our faces, and made an effort to arrange our neckties and change the set of our coats, but we were made to realise, more and more, that we looked hideous. The girls gave a sudden giggle and rushed back into the hall."

It was only when they got to their hotel rooms that the men understood why the women on the streets had avoided their gaze or fled outright. The faces staring back at them in the mirror attested to the hardship they'd endured: They "were drawn, and but a shade lighter than old copper kettles," Cook wrote; "our skins were rough, like nutmeg-graters; and our hair was long, stubborn, and liberally lined by bunches of gray, though the eldest among us was less than thirty-five years of age."* Their clothing, patched with leather and sailcloth and well suited to an Antarctic lifestyle, was suddenly a source of shame.

Visits to the tailor and the barber would improve their appearance, but the men's first priority was to fill their stomachs. After months of eating revoltingly insipid canned food and fatty, pungent Antarctic game, they craved fresh vegetables and the meat of grass-fed mammals. "I should be ashamed to confess the amount of beefsteak which we devoured," wrote Cook.

Once word got around that the *Belgica* had returned, a group of local dignitaries and diplomats met with the officers and bombarded them with questions: Had they reached the South Pole? Had they met Antarctic natives? The visitors then brought the explorers up to date on more than a year's worth of global events, including the Dreyfus affair in France; the Spanish-American War, which had been declared, fought, and settled in their absence; the disappearance of the Swedish balloonist and polar explorer S. A. Andrée over the Arctic; and Guglielmo Marconi's development of the wireless telegraph. "Marconi's discovery is particularly interesting to us," wrote de Gerlache, "as it will doubtless one day be of great use to polar explorers

---

*Henri Somers, the oldest of the men, was in fact thirty-six.

whom it will allow to correspond with rescue ships patrolling the open sea."

The expedition's mail had been forwarded to Melbourne, Australia, so there were only a few scattered, year-old letters awaiting the men in Punta Arenas. It would be days before Henri Somers, the only father among the men, would find out that his young daughter had died.

As soon as he had the chance, Tollefsen fled to the wildlands beyond Punta Arenas. Tollefsen's shipmates hoped that since his madness had been born on the Antarctic pack ice, it would subside with time and distance, as Van Mirlo's apparently had. But the Norwegian sailor only grew more unstable. He disappeared for days on end. When he ran out of food, he skulked back into town and loitered outside the door of de Gerlache's hotel. He begged the commandant for a few coins to buy provisions, then scurried back to his hiding place in the woods.

Tollefsen refused to return aboard the *Belgica*, even to get his belongings. He seemed to believe that the ship was haunted. He left behind a detailed diary, but we will never know what he confided to it: his fellow sailors chose to burn it rather than let posterity see the horrors and delusions it contained.

"These documents would have presented a certain interest," wrote Lecointe. "For my part, I declare that I had nothing to do with this act and blame those who directly or indirectly contributed to it."

Without the stamina or the funds to return to Antarctica, de Gerlache declared the expedition officially over in early April. He asked Amundsen to escort Tollefsen home on the next steamer bound for Europe. Though Amundsen remained cold toward de Gerlache and had never formally retracted his resignation, he agreed, bound by his responsibility to the crew. When they said goodbye, he and Cook promised to write and hoped to see each other again, if not in Norway or New York, then perhaps in some distant, frigid corner of the earth.

Lecointe, Racovitza, Arctowski, and Dobrowolski remained in South America for several months to pursue separate scientific projects and would find their own way back to Europe. Meanwhile, de Gerlache sailed the *Belgica* to Montevideo, and eventually back to Belgium, with a skeleton crew that included the mutinous Warzée, who had remained in Punta Arenas since his dismissal in December 1897 and begged to be rehired. Since the *Belgica* had used up all her coal and the expedition had no funds to buy more, de Gerlache relied on the wind alone. Crossing the Atlantic by sail took two and a half months and drained what little energy the commandant had left.

Cook left soon after for the Bridges estancia in Harberton to complete his anthropological study of the Fuegians. He had little awaiting him in Brooklyn. A few days after the *Belgica*'s arrival in Punta Arenas, Cook learned that his fiancée, Anna Forbes, had died the previous Easter.

BEYOND THE *BELGICA*

ON THE BRISK MORNING OF SUNDAY, NOVEMBER 5, 1899, DE GERLACHE sailed the *Belgica* up the Scheldt in the direction of Antwerp. As the ship approached the town of Doel, on the Dutch-Belgian border, the commandant saw a convoy of yachts cruising around the river bend to meet him. He heard cannon fire echo across the water and the distant din of "La Brabançonne." These were the same triumphant sounds that had accompanied the expedition's departure more than two years earlier. Bidding farewell that summer day in 1897, de Gerlache had scampered up the rigging with acrobatic agility and waved his cap energetically from the crow's nest. Today it was a very different man who saluted the welcoming flotilla. The *Belgica* had stolen his youth. While she looked resplendent for the occasion, in her new coat of ice-white paint, de Gerlache was stiff, weary, his features drawn and his hair grayer and sparser though he was only thirty-three.

At the head of the convoy, the *Princesse Clémentine,* the royal yacht, dispatched a rowboat to bring him aboard, along with Lecointe and several other officers and crew who had rejoined the *Belgica* for the occasion. On deck to greet them were ministers, senators, deputies, representatives of the Royal Belgian Geographical Society, top patrons, and the families of several of the men, among other notables. Amid the flurry of hurrahs, de Gerlache's bearded face twisted into a smile. He forgot how tired he was, forgot the lancing pain at his temples. He had dreamed of a glorious return for almost as long as he had dreamed of the Antarctic and was now mute with emotion. In front of him were the faces he had so often pictured while stranded on the desolate pack. There was his father, whose portrait had hung above his bunk; his mother, trying unsuccessfully to hold back tears;

his second mother, Léonie Osterrieth, beaming with pride. Lecointe, meanwhile, embraced his fiancée, Charlotte, to whom he had proposed on the eve of the *Belgica*'s departure.

A bitter wind forced the festivities to migrate into the yacht's lavish interior, where toast after toast was given to the glory of the explorers and their homeland. That the *Belgica* had failed to reach a record latitude or the South Magnetic Pole was dismissed as irrelevant. The expedition had charted new lands, completed more than a year's worth of scientific observations south of the polar circle, and survived an Antarctic winter—all historic firsts, and all in the name of Belgium. The Royal Geographical Society of Antwerp awarded its gold medal to de Gerlache and Lecointe. The accompanying speeches earned hearty applause, which swelled into deafening cheers when Jules de Trooz, Belgium's interior minister, announced that the king himself had named the expedition's officers and scientists knights of the Order of Leopold, the country's highest distinction. Lecointe may have smiled at the thought that he had already been inducted into a hallowed brotherhood, the Order of the Penguin, and wished that his fellow knights, Cook and Amundsen, had been there to share the moment. (They would receive their medals in the mail.) De Trooz asked de Gerlache's mother if she would do the honor of pinning the cross on the commandant's chest; she fell into her son's arms and wept with joy.

"The de Gerlache name appears not for the first time in our nation's history," said de Trooz, addressing the expedition leader. "It was borne by one of the founders of our independence. This great name, and the reputation attached to it, must have weighed heavily on you, but you have proven yourself, commandant, its worthy heir."

Attendees swarmed around the men, encircling and suffocating them much as the ice had. A journalist observing the festivities noted that the adventurers looked "disoriented" and "unsettled" by the attention. Following the ceremony, the guests and the explorers wandered through the *Princesse Clémentine*'s luxurious salons, chatted amiably, and ate a lunch so exquisite as to make one almost forget the taste of undercooked penguin. The setting couldn't have been further removed from the Antarctic, and the men were finally beginning to feel that the horrors of the pack were behind them.

But after about an hour, a commotion rippled across the yacht. Max Van Rysselberghe, the expedition's second mechanic, had fainted. He was sprawled on the ground, his heart palpitating as wildly as it had in the darkest days of winter. Doctors shouldered their way to his side and cleared a space around him. They lifted him and laid him down on a chaise longue, where he eventually regained consciousness.

The Antarctic had not finished with its victims. A journalist described the men, collectively, as "Captain Hatteras in flesh and blood." Though the writer meant the comparison as a celebration of their achievement, the evocation of Jules Verne's hero, who in the 1866 novel *The Adventures of Captain Hatteras* returns from the North Pole insane and spends the rest of his days in a madhouse, proved all too apt. Later that month, Johan Bryde, the Norwegian diplomat who had brokered the purchase of the *Belgica,* wrote de Gerlache about Tollefsen, to whom the commandant had sent a medal from King Leopold. "Poor Tollefsen has completely lost his head," Bryde wrote. "There is now talk of having him committed."

Tollefsen had a son with his sweetheart, Alette, and the two were married. Upon returning to Norway, Tollefsen had written to de Gerlache of his intention to establish a Belgo-Norwegian coal-mining colony on the remote Arctic island of Spitsbergen. But in the end, none of his dreams of leading a fruitful life would pan out. He was sent to a different kind of colony, a system of farms on the outskirts of Kristiania that employed and tended to the mentally ill. The surrounding town of Lier would become the site of an asylum notorious for its reliance on lobotomy and shock therapy, among other controversial treatments. Tollefsen was registered there for the rest of his life, along with the other patients living on the farms of Lier.*

---

* In 1981, a former nursing assistant named Ingvar Ambjørnsen published *23-salen,* a thinly disguised tell-all about the asylum that scandalized Norway with its vivid descriptions of patients strapped to gurneys with belts, left untreated, wallowing in their own filth, their chilling screams echoing through the halls. Several of the hospital's buildings closed soon after. The abandoned facilities, so decrepit they looked diseased, became a pilgrimage site for thrill seekers drawn to the macabre and the paranormal. The institution has since been razed, save for two of the original buildings, which are being converted into high-end apartments.

An official report of the expedition, published in Brussels in 1904, offered an explanation for Tollefsen's breakdown that could have been written by Poe: "One sailor [Van Mirlo] had fits of hysteria which bereft him of reason. Another, witnessing the pressure of the ice, was smitten with terror and went mad at the spectacle of the weird-sublime and in dread of pursuing fate."

Three months after informing de Gerlache of Tollefsen's worsening condition, Bryde had more grim news to share. Engelbret Knudsen, the cherubic twenty-four-year-old deckhand who had been among the sickest members of the expedition during the *Belgica*'s wintering, had died. Knudsen's death was a shock to the commandant, who considered him an exemplary sailor, and added to the remorse he likely felt over Tollefsen and the loss of Danco and Wiencke.

De Gerlache made every effort to conceal his own agony on the day of the *Belgica*'s return to Antwerp. He was rid of scurvy but remained gravely ill, crippled by fatigue, relentless headaches, and what Cook would call "nervous trouble." As the bells of the Cathedral of Our Lady rang in honor of the expedition, the commandant trudged through the jubilant sea of people that roiled between the pontoon and City Hall, where a formal reception was to be held. What would ordinarily have been a two-minute walk seemed to take an eternity as Antwerpians flocked around Belgium's unassuming new national hero.

More medals were given out at City Hall and, later, in Brussels. After all the ceremonies were over and all the decorations doled out, de Gerlache fled to the French Riviera with his mother to rest, at the insistence of his physician. He settled in Nice, at the Grand Hôtel des Empereurs. It would take him a year to recover.

The precise cause of his suffering remains a mystery. The scurvy that had ravaged him was now a distant memory. Like everyone else on board, he had experienced insomnia and cardiac symptoms during the monthlong night. But while most of his shipmates had recovered by the time they'd returned to South America, de Gerlache's ailment lasted well into 1900. One possible explanation lies in the baths of hydrocyanic acid that Cook used in the *Belgica*'s darkroom, which opened onto de Gerlache's cabin. The substance had been brought on board not to develop photographs—that was Cook's ingenious adaptation—but to euthanize animal specimens. Hydrocyanic acid, also known as prussic acid, kills by depriving cells of oxygen. (It would become the main ingredient in Zyklon B, the gas used in Nazi extermination camps during World War II.) As it happens, the early signs of low-grade cyanide poisoning closely resemble the symptoms the men of the *Belgica* were experiencing: headaches, fatigue, erratic heart rate, shortness of breath, confusion, vertigo. Survivors of such poisoning often exhibit long-lasting neurological effects.

In the early weeks of his convalescence in Nice, de Gerlache received a letter that buoyed his spirits. It was from Lecointe, who had taken a leading role in the Commission of the Belgica, an organization dedicated to analyzing and publishing the expedition's findings. (The effort would take forty years, so voluminous were the scientists' observations and the trove of specimens they brought back.) In his letter, Lecointe informed de Gerlache of his intention to recommend that the commission rename the voyage's most important discovery—the Belgica Strait—after its commandant.

"As you know, I am a 'grouch,' so nobody will consider my proposal a mere act of courtesy," Lecointe wrote. "I am convinced that my proposal is an act of justice." Today, the spectacularly beautiful 130-mile channel is known as the Gerlache Strait.

De Gerlache had more than lived up to the family name; he would become its most famous bearer. He had achieved the glory he'd so long craved not despite the terrible hardships he and his men endured, but because of them. His reckless gamble to enter the ice at the end of the austral summer had paid off, but he would never forget that it had done so at the cost of three lives and his own health.

The commandant never saw Antarctica again. Shortly after her return, the *Belgica* was taken to Ostend, where she was refit and cleared of rats at last. In 1905, she was sold to Prince Philippe, Duke of Orléans—a playboy adventurer and claimant to the French throne, were the monarchy to be restored—who hired de Gerlache to accompany him, as captain, on several Arctic expeditions. Years later, de Gerlache would oversee the construction of a magnificent barkentine called the *Mercator*, which would serve as a training ship for a new generation of Belgian sailors—furthering his lifelong mission to elevate his country's maritime profile. For the rest of his life, de Gerlache would remain an éminence grise of polar travel, content to advise participants in the heroic age of Antarctic exploration that had been kicked off by the *Belgica* expedition.

His name would make one more notable appearance in polar history. Shortly before the outbreak of the First World War, he teamed up with Lars Christensen, the Sandefjord shipbuilder who'd turned the *Patria* into the *Belgica,* to construct a new ship, the *Polaris,* on which he planned to lead polar-bear-hunting cruises for wealthy tourists. A three-masted barkentine clad in greenheart, she bore a sisterly resemblance to the *Belgica.* The *Polaris* was said to be among the strongest wooden vessels ever constructed. Yet in the end, de Gerlache had to back out of the partnership for financial reasons. Christensen sold the ship, at a loss, to the celebrated Anglo-Irish explorer Ernest Shackleton, who rechristened her the *Endurance.* In November 1915, she was crushed by the Antarctic pack ice and sank to the bottom of the Weddell Sea.*

From the moment he returned to Norway, Roald Amundsen began plotting his own expedition. The *Belgica* had been a crash course in polar exploration, and he was aching to apply the lessons he'd learned. "It was during this voyage that my plan matured," he would later write. "I proposed to combine the dream of my boyhood as to the North West Passage with an aim, in itself of far greater scientific importance, *that of locating the present situation of the Magnetic North Pole* [emphasis Amundsen's]." While the latter goal might gain the respect of a small circle of scholars, the blazing of a path from the Atlantic to the Pacific through the treacherous ice of the Canadian Arctic—a feat that had eluded explorers ever since the discovery of the New World—would thrill the public at large and earn Amundsen a heroic status on a par with Nansen, if not Cartier or Columbus.

---

*After Shackleton and his men drifted northward with the pack ice for nearly five months, they made the seven-day crossing to Elephant Island aboard the *Endurance*'s lifeboats. From there, Shackleton and five of his men sailed the sturdiest of those open boats, the *James Caird,* 720 nautical miles through raging seas to South Georgia Island to seek rescue, a sixteen-day journey that counts among the most impressive feats in the history of polar exploration.

Using his inheritance and what little credit he could scrounge—including a contribution from the *Belgica*'s guardian angel, Léonie Osterrieth—he purchased a scrappy twenty-nine-year-old, seventy-foot sloop named the *Gjøa,* among the puniest vessels in the golden age of polar exploration. He sailed from Kristiania in the wee hours of June 16, 1903, with a crew of six. The ship reached northern Canada's poorly mapped, ice-congested fragmentation of islands in early August. Amundsen followed a route slightly different from the one his childhood hero John Franklin had taken with the *Erebus* and the *Terror,* almost sixty years earlier. The nimble whaler was nonetheless stuck fast off King William Island for two winters in a row, not far from where the two British ships had sunk. But unlike Franklin, who stuck to Royal Navy protocol, Amundsen was determined from the beginning to survive on Arctic game and adopt Inuit modes of dress and travel. Cook's interventions during the *Belgica* expedition had convinced Amundsen of the benefit of living off the land in native style—and it was far more practical for 7 men (and a variable number of huskies) to do so than the *Belgica*'s 17, let alone Franklin's 130.

Amundsen and his crew built a hut on the shores of King William Island. Throughout their two-year stay, they maintained fruitful relations with local Netsilik tribesmen, who led the Scandinavians on hunting trips and, in exchange for Western goods, provided them with handicrafts, fresh game, sled dogs, and, for what the explorers considered a pittance, the right to sleep with their wives. (Amundsen would later maintain that he had urged his men, several of whom had families at home, to refrain from such activities.)

The men of the *Gjøa* made several attempts during the first year to locate the North Magnetic Pole, meandering across the ice as they followed the indications of an array of delicate instruments. But they were stymied by the brutal cold and their inexperience at running dogs. During the excursions on the Antarctic pack years before, Cook had convinced Amundsen of the primacy of dogs as a means of transportation across the ice. But it was the Netsilik who taught the Scandinavian explorers how to drive them. After they'd gotten the hang of it, Amundsen and a companion, Peder Ristvedt, managed in the spring of 1904 to reach the coordinates at which James Clark Ross, in 1831, had last pinpointed the magnetic pole. Yet the needles of their instruments kept pointing northward, proving definitively what was long suspected: that the magnetic pole is a moving target. A few weeks later, the two men reached the vicinity of the pole itself.

Though the explorers complained of boredom and cabin fever during the long Arctic night, they did not suffer as the *Belgica*'s men had. The proximity of Netsilik settlements—particularly Netsilik women—surely helped distract them. As a leader, Amundsen was overbearing, tyrannical, and occasionally petulant, marking a strong contrast with the retiring, lenient de Gerlache. (His men nicknamed him, somewhat derisively, "the Governor.") But perhaps the more consequential contrast was between the *Belgica*'s well-meaning but inept cook, Louis Michotte, and the *Gjøa*'s hard-drinking, Falstaffian chef, Adolf Lindstrøm, whose refined seal-meat stews were as delectable as Michotte's preparations were revolting.

The *Gjøa*'s humble size worked to her advantage, allowing her to glide over reefs and shoals that would have blocked a larger vessel. On August 17, 1905, she passed the easternmost point any ship heading east from the Bering Strait had ever reached. But the thaw would be all too brief. Just a few weeks later, the expedition was again beset and forced to spend nearly a year in the pack ice, during which one of the team's members fell ill and died. It wasn't until August 31, 1906, that the *Gjøa* sailed into Nome, Alaska, proudly flying the Norwegian colors.

When Cook showed up at Harberton in April 1899 to complete his study of the Ona and the Yahgan, Lucas Bridges was surprised to see that the *Belgica* had survived her Antarctic sojourn after all. The rancher informed Cook that his father, Thomas Bridges, had died in the meantime. But Lucas honored the late missionary's promise to Cook and handed over his manuscript for the Yahgan-English dictionary so the doctor could get it published. This was a remarkable act of faith: containing more than thirty thousand words, the dictionary was an invaluable record of a disappearing civilization. Thomas Bridges had not made copies.

Cook stayed in Argentina until the end of 1899. When he returned to New York, he was expected to deliver three in-depth monographs for the Belgica Commission. The first was to be an analysis of his medical observations during the *Belgica*'s wintering. The second would be an anthropological report on the Ona people. The third was titled "A Yahgan Grammar and Dictionary." In the official list of pending reports—printed on the back of each volume as it appeared— Cook is credited as the dictionary's author. There is no mention of Thomas Bridges. While the unmerited byline might have been an oversight, it would be cited years later as Cook's first brush with fraud. Lucas Bridges claimed that Cook had stolen his father's life's work and tried to pass it off as his own.

Whether that was truly Cook's intention is unknowable, since he never completed any of the three reports he was assigned to write. Once back in Brooklyn, he had other things on his mind. The death of Anna Forbes had left him as disconsolate and lonely as had that of her sister, Cook's first wife, Libby, a decade earlier. And though he reopened his medical practice, much of his clientele had found other doctors during his two-year absence. Once again, he sought escape in adventure.

Like Amundsen, he yearned to lead a major expedition of his own. But to mount one he would need fame and money, neither of which the three labor-intensive Belgica Commission reports he owed could provide, as they would never reach beyond a small cadre of academics. Instead, he got to work on a popular narrative of the Belgian Antarctic Expedition. It took him just a few months to write the manuscript. Published in 1900, *Through the First Antarctic Night* revealed Cook's prowess as a writer. The book was the first of the *Belgica* memoirs to come out, representing a significant breach in polar protocol: as Cook knew all too well after his falling-out with Robert Peary over the matter years before, it was the expedition leader's prerogative to publish first. De Gerlache took two years to complete his account, *Fifteen Months in the Antarctic,* considered in its time to be a magisterial literary achievement. Lecointe followed in 1904 with his own travelogue, *Au pays des manchots* [In the land of the penguins]. Cook's book sold exceptionally well and turned him into a minor celebrity in the United States.

A year or so after the book's publication, the doctor met a wealthy twenty-four-year-old widow named Marie Hunt and fell in love.

(Schumann's "Träumerei" was playing the first time they locked eyes.) In April 1902, Cook wrote to Amundsen to announce their engagement and, almost in apology, the end of his career as an explorer: "I expect to get married early in June and then my polar adventures will be at an end. The future Mrs Cook invites you to come and stay with us. . . . Come and let us show you N.Y."

Cook adopted Hunt's young daughter, Ruth, and soon afterward the couple welcomed a baby girl, Helen. Domestic life didn't curb Cook's wanderlust for long, however. Not only did Hunt encourage her husband's ambitions, but she also generously subsidized them. By the summer of 1903, Cook was back in the exploration game, leading an expedition to Alaska to climb Denali (then known unofficially as Mount McKinley), the tallest mountain in North America, which remained unconquered. Cook and his party trekked on horseback for three miserable months through uncharted brush and marshland at the base of the mountain, the rhythm of hooves syncopated by the sound of hands clapping mosquitoes against necks. They failed to find a practicable route to the summit, but in the process became the first men known to have circumnavigated the mountain.

Cook made a second attempt at the daunting peak three years later, with a team that included more-experienced alpinists. This time he claimed success. The triumph earned Cook the recognition he had long sought. Upon his return to New York, he was elected president of the newly founded Explorers Club. His second book, *To the Top of the Continent*, published in 1908, featured a photograph of the doctor waving the American flag above what appears to be the mountain's summit.

The life of an explorer is one of unquenchable thirst. While individual aims can be attained, the ultimate goal—something that exists not in some remote corner of the planet, but within a person's heart—is forever out of reach. Each feat must be succeeded by an even greater one. By 1907, Cook had decided what that greater feat would be. He made no announcement but quietly headed to Greenland, purportedly to guide a friend on a hunting expedition. Once there, he turned his eyes to the north.

. . .

It was one of the biggest scoops in history, with one of the longest headlines: "THE NORTH POLE IS DISCOVERED BY DR. FREDERICK A. COOK, WHO CABLES TO THE HERALD AN EXCLUSIVE ACCOUNT OF HOW HE SET THE AMERICAN FLAG ON THE WORLD'S TOP." On the morning of September 2, 1909, newsboys sold out of *The New York Herald* almost instantly. Much of the paper was devoted to breathless coverage of Cook's accomplishment: how he and two Inuit hunters reached the geographic pole by dogsled on April 21, 1908; how they spent the cruel Arctic winter marooned on Devon Island; how they survived a polar bear attack. President Taft sent his congratulations to Cook, as did Buffalo Bill. Children sent him letters asking if he'd seen Santa Claus.

Cook's coup was a global sensation, but Americans especially rejoiced. Within twenty-four hours, several midtown Manhattan establishments started serving the "Cook cocktail"—gin, lemon juice, egg white, maraschino, plenty of ice. A milliner in Chicago introduced the "Dr. Cook hat" for women, a two-foot-high dome of fur meant to evoke the rounded apex of the earth. Magazines and newspapers wired Cook, dangling eye-popping sums for the serial rights to the narrative of his journey. *Hampton's Magazine* offered the doctor $100,000.* The bidding quickly rose to $200,000, the following day to $250,000. Not to be outdone, William Randolph Hearst said he would double any amount Cook was offered. Yet Cook feared that publishing in Hearst's yellow press would "cheapen" the magnitude of his accomplishment. He rebuffed them all for the moment.

The explorer would not return to New York for another few weeks. On his way back from the Danish territory of Greenland, he laid over in Copenhagen, where he was showered with adulation. His features sharpened by months of starvation, his teeth chipped, Cook could barely squeeze past the quay, so thronged was it with top-hatted officials and bowler-hatted looky-loos. During his brief stay, he received an honorary doctorate from the University of Copenhagen. King Frederick VIII of Denmark threw a lavish reception for him, becoming the second monarch, after Belgium's Leopold II, to pay tribute to him.

---

* About $3 million in 2020 dollars.

Almost as soon as Cook's exploit was announced, it was thrown into question. A certain amount of skepticism was to be expected, since the achievement was virtually impossible to prove. The only witnesses were the two young Inuit hunters, who were not trained in astronomical observation and could therefore not confirm that they had arrived at the point where all meridians meet. Adding to suspicions was Cook's claim that he had made observations and measurements that would vindicate him, but that, fearing he might not survive the overland journey back to civilization, he had entrusted them to a friend in northern Greenland, who in turn had been forced to leave them behind. (They were never found.) Several polar experts, moreover, expressed doubt over Cook's seemingly superhuman rate of progress over the ice as stated in the *Herald*.

Yet for the most part, the public accepted and enthusiastically celebrated the attainment of the world's most coveted geographic prize. Fridtjof Nansen expressed faith in Cook, as did the doctor's former companions from the *Belgica*. "I am indignant at the idea that Dr. Cook's statement of his discovery is accepted as untrue by some people," Lecointe, by then head of the Royal Belgian Observatory, told the *Herald*. "I know Dr. Cook personally, and I vouch for his sincerity. He is truth itself." Amundsen, for his part, called his mentor's journey "the most brilliant sledge trip in the history of polar exploration."

Cook's moment of unchallenged glory as the conqueror of the North Pole lasted just four days. On September 6, Cook attended a dinner in his honor in Copenhagen. Between ovations, a man handed him a note on which it was written, "Peary says, 'Stars and Stripes nailed to the Pole.'"

If it bothered Cook that his former expedition leader turned archrival Robert Peary had staked a competing claim, he didn't let it show. "If Peary says he reached the Pole," Cook told a reporter, "I believe him!" He would later cable *The Herald*: "Two records are better than one." Cook was perfectly willing to share his laurels, especially since he purported to have reached the goal almost a year before Peary.

Three days later, Cook received two illustrious visitors in his room at Copenhagen's Hotel Phoenix. One was Otto Sverdrup, Nansen's longtime lieutenant, who had led his own Arctic expedition aboard the *Fram*. The other was Amundsen, who was also staying at the

Phoenix. The two old *Belgica* shipmates embraced. Emaciated from his journey, Cook disappeared in the arms of the hulking Amundsen. Since they'd last seen each other, ten years prior, they had both achieved the kind of fame they'd fantasized about while aboard the *Belgica*.

Sverdrup and Amundsen had come to congratulate the conqueror of the North Pole. To Cook, who had little sense of how the Peary news would play in the weeks to come, the visit was a heartening gesture of support. As crowds cheered outside Cook's window, the three men spoke of journeys past and future in an impromptu summit of polar legends.

Amundsen's conquest of the Northwest Passage had established him as the heir apparent to Fridtjof Nansen. Since then, he had announced plans and raised funding for an expedition that would attempt to reach the North Pole via the Bering Strait by emulating Nansen's historic drift aboard the *Fram* in the early 1890s. In a momentous passing of the torch, Nansen granted Amundsen use of that same sturdy, bowl-bottomed ship. With luck, the spiraling currents of the frozen Arctic Ocean would bring Amundsen to a high enough latitude that he could mush the rest of the way with dogs he planned to acquire in Alaska. Yet he recognized that Cook's and Peary's claims, made in such close succession, had stripped the North Pole of much of its prestige as a geographic trophy. He would be vying for scraps.

In the hotel room, Amundsen quizzed his former teacher about the northernmost regions of the earth, about the currents and the weather and the prospects of success. Cook expressed confidence that his friend could attain his goal but, perhaps sensing Amundsen's own misgivings, advised him to abort the expedition. At best, Amundsen could only hope to be the third man to the pole. The doctor instead recommended an audacious change of course.

"The North Pole is now out of the picture," he said bluntly. "Why not try for the South Pole?"

Amundsen was stunned. The idea had crossed his mind, but he'd kept it to himself. It was nevertheless in the ether. Earlier that year, Ernest Shackleton had established a new farthest-south record when he marched to within one hundred nautical miles of the South Pole before being forced to turn back for lack of provisions. The relatively short distance that remained untrodden was tempting to Amundsen, but it was well known that Shackleton's compatriot and rival, Robert Falcon Scott, was preparing a major expedition to close the gap.

Amundsen feared that Scott's head start and ample funds would make it an uneven contest. Yet Cook argued that Amundsen had a critical advantage over the Brit. "Scott doesn't know how to travel with dogs," he said. "Scott's overload will hang him. You know that the South Pole will never be reached except by dogs or wings."

Then there was the matter of etiquette. Amundsen felt honor-bound—to his expedition's backers, to the public at large, as well as to Nansen—to follow through on the mission he'd announced. More-over, according to unspoken rules of polar decorum, Scott could ex-pect to be given priority in reaching the South Pole, having long made his intentions clear. Yet Sverdrup argued that the contro-versy brewing over Cook's and Peary's claims to the North Pole had thrown those rules out the window. A competition between Scott and Amundsen would enthrall the public and lend even more glory to the eventual victor.

"Let's have a race," said Sverdrup.

Amundsen considered his friend's advice. He offered one last ob-jection, as if arguing with himself. "The *Fram* is not a good sea boat for the heavy South Seas," he said. "But this is the thing to do. Let me think it over."

Before leaving, Amundsen snatched a piece of Cook's personal sta-tionery on which, in his room, he wrote a note to Denmark's chief administrator for northern Greenland, asking for fifty sled dogs. He had made up his mind: he would no longer be going to Alaska.

Despite Cook's magnanimous offer to share North Pole glory, he could not talk his way out of conflict with Robert Peary. For Peary, who had made the North Pole his life's ambition, glory was a zero-sum game. He could win only if Cook failed. That Cook had even made an attempt at the prize to which Peary felt entitled was an inex-cusable betrayal. Peary would from then on assert that his erstwhile co-traveler had lied about attaining the North Pole. Cook, he said, "has simply handed the public a gold brick."

Since neither man supplied incontrovertible proof of his exploit, a coolheaded comparison of geographical data was out of the question. Instead, the story took the form of a bitter contest of character, primarily waged in the pages of *The Herald* (which backed Cook's claim) and *The New York Times* (which supported Peary's). The controversy was a war of attrition from which neither man's reputation emerged unharmed. Peary's camp—wealthier, better connected, more persistent than Cook's—ultimately prevailed. In an effort to expose Cook as a habitual liar, allies of Peary tracked down Ed Barrill, a Montana guide who had accompanied Cook on his second expedition to Denali. In exchange for a sizeable sum, Barrill confessed that the two men hadn't come close to the summit. He claimed that the image that graced Cook's memoir of the journey, *To the Top of the Continent,* was in fact a cropped photograph of a lesser peak, several thousand feet below.

In December 1909, Henryk Arctowski, the *Belgica*'s geologist, meteorologist, and oceanographer—and frequent laughingstock—weighed in on the controversy in a devastating series of articles in the Belgian newspaper *La Métropole*. While praising Cook's ingenuity, Arctowski doubted his commitment to accuracy. "Aside from his absolutely undeniable qualities as an explorer . . . Cook had decidedly exceptional powers of imagination," wrote the Polish scientist, alluding to the doctor's medical innovations in combating scurvy and depression aboard the *Belgica,* as well as his wild idea to break out of the Antarctic pack ice. But Arctowski questioned whether "Cook had acquired the mathematical and astronomical knowledge required to correctly determine the latitude and longitude of a given spot on the globe."

The death blow to Cook's honor was dealt that same month at the University of Copenhagen, which examined what little astronomical evidence he was able to supply and deemed it insufficient to confirm his attainment of the pole. No such hearing was held for Peary, but by that point, it didn't matter: Cook had been marked as a confidence man, among the kinder epithets thrown at him. Others included "monster of duplicity" and "monumental faker." Publishers rescinded their offers. New York's Explorers Club, of which Cook had been president, revoked his membership.

With Amundsen at her helm, the *Fram* left Norway on August 9, 1910, and headed south toward Madeira. This was no surprise, since Amundsen had announced plans to round Cape Horn before hooking north and sailing into the Arctic via the Bering Strait. But while in Funchal, where he was safely beyond the reach of his creditors, he made a stunning announcement to his men. They would still eventually head to the North Pole, he said, but would first take a detour—to the South Pole. They would challenge Scott to a race.

The abrupt change of course took the British by surprise. It also came as a shock to Nansen, who, at forty-eight, was still hoping to save the conquest of the South Pole for himself. To accomplish what he believed to be his destiny, Amundsen betrayed his hero, much as, twelve years earlier, he had turned against de Gerlache, whom he had admired so greatly.

After crossing the Southern Ocean, the *Fram* arrived at the Bay of Whales, along the Ross Sea, in January 1911. It had been more than a decade since Amundsen had last seen the Antarctic sea ice. He and his men built a hut near the lip of the Ross Ice Shelf, in which they lived for months as they prepared for their assault on the pole, sustained by Lindstrøm's delicious and antiscorbutic seal stews. On October 19, Amundsen, along with four men and fifty-two dogs, took off for the pole by sledge and on skis. Their goal was eight hundred miles away, at an elevation of more than nine thousand feet and with a range of much higher peaks blocking the way. Amundsen initially set a manageable pace of fifteen to twenty miles a day—between five and six hours of travel—to let men and dogs recover overnight. The Norwegian's sledging strategy was remarkably similar to the plan Cook had proposed aboard the *Belgica* for the Order of the Penguin's planned dash to the South Magnetic Pole.

While they felt deep affection for their dogs, Amundsen and his party shot the slowest ones at regular intervals and fed them to their brothers and sisters, even feasting on the meat themselves. The cold-bloodedly efficient method—which he, Cook, and Lecointe had first conceived during the *Belgica* expedition—kept the sledges light and allowed the men to arrive at the South Pole on December 14, well rested, well nourished, and scurvy-free.* With a series of sextant observations throughout the day, Amundsen verified that he had indeed arrived at latitude 90° south by measuring the height of the sun as it circled overhead.

"It is quite interesting, to see the sun wander round the heavens at so to speak the same altitude day and night," he wrote. "I think somehow we are the first to see this curious sight." This remark, confided to his diary, is an indication that Amundsen doubted both Cook's and Peary's claims to have reached the North Pole, where they would presumably have witnessed the same phenomenon. If his hunch was right, the North Pole remained up for grabs. His mental ledger of polar records had grown long since the list began during the *Belgica* expedition, and he'd just achieved an exploit to secure a permanent seat in the pantheon of human exploration. But there was always room for one more entry.

At that moment, Robert Falcon Scott was more than four hundred miles behind, dashing toward the pole by a different route. For the final stages of the journey, the headstrong captain had decided against using—and regularly killing—sled dogs, which he considered cruel and unsportsmanlike. Scott instead relied on Siberian ponies (also known as Yakut horses) to carry equipment over the Transantarctic Mountains. Unlike dogs, which release moisture by panting, ponies sweat profusely with exertion. Their perspiration froze in the sub-zero temperatures and incessant winds of the mountains. Incapable of moving any farther, all of Scott's remaining ponies had to be shot, and the five men were left to haul overloaded sledges themselves for hundreds of miles, an unfathomably arduous journey that left them in a state of extreme exhaustion and hunger, stricken with frostbite and incipient scurvy. Scott and his men arrived at the pole on January 17, 1912. The spot—a merely theoretical point on an endless, fea-

---

* Amundsen and his men also avoided snow blindness thanks to goggles based on those Cook had constructed after Inuit designs, using photographic filters as lenses.

tureless, lifeless expanse of white—was marked by a stomach-churning sight: a conical canvas tent above which floated the red, white, and blue Norwegian flag.

"The worst has happened," Scott wrote in his diary. "Great God! This is an awful place."

In the tent, Scott found a note from Amundsen:

Dear Captain Scott,
As you probably are the first to reach this area after us, I will ask you
kindly to forward this letter to King Haakon VII. If you can use any
of the articles left in the tent please do not hesitate to do so. With
kind regards I wish you a safe return.
Yours truly, Roald Amundsen

While he begrudgingly admired the tent's spare, wind-deflecting form, Scott saw it as a symbol of defeat. He considered its presence, like the note and the provisions within, a cruel gesture of pity by his Norwegian rival. He couldn't have known that it was Amundsen's nod to his friend and mentor: the tent had been designed by Cook, identical to the one the doctor had stitched together for the Order of the Penguin's trip across the sea ice in the winter of 1898. It was Amundsen's way of bringing Cook to the South Pole.

The Britons lingered at the pole for several days before turning back. Buffeted by snowstorms, tormented by frostbite, and plagued with bad luck, they made slow progress. Scott and his companions died of cold and starvation at the end of March 1912, a mere eleven miles from the next food depot.

After the newspapers and the scientific community turned against him, Cook decided to appeal to the American public directly. He became a fixture of the vaudeville circuit, touring the country to tell his version of the conquest of the North Pole. Sharing the stage in city after city with magicians, exotic dancers, animal wranglers, and minstrel acts, Cook put on an entertaining show, a pastiche of scientific lectures in which he goaded the audience to hiss at any mention of

Peary's skullduggery and the vicious press. But though he drank in the adulation, he had to have known that much of the applause was ironic. He had become a national punch line.

Cook's exploring days would come to an end. Few patrons would risk backing a suspected fraud, and he had squandered much of his wife's fortune on his expeditions. Tempted by the petroleum boom of the late 1910s, he tried to remake his life as an oilman, first in Wyoming and then in Texas, on the tenuous notion that his experience as a polar explorer qualified him as an expert in geology. In Fort Worth, he landed in a world rife with schemers, profiteers, and flimflam artists and found he fit right in. Cook turned his notoriety into an asset. With so much uncertainty and speculation in the petroleum business, companies would stake their legitimacy on the prestige of a respectable—or at least respectable-sounding—figurehead. (The brochures for one Texas oil concern, for example, prominently featured a man who called himself General Robert A. Lee, a courthouse janitor whose claim to fame was that he looked somewhat like General Robert E. Lee.)

In 1919, Cook founded the Texas Eagle Oil Company and became its main shareholder, reinvesting almost all of his earnings in it. Yet amid vicious competition in the area, he failed to strike oil. As he had many times before when faced with seemingly insurmountable obstacles, Cook doubled his resolve and found ingenious—if not entirely honest—ways around the problem. He formed the Petroleum Producers' Association (PPA), which bought up more than three hundred failing oil companies for pennies, in the hope that some of them would eventually strike a gusher and pay for the whole enterprise. In the meantime, however, he would need shareholders to stay afloat.

Cook and his team wrote florid marketing materials that promised Rockefeller-like profits to anyone who invested. They sent letters, in Cook's name, to shareholders of the bankrupt or moribund entities that made up the PPA and offered to let them convert their shares to Cook's company for 25 cents on the dollar—what one of his detractors would later describe as a "gigantic stock reloading scheme."

To gain his correspondents' trust, Cook cited his experience at both ends of the earth:

My life has been anything but a bed of roses; enduring hardships
from the North Pole to the Southern Hemisphere boundary; all
these bitter endurances without compensation, and for the sole and
only purpose of the extension of civilization and the betterment of
mankind, and I come to you with the above statistical facts, my
word of honor, reputation as a man, all these things in the form of
a positive guarantee for the purpose of helping you, knowing that
every man and woman on earth are dependent on investments
for their financial success.

At first the tactic worked, and the PPA was flush with money. By December 1922, its companies were capitalized at $380,861,000. But Cook spent money faster than he brought it in, much of it to pay for the company's fancy Fort Worth headquarters. With virtually no oil revenue to draw upon, Cook paid monthly dividends to shareholders by selling more shares. Cook believed that his oil wells would pay off eventually. The fact remains that his scheme was not much different from one of the most notorious swindles in American history, named after its originator, Charles Ponzi, convicted just two years earlier.

In April 1923, Cook was indicted on several counts of fraud. The federal prosecutor argued that the sole purpose of the PPA was to acquire lists of shareholders of defunct oil companies, who might be cajoled into investing in a new company. (This was not an uncommon technique during the wildcatting era. Almost as precious as black gold itself were the so-called sucker lists of potential dupes to whom oil promoters would send their overblown or outright fraudulent marketing materials.)

The trial captivated the nation for seven months. Cook's central defense was that he was guilty only of optimism. The virtue that had been his greatest asset on the Antarctic pack now became his downfall. He had every expectation that his company would strike oil at some point—in fact, he had invested every cent he had in it. But the federal judge, John M. Killits, an unsmiling, uncompromising Midwesterner, was not convinced. Referring to Cook as the Machiavelli of the twentieth century, he fined Cook $12,000 (which Cook claimed he didn't have) and condemned him to fourteen years and nine months in prison, by far the harshest sentence doled out for comparable crimes. Cook's fame allowed the judge to make an example of him. But it was almost as if Cook was being punished for a broader moral failing. The sentence, Killits implied, was retribution for Cook's having fooled the American people for so long. It was as much about Denali and the North Pole as it was about oil.

Cook was transferred from Fort Worth jail to Leavenworth penitentiary on April 6, 1925. He was by all accounts a model prisoner—aside from his irksome habit of washing just once a week, based on the medically dubious notion that bathing opened the pores up to disease. He took up embroidery as a hobby and, like so many things he set his mind to, mastered it. "The result of this needle work I prize today quite as much as the best of my literary efforts," he wrote. (The warden once submitted Cook's floral designs anonymously to a statewide contest, in which he won first place, beating out the housewives of Kansas.) He would later become the editor and principal writer of the *Leavenworth New Era*. Under his directorship, the weekly prison newspaper would change its name to *The New Era* and gain a national following. (His subscribers included the influential Baltimore editor and literary critic H. L. Mencken.) It covered topics that reflected his restless curiosity, from linguistics to male-pattern baldness. The paper became a platform for him to expound on the unconventional theories he had developed over the course of his life. In one article, for example, he revisited the idea of "a new ark" that he and Amundsen had concocted on the *Belgica*, arguing that there were enough penguins in Antarctica to solve global hunger, that their guano could fertilize the world's crops, and that farming them could provide plenty of good jobs.* In another, the doctor suggested that clothes prevented people in the civilized world from absorbing the sun's nourishing rays; flappers, with their swooping necklines, were on the right track. Wiser still were the nude natives he'd studied in Tierra del Fuego many years before.

Early in his sentence, Cook was tapped to cover the night shift at the prison hospital. There were other doctors serving time, many younger than he and more up-to-date on the latest medical develop-

---

*He would later send Danish prime minister Thorvald Stauning a lengthy proposal for transplanting penguins to Greenland.

ments. But most of them were barred from practicing, even in prison, because they had violated the Harrison Narcotics Act of 1914, which regulated the distribution of opiates and cocaine and made criminals of the physicians who continued to prescribe them irresponsibly. Since Cook's crimes were unrelated to his practice, he was selected as the night intern, a position he felt was beneath his qualifications but allowed him a shred of dignity.

Cook had his work cut out for him. Even at the height of Prohibition, the heroin and opium addicts at Leavenworth outnumbered the boozers and bootleggers. At night the prison walls would resonate with the agonized screams of addicts in withdrawal. One after the other, inmates would beg the doctor for a fix, or at least a sedative. Per Leavenworth policy, Cook largely ignored their pleas. His patients also included men who suffered from a kind of anemia he'd come to call "prison pallor." Conditions under Warden William Biddle were deplorable, with prisoners complaining of overcrowding, physical abuse, inedible food—and not enough of it. Many had discolored gums, brittle nails, and loose teeth, which the doctor recognized all too well as early signs of scurvy. In these cases, he recommended a treatment remarkably similar to the one he had prescribed to the men of the *Belgica*: regular exercise, a diet of vitamin-rich raw foods (including raw meat), and prolonged exposure to sunlight. As the ailing officers and crew of the *Belgica* had discovered long ago, he had a soothing, hypnotic effect on people, which might explain why his patients seemed to respond to his remedies, however unorthodox.

Ever since his experience on the *Belgica*, Cook had come to worship the sun. He believed that there was little it could not cure. It was a panacea against the devastations of the cold and the dark. And in his present state of mind, Leavenworth was the coldest place on earth.

On January 19, 1926, Cook was informed that he had a visitor. He had refused to let friends and family see him in prison, but this was no ordinary caller. If Cook's incarceration represented the long polar night of his soul, Roald Amundsen was the sun. The Norwegian explorer was touring the United States in preparation for his next expedition, an airship flight to the North Pole, and had stopped in Kansas to embrace his old *Belgica* comrade in his hour of misfortune.

The two men sat beside each other on a bench. Amundsen gripped Cook's hand and held on to it tightly. "I want you to know," he said at the outset, "even if all the world goes against you, that I believe in you as a man." Cook's hand remained in Amundsen's throughout their conversation. They reminisced about the *Belgica*, going through the ship's muster roll to determine who was still living and who had since died. They spoke of the connection between their adventures together in Antarctica and Amundsen's South Pole exploit.

The subject turned to women.

"You are a hard-headed bachelor," Cook teased. "How about the girl?"

Cook had hoped to elicit a mischievous smile. But Amundsen instead grew somber. "I suppose I ought to get married. After this voyage . . . then I will get married and go on another tour of exploration."

It was evident to Cook that the years had hardened Amundsen. The outrage in the British press over his perceived deception in challenging Scott had tarnished his honor. The subsequent suicide in 1913 of one of his fellow expeditioners, Hjalmar Johansen, whom Amundsen had denied a chance to join the pole-bound sledging party in punishment for perceived insubordination, further darkened the shadow of his achievement. An attempt to drift in the Arctic ice to the North Pole aboard the specially built *Maud* had been a humiliating, drawn-out failure, a farcical sequel to his glorious South Pole expedition.

Personal developments hadn't been much happier. Relentless financial troubles had led Amundsen to fall out with close friends, as well as with his brother and manager, Leon. Amundsen returned from the *Maud* expedition with two Inuit girls—the four-year-old, motherless Kakonita, whom he adopted, and an older girl named Camilla. He had grown fond of the children and intended to give them a better life in Norway. But bankruptcy soon forced him to send them back to live with Camilla's family in Russia. It had been a decade of heartbreak.

But by 1925, Amundsen had successfully revived his fortunes. In the spring of that year, he led a venture, along with an American explorer and financier named Lincoln Ellsworth, to reach the North Pole by means of two Dornier-Wal flying boats. When the expedition hadn't been heard from for weeks, the world believed the planes were lost, along with the six men they carried. In fact, the craft had landed on the sea ice within 160 miles of the pole. (*Highest northern latitude yet reached by air*, Amundsen inscribed in his now seemingly endless mental list of firsts.) The effort to get one of the planes airborne again was among the most admirable, if overlooked, feats of Amundsen's career, involving the shoveling of about six hundred tons of snow—on severely reduced rations—to clear a runway. In terms of the labor involved, and the low probability of success, it was second only to the *Belgica*'s epic escape from the pack ice in 1899.

Amundsen recounted that adventure to Cook, who for a moment was not in the dank confines of Leavenworth but in the open cockpit, alongside his friend.

"I wish that you could be with us on the next air voyage. We will cross the Pole the next time," Amundsen said.

Though Amundsen by now had far more, and far more recent, experience of the polar regions than Cook, he flattered his former teacher by asking for his opinion on the scientific value of flying to the pole. The doctor, who hadn't crossed either polar circle in nearly a generation, was attached to the old ways.

"When man takes to wings, he loses a biped perspective," Cook said. "This is the very base line of understanding."

Amundsen pointed out that, on the contrary, altitude could provide a useful overview, one that might at last vindicate Cook's claim to the North Pole. "Before we came down in the last flight," he said, "we could see near enough to the pole to gauge the general conditions there. All which I have seen verifies your report. The absence of land, the peculiar color of sky and ice, the absence of icebergs, the character of sea ice and direction of the drift."

Cook smiled ruefully. Amundsen's validation meant everything to the doctor, who had never ceased to claim that he had reached the North Pole.

The discussion turned to how they had both suffered at the hands of a fickle public and an unscrupulous press. Perhaps to avoid being overheard by prying guards, Amundsen switched to French. "Our lot has been a hard one," he said. "From the depths of poverty to the heights of glory. From brief spells of hard earned success to the scourge of condemnation. I have wondered for years how you stood it all. I have had the same, with perhaps not so much of the knife in it, but with quite as much of the pain of envy."

Amundsen continued in what Cook described as the language of the *Belgica*, a mix in this case of Flemish, German, and Norwegian: "There is a relation between the tongue and the harpoon. Both can inflict painful wounds. The cut of the lance heals. The cut of the tongue rots."

Cook was struck by the power of the sentiment. As he saw his companion's eyes well up, he began to cry as well.

"Men have stabbed you out of the darkness," Amundsen went on. "They have stabbed me in broad daylight."

There was a silence. Amundsen pressed Cook's hand and looked out the window into the dull winter day.

"I hate to see you here," he said. "Guard your health. Put in writing all your memories and notes. You and I have been in Hell many times before. Hell is a cold place, but the sunshine will be better because of the darkness there when you come out."

"How glad I am to have you talk that way," said Cook, "but Amundsen, I am now accused of having too much imagination."

"Keep it up, only fools' tongues wag that way."

After an hour, Amundsen rose, embraced Cook one last time, and said goodbye in Norwegian.

The afterglow of his visit would warm Cook for the rest of his time in Leavenworth. Like the first sunrise after the long Antarctic night, Amundsen had filled him with renewed hope and energy. He began writing his memoirs, in which he devoted a lengthy chapter entirely to his comrade from the *Belgica*. Cook titled his manuscript "Hell Is a Cold Place" and dedicated it to Amundsen.

The dialogue quoted here is from that unpublished manuscript. Yet there is something suspicious about it. Amundsen's long, metaphor-laden soliloquies (they go on for pages) bear much more resemblance to Cook's ornate prose than to Amundsen's dry, terse voice. Several

of the passages strain credibility: How, for example, could Amundsen
have pronounced a phrase as convoluted as the tongue / harpoon aph-
orism in three languages, only one of which Cook understood? Why
would he switch to French when he knew that, even after twenty
months on a Belgian expedition, Cook could hardly speak a word of
it? Moreover, the sentence "Hell is a cold place," here attributed to
Amundsen, appears in several other instances in Cook's memoirs,
each time in the mouth of a different person. (For instance, Lecointe
says it once, during the *Belgica*'s ordeal.)

The reader is left to wonder how much of Cook's recollection of
the visit is true. Some of it assuredly is; his deep love for Amundsen—
like Amundsen's for him—is beyond question. But as with so much
else about Cook's later life, it becomes nearly impossible to distinguish fact from fiction, especially with regard to his later, unverified
accomplishments.

The evidence strongly suggests that he didn't get closer to the
North Pole than a few hundred miles.* But we will never know for
certain—it is ultimately unprovable. Nor is it clear to what extent
Cook's slippery relationship with the truth is the result of malice.
Perhaps he *believed* he had been to the pole. Perhaps he believed he
deserved to have attained the pole, after what was undeniably a heroic journey.

Cook is an exemplar of a quintessentially American spirit, which
lies on the razor's edge between optimism and delusion, between audacity and deceit, imagination and flimflammery. This is the spirit
that pulled him out of the abject poverty of his youth and imbued
him with curiosity and ingenuity. It's the spirit that inspired him to
prescribe groundbreaking treatments to his *Belgica* shipmates without any evidence that they would work, and to plot an unprecedented
escape from the pack ice. It's also the spirit that convinced him he
could reach the North Pole and the summit of Denali and strike it
rich in Texas, and perhaps pushed him to bend the truth when he
failed to reach those goals.

If we can't fully trust Cook's transcript of his reunion with Amund-

* Robert M. Bryce, author of the extremely thorough *Cook & Peary: The Polar Controversy, Resolved*, makes a particularly convincing case for this.

sen, inasmuch as it seems fancifully reconstructed to support the doctor's claim to the pole, we have Amundsen's own account to rely on. A few days after the meeting at Leavenworth, the Norwegian's lecture tour had taken him to Fort Worth, where he gave an interview to a correspondent from *The New York Times*.

Amundsen's prison visit had made national news. That an explorer of his stature would deign to associate with the notorious fraud Frederick Cook reignited the North Pole controversy.

The journalist asked about Amundsen's impressions of Cook and what they had discussed.

"Poor fellow—he's old and about worn out," Amundsen said. "He never talked about his conviction, but only of the old times and my recent airplane trip in the Arctic country. He told me he was happy and was doing needle work for a pastime. What a pity! What a pity!"

Amundsen said he didn't know whether Cook deserved to be in prison, as he had not followed the case. But he was more voluble on the subject of Cook's qualities as an explorer.

"To me he always was a genius. When we were young men together in a Belgian Antarctic expedition I said that if any man ever reached the North Pole Dr. Cook would. . . . Cook was the finest traveler I ever saw."

What was he saying? That Cook *did* make it to the pole?

"I am of the opinion that his story of the discovery is just as plausible as was Peary's. . . . It is possible that neither of them actually reached the pole, but, regardless, it seems to me that Dr. Cook's claims were just as sound as Peary's."

Amundsen would have cause to regret his candor almost immediately. Following his statement that Cook and Peary had equally valid claims to the pole, the National Geographic Society—which had backed Peary during the controversy and remained a staunch supporter of him even after the explorer's death in 1920—rescinded its invitation to have Amundsen address the organization ahead of his next polar flight.

Amundsen claimed that he had been misquoted. What had offended the National Geographic Society was the implication that both Cook and Peary had been to the pole, meaning that Cook would have gotten there first. But the more revealing quote, which Amundsen never disputed, was the suggestion that "neither of them actually reached the pole." It was not a disinterested statement. By sowing doubt about both Cook and Peary, Amundsen was cleverly raising the stakes for his own upcoming poleward journey.

In the spring of 1926, Amundsen took off aboard the dirigible *Norge* with a sixteen-man team that included Lincoln Ellsworth and the airship's Italian designer and pilot, Umberto Nobile, who insisted on bringing along his yapping lapdog, Titina. The *Norge* reached the pole on May 12, 1926, and hovered over the spot long enough for Amundsen, Ellsworth, and Nobile to drop, respectively, the Norwegian, American, and Italian flags.

Just three days earlier, the American pilot Richard Byrd had returned from a flight over the Arctic aboard a trimotor monoplane, during which he circled the North Pole—or so he claimed. Doubts about his exploit were raised from the moment he landed. Recent examinations of his diary have vindicated the skeptics, showing that Byrd had attempted to erase sextant data that conflicted with his later typewritten report and would have placed him a good distance short of his goal. Likewise, in the 1980s, the National Geographic Society analyzed newly available documents related to Robert Peary's 1909 trek to the pole and concluded that he, too, most likely had falsified his record. If neither Cook, nor Peary, nor Byrd reached the Pole—as is the overwhelming consensus—then the prize belongs to Amundsen.

He had flown the Norwegian flag and blazed the Northwest Passage. His achievements exceeded the wildest dreams of his childhood, surpassed the accomplishments of his heroes—Nansen, Franklin, and his own father. But he found that his thirst had not abated. He didn't cry when there were no more lands to conquer. He raged. He turned his back to the horizon and gazed at the long trail of enemies he had left in his wake.

In the fall of 1927, Amundsen published *My Life as an Explorer,* a spiteful and uneven work that was less an autobiography than a settling of scores. He showered contempt on Nobile, whom he considered a pompous, reckless fop who had the audacity to demand equal credit for the *Norge*'s triumph. He lambasted the National Geographic Society's decision to punish him for his loyalty to Cook. He went after the British people, whom he called "a race of very bad losers" for accusing him of having beaten Scott to the South Pole by deceitful means.

The Norwegian's ire reached all the way back to the *Belgica* expedition. He reserved special scorn for de Gerlache, whom he never forgave for the contract the commandant had signed with the Royal Belgian Geographical Society excluding him from taking over the expedition in the event of its leaders' deaths. He wrote that by entering the pack ice at the onset of winter, de Gerlache and Lecointe "could not have made a greater mistake." Amundsen claimed that he had been against the decision to winter in the ice (his enthusiastic diary entries from the time directly contradict this) and that he ended up taking command of the expedition after de Gerlache and Lecointe became ill with scurvy (also patently untrue).

Amundsen's support for Cook, followed soon after by the publication of *My Life as an Explorer,* damaged the reputation of the famous Norwegian—and, by extension, of Norway itself. Mussolini's fury over the explorer's insults against Nobile and the Italian people was tolerable. More problematic was the reaction in Great Britain, which was among Norway's closest allies. Amundsen's former hero Fridtjof Nansen—by then an internationally revered academic, statesman, and Nobel Peace Prize winner*—was called upon to smooth relations.

"I do not understand Amundsen's conduct on the whole lately, there are several queer things which have happened, and the only explanation I can find is that something has gone wrong with him," Nansen wrote to the Royal Geographical Society's vice president, Hugh Robert Mill. "Now my impression is that he has entirely lost

---

*From 1921 until his death in 1930, Nansen served as high commissioner for refugees for the League of Nations, during which time he organized the distribution of so-called Nansen passports, an internationally recognized travel document that allowed hundreds of thousands of newly stateless people to cross national borders and seek asylum.

his balance, and that he is no more quite responsible for his actions. . . . I think there are various unmistakable signs of some kind of insanity."

This assessment was less a professional diagnosis (although Nansen did have a doctorate in neurology) than an effort at damage control. Yet it did make it clear that the Amundsen of 1927 was a far different, far more embattled and paranoid man than the young adventurer Nansen had first met on the deck of the *Belgica* thirty years before.

If Amundsen suffered from polar madness, it was of a different nature than the insanity that had afflicted Tollefsen and Van Mirlo, as well as so many polar explorers and station personnel since. It was caused not by the external forces that hold sway in extreme environments but by the ferocity of the inner forces—ambition, competition, perseverance, and an almost masochistic pursuit of struggle—that drove him to conquer such environments. These passions didn't subside simply because he reached his geographic goals.

The behavior that Nansen called "insanity," Amundsen would have described as simply defending his honor. His cold and taciturn manner concealed a poetic sensibility. He imagined himself as following a knightly code perhaps out of step with modern life. Not long after the publication of *My Life as an Explorer*, he would have a chance to demonstrate his commitment to this code. On May 25, 1928, he received word that the airship *Italia*, which Nobile had taken to the North Pole, had disappeared during its return trip. Without a second thought, Amundsen volunteered to come to his archrival's aid. Mussolini had let it be known that his services weren't needed. Yet the Norwegian's dashing gesture was as much about rescuing his own legend as it was about saving Nobile. That Nobile was a sworn enemy would make Amundsen's action seem all the more magnanimous.

Two weeks later, the survivors of the *Italia* wreck succeeded in establishing radio communication with the Italian support vessel *Città de Milano* cruising around Kings Bay. Nobile and eight men, most of them wounded, were stranded on the sea ice north of the Svalbard archipelago. Seven men were dead or unaccounted for. (Titina the dog was unharmed.) Several rescue efforts, by air and sea, were already under way. Yet Amundsen saw the opportunity, at fifty-five years of age, for one final coup—and a chance to see the ice again, perhaps for the last time. As he told an Italian journalist before leaving, "Oh! If you only knew how wonderful it is up there. That is where I want to die and I wish death would come to me in a chivalrous way, that it will find me during the execution of some great deed, quickly and without suffering."

On June 18, Amundsen and a crew of five climbed into a French-made Latham 47 flying boat docked in Tromsø, in the Norwegian Arctic. The motor rumbled to a start, the propeller spun, and the plane sliced across the water. It rose into the air and turned northward toward the Barents Sea. That was the last the world saw of Roald Amundsen.

To this day, neither the wreck of the plane nor the remains of the men have been found. (Nobile was eventually rescued.)

Cook was paroled in 1930, about halfway through his sentence. At age sixty-four, nearly blind in one eye, he had no adventures left in him. Not long after he was freed, he granted an interview to a freelance journalist named William McGarry. At one point, McGarry asked Cook for his thoughts on Amundsen's fate.

"It is quite possible," Cook replied, "that Roald Amundsen is still alive. He could have reached the North coast of Greenland, or Franz Josef Land. If so, he could live there indefinitely. Afoot, he was the master of all polar explorers, and he would have no great difficulty taking care of himself provided he reached a region where game abounds."

The old man thought of his journeys with his friend and let himself drift, on a floe of memory, to the pack ice of the Bellingshausen Sea.

AUTHOR'S NOTE

I FIRST HEARD OF THE *BELGICA* EXPEDITION IN THE SPRING OF 2015, while procrastinating at my desk at *Departures* magazine. I was flipping through the latest issue of *The New Yorker* when I found a headline that caught my interest: "Moving to Mars." It was about an ongoing experiment taking place on Hawaii's Mauna Loa—about as close as the earth gets to a Martian environment—in which six volunteers lived in isolation under a geodesic dome for a NASA-funded study on team dynamics, in preparation for eventual missions to the Red Planet. In classic *New Yorker* fashion, the author, Tom Kizzia, backed into the story. The first few paragraphs were about an expedition that took place 120 years ago, involving the first men to endure an Antarctic winter. Kizzia mentioned the "'mad-house' promenade" around the ship, a phrase that immediately jumped out at me. I was intrigued to find out what possible connection there might be between the *Belgica* and far-flung space exploration. But even more fascinating to me was the character of the physician, Frederick Albert Cook, known as one of America's most shameless hucksters, who through relentless ingenuity nevertheless managed to save the expedition from catastrophe. I've always been drawn to heroic antiheroes: Sherlock Holmes, Butch Cassidy, Han Solo. When I looked further into Cook's story and learned that he lived out his final days in Larchmont, New York, in a house I pass every time I walk my dog, it felt like a sign: there was no way I wasn't writing this book.

Thus began a five-year obsession that took me across the world, from Oslo to Antwerp to Antarctica, on the trail of the *Belgica* and her men. The narrative that unfolded before me, through diaries and other primary sources, turned out to be far richer than the simple good yarn I'd imagined at first. The expedition shaped two future giants of exploration, one rightly revered, Roald Amundsen, and one unfairly maligned, the aforementioned Cook. It culminated with an epic breakout from the tenacious Antarctic pack ice that, in its scale and ambition, rivals the greatest man-versus-nature struggles in history and literature. And its legacy proved much more consequential than the mere survival of (most of) its men.

One of the challenges I faced in re-creating a journey that took place so long ago, and in such extreme isolation, was getting access to the sensory quality of the experience. Not just what happened day to day, or what coordinates the ship reached along her circuitous drift, but what it must have been like for the men aboard, both to discover such splendors and to endure such hardship. To my delight, it soon became apparent that the *Belgica* voyage was among the most well-documented polar missions of the heroic age, in which no fewer than ten men kept detailed diaries or logs (even though one was later burned).

The first major breakthrough in my research came in the fall of 2018, when the filmmaker Henri de Gerlache, the commandant's dashing great-grandson and an explorer in his own right, invited me to his family's beautiful estate in the countryside outside Ghent.* There, he pulled out four large hardbound volumes—Adrien de Gerlache's log from the expedition. As Henri and I paged through the gently weathered books, we became engrossed, as if we were reading an adventure novel. To our right, under a grand staircase, was one of the *Belgica*'s sledges. As I ran my hand along its splintered edge, I told myself that it might have been one of the sledges Cook and Amundsen used on their death-defying treks across the pack. The story came alive to me that day.

The following morning, I headed to the Royal Belgian Institute of Natural Sciences in Brussels, a rather homely mid-century modern

---

* Exploration has become a de Gerlache family tradition. Adrien's grandsons, Jean-Louis and Bernard, have participated in a number of polar expeditions. Bernard's son, Henri, has traveled several times to Antarctica and has summited the tallest mountain on each of the seven continents.

building where much of the *Belgica*'s archives are held. I had an appointment with Olivier Pauwels, curator of recent vertebrates. Wearing a navy sweater-vest stretched over his paunch, the scientist exuded the wry world-weariness of a career civil servant, which failed to entirely obscure his abiding passion for the animal world. He threw on an ill-fitting white coat and led me down cluttered, decrepit hallways into the bowels of the institute's vast collection.

Zoological specimens accumulated over the institute's 175-year history are stored in a seemingly infinite, white-tiled labyrinth lined with wooden drawers and compartments, each one containing multiple individuals of a single species, either stuffed, jarred, or reduced to a labeled pile of bones. The aisles teemed with oversized taxidermy, a magic-realist menagerie organized with no apparent rhyme or reason, as if the animals were roaming freely. Twisting past a yak and a flock of flamingos, Pauwels at last arrived at the item number indicated on his clipboard. He slapped on a pair of blue latex gloves.

"Back in the day, these specimens were preserved in arsenic to ward off mites and insects," he said. The poison is still lethal a hundred years later.

Pauwels opened a large drawer and pulled out an emperor penguin captured and euthanized during the course of the *Belgica* expedition, one of many brought back to Belgium. Its eyes were missing and its feathers had lost their sheen, but the four-foot-tall bird, standing with exemplary posture, filled me with awe: this was the closest I'd get to meeting a member of the expedition. I wondered which of the *Belgica*'s men had killed it, and I tried to imagine how they had felt in that moment. I told myself that its meat had helped save their lives.

Over the next few hours, Pauwels guided me through much of the *Belgica*'s trove. We saw many more stuffed penguins—emperors, gentoos, Adélies—as well as seal bones and deep-sea fish preserved in jars of ethanol.

Pauwels took me to the invertebrates floor and showed me a slide containing a single, barely visible larva of *Belgica antarctica*, the only strictly terrestrial animal native to Antarctica, which the expedition's Romanian naturalist, Emile Racovitza, discovered. I was transported instantly to a rocky shore along the Gerlache Strait, in January 1898.

Beside me, Racovitza is hunched over a patch of lichen, brows furrowed, magnifying glass in hand, picking out insects.

In his address to the Royal Belgian Geographical Society on November 18, 1899, Georges Lecointe made it a point to emphasize that the expedition brought back much more than "one overwintering and two deaths." The contribution of the *Belgica*'s scientists to Antarctic scholarship cannot be overestimated. Racovitza cataloged thousands of specimens from hundreds of species of plant and animal life—moss, lichen, fish, birds, mammals, insects, pelagic organisms—many of them new to science. He documented penguin and seal behaviors in detail. His colleague, the Polish geologist Henryk Arctowski, discovered the deep abyss that lay between Tierra del Fuego and Graham Land. And together with his compatriot Antoni Dobrowolski, he compiled the first full year's worth of meteorological and oceanographic data south of the antarctic circle. It would take the Commission of the Belgica more than forty years to sort through and analyze the expedition's observations. Collectively, the scientists' findings form the basis of our understanding of the frozen continent, and all three men went on to distinguished careers.

The legacy of the *Belgica* voyage goes well beyond its scientific harvest. The mission was among the first truly international expeditions of the modern era, certainly the first to the polar regions. That achievement must be credited to de Gerlache, who despite his patriotism and military background was a pacifist at heart. He defied his compatriots' expectations that he hire only Belgians, instead recruiting the best men he could find, regardless of their citizenship. At a time when Western powers were racing to subdivide the world—a jingoistic frenzy that would lead to a world war within two decades—de Gerlache established a standard of global cooperation that persists in Antarctica to this day, unlike in the oil-rich and increasingly contested Arctic.

It is significant that de Gerlache declined to stake any claim of Belgian sovereignty over the strait that today bears his name. (Unlike, for example, James Clark Ross, who in 1841 formally took possession of Victoria Land on behalf of Great Britain.) In his belief that science transcended politics and borders, the commandant set the stage for more than a century of peace in Antarctica. Thanks to de Gerlache, and to his son Gaston, who led his own Antarctic mission in 1957–58, Belgium is a signatory to the Antarctic Treaty of 1959, which forbids all military activity on the continent. A subsequent accord, the Madrid Protocol of 1991, protects Antarctica's animals and natural resources against all forms of exploitation. Antarctica's example, in turn, prefigured such grand scientific endeavors as the International Space Station, where astronauts from rival nations collaborate peacefully, irrespective of terrestrial squabbles.

Where the *Belgica* was perhaps most influential was in illuminating the devastating physiological and psychological toll of far-flung exploration, which Frederick Cook so diligently chronicled. The science of the past 120 years has borne out the doctor's instincts.

Clinical studies on scientific and support personnel at year-round Antarctic bases have consistently yielded reports of physical and mental symptoms similar in kind, if not degree, to those experienced by the men of the *Belgica:* irregular heartbeat, fatigue, hostility, depression, memory loss, confusion, and cognitive slowing. There are also frequent accounts of a dissociative fugue state that leaves people looking blankly and unresponsively into the middle distance, known colloquially as the "Antarctic stare." One physician defines it as "a twelve-foot stare in a ten-foot room." This perfectly describes Adam Tollefsen's demeanor in the early stages of his madness.

Cook referred to these symptoms collectively as "polar anaemia." Researchers today use the term "winter-over syndrome," but it's essentially the same thing. A prevailing theory suggests the syndrome is a form of hypothyroidism, which is associated with depression and atrial fibrillation and could thus account for both the "cerebral symptoms" and the "cardiac symptoms" that most concerned Cook before scurvy took hold.* Thyroid hormones help the body regulate temperature and set its circadian rhythms. It's not difficult to see how

---

*Dr. Lawrence Palinkas, who analyzed clinical data from American men and women at Antarctica's McMurdo Station and Amundsen-Scott South Pole Station, posits specifically that the memory loss and other cognitive impairments he observed were related to a decline in levels of the thyroid hormone T_3, which helps determine how the body uses energy.

extreme cold and the prolonged absence of sunshine might throw the system off.

This is just a hypothesis. The causes of the syndrome remain puzzling more than a century after Cook first described it. Scientists believe physiological factors tell only part of the story. Stress due to confinement, isolation, boredom, unvaried food, and the psychosocial pressures that inevitably arise among small groups of people contributes in no small part to the psychological and cognitive symptoms experienced by Antarctic personnel. But in emphasizing the likelihood of a connection between winter-over syndrome and what is now known as seasonal affective disorder—a variation in mood that correlates with the dwindling of daylight hours—physicians today support Cook's belief that light plays an essential role in human welfare. His wild idea to have his ailing shipmates stand naked in front of a blazing fire is the first known application of light therapy, used today to treat sleep disorders and depression, among other things.

Though Cook is remembered today—if he is remembered at all—as the charlatan who lied about reaching the North Pole, he may yet find redemption in the next phase of human exploration: manned missions to Mars. The psychological challenges of such a voyage are every bit as daunting as the technical ones. As Roald Amundsen put it, "The human factor is three quarters of any expedition." Among the greatest threats future travelers to Mars are likely to face is an interplanetary version of winter-over syndrome. The unknown icescapes around the earth's poles—particularly Antarctica—seemed as remote and forbidding to nineteenth-century explorers as Mars does to us now. Not surprisingly, NASA has sought to draw lessons from polar expeditions, the closest thing in human history to a precedent for extended space travel. This was the context in which the *New Yorker* article I read in 2015 mentioned the *Belgica*.

For the past three decades, NASA has worked closely with Jack Stuster, a behavioral scientist and anthropologist best known for his 1996 book, *Bold Endeavors: Lessons from Polar and Space Exploration.* The *Belgica* is among Stuster's main case studies. Expeditions in which everybody died yield few practical lessons. The same goes for those— like Amundsen's South Pole run in 1911—that went off with nary a hitch. Far more instructive are those, like the *Belgica,* that encountered significant adversity and overcame it. Cook's observations, his warnings, his ad hoc remedies and recommendations, have directly influenced NASA operating procedures.

In his surveys of astronauts, for example, Stuster found that space travelers tire easily of their food and crave something crunchy.* This recalls Cook's complaint, "How we longed to use our teeth!" Taking a cue from the doctor, Stuster therefore suggests sourcing the widest possible variety of food. More generally, he encourages Mars-bound doctors to emulate Cook's resourcefulness and his insistence on maintaining a cheerful attitude.

"That's who I think of when I'm writing about the physician role," Stuster told me. "I think of Frederick Cook."

When we do reach Mars, we will, in some small part, have Cook to thank.

When I told a friend of mine, an editor whose advice I value dearly, that I planned to visit Antarctica for this book, he said, "What for? Why don't you just rely on the diaries?" I didn't know how to answer. The book, after all, is not a travelogue. My friend suspected I wanted to justify a bucket-list trip as a business expense. He was only partly right. I didn't know what I would find there, but I knew that, no matter how detailed the diaries were, I'd never be able to satisfactorily reconstruct the sights, sounds, and smells of Antarctica without experiencing them myself. I contacted the Chilean company Antarctica21 and splurged on a ticket for a weeklong cruise, departing mid-December 2018. Like de Gerlache and his men, I left from Punta Arenas. Unlike them, I flew over the tempestuous and notoriously nauseating Drake Passage by plane, a two-hour flight that landed at the Chilean-Russian research base on King George Island. From there my fellow cruisegoers and I boarded the *Hebridean Sky*, the seventy-passenger cruise ship that would take us across the Bransfield Strait to the channel discovered in 1898 by the men of the *Belgica*.

This was not a special concession to me. The weather around the

---

* Particularly hard to achieve in zero-gravity environments, where free-floating crumbs can find their way into the smallest crevices and disrupt machinery.

frozen continent is so unpredictable and so potentially dangerous that cruise companies never guarantee an itinerary ahead of time and instead defer to their ship captains to survey the winds and currents and determine the route each day. But the first-choice destination of virtually all the Antarctic cruises leaving from South America is the Gerlache Strait, one of the most sublime and photogenic places on the planet. Throughout my weeklong journey, I was struck by how familiar this landscape seemed to me. Save for the bluish tint of the ice, it looked virtually identical to Cook's black-and-white photographs. But as was soon made clear to me, the environment that the *Belgica*'s men explored is fast becoming a lost world.

On a misty afternoon halfway into my trip, a handful of passengers and I zipped across the channel on a Zodiac inflatable, cutting through light snowfall. We arrived in the lee of Danco Island, named after the *Belgica*'s second victim, Emile Danco. Penguins and humpback whales put on a show for us, as they did for the men of the *Belgica*. At first glance, nothing appeared to have changed here in 120 years. But a closer examination told another story.

At the helm of the Zodiac was Bob Gilmore, a geologist by training, hired to educate guests in the science of the Antarctic. As part of his job, he took measurements of temperature, salinity, and phytoplankton populations in the waters of the Gerlache Strait, which he communicated to academic and government institutions that monitor changes in the area but don't have the luxury of visiting regularly. Gilmore handed me a small tube and instructed me to fill it with seawater. I told myself this was the same work Racovitza and Arctowski performed here in the first blissful weeks of 1898. Gilmore squeezed a solution from an eyedropper into the sample to kill the organisms within it before the zooplankton had a chance to devour the phytoplankton. He screwed the top back onto the tube, the contents of which he would analyze back aboard our ship.

For the previous few years, the changes Gilmore had observed in these samples had been subtle but sobering. Warmer air temperatures had sped up the melting of glaciers. The increased flow of fresh water, in turn, had decreased the salinity of the strait. As a result, the structure of phytoplankton communities had shifted. The large diatoms that krill prefer to eat were being replaced by smaller diatoms that are better adapted to the less salty water. This trend has potentially catastrophic consequences: As the larger diatoms disappear, so might the swarms of krill that feast on them. As the krill go, so will the rest of this delicate ecosystem.

I was one of more than fifty thousand people to visit Antarctica in the austral summer of 2018–19. It wasn't lost on me that my very presence here—in particular, the emissions from the *Hebridean Sky* and dozens of ships like her—contributed directly to the endangerment of this magical place. The growing popularity of Antarctica as a tourist destination is understandable: for those who have the privilege to be able to visit, the experience is awesome and humbling. It is the last truly wild place on earth. Yet the very concept of Antarctic tourism is in some ways disheartening: thousands of people a year are drinking martinis and singing karaoke on the same waters that de Gerlache and his men navigated with such trepidation when they were the only people on the entire continent.

Powerful icebreakers and communication technology have made it safer to travel here. But it would be wrong to assume that the Antarctic has gotten any less menacing. The menace has simply transformed. The continent remains just as hostile to human life as it was in the age of de Gerlache and Scott and Shackleton. Only now its grasp extends well beyond the explorers foolhardy enough to venture into the ice.

For millions of years, Antarctica's glaciers have flowed into the sea, calving icebergs at a slow and sustainable rate. In the past few decades, that rate has rapidly increased as temperatures in the region have shot up to alarming levels. During a heat wave in February 2020, they reached a record 69 degrees on Seymour Island, at the tip of Graham Land. The less isolated Arctic is a harbinger of how climate change might soon affect the southernmost continent. In 2007, the Northwest Passage, which Amundsen took three years to muscle through aboard the tiny *Gjøa*, became navigable for the first time. It is expected that the North Pole will be clear of summer sea ice by 2050.

Antarctica's ice contains at least 80 percent of the fresh water on earth. If all of it were to melt, sea levels everywhere would rise by up to two hundred feet, drastically redrawing the world map. This may not happen in the near future—the Antarctic ice cap is more than a mile thick in places—but any sustained amount of warming will lead to sea-level rise that will obliterate coastal communities and cause incalculable suffering. The continent is a coiled spring loaded with tremendous destructive power.

If Poe and Verne were writing today, this is the nightmare scenario that would capture their imaginations. They would be drawn not to the ends of the earth, but to the end of the earth. Just as the *Belgica*'s men answered the call of fiction to elucidate the mysteries of the Antarctic, it is now up to scientists and explorers to blaze the path ahead. May they have the audacity of Adrien de Gerlache, the fortitude of Roald Amundsen, and the gumption of Frederick Cook. Like the *Belgica*, we have sailed heedlessly into a trap of our own making, but if that expedition proved anything, it's that we need never resign ourselves to doom. *Audaces fortuna juvat!*

ACKNOWLEDGMENTS

WHEN I EMBARKED ON THIS PROJECT, THE ANTARCTIC WAS AS BLANK in my mind as it was on world maps in the late 1800s. Save for a few factoids and names—Amundsen, Scott, Shackleton—I knew nothing of its history or geography. I had even less of an idea of how to write a book. But, in my Gerlachean optimism, I figured it couldn't be too hard to find my way through the fog. Five years later, it's clear I would have been dashed against the rocks without the many people who helped guide me.

I can never properly repay the men and women who shared their time and knowledge simply out of a shared passion for the subject. My thanks go out in particular to fellow *Belgica* historian Jozef Verlinden, who from the moment we met over beers in Brussels's Grand Place has been unfailingly generous, and to Anne Melgård, of Norway's National Library, whose archival sleuthing turned up treasure after treasure. Thanks as well to Robert Headland of the Scott Polar Research Institute for patiently answering every question I had on the history and science of Antarctica, and to the other experts I consulted: Jack Stuster, Lawrence Palinkas, Susan Kaplan, Sarah Kennel, Kenneth LaMaster, David Rose, and Dan Oren. And *veel dank* to Kurt Van Camp, director of the New Belgica project, for the last-minute ride to Antwerp. Favors big and small were the wind in my sails.

I'm especially grateful to Henri de Gerlache, Bernard de Gerlache, and Jean-Louis de Gerlache for graciously allowing me to consult their ancestor's papers and logbooks; to Claude De Broyer, for granting me access to the expedition's archives at the Royal Belgian Institute of Natural Sciences; and to Georges Lecointe's descendants for our spirited exchanges.

The multilingual trove of archives they helped me unearth would not have done me much good without translators, namely Sean Bye, Emma Pressley, Elin Melgård, and Tomasz Poplawski. And a hat tip to Markus Voelker for confirming that my high school German (and Google Translate) hadn't led me astray.

It wasn't until the revision stage that I began working with the intimidatingly brilliant fact-checker CB Owens, who saved me from a number of embarrassing errors, tracked down 120-year-old documents that had eluded me for years, and revealed to me only *after* I'd hired him that he read Norwegian.

The project would have remained an icy glimmer in my eye were it not for the team at Aevitas Creative Management—particularly my indefatigable agents, Todd Shuster and Justin Brouckaert, and my former boss at *Esquire,* David Granger—whose enthusiasm for this story was equaled only by their high expectations. Higher still were those of my editor, Kevin Doughten, who would become my closest collaborator. He and everyone at Crown—from Lydia Morgan to the publicity team to art directors Christopher Brand and Elena Giavaldi, book designer Simon Sullivan, and copy editor Barbara Jatkola—brought to life the kind of book that I'd long dreamed of writing.

Many friends and colleagues supported and advised me along the way. I can only mention a few: Alex Ros, of Open Sky Expeditions, who helped arrange my trip to Antarctica (and almost got me mauled by a puma in Patagonia); Ed Couch and John Lopez, respectively the angel and the devil reading early drafts over my shoulder; my colleagues at *Departures,* notably Jeffries Blackerby, Maura Egan, and Rebecca Stepler; and Justin Bishop, who took my author's photo and gave me a taste for the cold.

My deepest thanks go to my family. To my father, who showed me the ropes. To my mother, my most assiduous reader. To Jessica Levine, my partner and greatest love. And to my daughters, Maya and Leila, who have no idea how much they inspire me.

SELECTED BIBLIOGRAPHY

ARCHIVAL COLLECTIONS

Belgian Antarctic Expedition. Archives. Royal Belgian Institute of Natural Sciences. Brussels.

Cook, Frederick A. Leavenworth Federal Penitentiary inmate case file. U.S. National Archives and Records Administration. College Park, MD.

Cook, Frederick A. Papers. Library of Congress Manuscript Division. Washington, DC.

Cook, Frederick A. Papers. Stefansson Collection on Polar Exploration. Dartmouth College. Hanover, NH.

De Gerlache Family Collection. Zingem, Belgium.

Frederick A. Cook Society Records. Byrd Polar and Climate Research Center Archival Program. The Ohio State University. Columbus.

Library and Archives. Norwegian Maritime Museum. Oslo.

National Archives of Norway. Oslo.

National Library of Norway. Oslo.

Osterrieth, Léonie. Belgian Antarctic Expedition archives. FelixArchief. Antwerp.

Royal Belgian Geographical Society. Archives. Université libre de Bruxelles. Brussels.

BOOKS AND JOURNAL ARTICLES

Amundsen, Roald. *My Life as an Explorer*. Garden City, NY: Doubleday, Page & Company, 1927.

———. *The Northwest Passage: Being the Record of a Voyage of Exploration of the Ship "Gjöa."* New York: E. P. Dutton, 1908.

———. *The South Pole: An Account of the Norwegian Antarctic Expedition in the "Fram."* 1910–1912. Two volumes. Translated by A. G. Chater. London: John Murray, 1912.

Anthony, Jason C. *Hoosh: Roast Penguin, Scurvy Day, and Other Stories of Antarctic Cuisine.* Lincoln: University of Nebraska Press, 2012.

Arctowsky, Henryk. "The Antarctic Voyage of the Belgica During the Years 1897, 1898, and 1899." *The Geographical Journal,* no. 18 (July–December 1901).

———. Die antarktischen Eisverhältnisse: Auszug aus meinem Tagebuch der Südpolarreise der "Belgica." 1898–1899. Gotha, Germany: Justus Perthes, 1903. (Translations by author.)

———. "Aurores australes." Résultats du voyage du S.Y. Belgica en 1897–1898–1899. Rapports scientifiques, Météorologie (1901).

———. "Exploration of Antarctic Lands." *The Geographical Journal,* no. 17 (January–June 1901).

Astrup, Eivind. *With Peary Near the Pole.* Translated by H. J. Bull. London: C. Arthur Pearson, 1898.

Beattie, Owen, and John Geiger. *Frozen in Time: The Fate of the Franklin Expedition.* New York: E. P. Dutton, 1987.

Bergreen, Laurence. *Over the Edge of the World: Magellan's Terrifying Circumnavigation of the Globe.* New York: William Morrow, 2003.

Bomann-Larsen, Tor. *Roald Amundsen.* Translated by Ingrid Christophersen. Thrupp, Stroud, Gloucestershire, UK: Sutton, 2006.

Bown, Stephen R. *The Last Viking: The Life of Roald Amundsen.* Boston: Da Capo Press, 2012.

———. *Scurvy: How a Surgeon, a Mariner, and a Gentleman Solved the Greatest Medical Mystery of the Age of Sail.* New York: Thomas Dunne Books, 2003.

Bridges, E. Lucas. *Uttermost Part of the Earth: A History of Tierra del Fuego and the Fuegians.* 1948. Reprint, New York: The Rookery Press, 2007.

Bryce, Robert M. *Cook & Peary: The Polar Controversy, Resolved.* Mechanicsburg, PA: Stackpole Books, 1997.

Chapman, Anne. *Hain: Ceremonia de iniciación de los Selk'nam de Tierra del Fuego.* Santiago de Chile: Pehuén Editores, 2009.

Cook, Frederick Albert. "The Antarctic's Challenge to the Explorer." *The Forum,* no. 17 (June 1894): 505–512.

———. "The Great Indians of Tierra del Fuego." *The Century Magazine,* no. 59 (March 1900): 720–729.

———. *My Attainment of the Pole: Being the Record of the Expedition That First Reached the Boreal Center, 1907–1909. With the Final Summary of the Polar Controversy.* 1911. Reprint, New York: Mitchell Kennerley, 1912.

———. "My Experiences with a Camera in the Antarctic." *Popular Photography,* February 1938, 12–14, 90–92.

———. "A Proposed Antarctic Expedition." *Around the World,* no. 1 (1894): 55–58.

————. *Through the First Antarctic Night: A Narrative of the Voyage of the Belgica Among Newly Discovered Lands and Over an Unknown Sea About the South Pole.* 1901. Reprint, New York: Doubleday, Page & Company, 1909.

————. *To the Top of the Continent: Discovery, Exploration and Adventure in Sub-arctic Alaska. The First Ascent of Mt. McKinley, 1903–1906.* New York: Doubleday, Page & Company, 1908.

Darwin, Charles. *Voyage of the Beagle.* 1839. Reprint, New York: Penguin Books, 1989.

Decleir, Hugo, ed. *Roald Amundsen's Belgica Diary: The First Scientific Expedition to the Antarctic.* Translation by Erik Dupont & Christine Le Piez. Norfolk, UK: Erskine Press, 1999.

Decleir, Hugo, and Claude De Broyer, eds. *The Belgica Expedition Centennial: Perspectives on Antarctic Science and History.* Brussels: Brussels University Press, 2001.

De Gerlache, Adrien. "Fragments du récit de voyage." Résultats du voyage du S.Y. Belgica en 1897–1898–1899. Rapports scientifiques, 1938.

————. *Quinze mois dans l'Antarctique.* Brussels: Imprimerie scientifique Ch. Bulens, 1902. (Translations by author.)

Dobrowolski, Antoni Boleslaw. *Dziennik wyprawy na Antarktydę (1897–1899).* Edited by Irena Łukaszewska & Janusz Ostrowski. Wrocław-Warsaw-Krakow: Zakład Narodowy im. Ossolińskich, 1968. (Translations of select passages provided to author by Sean Bye and Tomasz Poplawski.)

————. *Wyprawy polarne: Historja i zdobycze naukowe.* Warsaw: Henryka Lindenfelda, 1914. (Translations of select passages provided to author by Sean Bye.)

Dodds, Klaus, Alan D. Hemmings, and Peder Roberts, eds. *Handbook on the Politics of Antarctica.* Cheltenham, Gloucestershire, UK: Edward Elgar Publishing, 2017.

Drinker, Henry S. *Tunneling, Explosive Compounds, and Rock Drills.* New York: John Wiley & Sons, 1882.

Du Fief, Jean, ed. *Bulletin de la Société Royale Belge de Géographie,* no. 24 (1900): 1–531.

Dunn, Robert. *The Shameless Diary of an Explorer.* 1907. Reprint, New York: Modern Library, 2001.

Dyer, George L. *The Use of Oil to Lessen the Dangerous Effect of Heavy Seas.* Washington, DC: Government Printing Office, 1886.

Fletcher, Francis. *The World Encompassed by Sir Francis Drake.* London: Nicholas Bourne, 1652.

Freeman, Andrew. *The Case for Doctor Cook.* New York: Van Rees Press, 1961.

Headland, Robert Keith. *A Chronology of Antarctic Exploration: A Synopsis of Events and Activities from the Earliest Times Until the International Polar Years, 2007–09.* London: Bernard Quaritch, Ltd., 2009.

Henderson, Bruce. *Peary, Cook, and the Race to the Pole*. New York: W. W. Norton & Company, 2005.

Hochschild, Adam. *King Leopold's Ghost: A Story of Greed, Terror, and Heroism in Colonial Africa*. New York: Mariner Books, 1999.

Huntford, Roland. *The Last Place on Earth: Scott and Amundsen's Race to the South Pole*. 1979. Reprint, New York: Modern Library, 1999.

———. *Two Planks and a Passion: The Dramatic History of Skiing*. London, New York: Continuum, 2008.

Kløver, Geir O. *Antarctic Pioneers: The Voyage of the* Belgica *1897–99*. Oslo: The Fram Museum, 2010.

Lansing, Alfred. *Endurance: Shackleton's Incredible Voyage*. 1959. Reprint, New York: Basic Books, 2014.

Larsen, Carl Anton. "The Voyage of the 'Jason' to the Antarctic Regions." *The Geographical Journal*, no. 4 (July–December 1894): 333–344.

Lecointe, Georges. *Au pays des manchots: Récit du voyage de la "Belgica."* Brussels: Oscar Schepens & Cie, 1904. (Translations by author.)

———. "Mesures pendulaires." Résultats du voyage du S.Y. Belgica en 1897–1898–1899. *Rapports scientifiques*, Physique du Globe (1907).

———. *La navigation astronomique et la navigation estimée*. Paris, Nancy: Berger-Levrault & Cie, 1897.

———. "Travaux hydrographiques et instructions nautiques." Résultats du voyage du S.Y. Belgica en 1897–1898–1899. *Rapports scientifiques* (1907).

Marinescu, Alexandru, ed. *Belgica (1897–1899): Emile Racovitza—lettres, journal antarctique, conférences*. Bucharest: Fondation Culturelle Roumaine, Collection le Rameau d'Or, 1998.

Marinescu, Alexandru. *Le Voyage de la "Belgica": Premier hivernage dans les glaces antarctiques*. Paris: L'Harmattan, 2019.

Martin, Stephen. *A History of Antarctica*. Kenthurst, New South Wales, Australia: Rosenberg Publishing Pty Ltd, 2013.

Nansen, Fridtjof. *Farthest North*. London: Archibald Constable and Company, 1897.

Oren, Dan A., Marek Koziorowksi, and Paul H. Desan. "SAD and the Not-So-Single Photoreceptor." *The American Journal of Psychiatry*, no. 170 (December 2013): 1403–1412.

Palin, Michael. *Erebus: The Story of a Ship*. London: Hutchinson, 2018.

Palinkas, Lawrence A. "Psychological Factors and the Seasonal Affective Disorder." Reports on the Conference on Polar and Alpine Medicine, presented at the Explorers Club, New York City, September 25, 1999, 11–22.

Palinkas, Lawrence A., and Peter Suedfeld. "Psychological effects of polar expeditions." *The Lancet*, no. 371 (January 12, 2008): 153–163.

Peary, Robert E. *Northward Over the "Great Ice": A Narrative of Life and Work Along the Shores and upon the Interior Ice-Cap of Northern Greenland in the Years 1886 and 1891–1897*. New York: Frederick A. Stokes, 1898.

Pergameni, Charles. *Adrien de Gerlache: Pionnier maritime—1866–1934*. Brussels: Editorial-Office H. Wauthoz-Legrand, 1935.

Poe, Edgar Allan. *The Narrative of Arthur Gordon Pym of Nantucket*. New York: Harper & Brothers, 1838.

Poplimont, Ch. La Belgique héraldique: recueil historique, chronologique, généalogique et biographique complet de toutes les maisons nobles reconnues de la Belgique, vol. 4. Paris: Imprimerie de Henri Carion, 1866.

Pyne, Stephen J. *The Ice: A Journey to Antarctica*. Iowa City: University of Iowa Press, 1986.

Racovitza, Emil. "Cétacés." Résultats du voyage du S.Y. *Belgica* en 1897–1898–1899. *Rapports scientifiques*, Météorologie (1903).

———. "Vers le Pôle Sud: Conférence faite à la Sorbonne sur l'Expédition Antarctique Belge, son but, ses aventures et ses résultats." Causeries scientifiques de la Société zoologique de France, no. 7 (1900): 175–242.

Schelfhout, Charles E. *Les Gerlache: Trois générations d'explorateurs polaires*. Aix-en-Provence: Editions de la Dyle, 1996.

Sides, Hampton. *In the Kingdom of Ice: The Grand and Terrible Polar Voyage of the USS* Jeannette. New York: Doubleday, 2014.

Smith, Percy S. "Hawaiki: The Whence of the Maori." *The Journal of the Polynesian Society*, no. 8 (1899): 1–48.

Stuster, Jack. *Bold Endeavors: Lessons from Polar and Space Exploration*. Annapolis, MD: Naval Institute Press, 1996.

Verlinden, Jozef. *Discovery and Exploration of Gerlache Strait*. Bruges, 2009.

———. *Poolnacht: Adrien de Gerlache en de Belgica-expeditie*. Tielt, Belgium: Lannoo, 1993.

Verne, Jules. *Le sphinx des glaces*. Paris: Bibliothèque d'éducation et de récréation, 1897.

———. *Vingt mille lieues sous les mers*. Paris: Bibliothèque d'éducation et de récréation, 1870.

Walke, Willoughby. *Gunpowder and High Explosives*. Washington, DC: Government Printing Office, 1893.

Wharton, Charles S. *The House of Whispering Hate*. Chicago: Madelaine Mendelsohn, 1933.

A NOTE ON SOURCES

Between leaving Isla de los Estados on January 14, 1897, and returning to Punta Arenas on March 28, 1899, the men of the *Belgica* had no means of contacting another human being. As a consequence, my sources for the bulk of this story were necessarily limited. Fortunately, many of the expeditioners kept some kind of record, and most of the surviving accounts are surprisingly rich in color and detail.

For the chapters chronicling the journey itself, I leaned heavily—though far from exclusively—on four primary sources: Frederick Cook's rollicking *Through the First Antarctic Night;* Roald Amundsen's diary, almost Hemingway-esque in its austerity and machismo; *Fifteen Months in the Antarctic,* Adrien de Gerlache's elegant narrative; and Georges Lecointe's *Au pays des manchots* (In the land of penguins), wry and winking, and occasionally quite moving. All translations of French-language sources are my own.

Many details are drawn from the diaries of the three eastern European scientists aboard. Henryk Arctowski also wrote extensively of the voyage upon his return, notably in *The Geographical Journal.* Emile Racovitza left behind a series of writings and lectures that are frequently laugh-out-loud funny, even to modern ears. Antoni Dobrowolski's recollections are particularly revealing, containing moments of powerful lyricism as well as unvarnished vulgarity.

The perspective of the crew was sadly not as well documented as that of the officers and scientists. I was lucky to chance upon Carl August Wiencke's journal, which has to my knowledge never previously been cited. It's a poignant document, full of hope and deep reflection, and its abrupt end on January 22 still puts a ball in my throat. Johan Koren kept a diary as well, though he stopped confiding in it soon after the expedition arrived in the Antarctic—it's instructive mainly for its excellent drawings.

Then there is the commandant's log, which, though often drily descriptive, as such documents tend to be, features elements of un-adorned poetry.

Most of the archives from the journey are at the Royal Belgian Institute of Natural Sciences in Brussels. They contain documents related to the expedition's conception, as well as an illuminating trove of letters and memoranda exchanged with de Gerlache while the ship was confined to the ice, and the commandant largely to his cabin. This correspondence is described at length in Chapter 14.

De Gerlache was at his most candid when writing to Léonie Oster-rieth. Her papers, at the Felix Archive in Antwerp, shed much light both on the leadup to the expedition and on the commandant's con-valescence.

A compulsive writer, Cook wrote several voluminous, hopelessly disorganized unpublished memoirs, held at the Library of Congress in Washington, DC. They include *Hell Is a Cold Place* (about his polar experience); *Out of the Jungle* (about life in Leavenworth penitentiary); and *Peeps into the Beyond* (ethnographical and metaphysical musings based on his wide-ranging travels). The Cook collection at the Li-brary of Congress also contains biographical notes kept by his daugh-ter, Helen Cook Vetter, who dedicated much of her life to salvaging her father's reputation.

For decades, the Frederick A. Cook Society pursued the same goal. Its records—bequeathed to the Byrd Polar and Climate Research Center at Ohio State University—contain many valuable documents. Especially useful were the interview notes taken by Cook's biogra-pher, Andrew Freeman.

Freeman's *The Case for Doctor Cook,* from 1961, was one of several books I relied on to fill out the life and times of my three main char-acters. Details on Cook's life before and after the *Belgica* were plucked from *Cook & Peary: The Polar Controversy, Resolved,* by Robert M. Bryce, one of the most exhaustively researched works of nonfiction I've ever encountered. To fully render Amundsen, I turned primarily to two terrific biographical works: Roland Huntford's *The Last Place on Earth,* and Tor Bomann-Larsen's *Roald Amundsen.* My portrait of the commandant, meanwhile, draws in part from *Les Gerlache,* a beautifully assembled volume written by Charles Schelfhout in close consultation with de Gerlache's son, Gaston.

Remarkably few full-length books have been written specifically about the voyage, and none in English. The world of *Belgica* enthusiasts is a small but passionate one, and I benefited in particular from the work of two historians. One is the late Romanian scholar Alexandru Marinescu, whose opus on the expedition, *Le voyage de la "Belgica,"* was published as I was in the end-stages of the manuscript. The other is the Flemish author Jozef Verlinden, who has written a number of books on the subject.

I pored through hundreds of newspapers from both sides of the Atlantic. The Belgian papers, as de Gerlache knew all too well, covered the expedition in depth. Their dispatches contributed greatly to my descriptions of the ship's departure from and return to Antwerp. Even articles published during the *Belgica*'s absence were eye-opening, if entirely invented. In the spring of 1898, papers around the world printed reports of the *Belgica*'s demise: the ship's grounding in Beagle Channel had morphed, through an international game of telephone, into a horrendous shipwreck. (Cook's fiancée, Anna Forbes, died in Brooklyn less than a week after *The New York Herald* announced that the *Belgica* was lost.)

Any dialogue within quotes appears as such, verbatim, in primary sources. Approximated or paraphrased dialogue is set in italics. Descriptions of internal thoughts are drawn directly from the thinker's own words or writings. The rare occasions on which I was forced to speculate are indicated with qualifying language, and always informed by logical deduction and scrupulous research.

I should account for a few passages that include details appearing in no other secondary accounts of the expedition. The incident, early in Chapter 3, when an exhausted Van Mirlo brandishes a gun on deck, comes from Wiencke's journal entry for September 3, 1897. The bloody forecastle fight in the port of Montevideo was described by Wiencke and Dobrowolski in their diaries, likely through a drunken haze. The confrontation between de Gerlache and Van Damme that led to the near mutiny in Punta Arenas is taken from the commandant's log entry for December 9, 1897. The scene, on January 2, 1898, when Danco cries as he hoists the Belgian flag to the top of the mast, is informed by Dobrowolski's narrative in *Wyprawy polarne: Historja i zdobycze naukowe*, which conflicts slightly with Lecointe's memory. Cook's insincere warning that the long Antarctic night would render the men impotent is recounted in *Peeps into the Beyond*. Lecointe's brush with death in July 1898, from Chapter 12, combines dialogue from *Au pays des manchots* and *Hell Is a Cold Place*. Details on Adam Tollefsen's grim fate following the expedition, as related in the epilogue, come from public records held in Norway's National Archives. Cook and Amundsen's reunion in Copenhagen's Hotel Phoenix in September 1909 weaves together sections from *Hell Is a Cold Place* and segments of Cook's interviews with Freeman.

History, like individual memory, is by nature inexact. Whenever there was a conflict between primary sources, I deferred to a hierarchy of credibility: the sources written soonest after the events they describe—like the diaries or de Gerlache's log—were given precedence over published accounts written months or years later. Among the memoirists, de Gerlache and Lecointe struck me as more believable than Cook, who couldn't resist the occasional embellishment and wasn't an especially diligent note-taker, as the world would discover. My fact-checker, CB Owens, put it succinctly: "between Cook and Other Guy, I tend to believe Other Guy."

The question of when, and when not, to trust Cook bedeviled me. It seems that Cook grew increasingly untrustworthy with age. We will never know for sure whether he faked the ascent of Denali or the attainment of the North Pole, but, having read thousands of pages of his fanciful writings from prison, I tend to believe that he forcefully bent the truth about many of his later achievements. Yet when it comes to the *Belgica,* one of the proudest chapters of his life, there's evidence that Cook wasn't a wholly unreliable narrator. Unlike on Denali and the North Pole, there were many witnesses to the events he described, several of whom published their own books. *Through the First Antarctic Night* was the first of the *Belgica* memoirs to come out, yet none of the accounts that followed meaningfully contradicted Cook's version.

Not, at any rate, until 1909, when Arctowski wrote a series of articles in *La Métropole* questioning Cook's attainment of the North

Pole—and his honesty in general. He accused the doctor of, among other things, having fabricated the story of the death of Nansen the cat in *Through the First Antarctic Night*. According to Arctowski, Cook had never met Nansen, who had been thrown overboard well before the doctor joined the expedition. This troubled me greatly until I read Wiencke's diary, which mentioned the cat-throwing incident. Only that poor cat's name, per Wiencke, was Sverdrup. Nansen was another cat, who survived, at least for a time. Cook was vindicated!

Or maybe not. Perhaps his recollections, like penguin meat, are best swallowed with a heap of salt. But there is one fact on which all of the men of the *Belgica*, even Arctowski, agreed: none would likely have survived the Antarctic winter without Cook. Amundsen's undying loyalty to the doctor remains to me the ultimate proof that, at least with regard to the *Belgica*, Cook deserves the benefit of the doubt.

INDEX

ABOUT THE AUTHOR

JULIAN SANCTON is a senior features editor at *Departures* magazine, where he writes about culture and travel. His work has appeared in *Vanity Fair, Esquire, The New Yorker, Wired,* and *Playboy,* among other publications. He has reported from every continent, including Antarctica, which he first visited while researching this book. He lives in Larchmont, New York, with his partner, Jessica, and their two daughters.

ABOUT THE TYPE

This book was set in Dante, a typeface designed by Giovanni Mardersteig (1892–1977). Conceived as a private type for the Officina Bodoni in Verona, Italy, Dante was originally cut only for hand composition by Charles Malin, the famous Parisian punch cutter, between 1946 and 1952. Its first use was in an edition of Boccaccio's *Trattatello in laude di Dante* that appeared in 1954. The Monotype Corporation's version of Dante followed in 1957. Though modeled on the Aldine type used for Pietro Cardinal Bembo's treatise *De Aetna* in 1495, Dante is a thoroughly modern interpretation of that venerable face.

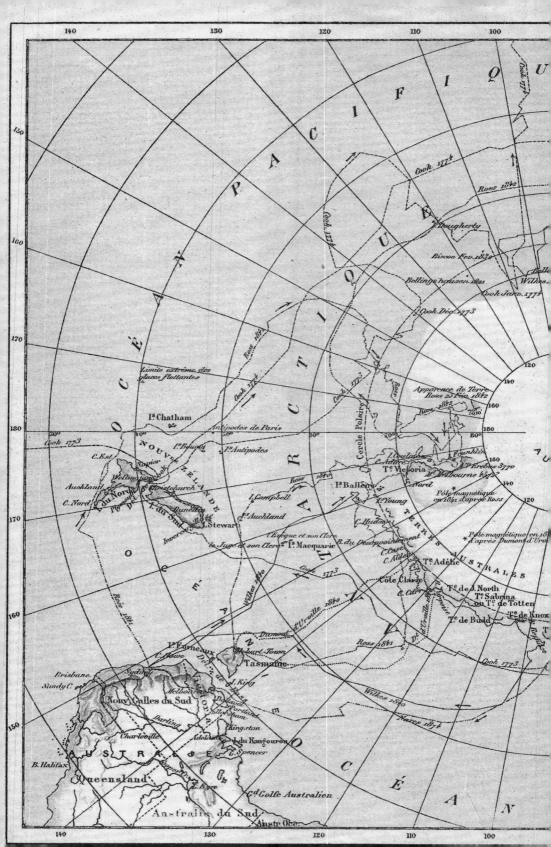